FRAMING CONTRACT LAW

Victor Goldberg

Framing Contract Law

An Economic Perspective

HARVARD UNIVERSITY PRESS
Cambridge, Massachusetts, and London, England

First Harvard University Press paperback edition, 2012

Library of Congress Cataloging-in-Publication Data

Goldberg, Victor P.
    Framing contract law : an economic perspective / Victor Goldberg.
       p.   cm.
    Includes bibliographical references and index.
    ISBN 978-0-674-02312-3 (cloth:alk. paper)
    ISBN 978-0-674-06392-1 (pbk.)
    1. Contracts—Economic aspects—United States.   2. Negotiation in business—United
States.   3. Commercial law—United States.   I. Title.

    KF889.G65   2006
    346.7302—dc22   2006046187

To Linda

Acknowledgments

A number of the essays in this book have been published before in one form or another. Editing of some of those has been very light, taking the form of pruning the excessive footnotes so beloved by law review editors. Others have been substantially revised, and about one-third are new. The essays span more than two decades. Over that period I have received helpful comments from many colleagues at Northwestern and Columbia and from participants in workshops at numerous law schools. I apologize in advance to those whose inputs I have inadvertently failed to acknowledge: Zvi Adar, Barry Adler, Jack Ayer, Bob Bennett, Lisa Bernstein, Randy Bryan Bigham, Barbara Black, John Bogel, Alan Brownstein, Steve Burton, George Chandler, William Chernenkoff, Marvin Chirelstein, Dan Davis, Mel Eisenberg, Chris Fargo, Allan Farnsworth, Dan Fischel, Mark Gergen, Ron Gilson, Scott Gluck, Jeff Gordon, Phil Hacker, Alice Haemmerli, Henry Hansmann, Paul Hong, Kenny Jones, Avery Katz, James Killmond, Ben Klein, Ken Kleinberg, Chuck Knapp, Michael Knoll, Saul Levmore, Ian Macneil, David Matta, Thomas McCarthy, Tom Merrill, Jim Mooney, Jim Murtaugh, Jerome Mushkat, Jeff Perloff, Dan Raff, Carol Sanger, Mel Sattler, David Schizer, Alan Schwartz, Bobby Schwartz, Bob Scott, Steve Shavell, Linda Silberman, Richard Speidel, Kevin Stemp, Bill Stempel, Sarah Stewart, Jodi Stillman, George Triantis, Charles Updike, Mark Weinstein, William Whitford, Steve Wiggins, Jeff Williams, Michael D. Young, and Kyle Zipes. I also owe thanks to my Contracts students over the last decade who have suffered through my efforts to work out my thoughts. Some of the research for this project was supported by the Milton Handler Research Fund at the Columbia University School of Law.

The earlier versions of these essays are as follows; full citations of the articles are given in the References. In some instances, material has appeared in more than one place: Introduction, Goldberg 1990, 2005; Chapter 1, "The Net Profits Puzzle," Goldberg 1997b; Chapter 4, "Satisfaction Clauses," Goldberg 2000b; Chapter 5, "Discretion in Long-Term Open Quantity Contracts," Goldberg 2002a; Chapter 6, "In Search of Best Efforts," Goldberg 2000a; Chapter 8, "The 'Battle of the Forms,'" Goldberg 1997a; Chapter 10, "Expectation Damages and Property in the Price," Goldberg 1989, 2005; Chapter 12, "An Economic Analysis of the Lost-Volume Retail Seller," Goldberg 1984a; Chapter 14, "A Reexamination of *Glanzer v. Shepard*," Goldberg 2002b; Chapter 16, "*Bloomer Girl* Revisited," Goldberg 1998; Chapter 18, "Price Adjustment in Long-Term Contracts," Goldberg 1985; Chapter 19, "Impossibility and Related Excuses," Goldberg 1988; Chapter 20, "*Alcoa v. Essex*," Goldberg 1985.

The author and publisher gratefully acknowledge permission to reprint the following:

Victor P. Goldberg, "The 'Battle of the Forms': Fairness, Efficiency, and the Best Shot Rule," *Oregon Law Review* 76 (1997): 155–171.

Victor P. Goldberg, "Bloomer Girl Revisited, or How to Frame an Unmade Picture," *Wisconsin Law Review* 1998: 1051–1084.

Victor P. Goldberg, "Discretion in Long-Term Open Quantity Contracts: Reining in Good Faith." This work was originally published in 35 *U.C. Davis Law Rev* 319–385, copyright 2002 by The Regents of the University of California. Reprinted with permission. All rights reserved.

Victor P. Goldberg, "An Economic Analysis of the Lost-Volume Retail Seller," 57 *Southern California Law Review,* 283–298 (1984), reprinted with the permission of the *Southern California Law Review.*

Victor P. Goldberg, "Economic Reasoning and the Framing of Contract Law: Sale of an Asset of Uncertain Value," *Revue d'Economie Industrielle* 92(2000): 111–123.

Victor P. Goldberg, "Impossibility and Related Excuses," *Journal of Institutional and Theoretical Economics* 144(1988): 100–121. With kind permission of Springer Science and Business Media.

Victor P. Goldberg, "In Search of Best Efforts: Reinterpreting *Bloor v. Falstaff,*" 44 St. Louis U.L.J. 1465 (2000). Reprinted with permission of the Saint Louis University *Law Journal* © 2000. St. Louis University School of Law, St. Louis, Missouri.

Victor P. Goldberg, "The Net Profits Puzzle," *Columbia Law Review* 76 (1997): 524–550.

Victor P. Goldberg, "Price Adjustment in Long-Term Contracts," *Wisconsin Law Review* 1985: 527–543.

Victor P. Goldberg, "A Reexamination of *'Glanzer v. Shepard':* Surveyors on the Tort-Contract Boundary," *Theoretical Inquiries in Law* 2(2002): 476–510.

Contents

Introduction

I have been teaching the first-year Contracts course for a number of years now. As one of the small band of Contracts teachers trained in economics (and the even smaller band without a law degree), I come to the case law from a somewhat unorthodox angle. I sometimes find myself exasperated by various features of the reported decisions, including, but not limited to, the outcomes. Too often I find the facts as stated to be incomplete, irrelevant, or inaccurately stated. Absent a framework for organizing the inquiry, the courts often fail to ask the relevant questions, in no small measure because both the courts and the lawyers who present the case exhibit a lack of understanding about the underlying economics of the transactions in dispute.

At about the same time that I began teaching contract law, Ron Gilson and I, along with some colleagues, were developing a transaction-oriented course—Deals: The Economic Structure of Complex Transactions, known informally as Deals. The central theme of Deals is that transactions that appear very different on their face—long-term supply contracts, securitizations, corporate acquisitions and divestitures, and so forth—present many of the same problems, and similar tools can be employed to deal with them. The transactional lawyer is, in effect, a transaction-cost engineer, designing structures to cope with problems such as information asymmetry, moral hazard, and the like. It has become clear to me that there is a significant disjunction between the intellectual frameworks of the transactional lawyer structuring deals and the litigator interpreting those transactional structures after problems have arisen.

The central conceit of the chapters comprising this book is that the theoretical framework of the transaction-cost engineer is appropriate for analyzing contract disputes and for developing contract doctrine—at least for business to business transactions. The analysis relies heavily on recent developments in economics. However, those accustomed to seeing the economics of contract law as being permeated by the concept of efficient breach and the technique of formal mathematical modeling will be surprised to find very little of the former and none of the latter. The economic analysis here focuses on the transaction. I ask: Why might reasonable, profit-seeking actors structure their relationship in a particular way? How should the answer to that question affect the interpretation of a contract or suggest the appropriate contract law rule? Hereafter, when I invoke "economics" I mean this particular brand of economics. The features of that brand will emerge in the course of this book.

The best way to demonstrate the usefulness of the transactional framework is to apply it. Most of the chapters comprising this book analyze particular cases, with an emphasis on cases common to many Contracts casebooks. The chapters come at the subject from different angles. Some involve going back to the briefs and record of a case in an attempt to understand what actually happened and how the court came to frame the story in the way it did. Others take the facts as stated by the courts as a jumping-off point. While the methods vary from chapter to chapter, the theme remains constant.

Like virtually all contracts scholars, I start with the presumption that the purpose of contract law is to facilitate private ordering. The parties are the best judges of their interests, and the law should, as much as possible, stay out of the way. There are exceptions—there might be good reasons to discourage or prohibit certain classes of promises (for example, disclaimers or promises to commit illegal acts) or to be suspicious of the manner in which agreements have been reached (for example, the battle of the forms or duress). Still, the facilitation of voluntary exchange remains the primary goal of contract law. Voluntary exchange is not a zero-sum game; it allows parties to achieve gains from trade. The parties enter into their agreement because they each expect to be better off. They might, of course, turn out to be wrong. It might have seemed a good idea at the time, but conditions might have changed, leaving one party to regret having entered into the agreement. Or one party might simply have misperceived the possible outcome. Had it known more (or been a more intelligent processor of available information), it would not have entered into the deal. Regardless, the basic presumption that there are gains from trade is the economic foundation for a facilitative law of contract.

The facilitative nature of contract law means that if parties don't like a particular rule, they can change it. Formal contract law provides only a set of default rules. If drafting around the rules were always easy, then the precise content of the rules would be of little consequence. Economic analysis would be of value to transactional lawyers, but less so for judges and litigators, although the analysis would still be useful for interpretation. Not everything, however, is negotiable. At the extreme, some rules are mandatory. More generally, default rules can be sticky either because the law imposes hurdles to drafting around the defaults or because of nonlegal factors (for example, the costs of negotiating). The stickiness of the defaults, which includes the uncertainty that any particular deviation will survive in litigation, means that in at least some instances the default rules will matter.

Whether parties do contract around a particular rule provides a test of the economic sense of a rule. If parties routinely accept the rule, and the legal barriers to contracting around the default are low, then there ought to be at least a presumption that the court (or legislature) got it right. So, when I argue below that the lost profits remedy is too liberal (Chapter 12) or that certifiers of quantity or quality should not be liable for the consequential damages arising from erroneous measurement (Chapter 14), the failure of contracts to conform with my expectations necessitates my providing a satisfactory explanation of the divergence between theory and practice.

Months might pass between the time the parties enter into a contract and the date it is to be performed. Performance itself might take place over time. As time passes, things change—both conditions and the information available to the parties. The recurring theme in these chapters is that because contracting takes place over time, contracts will have to determine how to respond to the changed circumstances. Some changes are simply the inevitable risks of doing business, risks assigned by the contract. The more interesting questions concern adaptation as new information is revealed, termination being the extreme form of adaptation. The contract could give one or both parties the explicit right to terminate, perhaps for a price. The right could be unconditional, or it could require a specific trigger (for example, an excusing circumstance). The right to terminate could be implicit—the right to breach and pay damages. The contract could give one party discretion to adapt, and it could require that party to compensate the other if the adaptation would impose costs on it.

In Part I, I begin with a short note sketching the analytical tools that will be used throughout the book. I then go into greater depth examining a puzzle: Why is it that in the movie business the compensation of many of the actors, writers, and producers is based in part on "net profits," despite the widespread belief that Hollywood accounting means that most movies will never show any net profits? This provides a fairly painless introduction to a number of the themes developed in the rest of the book, particularly the importance of adapting to new information; it has the added virtue of touching on one area of contract law not otherwise covered in this book—unconscionability.

Parts II and III focus on problems involving fuzzy language, in particular the abuse of "good faith" and "best efforts." In a number of cases courts have dealt with the apparent lack of consideration by invoking an implied duty of good faith. This I believe to be a mistake, although in the long run it does not do much direct harm, since by and large these are agreements that the parties easily could have made enforceable without any such implication. The interesting problem is not whether the agreements are enforceable, but what is to be enforced. By imposing a near-mandatory "good faith" or "best efforts" duty on the promisor, the law raises barriers to efficient contracting. The consideration cases, including the classic *Wood v. Lucy, Lady Duff-Gordon,* are the focus of Part II.

Interpretation is the theme of Part III. I return to "good faith" and the treatment of variable quantity contracts (for example, requirements contracts). Having found that a contract exists, courts then have to interpret what it means. Variable quantity contracts grant one party discretion in determining the quantity for good reason—to facilitate adaptation to changing circumstances. To protect the interests of the counterparty, the contracts almost always impose limits on the quantity-determining party's discretion. Notwithstanding that, the courts have taken to invoking good faith to impose different limits, undoing the allocation worked out by the parties. I next show how the one "best efforts" case that makes it into the casebooks *(Bloor v. Falstaff)* poses the wrong question and comes to the wrong conclusion. The two remaining chapters in Part III concern very different interpretation issues. First, I consider the role of custom and usage in interpreting a contract. I explore the notorious *Columbia Nitrogen* decision in which the court claimed that the apparently clear and unambiguous language of the contract regarding the minimum quantity could be modified by alleged custom and usage and the course of dealing of the parties. I conclude Part III with my proposal for coping with the "battle of the forms" problem—the "best-shot" rule.

In Part IV, the discussion shifts to remedies. My primary focus is on monetary damages. However, I begin with an examination of the specific performance remedy in the context of *Campbell Soup v. Wentz*. The court would have granted specific performance, but for its conclusion that the contract was unconscionable. However, the court's misunderstanding of the contract made it doubly wrong. It erred both in finding the contract unconscionable and in identifying the rationale for awarding specific performance.

The balance of Part IV focuses on the damage remedy. While a common criticism of contract law is that the remedies are undercompensatory, I argue that in many instances the opposite is true. The standard remedy is expectation damages, and the usual statement of the rule is that expectation damages should make the victim of the breach as well off as she would have been had the contract been performed. I would propose instead that the question be: What remedy would reasonable parties have put in the contract in the first place? The remedy is (or, rather, ought to be) just another contract term for the parties to choose in designing their relationship. The two questions give the same answer when the remedy is the contract price-market price differential (what I refer to as the narrow expectation interest). But in other instances, notably the "lost-volume" seller's lost profits and "foreseeable" consequential damages, making the victim whole would produce an overcompensatory remedy. Ironically, in the one instance in which some commentators complain about overcompensatory remedies—awarding the contract-market differential to a hedged middleman—I argue that these commentators are wrong.

The decision to breach can be viewed as an option, with the damage rule establishing the price of the option. Katz (2004) and Scott and Triantis (2004) make a persuasive case for this. The line between this implicit option and more explicit options is an artificial one. Two casebook favorites— *Parker v. Twentieth Century-Fox* and *Wasserman v. Township of Middletown*— were treated by the courts as raising difficult questions regarding remedies for breach. Properly framed, they are easy cases in which there was no breach, only the exercise of an option. Although they invariably appear in casebooks in the chapter on remedies, I have broken these out into their own section in Part V. It should become clear, however, that the label has no bearing on the appropriate analysis.

When circumstances change, a disadvantaged party might ask the court to excuse its performance, or at least modify it. The many variations on the excuse doctrine are the subject of Part VI. Force majeure clauses are not mere boilerplate. There is an economic logic to them that provides the basis of the analysis of the excuse cases where the contract is silent. I argue that the standard warhorses, *Taylor v. Caldwell, Krell v. Henry,* and the Suez Canal cases, were rightly decided, but I suggest an alternate route to those outcomes. The court's analysis in *Alcoa v. Essex* was dubious, but the deeper problem was that the transactional lawyers had written a badly flawed contract. The main flaw was not, however, the one on which the court focused. In the final chapter in Part VI, I consider the case generally cited for the proposition that if performance is "too expensive" it will be deemed impractical and therefore the party will be excused: *Mineral Park v. Howard.* When properly framed it is clear that the impracticality was irrelevant. Holding the promisor to the bargain would have led to the efficient outcome and would not have been unduly burdensome to the promisor.

Economic analysis, whether right or wrong, will not be of much use in deciding cases if its application requires training and skills beyond those of judge and jury. In some instances, the economics simply helps pose the proper question. Litigation is storytelling, and if the parties use the right framework, the answer becomes obvious. The following chapters are full of examples of such clean kills, for example, *Parker v. Twentieth Century-Fox, Bloor v. Falstaff, Feld v. Levy, Tongish v. Thomas,* and *Mineral Park v. Howard.* Perhaps the most useful role of my proposed framework is in providing a plausible rationale for classes of contract clauses that can shield them from judicial modification or nullification with interpretative tools like "good faith" or trade usage. To the extent that the moral of such analyses is "don't meddle," the economics makes the court's task easier. I do not mean to suggest that the analysis will inevitably make life easier—there is some pretty tricky stuff yet to come. But my belief is that a little economics can go a long way in helping to decide contract disputes.

One source of tension in contract law concerns the weight that should be given to factors beyond the actual wording of the contract in dispute. Variations on this problem crop up in many forms: objective versus subjective theories of interpretation; the parol evidence and plain meaning rules; the incorporation of trade usage and custom into agreements (and, more generally, the inferences that formal adjudications can make from the informal resolution of disputes). I do not want to confront these issues directly, although I lean toward the objective view and am quite skeptical regarding trade usage and custom. The reasons for this will, I hope, become clear after we work through the analysis. For now it is sufficient to acknowledge that these views appear to be in conflict with my theme, namely, that placing transactions in their economic context is necessary for the proper resolution of disputes, and that part of my task will be to resolve that apparent conflict.

Some of these chapters have been published before, not always in easily accessible places. These are hardly sacred texts, and I have edited and, in some instances, revised them. In particular, I have eliminated some of the over-footnoting common to law review articles. By putting these chapters together in one place, with some connective tissue, I believe the power of a transactionally sensitive economic approach to contract law will become apparent. If the book works as I hope it will, on a first reading many of the arguments should seem counterintuitive and wrong. But on further reflection the same arguments should appear obvious, if not trivial. Because of the focus on individual cases, I have had to sacrifice breadth for depth. Still, I believe that the chapters cover a broad enough spectrum of the case law to illustrate the virtues of the transactional framework for analyzing both specific contract disputes and broader issues of contract doctrine.

The book is, first and foremost, a work of scholarship aimed at contracts scholars. I have tried to write it in such a way as to make it (or at least most of it) accessible to a wider audience. First, of course, it is meant for those who teach contract law. For them it can be both a sword and a shield. On my more optimistic days I think of it as a sword, providing a framework for analyzing contract law questions. When in a more cynical mood, I believe it can at least shield the professor from the embarrassment of being blindsided by a student who has read the book and can show why the professor has the facts or the interpretation (or both) wrong. I would hate to be teaching *Wood v. Lucy* and have a student inform me that months before entering into his arrangement with Lucy, Otis Wood had sued another client for breach of a contract that included an explicit best efforts clause. That leads to the second audience—first-year contracts students. To be sure, some of the analysis here will be hard going for One L's, but I believe that enough of it is accessible to make the book a worthwhile supplement to a first-year course. For students it provides both a way of thinking about contract law and an introduction to the transactional side of lawyering, which is underrepresented in the three-year curriculum and otherwise absent in the first year.

Influencing how faculty and students frame contract questions is a deep investment in legal change. My other audiences—lawyers and judges—are more directly involved. While they have the potential for an immediate impact, their contact with contract law is more episodic. Unlike corporate law, there is no specialized bar. For the Delaware bench, keeping up with the corporate law literature is essential. They engage in an ongoing dialogue with academics and a group of high-powered lawyers who keep up with the literature and feel comfortable incorporating concepts from the literature in litigation. Since contract disputes typically account for only a small portion of the case load for both judges and lawyers, their incentives to engage with the literature are less keen. Contract law's place in the general lawyer's mind was driven home to me a few years ago when I was being deposed. After I alluded to the "famous case of *Hadley v. Baxendale*," my interrogator (a good lawyer and a Columbia grad, by the way) said, "Excuse me, professor, but I'm not familiar with that case." So, while my target audience includes practitioners and judges, I am mindful of the fact that making inroads here will not be easy.

PART I

Some Concepts

Contracts necessarily deal with an uncertain future. Bad things (fires, wars, floods) can damage the subject matter of the contract or can make performance of the contract more difficult. Changing market conditions might result in large price changes or make continued performance unnecessary or even foolish. Contracts assign responsibility for these risks, and, broadly speaking, the responsibility is assigned to the party that can best manage the risks. Management can include the purchase of insurance or the use of financial derivatives, but it includes much more. The contract can grant one party discretion to adapt to new information along with establishing constraints upon the exercise of that discretion. Compensation can be made contingent upon outcomes. As we go through the cases in the following chapters, we will find a variety of devices for managing risk.

While some of the future risks stem from factors beyond the parties' control (weather, wars, etc.), others do not. Even if factors like the weather are exogenous, their economic consequences need not be. A cold winter might make shipping grain impossible, but the losses to the buyer depend upon the extent to which it relied on the particular shipment. The buyer could, for example, have held a larger inventory of grain or had access to mills (by ownership or contract) that were less vulnerable to the weather. The same actions could have dampened the economic consequences of a failed delivery caused by the negligence of a carrier (as, for example, in *Hadley v. Baxendale*).

A particular set of risks involves the behavior of the parties. What if one party refused to perform or behaved in a manner that reduced the gains from entering into the contract in the first place? These problems recur in a variety of contexts, and they will show up in most of the case studies

9

that form the core of this book. I will introduce some of them briefly here, as I suspect the reader is anxious to get to the meat of the analysis.

Two concepts have their origins in the insurance business—adverse selection and moral hazard. The first arises because of asymmetric information—one party knows more than the other. The second arises because insurance changes the incentives of the insured, thereby changing the outcome. A classic example of the former is the purchase of life insurance by a terminally ill person; arson for hire is a standard illustration of the latter. The negative nomenclature reflects the perspective of the insurance industry.

The problems go well beyond the insurance context. Adverse selection problems appear in two contexts. First, in contracts for the sale of goods, if a seller cannot fine-tune the warranties it offers, it will be providing the same warranty package for customers who might have very different exposures. Those with significant exposures would be subsidized by the rest. Buyers with low expected damages might find themselves priced out of the market. They will try to distinguish themselves from the rest, and those with high expected damages will try to be included in the same pool as the others. Sellers will engage in strategies to identify the different risks, price them, and assign responsibility for them.

Second, in sales of complicated assets (for example, a corporate division or an office building), the seller will often know more than the buyer. The buyer, fearing that he might be buying a "lemon," will discount his offer accordingly. The seller, anticipating this, has an incentive to provide the buyer with assurance as to quality. There are numerous devices available to the seller: for example, representations and warranties, guarantees, and contingent compensation. The more quality assurance it receives, the more the buyer would be willing to pay. In some instances the buyer might turn out to be the more effective producer of information, and the contracts would reflect this.

The generalized notion of moral hazard is that the party making the decisions does not bear all the consequences. So, for example, the owner of a highly leveraged corporation (that is, one with a high level of borrowing and limited liability) will get all the upside if things go well, but if things go poorly the losses fall on the lenders. Unless the loan contract places some constraints on the owner's subsequent behavior, his incentive is to take risky projects. If the project succeeds, he wins; if it fails, the lenders lose. If one party sells a machine at a fixed price with delivery to take place three months later, the seller has three months in which to use and abuse the machine without bearing the adverse consequences; conversely, if it sold the machine under warranty, the buyer's incentive would be to use the machine aggressively, since the seller would bear the costs of the abuse. Again, contracting parties should anticipate these incentives and design their relationships to cope with the problems they produce.

I want to introduce only one more concept here before we begin. In complicated business transactions, decisions are often made sequentially. As new information comes in, projects are revised, postponed, or abandoned. Contracts will reflect a balancing of the parties' reliance on the continued performance of the other against the benefits of maintaining the flexibility to adapt as new information becomes available. Finance scholars refer to the problem as one of "real options." (See Scott and Triantis 2004). There are benefits to deferring decisions until more information becomes available (the value of the real option), and there are also costs. If the benefits and costs are both borne directly by the decision maker, it has the incentive to economize appropriately (equate the incremental benefits with the incremental costs). If the benefits and costs are borne by different parties, the balancing must be done by contract. The balancing task is made more difficult by "rent-seeking"—the parties' incentives to pursue their private interest, even if the possibility of their doing so would reduce the value of their deal. Contracts can establish mechanisms for adaptation or assign the task of adapting to one of the parties, perhaps placing some constraints on the exercise of that discretion. Those mechanisms include granting one party limited discretion to make adjustments, setting up governance mechanisms, assessing penalties for termination or breach, and excusing performance under certain circumstances.

I mentioned risk a number of times in the preceding paragraphs. I did not, however, mention risk aversion. The omission was deliberate because the concept is almost always unhelpful in understanding contracts and contract law. I have spelled out the reasons for my "aversion to risk aversion" elsewhere, and I will not rehearse them here. (See Goldberg 1990, 2005.) Much of the intuitive appeal of risk aversion, especially to law professors, derives from a misunderstanding. Most people are averse to downside risk—they don't like bad outcomes. But risk aversion means something quite different. It is a proposition about individual preferences: given the choice between two outcomes with the same mean and a different variance, people will prefer the one with the smaller variance. So, for example, when given a choice between receiving $100 with certainty or a 50:50 chance of getting $200 or zero, a risk averse person would choose the former. My contention is that the analysis of contracts between business entities should not be based on risk preferences, but on risk management.

In a book built around close analysis of cases, I have chosen to open with a contracting puzzle, the persistence of net profit compensation in the movie business. I have a number of reasons for this choice. First, the problem illustrates nicely how an atheoretical analysis unguided by economic theory can easily veer off in the wrong direction. Second, the sequential nature of decision making is obvious in the filmmaking context; the movie studios must inevitably deal with the problem of adapting (or abandoning) the project as new information appears. The analysis amplifies the terse description of the "real options" problem noted above. Third, the division of revenues between the studio and others (talent and exhibitors) illustrates how parties might deal with moral hazard, adverse selection, and incentive problems. Fourth, the movie business background will come in handy when we reach the *Bloomer Girl* case (Chapter 15). Fifth, even though the case law is not the main focus of the chapter, there has been litigation arguing that net profits compensation was unconscionable. Indeed, one of the cases has even made it into a casebook. (See Frier and White 2005, pp. 457–465.) *(Batfilm Productions, Inc. v. Warner Bros., Inc.)* And, finally, the movie business is fun; readers will have an easier time relating to it than, say, to a coal-fueled electric power plant. It is a relatively painless way to get a handle on the basic theoretical concepts.

I should note that the chapter was first published in 1997 and that the references to specific films and the industry statistics are somewhat dated. Both the production and marketing costs of major films have increased substantially in the last few years. The sources of film revenue have shifted dramatically, with the share of domestic box office shrinking, while tape, DVD, and foreign box office revenues have been increasing. For a readable discussion of the changing nature of the business, see Hayes and Bing 2004. Despite all the changes, the chapter's basic themes remain sound.

CHAPTER 1

The Net Profits Puzzle

It is not uncommon for Hollywood talent—producers, writers, and actors—to have part of their compensation based on "net profits." Since Art Buchwald's well-publicized lawsuit against Paramount *(Buchwald I, II and III)* concerning the lack of net profits for *Coming to America,* the common perception has been that net profits are illusory; Hollywood accounting will assure that films will fail to show a profit and net profits participants will go away empty handed. That perception is bolstered by the failure of other apparent successes, such as *JFK* and *Batman,* to show positive net profits. While data are difficult to come by, industry insiders suggest that of the approximately 130 major studio movies made each year, fewer than 20 will pay off for the net profits participants. The low likelihood of a payoff raises an obvious question: Why bother? Why not simply pay a fixed fee and eliminate the ephemeral contingent compensation? And why, despite recent legal attacks on net profits clauses, have the studios continued to include them in contracts? The persistence of the net profits deal and the studios' vehemence in defending it as an essential element in the way Hollywood does business suggest that there might be some method to the apparent madness.

One line of explanation has been presented in litigation on behalf of disgruntled net profits (non)recipients. The compensation arrangements are said to reflect the power of the studios to impose their will upon the talent; the talent is powerless to vary the unconscionable terms presented them. This argument was accepted by one trial court in *Buchwald II* but rejected by another in *Batfilm Productions, Inc. v. Warner Bros.* Although some commentators have found this argument persuasive, the unconscionabilty analysis fails to explain why, if studios have the power ascribed to them, they would choose to exercise it in such a peculiar way.

Part of the explanation is that the fate of net profits participants is not as bleak as the public perceives it to be. The conventional wisdom in Hollywood is that if a film without major stars succeeds, the net profits participants are likely to receive some contingent compensation. If, however, the film has "gross participants" (major stars whose compensation is in part a function of the film's gross receipts), the net participants' recovery is far less likely. In many instances, the gross participants are added to a project after the net participants have entered into their contracts with the studio. Solving the net profits puzzle thus requires an explanation of four things: (1) why net profits participants would agree to give up their contingent compensation if gross participants are subsequently added to the project; (2) why studios want to maintain the option of adding gross participants to the project; (3) what function the expectation of net profits serves; and (4) why that function is less important when there are gross participants in the project.

Timing in the movie business, as elsewhere, is (almost) everything. Movies are assembled sequentially. Some people sign on early, before the project has taken shape, while others come in much later. Some, like screenwriters, perform most of their task at the outset. Others, notably the distributor, make the bulk of their contribution after production is nearly complete. The net profits participants (for example, the producer) usually sign on before they know either the identity of the other participants or the precise nature of the project. Having agreed to receive part of their compensation in the form of net profits, they are concerned with protecting their contingent claim from dilution, much as an investor in a corporation's debt would be concerned about subsequent changes in the firm's capital structure. However, net profits participants, like their less artistic counterparts, do not want absolute protection; they would agree, ex ante, to dilute their claims under certain circumstances if that dilution were to increase their expected earnings. I will argue that by sacrificing some of their back-end compensation when gross participants are added to a project, net participants can make themselves better off both directly, by increasing their expected earnings, and indirectly, because the studio is willing to pay for the resulting increased flexibility.

That accounts for only one blade of the scissors: Why would net profits participants be *willing to give up* most or all of their contingent earnings? The remaining question is *why would they want* a contract with net profits in the first place? Why make a portion of their compensation contingent

upon the film's commercial success, particularly on the contractually defined net profits? Timing, again, is a critical factor. Because the contributors
to a movie's commercial success do not make all their contributions simultaneously, the compensation scheme will be tailored to induce effort at the
appropriate time. The studio must make substantial distribution expenditures after most of the net profits participants have performed, and the
smaller its share of the revenue stream, the weaker its incentives to promote the film. Still, the studio would like to set aside some of the upside
to influence the post-completion promotional behavior of the talent and to
better contain some of the pre-completion costs as well.

The argument proceeds as follows: Section 1 sets the stage by giving some
background information on contingent compensation in the movie business. Section 2 critically evaluates the unconscionability attack on net
profits clauses. Section 3 then suggests that net profits participants are made
better off ex ante by providing studios with the flexibility to add gross
participants to a project. Section 4 shows how the contingent compensation
is structured to provide incentives at the appropriate time. The concluding
section explains why studio films have in recent years been less likely to
produce net profits.

1. Net and Gross Participations

The "net profit" is a defined contractual term that differs substantially from
generally accepted definitions of profit. A film could, therefore, be profitable
for the studio even though the calculated net profits turn out to be a large
negative number. The misleading terminology is responsible for some of the
confusion regarding net profits participations. Nochimson and Brachman
(1996, p. 1) note:

> The subject of contingent compensation in the theatrical motion picture
> business is most customarily associated with the phrase *net profits* and this
> is where the trouble usually begins. Net profits conjures up in the minds
> of profit participants an accounting concept, and when these expectations
> are not realized, the [studio] is accused of chicanery and sometimes worse.
> What must be kept in mind . . . is that net profits participation[s] . . . are
> negotiated contractual definitions which have evolved within the motion
> picture industry and have little to do with real profit of a picture as mea-
> sured by generally accepted accounting [principles].

Although there were some net profits contracts in the heyday of the studio system (pre-1948), Jimmy Stewart's contract for *Winchester '73* in 1950 is generally viewed as the first modern net profits agreement. With Universal Studios financially strapped, Stewart agreed that instead of receiving his usual fee of $250,000, he would defer his compensation and receive 50% of the net profits, defined in the contract as the film's gross revenues less twice the "negative costs" (the cost of producing the film, as distinguished from distribution costs). Stewart's contract differed from the now-standard net profits agreement in two respects. First, the standard agreement contains a fixed compensation component, payable regardless of the film's subsequent success. Second, the standard net profits agreement determines "costs" in a quite different manner that results in the film achieving net profits (attaining breakeven) at higher revenue levels than under Jimmy Stewart's formula.

The studio is the distributor of the film. To simplify somewhat, the basic net profits formula subtracts from the studio's adjusted gross receipts[1] the production costs, distribution expenses, distribution fees, and interest. If that number is negative, it is disregarded. *Production costs,* also called *negative costs,* are all costs directly attributed to the particular film (plus overhead). For the major studios in 1995, such costs averaged over $36 million per film. Production costs include the payments to all other participants in a film, including the contingent compensation of gross participants. So, for example, since Eddie Murphy had fifteen gross points for *Coming to America* (that is, he received 15% of the gross receipts), every dollar of revenue the film generated pushed the net profits breakeven point back 15 cents. (Actually, it recedes even further, since the studio will assess a 15% overhead charge on the additional cost and will also charge interest on it.) Thus, if a film has significant gross participants, the breakeven point quickly recedes. Almost all the box office smashes that failed to produce net profits had significant gross participants.

Distribution expenses, principally production of prints and advertising, averaged about $17 million per film in 1995. Distribution expenses are identifiable costs attributable to the particular film (again, plus overhead). *Distribution fees* are not related directly to specific costs. Rather, they are assessed as a percentage of receipts, with the percentage varying with the source. So, distribution fees for a particular film might be 30% for domestic box office, 40% for foreign box office, 25% for domestic network television, and so forth. As with gross points, an increase in revenue increases the distribution fee and shifts out the breakeven point.

The distinction between net and gross participations is not as significant as might at first appear. In both instances, the participant receives a fixed fee and contingent compensation that comes into play after a breakeven point. It is the nature of the breakeven point that distinguishes net and gross participations. The net participants have a "rolling breakeven" that depends upon costs, receipts, and the distribution fee. The so-called first-dollar gross participation is set off against the talent's fixed fee (which operates as a nonrefundable advance against earnings).[2] The first-dollar gross participant has a fixed breakeven point—the advance (the fixed fee) divided by the sharing rate—that depends on receipts only. So, for example, for *Coming to America* Eddie Murphy would have received no contingent compensation until the film's gross revenue exceeded his advance ($8 million) divided by his 15% share, or $53 million. The first-dollar deals go to the superstars, who in 1996 were commanding over $10 million, or in some instances $20 million, in advances.[3]

Other variations that go under the gross participation rubric are, essentially, net profits deals with a lower breakeven. As in the standard net profits arrangement, the contingent compensation is in addition to the fixed fee. The director of *Coming to America*, John Landis, for example, received 10% of gross above a negotiated breakeven point determined by subtracting a 20% distribution fee and only certain production costs from the gross receipts. (O'Donnell and McDougal 1992, pp. 296–297) These deals could also subtract certain distribution costs from the gross; or they could, like Jimmy Stewart's deal, define breakeven as a multiple of production costs. In most such arrangements, after breakeven is reached, no further distribution fees are charged against the participant. Participants in these modified gross deals will reach breakeven sooner than the net profits participants. Their contingent compensation will be included in the production costs in the net profit definition, so these payments too will shift out the breakeven point for the net participants.

The accounts of *Coming to America* illustrate how a successful picture can fail to produce net profits. By the end of 1989, Paramount had received $125 million. Negative costs, excluding gross participations, were $47 million, distribution costs $36 million, and distribution fees an additional $42 million. Eddie Murphy's gross points had yielded about $10 million, and

Landis's an additional $1 million. With interest of $6 million, the accounts showed the movie to be still about $18 million in the red. Of each additional dollar of revenue received, about one-third would go toward reducing that deficit. Even if Murphy and Landis had received only their fixed fees, there still would have been no net profits.

Forrest Gump provides another example. By the end of 1994 Paramount had received about $191 million. In the next six months it took in over $100 million more not counting revenues from the videocassette, sound track, and licensing fees on such products as Forrest Gump wristwatches and cookbooks. (Munk 1995, pp. 42–43) Some of these ancillary revenues would be included in *Gump*'s revenues for determining the film's net profits. (Sandler 1995, p. 7) Distribution costs were about $73 million. Distribution fees (32% of the gross) were about $62 million. Negative costs, before taking into account gross participations by Tom Hanks and director Robert Zemeckis, were about $66 million. The gross participants each were entitled to 8% of the gross and had received about $20 million each (with Paramount reckoning 15% overhead on that as an additional negative cost). After including an additional $6 million for interest, the picture remained over $60 million short of the breakeven point.[4]

The studios undoubtedly set themselves up for ridicule by misnaming the back-end compensation as a share of "net profits."[5] Some elements of the compensation scheme are directly related to costs, but others, notably the distribution fee and various overhead charges, are not. The formula will fail to show net profits until long after a movie is profitable in more familiar terms. If the film has significant gross participants, it is likely that even if the film is a box office success, it will fail to record net profits. Note that it is not the gross formula per se that prevents the net participants from receiving back-end compensation. If Eddie Murphy's contract called for an $18 million flat fee and no gross points, Art Buchwald would have fared just as poorly. Buchwald lost because of the *size* of the claims of those ahead of him in the queue, not the *shape* of those claims. Since the size and shape are correlated (big earners get gross points), for our purposes the distinction does not much matter.

The breakeven point depends on the presence of gross participants and on the magnitude of the production and distribution budgets. These are interrelated. Big stars are not substitutes for production and distribution expenses; they are complements. If a studio adds a gross participant to a film, other things being equal, the negative costs (net of that star's compensation) and distribution costs increase. Bigger stars appear in films with bigger production budgets. Films with bigger production budgets will have bigger distribution budgets as well. Consequently, adding a gross participant to a film has a magnified effect on the rate at which the breakeven point recedes. Still, on occasion net profits participants do win. Some films—for example, *Flashdance, Airplane,* and *Grease*—have paid off handsomely. (O'Donnell and McDougal 1992, p. 410) In *Buchwald II* (p. 20), Paramount introduced evidence showing that in the previous fifteen years it had paid out over $150 million to eighty-nine net profits participants in twenty-nine movies.

2. Unconscionability

Haggling over net profits accounts has long been a Hollywood sport, and the disputes often end up in litigation. But only recently has the basic contract come under attack. In this section, I will describe briefly the litigation regarding three films—*Coming to America, Batman,* and *JFK*—in which disappointed net profits participants attacked the validity of the standard studio agreements.

The *Coming to America* story has been told in an entertaining book co-authored by the plaintiffs' attorney, Pierce O'Donnell. Producer Alain Bernheim entered into an agreement with Paramount Studios giving the studio the option to develop a treatment by humorist Art Buchwald originally entitled *It's a Crude, Crude World,* subsequently rechristened *King for a Day.* The movie, if made, would have been produced by Bernheim. Paramount abandoned the project, but then produced *Coming to America,* which Bernheim and Buchwald claimed was based on Buchwald's original treatment. In a hotly disputed and well-publicized trial, the court held that *Coming to America* was indeed based on Buchwald's treatment and that Paramount had breached its contract. If damages had been assessed as per contract, the plaintiffs would have won their fixed fee, a combined $265,000, plus their share of the net profits. That share, however, would have been worthless, since the movie never earned net profits by Paramount's accounts. In the trial's second phase, the plaintiffs succeeded in having the compensation formula based on net profits declared unconscionable. In a third phase *(Buchwald III),* the court rewrote the contract, determining that Bernheim was due $750,000 and Buchwald $150,000. While the case was on appeal, the parties settled, reportedly for $825,000. Total litigation costs have been estimated at $12 million. (Welkos 1995b, pp. D2, D11)

Both plaintiffs had been represented by agents when they entered into the deal; Bernheim's was Roger Davis, executive vice president of the William Morris Agency, a significant figure in the industry. Bernheim received $10,000 as a development fee and would have received an additional $150,000 if the film had been produced; this latter fee would have increased to $200,000 if he had produced another movie after entering into this contract but before commencement of principal photography. In addition, he would have received 35% of net profits (which would have increased to 40% if he had produced another movie). However, his net profits share could have been reduced to 17.5% if other net or gross participants had been added to the project. This reduction of the net profit rate was set out in a standard term in a producer's contract, the so-called consultation clause. Paramount agreed to consult with him about adding gross and net participants to the film if doing so would reduce his share, but Paramount's decisions on such matters would be final. Paramount paid Buchwald $10,000 for a standard one-year option. If the option were exercised, Paramount would pay $50,000; it would pay an additional $15,000 upon commencement of principal photography and 1.5% of the net profits.[6]

Judge Schneider held that the contract (or at least seven clauses of the standard net profits agreement) was unconscionable. He did not claim that Buchwald and Bernheim had been snookered in any way. They were, after all, represented by sophisticated agents. However, Bernheim, said Schneider, lacked "clout." (*Buchwald II*, p. 542) Because of the "inequality of bargaining power" between Paramount and Bernheim, the contract terms were substantially dictated by the studio. (*Buchwald II*, p. 11) Calling the contracts oppressive and one-sided, Judge Schneider held that if the contracts reallocated risk in an unreasonable way they could be deemed unconscionable. He concluded that seven specific cost items relating to overhead and interest were not justified by Paramount and were therefore unconscionable. (*Buchwald II*, pp. 550–551)

The court's reasoning was fuzzy at best. It was apparently driven by the belief that Paramount had to justify the various pieces of its cost formula. Paramount had argued that it needed to recoup more than its costs on its few big successes because winners had to subsidize losers. Paramount invoked this argument, dubbed the "risky business" defense, to explain why the breakeven for net profits participants came so late, but ultimately dropped the argument, apparently to avoid disclosure of confidential information regarding the profitability of its films. (O'Donnell and McDougal 1992, pp. 435–436, 440–442, 450–452, 460)

Paramount's silence left an explanatory vacuum. That vacuum was decisive for Judge Schneider:

> So long as Paramount maintained its net profit formula was justified by the nature of the motion picture industry, the court felt an inquiry into Paramount's profitability was necessary and proper. In effect, Paramount was arguing that the net profit formula was justified in order to properly allocate the risks between Paramount and Bernheim, Paramount's position being that it bore substantially all of the risks. The court reasoned that if Paramount's representations as to its profitability were untrue, i.e., if it really ran no meaningful risk because of the profit structure of its business, then its argument that the net profit formula was justified would fall by its own force. (*Buchwald II*, p. 547, n.4)

Buchwald's lawyers and some sympathetic commentators argued that moviemaking (at least by the major studios) was not so risky because many, perhaps most, films made money. (O'Donnell and McDougal 1992, pp. 415, 432–433) The high distribution fee and other features of the net profits deal were not necessary for the winners to compensate for the losers, since there were few losers. But this misses the point. Regardless of what fraction of films made money (by some accounting definition), it is surely correct that there is a large variance in the earnings of films. If money is to be invested in the film industry, where some films do relatively poorly and many projects do not make it to the screen at all, firms have to expect to take in enough revenue on their successes (and their limping successes and their failures) to justify making the investment. But this is true regardless of whether the studio shares revenue with the talent. Thus, while Paramount's basic point was undoubtedly correct—making movies is indeed a risky business—its truth has no bearing on the questions of whether the studio should share revenue with the creative talent and how it should do so.

Paramount might have to justify its investment decisions to its shareholders, but why must it justify particular contract terms to anyone? Surely, the creative talent has no natural right to a piece of a successful movie. The right is determined by contract, and there is no reason that contractually defined terms need conform to some court-proposed definition of costs or profits (as in the seven terms identified by the court). The court implicitly adopted the position that (a) people with a lot of clout (Eddie Murphy) can bargain for gross points and are therefore not victims of unequal bargaining power; (b) people with some clout (Alain Bernheim), who get net points but cannot bargain over the terms, are victims of unconscionable contracts and are entitled to have them rewritten by the courts; and (c) people further down the food chain with no clout, who receive no net points, cannot complain about their compensation because none of the unconscionable clauses are included in their contracts. Making the decision even more peculiar, the court failed to find the distribution fee itself unconscionable. Deleting the cost elements identified by the court and increasing the distribution fee by a few percentage points would yield essentially the same outcome, but, following the court's logic, such an agreement would survive an unconscionability claim.

Two years after the *Buchwald II* decision, and one year before the case finally settled, another California court held that the net profits clause in the contract of the producers of *Batman* was not unconscionable.[7] In 1979, Benjamin Melniker and Michael Uslan obtained an option on the motion picture rights to the Batman comic book characters. They made a development and production deal with Casablanca Productions which was amended nine years later so that the film could be made with Warner Bros. Their fixed compensation as executive producers for *Batman* was $300,000. In addition, they received a $100,000 deferment, payable after the film generated a certain level of receipts, plus 13% of the net profits. Although one of the biggest box office successes in history, the picture remained $20 million in the red. Represented by Pierce O'Donnell, the same lawyer who represented Art Buchwald, the two producers sued Warner for $8 million.

In finding for Warner, the court made clear that the plaintiffs were not naive beginners, but rather were wise to the ways of Hollywood. "Mr. Melniker negotiated the Warner Agreement on his and Mr. Uslan's behalf. No one is less likely to have been coerced against his will into signing a contract like the Warner Agreement than Mr. Melniker. This former general counsel and senior executive of a major motion picture studio (Metro-Goldwyn-Mayer) knew all the tricks of the trade; he knew inside and out how these contracts work, what they mean, and how they are negotiated." (*Batfilm*, p. 4) The court rejected the claim that the unfairness of the contract made it unconscionable:

At the core of plaintiffs' case is their argument that the contract was not fair to them because Warner Bros. and others earned millions of dollars on *Batman* and plaintiffs did not. The answer to that argument is that ever since the King's Bench decided *Slade's Case* in 1602, right down to today, courts do not refuse to enforce contracts or remake contracts for the parties because the court or the jury thinks that the contract is not fair.

That principle is not some medieval anachronism. This society, this country, this culture operates on the basis of billions of bargains struck willingly every day by people all across the country in all walks of life. And if any one of those people could have their bargain reexamined after the fact on the ground that it was not fair or on an assertion that it was not fair, we would have a far different type of society than we have now; we would have one that none of the parties to this case would like very much. (*Batfilm*, pp. 4–5)

Despite the rhetoric, the court did consider the plaintiffs' complaints about specific charges (mainly overhead and interest), but ultimately rejected them for the following reason:

[T]he plaintiffs failed to prove that historically Warner Bros.' indirect general administrative expenses for motion picture production and advertising—"overhead"—do not equal or exceed the amount charged under the "Net Profits" definition, namely, 15 percent of production costs and 10 percent of advertising expenditures. As a matter of fact, plaintiffs conceded that they could not show that the overhead charges under the "Net Profits" definition exceeded Warner Bros.' actual overhead costs, taken as a whole. (*Batfilm*, p. 7)

If the contract had defined production cost overhead as 15% even if in fact it was 2%, why should this matter, so long as the complaint was not that Warner Bros. defrauded the producers with a devious definition or overly aggressive accounting? That is, so long as Hollywood professionals know that charges labeled "overhead" in a net profits agreement need bear no relationship to any costs actually incurred by the studio, proof that the overhead charge is not grounded in reality should gain the plaintiff nothing. It seems odd to suggest that a gross mismatch between contract overhead and "actual overhead" would make a contract unconscionable, especially if the studio could rename the overhead as "a gratuitous fee that we assess just because we want to."

A third case involving a suit over net profits was filed in November 1995 by the estate and heirs of Jim Garrison, which had yet to receive net profit payments from *JFK,* a film based on Garrison's 1988 book of the same name, despite the film's gross of over $150 million. The suit upped the ante: it was a class action against seven major studios and the Motion Picture Association of America, and it included antitrust causes of action (price fixing and concerted refusal to deal). The plaintiff class included more than 2,000 authors, screenwriters, actors, producers, and directors who had entered into standard net profits contracts. The complaint included the familiar litany of unreasonable overhead and interest charges. Labeling net profits "a scam that has endured nearly a half century," the complaint asserted that the studios worked in concert "to fix, lower, maintain or stabilize the prices they paid to Talent." (*Garrison v. Warner Bros.*, First Amended Complaint, pp. 2, 11) The suit ultimately failed when the class was denied certification.

It is hard to imagine how a conspiracy fixing the back-end compensation of some of the talent could possibly benefit the studios. The back-end compensation is only a small piece of the reward; indeed, as the Garrison family learned, it can be a vanishingly small part of the compensation package. What purpose could be served by conspiring to fix the tail while the dog remains freely negotiated? Why agree on a rather convoluted contingent compensation clause when it would surely be simpler to agree to give no back-end compensation at all?

While I obviously do not think the unconscionability or antitrust complaints have legal merit, that is beside the point. Neither "theory" helps answer the central questions: Why make any of the compensation of this class of talent contingent on the commercial success of the film? And why does the class's breakeven point depend so much on the presence of superior (more marketable) talent—the gross participants? Neither "studio power" nor "conspiracy" is a sufficient answer to these questions. The expected value of the talent's compensation package will depend upon the studio's evaluation of the individual's ability to sell tickets, and the relevant alternatives. That market value is the talent's "power." Eddie Murphy could command $8 million in straight salary; Alain Bernheim could not. Eddie Murphy could balk at the studio's standardized terms; Alain Bernheim could not. Eddie Murphy could demand first-dollar back-end compensation; Alain Bernheim could not. The price of the talent is correlated with the quality of its contingent compensation: high-priced talent takes gross, lower priced talent takes net, and still lower priced takes naught. Treating the marketability of the talent as a manifestation of unconscionability simply obscures the real question: Why do we observe this *form* of payment?

3. Why Give Up Net Points?

Assume for the moment that making a portion of the talent's compensation contingent upon net profits serves a useful function, a point I will develop in the next section. Here I ask why a net profits participant would be willing to sacrifice some or all of those net profits in certain circumstances. To simplify the discussion, I will focus on a particular net participant, a producer like Alain Bernheim.

Movies are put together sequentially, with the producer typically signing on to the project before most of the other participants are even known. The producer's compensation typically will be in at least three pieces. The producer will receive a fairly modest development fee to begin the process of shepherding the basic concept to the screen. Most movie projects never make it to the screen, so it is quite likely that a producer will devote months of his time to a project and end up receiving only the modest development fee. If the project advances far enough for the studio to make a serious commitment, the producer's deal becomes "pay or play." That is, the studio makes a commitment to pay the producer a further sum even if the project is not completed. The studio reserves the right to either abandon the project or replace the producer, but if it does either, it must pay the producer the second installment, usually called the fixed compensation, which will be a substantial amount. Bernheim's fixed compensation, recall, was $200,000. If the producer remains with the film, and it is produced, he receives the fixed component and he also becomes eligible for the third component, the back end contingent compensation, which for most producers would come in the form of net profits.

If the movie is made with no-name talent and it succeeds at the box office, the back-end could be substantial. The producer has, in effect, a priority claim on a possible future stream of income from the project; he does not want the studio to enter into subsequent contracts that might water down his claim. In this sense, he is like an investor in a corporation's debt who wants to prevent subsequent revisions of the firm's capital structure that would reduce the value of the claim. Like the investor, the producer recognizes that there will be some situations in which diluting his claim will still increase his expected future income. In particular, he might be willing to give up net points or move the breakeven point back (or both) if superior talent is brought into the project. Mel Sattler, an industry veteran and expert witness for Paramount in *Buchwald*, put the point well:

[P]roducers do not complain about the studio's decision to grant "Net Profits" participations even though they reduce the producer's share. . . . [T]he producer knows in advance that he will be trading his contractually allocated "net" points to obtain the services of a proven talent. That increases the likelihood that the motion picture will be produced (which triggers payment to the producer of his "up front" fixed compensation) and be successful.

The situation is no different in the case of a so-called "Gross" participant. Obviously, a talent that commands a "Gross" deal has enjoyed even greater success than the talent that only receives a "Net" deal. The producer is even more delighted to have a major "star" involved in a project. (*Buchwald I*, Declaration, pp. 36–37)

The consultation clause in which the producer agrees in advance to reduce his net points from around forty to around twenty if net or gross participants are subsequently added to the project is one manifestation of this ex ante agreement to reduce the producer's share. A second is the outward shift of the breakeven point if high-priced talent (especially talent that could command gross points) is added to the project.

Adding high-priced talent does more than simply increase the likelihood that the movie will be made. There is also a greater likelihood that the movie will be a commercial success. While the success might not be sufficient to yield net profits given the higher breakeven point, it can still redound to the producer's financial benefit. If the movie is a success, the probability that the producer will be offered another project increases; so too, most likely, will his fixed compensation on the subsequent picture. Successful movies are more likely to breed sequels, and—since the producer's contract typically gives the producer the option to participate in sequels—provide additional compensation. Melniker and Uslan, for example, were given executive producer credit on all the *Batman* sequels. Bernheim's contract itself illustrated the link between actually making a picture (regardless of its commercial success) and the size of fees for subsequent movies. Both his fixed fee and his net profit share would have increased had he merely begun another picture before *Coming to America* was set for production. Winston Groom's experience following the success of *Forrest Gump* provides a vivid illustration of the financial possibilities stemming from a smash hit. His novel sold only 9,000 copies when it first appeared about a decade before the film. After the movie it sold about 1.8 million copies in paperback and an additional 36,000 in hardcover. A second book of "Gumpisms" sold an additional 600,000 copies. (Welkos 1995a, p. A1)

Thus, adding a star worthy of gross points to a project will increase the producer's expected future earnings even though it means that he is much less likely to see back-end compensation from the picture. It might seem counterintuitive that an agreement to forego one piece of compensation under certain conditions would redound to the producer's benefit, but this is just another variation on a common theme: by agreeing in advance to allow its interest to be diluted under specified conditions, a party can be better off than if it had insisted upon absolute protection.

Even if he received no *direct* benefits from sacrificing the back-end compensation, the net profits participant could benefit indirectly. Because the studio values the option to add gross participants, the compensation paid to net profits talent already reflects a premium for that option. In other words, if the studio were denied the option to add gross participants, then the producer's fixed compensation would likely be less. The studio, the major claimant on the project's future revenue stream, wants the ability to adapt as new information and opportunities come along. On the downside, it maintains the option to abandon the project altogether. Exercising this option can be quite expensive if the project has gone far enough along so that the major players are "pay or play." When Paramount abandoned (it thought) *King for a Day*, it had spent over $400,000 and had not yet made the picture "pay or play." (O'Donnell and McDougal 1992, p. 295) On rare occasions studios have killed a project after the entire film was shot. The studio needs the flexibility to adapt as scripts are rewritten, particular talent becomes available, or the concept switches from, say, a made-for-TV movie to a big screen star vehicle. The pay or play clause, for example, preserves (at a hefty price) the studio's option to substitute talent better suited to the new circumstances. (See Chapter 15.) Had Paramount made *King for a Day* "pay or play," it could have replaced Bernheim as producer, but only if it paid him his fixed compensation ($200,000).

The option to add high-priced talent is an extremely valuable one. The consultation clause provides for that option according to a predetermined pricing formula. If a net profits participant is added, most or all of his share will come out of the producer's share. If a gross participant is added, both the studio and the net participants dilute their claims to the future earning stream. The studios could, of course, sweeten the deal for the producer by altering the compensation package when the project changes direction. Bernheim's agent suggested that they always do so, surely a litigation-induced exaggeration. A voluntary increase in the producer's compensation might well be in the studio's long-term interest (maintaining good will), but it is doubtful that as a general rule the studio would choose to increase the producer's direct compensation at precisely the moment that the producer's relative contribution to the film's commercial success has been diminished. In any event, if the studio does choose to sweeten the deal, the new compensation package will almost certainly have a higher breakeven point.

4. Why Take Net Points?

We have a reasonable explanation of why net profits participants might be willing to give up some or all of their back-end compensation when star talent capable of commanding gross points is added to a project. That leaves the prior and more general question: Why use net profits compensation in the first place? Why give Art Buchwald 1.5% of the net for a treatment or Alan Bernheim 17.5% of the net for producing a film? Why, for that matter, give Eddie Murphy 15% of the adjusted gross? Why doesn't the studio simply pay everyone fixed fees and take 100% of the revenues for itself, and why wouldn't the talent prefer that?

A Brief Digression

It is useful to step back and put things in perspective. Contingent compensation is not confined to the contracts between studios and talent. It is endemic in the movie business throughout the distribution chain. It is even the rule in the sale to distributors of completed, low-budget, independent films, a point to which I shall return below. In the standard distribution contract, the exhibitor receives a contractually determined share of the box office gross. The standard subdistributor contract for foreign distribution also involves a sharing rule, typically based on the net rather than the gross. Before turning to our particular problem—the studio-talent contract—it will be instructive to investigate why these contracts take the form they do. The critical feature is the relationship between the timing of the parties' performance and their compensation.

Consider first the contract between the distributor (for example, Paramount) and the exhibitor (the local theater). The exhibitor could pay a fixed fee for the movie and keep all the revenues for itself, or it could simply charge a flat rental fee for the space, with the distributor then receiving all the revenue. Typically, the parties avoid these extremes, dividing the revenues roughly evenly after subtracting out the so-called house nut—a fixed amount subject to negotiation that ostensibly covers the exhibitor's fixed costs. (Some exceptions to this rule will be discussed below.) The sharing arrangement reflects the fact that the size of the revenue stream is influenced by the efforts of both the distributor and the exhibitor. The distributor launches a massive advertising campaign shortly before a film is released. The exhibitor markets the movie locally (some of this expense being footed by the distributor through cooperative advertising). By maintaining a large stake in the outcome for both distributor and exhibitor, the sharing formula gives to both an incentive to provide selling effort. Technically, the parties face a two-sided moral hazard problem since the outcomes depend on the efforts of both.

Their efforts are not provided simultaneously, the distributor's effort being more significant in the beginning. The sharing formula reflects that timing. Since the selling effort of the distributor is more heavily front-loaded, a constant sharing formula would give the exhibitor a poor return on its marketing efforts in the later stages of a film's run. It would be inclined to terminate a run early since it would bear nearly all the incremental marketing costs at this stage yet reap only a portion of the gains. Distribution contracts account for this timing asymmetry by reducing the distributor's share as the length of the run increases. Thus, the typical distribution agreement gives the distributor the greater of two figures. Either it receives 90% of the box office receipts in excess of the house nut or it receives a floor that is typically 70% of box office receipts in the first two weeks and that is gradually reduced to about 35% to 40% by the eighth week.[8] "In the earlier, high-grossing weeks of a run, the 90/10 calculation prevails, while in later weeks the percentage minimums are invoked." (Reardon 1992, p. 314) The sharing formula is tilted to provide a larger share of the compensation to the party whose effort is most significant at a particular phase of the film's life.

The few exceptions illuminate the purpose behind the arrangement. On occasion the exhibitor pays a fixed fee for the film and keeps all the box office receipts. Typically this would occur for a small theater showing a late run, long after the distributor's promotional efforts have ceased. At the opposite extreme, distributors sometimes engage in "four-walling," renting the theater at a fixed fee and keeping all the box office receipts. The four-walling distributor will engage in a massive advertising campaign on local television, essentially taking over most of the local exhibitor's marketing tasks. (Vogel 1994, p. 73)

The foreign distribution contract also phases the compensation to reflect the timing of the parties' efforts. The studios often enter into foreign distribution arrangements with subdistributors before the movie is completed. When arranging its foreign distribution, a studio could purchase distribution services from the subdistributor for a flat fee. It does not. Instead, the studio enters into a sharing arrangement in which the subdistributor gives the studio a fixed payment plus half the net profits (derived by subtracting from the subdistributor's revenues the initial payment, the local distribution costs, and a distribution fee). (Yeldell 1987, §18.02(c)(2)) In effect, the studio accepts from the foreign subdistributor the same deal that the studio gives to the net profits participants like Bernheim and Buchwald. The compensation can be broken down into three pieces. First, the studio receives a lump sum based on expectations of the yet-to-be-made movie's marketability in the local market. The subdistributor then receives all the revenues until the breakeven point is reached. Finally, after breakeven the revenues are divided on a roughly fifty-fifty basis. The breakeven point increases as the subdistributor's distribution costs rise—it is a "rolling breakeven."

The division of the first two pieces is nicely coordinated with the timing of the effort of the two parties. The phasing of the compensation is even more extreme than in the distributor-exhibitor contract. Virtually all the studio's efforts to influence the box office in the local market have been made long before the movie appears there. In a typical release pattern, the film will be shown in foreign markets some months after it first appears in the American market. The subdistributor, when determining how much marketing effort to put behind a particular film, finds that it (and its local exhibitors) will receive all of the rewards from local effort up to the breakeven point. Only after breakeven does the subdistributor share with the studio. But that raises the natural question: Why stop there? Why water down the subdistributor's incentives by giving the studio half the net revenues after breakeven has been reached?

Part of the reason, of course, is that a rolling breakeven arrangement does not water down the incentives very much. True, at the planning stage, when the subdistributor is planning its local distribution budget, truncating the earnings stream reduces the expected value of its marketing expenditures. If the marketing decision were completely irreversible, then perhaps the truncation would result in a somewhat smaller expenditure. But the decision, almost certainly, is not irreversible. As new information becomes available, the subdistributor can adapt its marketing plan accordingly. And at that stage, the rolling breakeven means that so long as the expected incremental revenues exceed the subdistributor's expected incremental costs, it will be willing to expand its marketing effort. By giving the subdistributor a large share of the incremental benefits, the arrangement creates a larger pie for the studio and sub to share.

There are three additional explanations for the sharing arrangement. First, since the foreign distribution agreement is often made at an early stage in the project, giving the studio some of the contingent compensation heightens its incentive to produce a film that will appeal to the foreign market. That is, incentives affect not only effort but artistic judgment as well. Second, if the parties must agree on a single price for an asset of uncertain value (the unfinished film), they have an incentive to economize on the production of information about the value of that asset; sharing reduces the value of an informational advantage, allowing the parties to spend less in pursuit of special information and also allowing them to consummate the deal earlier, with less information revealed. (See Barzel 1982; Kenney and Klein 1983; and Goldberg (1997c.) Third, by accepting some of its compensation in a contingent form, the studio assures the subdistributor of its belief in the quality of the film. The studio is like the seller of a firm who takes part of the price in the form of an "earnout," making part of its payment contingent upon the future success of the asset (the firm or the film). We will see this argument again in the analysis of *Bloor v. Falstaff* (Chapter 6).

The Studio-Talent Contract

The studio's role vis-à-vis the foreign subdistributor is just the opposite of its role vis-à-vis the talent. Virtually all the subdistributor's effort comes after the studio has made its contribution to the project. Virtually all the talent's effort comes before the studio's marketing effort. The studio is responsible for the production and marketing costs, and the deferred break-even assures the studio that it will receive most of the revenues arising from an increase in either production or distribution expenses. The studio receives 100% of revenue until breakeven, just as the subdistributor does vis-à-vis the studio in the foreign distribution. The studio's incentives to develop and exploit the property are preserved by allowing it to reap almost all the rewards. Again, the puzzle is not why the talent get *so little* of the profits; the question is why they get any.

The studio does not take all the upside; it shares net profits above the contractually defined breakeven point. The reasons are variations on the themes noted above. For the author of a treatment (like Buchwald), whose contribution is completed before the project has taken shape, making a piece of the compensation contingent simplifies the valuation problem. The sale can be completed before either party has determined how (or whether) the property might be developed.

For a producer who remains with the project, the opportunity to share in net profits serves as a goad both to improve quality and to control costs. The producer will often maintain considerable control over the film's costs. Making some of the compensation depend upon cost containment encourages him to balance the benefits of lower costs against those of increased quality and gross revenue. Indeed, a producer's contract often includes an "overbudget penalty clause," which reduces the producer's share of net profits if the film is over budget by more than a specified amount. As gross participants are added to the project, the producer's influence over both cost and quality of the final product decreases and the incentive effects of the net profits carrot are, naturally, weakened. That is, when there is no exceptional talent taking gross points, the net profits clause provides some incentives to the talent who have a significant impact on the outcome; the incentive effects of the net profits clause fade away precisely when that intermediate-level talent has less impact on the outcome.

The larger the share of the distribution budget allocated to the post-release period, the more important are the studio's incentives at the margin. If the studio has the option of continuing to spend on promotion, it is more likely to do so the greater its share of the rewards from that promotion. Because their commercial success depends critically upon the opening weekend's box office receipts, films with top talent allocate a larger share of their promotion-distribution budget to the pre-release phase than do films staffed with lesser talent. Indeed, the presence of the top talent is itself a critical element in the film's marketing. The presence of Eddie Murphy, Arnold Schwarzenegger, or a handful of other top stars can by itself assure a film an opening on a significant number of screens. Moreover, those stars can make a substantial contribution to the marketing of the film, promoting the film to exhibitors to assure wide distribution and to potential viewers on the talk show circuit. By giving these top stars a share of first-dollar gross, a studio encourages promotional effort. The marketing efforts of Schwarzenegger and Reese Witherspoon in *Terminator 3* and *Legally Blonde 2*, respectively, are well documented in Hayes and Bing (2004).

Because the bulk of the marketing budget of a film with gross participants has been committed prior to the release of the film, the adverse incentive of, in effect, taxing the return on the studio's post-release marketing effort is muted. On the other hand, films with less exceptional talent will, in general, have more modest openings, and their commercial success will depend more on building an audience over time. A considerable portion of the studio's marketing effort will be concentrated on the post-release period, during which the studio will have to balance the expected benefits of spending an additional marketing dollar against the costs. Efficient exploitation of this type of movie is enhanced with a rolling breakeven, which allows the studio to recoup its incremental post-release marketing expenditures before sharing any revenues. Thus, the pattern of contingent compensation that we observe—first-dollar gross for top stars, adjusted gross for the next tier, and net for the next—is consistent with the timing of the studio's marketing effort.

Most net profits participants enter into their contracts long before the picture is completed. The net profits structure reflects the timing of their contributions to the commercial success of the movie and the importance of maintaining incentives at the various stages of the project's life, particularly the incentives of the distributor. There is one notable class of exceptions—independent films sold to distributors after completion—and this class enables us to view the net profits clause from a different angle. Independent producers will typically produce a film without having prearranged the distribution rights. They will then try to market the film to a distributor, often by exhibiting it at a festival. While most such films are small, relatively inexpensive, and of dubious commercial value, a few achieve commercial success, for example, *She's Gotta Have It, Reservoir Dogs, sex, lies, and videotape, Roger & Me,* and *Hoop Dreams.* (Pierson 1995, pp. 62–66, 127–128, 149–150, 210–211, 323–327)

These deals virtually always include net profits. (Deutchman 1992, p. 324) The producer buys services from a distributor just as the distributor buys services from the foreign subdistributor. Rather than paying directly for the service, the producer receives a fixed fee and the distributor keeps all the revenue until breakeven, after which the revenues are divided. The contract comes too late in the project's life for the net profits to influence the producer's behavior in making the original print. Still, net profits can influence the producer's behavior in two respects. Between the date of acquisition and the film's commercial release, the film can be reshaped in various ways to make it more marketable. For examples, see Pierson's (1995, pp. 66–78, 152–176) discussion of the post-acquisition, pre-release changes in *She's Gotta Have It* and *Roger & Me*. The producer can also play an active role in promoting the film. Michael Moore, for example, agreed to be available for a six-month period to promote *Roger & Me*.[9] The producer's continuing role in the commercial success of the film goes a long way toward explaining the use of contingent compensation for the sale of a "completed" film. As noted above, the net profits formula maintains the distributor's incentives at the margin. For every dollar spent by the distributor, the first $1.30 or so (depending on the distribution fee) of revenue goes to the distributor. This is of crucial importance for small, independent films since such a large share of their promotional budget is allocated to the post-release period.

Net profits compensation for the independent producer-director might play two other roles as well. In part, the contingent compensation bridges a difference of opinion. If the producer's view of the commercial value of "his baby" is systematically more rosy than that of the distributors, the expected value of the back end will be greater for the producer than for the distributor. This explanation relies upon the systematic relative optimism of the producer-director. Alternatively, by reducing the value of divining the right price, net profits can serve to reduce the costs of haggling over the film's commercial value. Pierson (1995, pp. 139–165) provides an extensive description of the haggling over the advance for *Roger & Me*.

5. Conclusion: The Diminishing Likelihood of Net Profits

The public perception of net profits clauses is, I think, that talent are entitled to a share of the earnings of a film and that the studios have manipulated the clauses to make it unlikely that the talent will reap their just rewards. I start with the notion that it is not at all obvious that any contingent compensation is in the interests of the talent because any sharing rule waters down the studio's incentives to spend money on producing and promoting the picture. The harder question, I have argued, is why the studio shares as much of the film's revenue stream as it does with the talent. I conclude that giving the net profits participants a share of the back end sharpens their incentives both while the film is being produced and afterward if they are to be involved in promoting the film. It also facilitates early contracting in the context of imperfect and asymmetric information. The fact that the studio-talent clause is structurally close to the studio-subdistributor contract (but with the studio taking the back end in the latter) suggests that the clause is being used to resolve the same problems there.

Granted that there are satisfactory reasons for sharing some of the film's contractually defined net profits, the question that naturally arises is why the formula results in so few payouts. It is part of the semantic confusion in this industry that the largest component of the net participant's expected compensation is labeled "fixed" but is, in fact, contingent. Most projects are terminated early, with the net participants receiving modest development fees but no fixed fees. Of those projects that do make it to the screen, in most instances the net participants receive only their fixed fee. Net profits participants, I have argued, agree in advance to give up their priority to claims on the future revenue stream in certain circumstances. In particular, when a gross participant is added to the project, even though the likelihood of receiving net profits from a successful movie might fall, the expected value of the net profits participant's overall contract will increase. The gross participant's presence increases the likelihood that the project will actually go into production, and that means that the net profits participant is more likely to receive her fixed compensation.

Not only is the likelihood that a studio film will yield net profits low, but industry observers agree that the likelihood of a payout has declined in the past two decades. In part, this is attributable to rising production and distribution costs. In addition, there has been an increased skewing of earnings, with the payments to top stars increasing relative to those going to the net participants. The value of top stars has been enhanced both because domestic box office revenues have become more dependent on a film's performance in its opening weeks and because foreign exhibition accounts for a much larger share of receipts today than in the past. As a consequence of these two factors, the breakeven point for net profits participants has been receding, commensurate with their decreased contribution to the commercial success of a movie.

PART II

Consideration

Which promises will be enforceable at law? The primary doctrinal answer at common law is those promises for which there is consideration. Like many contracts scholars, I am not particularly enamored with the doctrine, which seems to draw the boundary in a way that has little to do with function. If we were starting with a clean slate we could probably design a system that would enable parties to make clear their intention whether or not to have a transaction legally enforceable. But so long as the doctrine provides a fairly sharp boundary as to what is enforceable, where the boundary lies shouldn't matter very much. The parties can take the rule into account and choose whether they should provide explicit consideration. I don't intend to reinvent the wheel; I take the basic doctrine as given and focus only on the fringes. In particular, I am concerned with attempts to finesse the illusory promise problem.

Economic actors often attempt to arrange their affairs so that there is no enforceable promise. For example, early automobile franchise agreements were held unenforceable for want of mutuality. The auto manufacturers could have redrafted to resolve that problem but chose not to do so since they preferred that their arrangements be terminable at will. As Kessler (1957, p. 1149) noted:

An initial block confronting dealers lay in the argument that a franchise, marked by the absence or indefiniteness of obligations, was not a valid and enforceable contract. Until recently, the validity issue was continuously raised in franchise litigation, the defendant manufacturer almost invariably arguing that the agreement lacked mutuality. . . .

For many decades, the invalidity argument may have been the most powerful weapon available to manufacturers in defending damage suits by dealers. It was honored by most courts, provided the manufacturer engaged in careful draftsmanship.

Clearly, the automobile manufacturers desired that their agreements not be enforceable, and their dealers knew (or should have known) that. The dealers were not willing to pay enough to change the manufacturer's minds. It should not have required "careful draftmanship" to achieve a simple result. Nor should it have been necessary to use an oblique doctrinal tool to do so.

If a promisor said, in effect, I will do X if I want to, the promise would be illusory and a court would conclude that there was no contract. Some agreements that seemed on their face to be legitimate deals—requirements contracts, full output contracts, and exclusive contracts—were held to be unenforceable in the early twentieth century. The doctrinal response was to imply two Band-Aids: (a) good faith and (b) reasonable or best efforts. These were, I believe, a big mistake. The chapters in Part II, and one of the chapters in Part III, show why.

The Band-Aids were codified in the Uniform Commercial Code in §2–306. Since I will be referring to these often in Parts II and III, that Code section and the pertinent Official Comments are reproduced here.

> UCC 2–306 (1) A term which measures the quantity by the output of the seller or the requirements of the buyer means such actual output or requirements as may occur in good faith, except that no quantity unreasonably disproportionate to any stated estimate or in the absence of a stated estimate to any normal or otherwise comparable prior output or requirements may be tendered or demanded.
>
> (2) A lawful agreement by either the seller or the buyer for exclusive dealing in the kind of goods concerned imposes unless otherwise agreed an obligation by the seller to use best efforts to supply the goods and by the buyer to use best efforts to promote their sale.

Comments

2. Under this Article, a contract for output or requirements is not too indefinite since it is held to mean the actual good faith output or requirements of the particular party. Nor does such a contract lack mutuality of obligation since, under this section, the party who will determine quantity is required to operate his plant or conduct his business in good faith and

according to commercial standards of fair dealing in the trade so that his output or requirements will approximate a reasonably foreseeable figure. Reasonable elasticity in the requirements is expressly envisaged by this section and good faith variations from prior requirements are permitted even when the variation may be such as to result in discontinuance. A shut-down by a requirements buyer for lack of orders might be permissible when a shut-down merely to curtail losses would not. The essential test is whether the party is acting in good faith. Similarly, a sudden expansion of the plant by which requirements are to be measured would not be included within the scope of the contract as made but normal expansion undertaken in good faith would be within the scope of this section. One of the factors in an expansion situation would be whether the market price had risen greatly in a case in which the requirements contract contained a fixed price. Reasonable variation of an extreme sort is exemplified in *Southwest Natural Gas Co. v. Oklahoma Portland Cement Co. . . .*

3. If an estimate of output or requirements is included in the agreement, no quantity unreasonably disproportionate to it may be tendered or demanded. Any minimum or maximum set by the agreement shows a clear limit on the intended elasticity. In similar fashion, the agreed estimate is to be regarded as a center around which the parties intend the variation to occur.

4. When an enterprise is sold, the question may arise whether the buyer is bound by an existing output or requirements contract. That question is outside the scope of this Article, and is to be determined on other principles of law. Assuming that the contract continues, the output or requirements in the hands of the new owner continue to be measured by the actual good faith output or requirements under the normal operation of the enterprise prior to sale. The sale itself is not grounds for sudden expansion or decrease.

5. Subsection (2), on exclusive dealing, makes explicit the commercial rule embodied in this Act under which the parties to such contracts are held to have impliedly, even when not expressly, bound themselves to use reasonable diligence as well as good faith in their performance of the contract. Under such contracts the exclusive agent is required, although no express commitment has been made, to use reasonable effort and due diligence in the expansion of the market or the promotion of the product, as the case may be.

The illustrations to §77 of Restatement (Second) Contracts make the same point:

8. A promises to sell his output or buy his requirements of a specified type of goods from B on specified terms. A's promise is consideration for a return promise by B. A must operate his plant or conduct his business in good faith and according to commercial standards of fair dealing in the trade so that his output or requirements will approximate a reasonably foreseeable figure.

9. A promises to pay B half of any profits he derives from the sale of goods manufactured by B; in return B promises that A shall have the exclusive right to market such goods. The promises are consideration for each other, since the agreement for exclusive dealing imposes an obligation on A to use best efforts to promote sale of the goods and on B to use best efforts to supply them.

Good faith and best efforts solve the lack-of-consideration problem, but neither was necessary for that narrow purpose. There are plenty of drafting techniques available to contracting parties who want their agreement to be enforceable. The problem is not whether the agreements are enforceable, but what is to be enforced. By imposing a near-mandatory "good faith" or "best efforts" duty on the promisor, the law raises barriers to efficient contracting. Good faith and best efforts are very fuzzy standards. It is hard enough to interpret an express good faith or best efforts promise. The difficulties are compounded when the promise is implied.

I begin Part II with an analysis of a classic, *Wood v. Lucy, Lady Duff-Gordon*. Cardozo's solution to the lack-of-consideration problem provided the basis for both the Code and Restatement responses noted above. I had originally thought that the case would be a great vehicle for analyzing incentive structures and the free rider problem. However, the economics turned out to be less interesting than the history. Cardozo had virtually no facts to work with when fashioning his opinion. Had he been informed about another of Wood's contracts, he would have found the case for implying reasonable efforts less compelling. Whether the court should have found an enforceable agreement without invoking the implied best efforts clause remains a close question. The deeper problem with the opinion is the impact it has had on the interpretation of agreements generally, including those for which the existence of consideration was not an issue.

While *Wood v. Lucy* remains a casebook favorite, the second case, *Oscar*

Schlegel Manufacturing Company v. Peter Cooper's Glue Factory, seems to be fading from the repertoire. This is unfortunate because it appears to present the ultimate horror story—the requirements contract with no limits and a buyer dramatically increasing its purchases in response to a soaring market price. I say "appears" advisedly. If the seller's obligation were truly unbounded, the transaction would make no economic sense. However, a careful reading of the case reveals that the buyer's discretion was not unbounded, and that there was a coherent economic rationale for the transaction. The court left the buyer with no remedy. I suggest two theories under which the buyer should have recovered; neither requires invocation of good faith or reasonableness.

The final chapter of Part II concerns the use of satisfaction clauses in real estate transactions. In particular, I focus on *Mattei v. Hopper*, in which the buyer had the option to proceed with a purchase, subject to its obtaining satisfactory leases for a potential shopping center. As in *Wood v. Lucy*, courts have invoked good faith to find these agreements enforceable. That approach obscures the underlying economics of the transactions. Producing information is costly, and in some instances the most efficient producer of the information would be the potential purchaser. But if the potential purchaser produced the information before entering into an enforceable agreement, the seller could take advantage of the information and leave that potential buyer holding the bag. The contract provides a simple mechanism for encouraging the potential purchaser's production of the information.

CHAPTER 2

Reading *Wood v. Lucy, Lady Duff-Gordon* with Help from the Kewpie Dolls

Everyone knows about *Wood v. Lucy, Lady Duff-Gordon*. It is in virtually every Contracts casebook and is still widely cited by courts.[1] In a decision marked by rather colorful language, Cardozo found consideration for a promise despite the fact that, if read literally, the contract bound Otis Wood to do nothing. Although Wood had not overtly promised to do anything, a promise could fairly be implied, said Cardozo. "His promise to pay the defendant one-half of the profits and revenues resulting from the exclusive agency and to render accounts monthly, was a promise to use reasonable efforts to bring profits and revenues into existence." (p. 92) When I first began this project I thought this an easy case. Cardozo got the result right, but for the wrong reasons. The consideration lay not in the implied promise to use reasonable efforts, but in the contract's incentive structure. I had assumed that Wood, the professional repeat player, had used a standardized form slightly customized for this particular client, and that in that era, parties had not yet thought of making explicit promises to use reasonable or best efforts.

It turns out that I was quite wrong. Fortunately for posterity (less so for Wood), he was involved in one other piece of litigation against a different client, Rose O'Neill, the mother of the Kewpie doll, who, he claimed, had breached a contract in which he was to be the exclusive agent. The differences between his contract with Lucy and that with Rose O'Neill show that there was no need for a court to imply a promise to use any particular level of effort—the parties were quite capable of doing so themselves and apparently chose not to do so.

Moreover, even if Wood and Lucy had a valid, enforceable contract, it is not clear which of Lucy's actions amounted to a breach. She entered into endorsement contracts with at least two third parties, Sears, Roebuck & Co.

43

and Chalmers Motors, during the term of Wood's exclusive deal, but entering into those transactions did not necessarily violate her agreement. It depends on what you mean by "exclusive." The Kewpie contract suggests that "exclusive" is a lot more ambiguous than it looks. Indeed, the Kewpie definition makes it more likely that Lucy had not entered into an enforceable bilateral contract. Cardozo's claim that to hold otherwise would put Lucy at the mercy of Wood, oft cited as the basis for inferring an obligation, is undercut if the Kewpie definition were to hold.

In Section 1, I analyze *Wood v. Lucy* in light of the prior Kewpie contract. I provide some historical background on the parties, and details about both contracts and the litigation. If Cardozo had all this information available to him, I conclude that he would most likely have held that there was no enforceable agreement.

Does it matter whether Cardozo got it right? That is the subject of Section 2, and the answer is that for his ostensible purpose—finding consideration when there is no other source—probably not much. I say that despite the decision's enthusiastic reception and its being the basis for UCC §2–306(2) and an illustration in Restatement (Second) of Contracts. Since it would be easy enough for the parties to incorporate an explicit form of consideration into their agreement, at most the *Lucy* rule provides protection for lazy or sloppy drafting. On the negative side, it exposes parties to the risk that some overzealous court will find an enforceable contract where none was intended.

However, *Lucy*'s reach has been extended beyond this limited purpose, and therein lies its adverse impact. It imposes an ill-defined standard on an ill-defined set of promisors. The meaning of an implied efforts clause (reasonable, best, or otherwise) is, at best, unclear. To make matters worse, some courts have chosen to impose an implied efforts clause even in instances in which there is a separate source of consideration. Doctrinal evolution, unchecked by any sensitivity to the economic context, has produced an incoherent mess. The nature of this mess will be sketched out in Section 2.

1. Wood v. Lucy

The Players

Because the case record is so sparse, I have supplemented it with material from a wide variety of sources: paper, Internet, and human (or at least their e-mail manifestations).[2] I begin with a bit of biographical background.

Lucy, Lady Duff-Gordon.   As Cardozo put it, Lucy "styles herself 'a creator of fashions' [whose] favor helps a sale." And so she was. Cardozo was not, as Llewellyn (1962, pp. 637–638) argued, making a rhetorical dig in order to incline his readers against her. This was how she was described in the contract, and this is how she billed herself to the public. She had an illustrious career as a fashion designer in the early twentieth century, providing elegant gowns to European royalty (including the queens of England and Spain) and leading entertainers (including Irene Castle and Mary Pickford). She was the first British-based fashion designer to achieve an international reputation. In addition to her couture business, she wrote columns on fashion for the Hearst newspapers, *Good Housekeeping,* and *Harper's Bazaar.* In these columns she referred to herself as the "greatest living creator of fashions." She and her second husband, Cosmo Duff-Gordon, survived the *Titanic,* although their reputations were tarnished by the manner in which they survived. Cosmo was accused of bribing the sailors to secure positions in the lifeboats. The accusation generated considerable negative press coverage ultimately leading to a formal board of inquiry. While the charges were not proved, the suspicion remained.

However, the incident did not affect Lucy's business adversely. Her arrangement with Otis Wood was, it appears, one element in a repositioning strategy, aimed at broadening her market, reaching women of more modest (but not very modest) means. Her entry into an agreement with Sears, Roebuck & Co. (described below) was another manifestation of that strategy. In the 1920s she suffered some business reversals and eventually went bankrupt. Lucy's life has been documented in a number of places, most recently in the forthcoming biography by Randy Bigham, so I need not provide more detail.

While Lucy was a famous public figure, Otis was not exactly chopped liver. He came from a prominent, wealthy, and controversial family. Although his family background has no bearing on the case, it is too colorful to ignore entirely. For those uninterested in such gossip, I recommend skipping the next few pages. For those more curious, here are a few branches from his family tree.

Father Fernando.   Otis's father was a three-time mayor of New York. He amassed a considerable fortune early in his career in shipping and later in New York real estate. He married Otis's mother (his third wife) when he was forty-eight and she was sixteen. He fathered many children; his biographer reckons somewhere between fourteen and seventeen, although his

New York Times obituary listed only three, none of whom was Otis. A *New York Times* article on the centenary of his birth began: "Of all the Mayors of New York City from the beginning of the century up to 1881 [the year of his death] the names of only two have passed into tradition—DeWitt Clinton and Fernando Wood." He merited almost an entire chapter in *Gangs of New York* (Asbury 1928, pp. 96–107) and a bit part in the movie of the same name. He was the first mayor elected by the Tammany Hall machine, although he later broke with it. He was instrumental in the development of Central Park. During the Civil War he was a leading "peace Democrat," sympathizing with the South and strongly opposing abolition. His opposition to the war and his battles with Albany led him to propose that New York City secede from the Union on the eve of the war. His position on the crucial issue of the day was laid out starkly in a speech made while serving as a congressman during the war: "This is a government of white men made by white men for . . . the protection of the states and the white people thereof. . . . Yet it is proposed to oppress the white and elevate the social and political condition of the black race. . . . Under the organic law slaves are property. They have no other status in the Constitution and as property cannot be taken except by giving just compensation in return." He is credited (blamed) for being one of the leaders of the New York draft riots, although his brother Benjamin likely played a larger role.

In 1867, Wood and Boss Tweed secured a nomination to the New York Supreme Court for Albert Cardozo. Shortly thereafter Cardozo ruled in Wood's favor in the so-called Wood Lease case *(New York v. Wood)*, a controversial decision in which Wood was accused of procuring a lucrative lease arrangement from the city by fraud or bribery; the judge rejected the city's evidence on technical grounds, giving a directed verdict for Wood. (Cardozo subsequently resigned from the bench when confronted with impeachment for misbehavior in other cases.) A half century later Albert's son, Benjamin, found in favor of Fernando's son, Otis. Fernando spent the last two decades of his life in the House of Representatives, eventually becoming chairman of the Ways and Means Committee. He died while still in office in 1881.

Uncle Ben.   Fernando's younger brother Benjamin was, for the forty years prior to his death, the publisher and editor of the *New York Daily News*, which under his leadership grew to have the largest circulation of any newspaper in the country. He served two short stints in the House of Representatives. His views on the war, race, emancipation, and the draft were, if anything, more extreme than his brother's. Both he and his newspaper were in constant battle with Lincoln (whom he labeled a dictator) during the war. The paper was forced to suspend publication for over a year, and he was at various times threatened with both arrest and court-martial.

In his later years he spent little time with the newspaper, but continued to receive a large income from it, much of which he gave to his second wife, Ida. When in 1899 his income diminished, his wife gave him $100,000 on condition that he turn the newspaper over to her, which he did. He died the following year.

The Wacky Widow.   Ida and Benjamin had been prominent members of the New York social scene. Ida accumulated a substantial fortune, so that by the time of her husband's death her holdings were well over $1 million. She suffered some financial losses in the Panic of 1907, and panic she did. She sold the newspaper, withdrew $750,000 from the banks, and, along with her sister and daughter, moved into the Herald Square Hotel, from which, for the next quarter century, she did not venture out. The women shared two rooms, cooked their own meals, and saw no one. She died in 1932 at the age of ninety-three. Her sister and daughter predeceased her, setting the stage for a notorious battle for her fortune upon her death.

After her sister's death, Ida's nephew Otis reentered her life. He instituted proceedings to declare her incompetent, and to be named her guardian. He succeeded. The case generated considerable press coverage, as did the subsequent battle over her estate. Ida, who became known as the Recluse of Herald Square, died within a year of Otis being named her guardian. Despite her irrational fear of poverty, it turned out that she was still extremely wealthy. Her rooms contained trunks of items, including lots of junk (for example, bushels of hotel soaps) and some very valuable jewelry (one piece was appraised at $38,000). She also had substantial amounts of cash. Sewn into the lining of one garment was an envelope containing fifty very old $10,000 bills. Total cash holdings exceeded $750,000, including some that was actually hidden in the mattress. Upon her death, Otis was initially named the administrator of the estate. Her will left her entire estate to her sister and daughter, but because they were both deceased, the court treated her as having died intestate. This precipitated a battle over the estate that dragged on for seven years with over 1,000 hopefuls making claims. Early on in the battle Otis was ousted as administrator, and he and others from

Benjamin's side of the family were denied any share of the estate. Ultimately, ten of Ida's relatives received equal shares of the estate, which was valued at $877,500.

Brother Henry.   Henry A. Wise Wood, one of Otis's many brothers, was a successful inventor and businessman and a political gadfly. He was the inventor of the high-speed printing press. According to his obituary in the *New York Times,* he "invented much of the intricate modern machinery that makes possible the large circulation of daily newspapers today." His prominence in the business is indicated by his appointment as chairman of the Code Authority for the newspaper machinery industry under the National Recovery Act. He also was a noted aeronautical engineer. He was a strong supporter of America's entry into World War I and a harsh critic of President Wilson's policies both before the United States entered and after the armistice. He vigorously opposed America's entry into the League of Nations and petitioned Congress to impeach President Wilson. He died in 1939, less than one month before his younger brother, Otis.

Otis Fenner Wood.   By contrast to these folks, Otis appears to be the bland sheep of the family. Born in the same year that Albert Cardozo decided the "Wood's Lease" case, Otis died a bachelor in 1939. His business career spanned almost fifty years, but from the few shards of historical material available, we can't say whether the promotion/agency activity promised to Lucy was a core part of his business or merely a sideline. We know how he characterized his business affairs. His contract with Lucy asserts that he "possesses a business organization adapted to the placing of . . . endorsements." In his brief he states that he "has been for over a quarter of a century engaged in the business of advertising and promoting and securing a market for novelties, ideas and plans for the promotion of trade in addition to the marketing of special articles for newspapers and other publications, throughout the United States and other parts of the world." (Plaintiff Brief [PB], pp. 1, 2) The evidence with regard to the second half of his statement syndication is pretty clear; there is less of an obvious fit between the first half (promotion, alas, the relevant half) and the limited descriptions of his other business background. He began his career writing for the *Philadelphia Inquirer.* His first known employment in New York was as cofounder of a firm engaged in lithography in Manhattan in 1892. Within a few years, business directories have him listed as both a lithographer in Manhattan and a publisher in Staten Island (his home). In 1901, the Types Publishing Company, of which he was one of three directors, was dissolved. (The other two directors were his younger brother Benjamin and Benjamin's brother-in-law E. F. Hutton, who founded the eponymous brokerage house a few years later.) There is no evidence as to when the publishing company was formed, what it did, or what Otis's role was other than as a director. By the time of the *Lucy* litigation, he is listed in business directories as the president of two corporations, one on Staten Island and a second in Manhattan. The latter, identified as a newspaper syndicate, was most likely his primary business. His obituary, over two decades later, noted that he was still associated with the syndicate.

Rose O'Neill. We have no idea how many other clients Wood had, but of one we are certain. Less than two years before entering into the contract with Lucy, Otis entered into an agreement with Rose O'Neill to promote her Kewpie dolls, and two months before the Lucy deal, he sued O'Neill for breach. O'Neill was a prominent illustrator with hundreds of illustrations in *Puck* and other major periodicals. She also did illustrations for advertisements, Kellogg's Corn Flakes and Jell-o being two of her more significant clients. She illustrated books, wrote books, and wrote poetry. In 1907, she divorced her second husband, the author and playwright Harry Leon Wilson (hence the name of the case, *Wood v. Wilson*). Two years later, she published drawings of Kewpies along with some of her poetry in the *Ladies Home Journal*. They were a big hit, indeed a phenomenon. Rose had copyright and trademark rights in the Kewpies, and in March 1913 she obtained patent rights. Weeks later she entered into her contract with Otis, and shortly thereafter production of Kewpie dolls commenced. Kewpies were everywhere. As she wrote in her autobiography, there were "Kewpies holding candlesticks, ash-trays, ink-pots, umbrellas, puppies, kittens, rabbits, Easter-chicks. They were painted on dishes and cards, fans, and all sorts of objects. They appeared on buttons, jewelry, children's clothing, toy furniture." (O'Neill, 1997, p. 110) Various sources have her Kewpie royalties at about $1.4 million, although some suggest that was over her lifetime, while others suggest that she received that amount within one year. I suspect the first is closer to the truth, but it doesn't much matter. The main point is that the Kewpies were an instant success and her royalties were huge. (The fact that she managed to spend it all and die relatively poor need not concern us.)

The Contracts

My initial presumption was that Wood had a standard contract and that Lucy had accepted it with minimal revisions, but, as I noted earlier, this was not the case. These two contracts, at least, looked very different, although they treated some issues in a similar way, albeit with very different language. I first describe the two contracts and the litigation in the two cases. Then I turn to the analysis. Neither contract is presented in the published decisions. However, they can be found in the very slim records available to their respective courts, although the courts in neither case had access to both contracts. The Lucy contract was reproduced in the Amended Complaint at pages 5–8; the Kewpie contract was reproduced as Appendix A to Wood's Affidavit at pages 15–20.

Lucy.   The Kewpie dispute was already in the courts when Wood entered into his agreement with Lucy. I suspect that the form the contract took was to some degree influenced by the problems arising under the Kewpie contract, but there is no direct evidence of that. Wood's counsel asserted that the "contract . . . was drawn by the parties themselves and without 'the technical accuracy and with obvious attention to details' that an inspection of the contract will reveal, which would have avoided any controversy between the parties thereto." (PB, p. 11) I find it hard to believe that the contract was the work of the parties, not of lawyers. Counsel's argument was no doubt designed to take advantage of a precedent, *Booth v. Cleveland Mill Co.,* that relaxed the standard for finding consideration because the contract language was informal and colloquial. We do not know which law firms were involved in drafting the agreements; we do know, however, that Wood used different law firms to litigate the two cases. In *Wood v. Wilson* he used Kelley & Becker, and in *Wood v. Lucy, Lady Duff-Gordon* his lawyer was John Jerome Rooney (a published poet and, subsequently, a judge).

The contract, dated April 1, 1915, was an evergreen contract, one that is renewed automatically unless either party gives appropriate notice of nonrenewal; here the term was one year and the notice period ninety days. Unlike the Kewpie contract, Lucy's contract included recitals regarding what each party brought to the arrangement:

> Whereas, the said Otis F. Wood possesses a business organization adapted to the placing of such endorsements as the said Lucy, Lady Duff-Gordon, has approved

Whereas, [she] occupies a unique and high position as a creator of fashions in America, England, and France

Whereas, her personal approval and endorsement over her own name of certain articles and fabrics used not only in the manufacture of dresses, millinery and other adjuncts of fashion, but also divers other articles of use to people of taste has a distinct monetary value to the manufacturers of such articles

Whereas, [her] approval and selection of certain articles and fabrics used in the manufacture of her model gowns, millinery and other adjuncts of fashion which she designs has a distinct monetary value to the manufacturers of such articles used

Whereas, [she] creates from time to time different articles, such as parasols, belts, handbags, garters, etc., etc., and these also have a distinct monetary value independent of their specific use in her own dress creations sold at her own houses of 'Lucile'

Wood had the exclusive right to place endorsements and negotiate terms and conditions as well as the exclusive right to sell or license rights to ancillary fashion items. However, all such deals were subject to the judgment of Lucy or her personal business adviser, Abraham Merritt, that the deals be "most advantageous to the said Lucy, Lady Duff-Gordon and the said Otis F. Wood." The exclusivity covered articles of clothing, various inputs (e.g., fabrics), and accessories. There were some itemized exceptions: any of her contracts executed or pending, moving pictures, theatrical projects, performances, lectures, distribution of photographs of her gowns, articles or books. If a contract with a client went beyond the term of the contract, Wood would continue to receive his share of the profits during the life of the client agreement; however, if that client renewed following termination of the Wood-Lucy agreement, Wood would not be entitled to a share of the proceeds. The costs of obtaining and protecting intellectual property were to be borne equally. Wood could not initiate a suit to protect the intellectual property without her consent. Presumably, the decision to defend a suit or to manage the litigation once it had begun was in his hands, although the contract is silent on that.

All revenues under the contract were to be paid to Wood, who would then pay Lucy her share. The revenues were to be shared equally. "IT IS AGREED, that all profits and revenues derived under any contracts made with third persons hereunder are to be paid over and collected by the said

Otis F. Wood, and that all said profits and royalties are to be divided equally between the parties hereto." He was to account to her monthly for all moneys received by him. Any costs incurred by Wood in promoting Lucy were for his own account.

Kewpies.   The initial contract with O'Neill was a three-year exclusive contract dated March 19, 1913. That contract is unavailable. The dispute was over the amended contract dated April 21, 1914. My presumption, based on the following language, was that only Wood's share, not the basic structure of the contract, was affected by the amendment, but of that we cannot be certain: "Whereas the parties heretofore have by correspondence made certain modifications . . . whereby in certain particulars the compensation of [Wood] has been increased."

Some of the terms were similar to those in the Lucy contract. Wood had the exclusive right to negotiate sale and disposition of Kewpies, to represent her in all publicity in connection with Kewpies, and to promote sales, licenses, and rights for "Kewpie forms and figures made up into all kinds and classes of merchandise." As in Lucy's contract, there were exceptions: production of art prints, wallpaper, books, and all customary book rights including "Kewpie Kut-Outs." She had the right to refuse any deal that he arranged: "[N]o contract or agreement shall be binding . . . until it shall be so signed by her." The contract had the same sort of continuation arrangement as Lucy's. The language was different, but the results the same. Compare: "IT IS AGREED, that in the event any arrangement is made with the third party running longer than the time stated in this agreement, that the said Otis F. Wood is to share in the returns from same during his lifetime of such agreement, and the said Otis F. Wood's rights hereunder are not to cease at the expiration of this agreement." (Lucy) "The said compensation to [Wood] . . . shall continue throughout the period of any such contracts and agreements, although the period of the said contracts and agreements be longer than the period covered by this instrument." (Kewpies) The costs of acquiring or protecting patents, trademarks, and copyrights were to be borne in proportion to division of royalties between them, although unlike Lucy, O'Neill did not have any control over the decision to bring suit. While in the Lucy contract all revenues were to go first to Wood, who would then pay Lucy her share, in the Kewpie contract all revenues were to be paid to a named trustee, who would then disburse the funds to both Wood and O'Neill.

Two other differences were of much greater significance, putting a new spin on the Lucy contract. First, the Kewpie contract included a "best efforts" term: He "will use his best efforts and devote so much of his time as shall be necessary diligently to promote the sale or licenses and rights for said 'Kewpies' in all materials, and that in agreements for the manufacture and sale of said 'Kewpies' which he shall negotiate, he, as her agent, will use his best efforts to obtain, and will obtain, for [her] the highest possible royalty." The existence of an explicit "best efforts" promise in the Kewpie contract makes Cardozo's implication of such a promise in Lucy's contract (entered into only one year later) at least problematic.

Second, the compensation arrangement was different and somewhat more complicated. Apparently, after the initial success of the Kewpie dolls, the parties amended the agreement to increase Wood's share. (I don't know why; the more natural thing to do would be to reduce his share, since her input was responsible for most of the success.) Under the new arrangement, for five contracts that had already been procured and for all subsequent business obtained by Wood, he would get 40%. For business obtained by her without his assistance, Wood would get 20%; the burden of proof as to who generated the business would be on her. The clear implication of this formula is that "exclusive" refers only to other agents. O'Neill had the right under the agreement to enter into deals directly, but if she did so, Wood would still get 20% of the revenue. The exclusivity appears to mean only that she was not free to work with another agent to generate business. The significant point is that even though the contract labeled Wood's right "exclusive," it clearly presumed that Rose O'Neill was free to develop business on her own.

Other Forms. It is possible that one or both of Wood's contracts were based on standard forms in common use in this period. However, I think that unlikely. I reviewed three contemporaneous form books (Cowdery 1905; Jones 1909; and O'Malley 1916) and found that none included a form covering this type of relationship. The closest was a contract between a company and a retailer which required that the "retailer shall use his best endeavors and skill to procure the greatest possible sale of all such goods which he shall be employed to sell" and that "he shall act in such manner as he may believe to be most advantageous to the company."[3] (Jones 1909, p. 94) Exclusivity was the opposite of the Wood contracts: "Said retailer shall devote his whole time and attention exclusively to said agency, and shall not engage in any other business whatsoever." (Jones 1909, p. 96) That same form book also included a number of patent license arrangements and mining agreements, most of which included a royalty, a fixed payment, and a minimum usage requirement. (Jones 1909, pp. 114–115, 481–484, 730–745) So, although there were no forms that matched Wood's business needs, there were some dealing with contingent compensation and unspecified levels of effort. And in these, the parties surmounted the consideration hurdle with fixed fees and/or minimum levels of effort (or results). They would not have to fall back on their agreements being "instinct with an obligation."

The Litigation

Unfortunately, neither case advanced very far, so the records are slim. Still, there are some useful tidbits.

Kewpie.   The Kewpie litigation involved only a procedural question—could Wood get O'Neill to give some pre-complaint testimony. The answer: No. Bits of the story emerge from the various affidavits and briefs, and from these I can put together at least some indication of what was going on. Wood served O'Neill with a summons in January 1915. (My proceduralist sources tell me that this was an appropriate way of initiating litigation in New York at the time. The filing of the complaint could come later.) Shortly after the April 1914 renegotiation of the contract on terms more favorable to Wood, the parties seem to have had a falling out. In one of her affidavits she states: "Mr. Wood alleges . . . that I have refused to have business dealings with him. I am free to admit that it is most distasteful for me to meet Mr. Wood personally. When I took up my residence in New York City last June I requested Mr. Wood to come see me which he did. At that time I asked him to advise me concerning the performance of his obligations to me as my exclusive agent. . . . This he refused to do, and his manner of refusal was such that I have never again requested him to discuss personally with me any matters relating to the Kewpie business."

At about that time she appointed her sister, Callista, to attend to her business affairs, a fact that she acknowledges in her autobiography. Otis Wood, I should note, does not appear in that autobiography. He claimed that Callista's appointment violated his right to be the exclusive representative; she said that Callista's role was not that of an agent, and her appointment was, therefore, consistent with the contract. There is not enough material in the record to settle this dispute.

Wood alleged that there might have been other agents appointed, but he had no proof. Indeed, he claimed that he needed O'Neill's pre-complaint testimony on this matter to properly draft a complaint. He also alleged that royalties that should have been paid to the trustee had been paid directly to her. She denied that, claiming that the only funds paid directly to her, prior to the commencement of this litigation, were for matters not covered by his contract. O'Neill took the position that once Wood had brought suit for a breach of contract, she was free not to perform. So, she was free to hire other agents and to inform all third parties that they should no longer send royalty payments to the trustee, but should send them directly to her. (The trustee resigned at the end of April 1915.) Wood, she claimed, had no further right to royalties, only to damages for breach.

Determining damages for breach could be pretty tricky. Wood's claim appears to be that he would have been able to get 20% of her actual royalties. Her counsel argued for less: Wood "had no vested interest in any royalties. He was entitled to a percentage of them as compensation for his services only in case of his performance during the entire term of the agreement of all of his obligations. The question of his performance is at issue in this action." (Defendant Brief [DB], p. 7) If at trial it was found that she had not breached at the time he filed his claim, then, arguably, he breached his best effort obligation and would have no claim to future royalties.

She went further than this, counterclaiming that he had failed to use best efforts. "[T]he plaintiff has failed and refused to use his best efforts and devote as much of his time diligently to promote the sale of licenses and rights for the said Kewpies as he had agreed to do; . . . he has failed and refused to use his best efforts to obtain, nor has he obtained for the defendant the highest possible royalty in agreements which he, as agent, had negotiated for the defendant." The counterclaim is somewhat ambiguous in that it does not say whether the failure to use best efforts preceded Wood's filing a claim. Regardless, she asked for damages of $10,000. (In his complaint he was asking for $50,000.) The court never had to face these issues. Wood lost his motion and the case disappeared. If O'Neill paid anything to settle the case, there is no record of it.

Lucy.   It appears that Wood's performance in the first term of the contract was satisfactory. According to Randy Bigham, Wood succeeded in placing a number of commercial endorsements, including a new Manhattan retail outlet, Bedell Fashion Shop,[4] Essanay Film Studios, Mallinson Silks, the Model Brassiere Co., Heatherbloom Petticoats, Hartmann Trunks, and O'Conner-Goldberg Shoes. Things began to unravel in year two when Lucy bypassed Wood and directly entered into a contract with Sears, Roebuck & Co. The Sears ad announcing the new arrangement appeared in the October 1916 *Ladies Home Journal*. The Sears deal was an attempt to reach an entirely new market. The advertisement, in the form of an interview, gives Lucy's rationale:

> Yes, of course, I have designed gowns for most women of note in the world, I suppose—Queen Mary of England, Queen Victoria of Spain, the Duchess of Roxborough, for coronation ceremonies and millionaire's weddings—and I shall continue to do this through the 'Lucile' establishments in London, Paris, New York, and Chicago.
>
> But what of that? It is nothing. This other it has been *my one dream* to make clothes for the women who have *not* hundreds of dollars to spend on one frock. They have not come to me naturally because they could not through the house of 'Lucile.' But now these men in Chicago who have grasped my idea are giving us our opportunity to reach each other. I am going to design clothes for the women who have twenty-five or fifty or ten dollars to spend. The garments will be made up under my personal supervision and this great Chicago house of yours will then pass them on to these women. Oh, I can help them so much with their clothes! Won't you tell them so for me?

There is some controversy as to how successful the Sears move was. The two extreme versions are embodied in the following quotation.

> It is reasonable to assume from what is known of Sears, Roebuck's general merchandising philosophy, that, with the rare exceptions like groceries, those items which held sway in the catalogue for any length of time met with reasonable satisfactory public response—sufficient, at least, to pay their way in space consumed. There were, however, several ventures in this period which met with less fortunate results—and did not long remain in the catalogue. One of these, launched in 1916, was the "Lady Duff-Gordon" line of women's style clothing. Lady Duff-Gordon, one of the best-known fashion stylists in America, was engaged by Sears, Roebuck to design fairly expensive clothes for women. One magazine reported the arrangement in these terms:

Lucile, the trade-name of Lady Duff-Gordon, has become a name to conjure with. She has designed frocks for the queens of Europe and wives of America's finance kings, for millionaire weddings, for stage stars and grand opera prima donnas, for coronation fetes and the like. Her name has been tied up inseparably . . . with smartness and elegance. And now comes a great mail-order house, Sears, Roebuck & Company, of Chicago, hires Lucile to design clothes for its patrons at prices ranging from $20 to $45, and sells the same in huge quantities. Romance and a sense of surpassing smartness are thus brought into the remotest homes that the Sears-Roebuck catalogue reaches. . . . The great mail order house stimulates its movement of women's wear to a degree that could probably never have been attained in any other way. Sears-Roebuck puts on the "dog" and multitudes of women put on Sears-Roebuck clothes. (Fuessle 1916, p. 54)

Fuessle's reference to Sears, Roebuck selling those exotic creations "in huge quantities" could hardly have been farther off the mark. The venture into Continental fashions for the farm wives of the Plains was a resounding failure. Lady Duff-Gordon christened each of her creations with a name. One gown was titled "I'll Come Back to You." Company records, according to former employees, bore the name out in cold statistical terms; two were sold, and both came back. (Emmet and Jeuck 1950, p. 225)

The truth lies somewhere in between. Sears sold about $90,000 worth of Lucy's dresses in six months at about $26,000 less than it paid for them. While the venture ultimately turned out poorly for Sears, it was, at least initially, pretty good for Lucy. Her biographer, Randy Bigham, says that in the first season her collection almost completely sold out, but that it did less well in the second (and last) season.

Wood's complaint cited Lucy's contracts with Sears and Chalmers Motors. The logic behind her deal with Sears is easy to understand. Less obvious is her deal with Chalmers Motors. What, one might reasonably ask, does a dress designer have to contribute to automobile sales? Her answer is in the opening lines of a full-page advertisement in the *Saturday Evening Post* signed by Lucy:

I have been engaged by the Chalmers Motor Company to select materials for furnishing the interiors of their new closed cars.

As for myself—I am not interested in the exterior of this Chalmers town car. If external things interest you, glance at the picture.

Neither am I concerned in the least with the motor. I know not and care not whether it be what mechanical men call a six, a 22, or a 3400. *Les détails m'ennuie.* I leave them to Monsieur Chauffeur.

My only interest is in the vitally important thing—the interior. All important because there is where I have to sit. It is my sun-parlor on wheels, and if colors clash or upholstery fabric grates on my nerves, how am I to love the car?

Nothing can recompense for poor taste.

The Sears dresses were marketed to the middle class; they were generally in the $20–45 price range. Given that per capita annual income at the time was $450 (Johnston and Williamson 2002), this was a considerable part of the farmer's wife's budget, which probably explains why Sears dropped the line. Nonetheless, it was at least within the reach of the mass market. Not so the Chalmers car with its list price of $2,480. Those able to buy such a car could, no doubt, leave the mechanical details to Monsieur Chauffeur.

In his complaint, dated December 7, 1916, Wood asserted that Lucy had violated the agreement by entering into at least these two contracts and having the revenues from them paid directly to her. The case raced through the courts. Her motion for judgment on the pleadings was denied on January 6, 1917. That decision was reversed in Appellate Division on April 20, 1917, by a unanimous court which held the agreement void for want of mutuality. It was argued before the Court of Appeals on November 14, 1917, and in a 4–3 vote, Cardozo issued the opinion for Wood on December 4, 1917, just shy of one year from the filing of the complaint.

The complaint is a bit fuzzy as to what constituted the breach. It seems to suggest that by entering into the Sears and Chalmers (and perhaps other) contracts Lucy breached. Two other alternatives are hinted at. First, she entered into those contracts "without the knowledge or consent of plaintiff." Second, the revenue from those other contracts did not go directly to Wood to be divided equally between them. If we take the Kewpie definition of "exclusive," Lucy could bypass Wood and directly enter into endorsement contracts with third parties. Contracting with Sears would not have been a breach; having an agent arrange the Sears transaction or having the Sears payments go directly to her instead of Wood would be a violation.

This interpretation of "exclusive" is not unique to the Kewpie contract. In *Commercial Wood & Cement Co. v. Northampton Portland Cement Co.,* cited by the Appellate Court and in the briefs of both parties, the plaintiff was to be the "sole selling agent of the entire output of cement of the defendant for the period of five years." Even if the plaintiff did nothing, the court noted, "it could be entitled to demand from the defendant a commission . . . upon all cement that the defendant manufactured and sold." "Sole," like "exclusive," did not seem to preclude sales by the defendant.

However, in another contemporaneous case, "exclusive" did preclude sales by the defendant. In *Ehrenworth v. George F. Stuhmer & Co.*, a baker of pumpernickel agreed to sell all his bread in one area of Brooklyn through a single distributor who, in turn, had agreed that he would carry the pumpernickel of no one else. After the bakery expanded, it began to sell directly, and the distributor claimed that this amounted to a breach. The New York Court of Appeals agreed, and it found mutuality in the oral contract for so long as both parties remained in business. That breach occurred in March 1915, just before Wood entered into his contract with Lucy. A few years later, in a 4–3 decision (Cardozo in the majority), the court found for the distributor. The definition of exclusivity was not challenged; it was simply assumed that selling direct would violate the distributor's exclusivity.

Wood's response to the claim that there was no mutuality was, first, that he had made an express promise to do something, and if that promise were not sufficient, "the doctrine of implied covenant, where the minds of the parties have clearly met . . . is sufficient to uphold the agreement between the parties in this case." Regarding the express promise, Wood argued: "The Court must say whether such a promise can be put aside by plaintiff *at his mere whim;* or whether such a promise does not carry with it the use *of a reasonable and just exercise of the judgment of plaintiff* for the protection of the joint property of plaintiff and defendant in the subject matter of the contract." Alternatively, Wood argued, one could imply a duty to use "best endeavors and efforts" to provide sufficient consideration. Cardozo did not have to invent his effort standard from scratch.

The defense argued that, because Wood had not bound himself in any way, there was no mutuality of obligation, and, hence, no consideration. It was improper to infer a best efforts obligation, and the exclusion of any such obligation was a deliberate choice.

The agreement was drawn by this appellant, with clear language, tending to show the operation of the minds of the parties at that time. It is clearly visible that the contract was so drawn and worded with the express purpose and intention of avoiding any liability on the part of this appellant. There was no intention at any time that this appellant be compelled to perform any act or to pay damages in the event of any breach. It was simply a contract to measure compensation for any services that he might render in procuring articles for endorsement by this respondent. It was part and parcel of his advertising business, conducted by him in the ordinary course of business. The intention was that he be paid only for obtaining results and for business procured by him. The intention was not that he receive remuneration for the work performed by others. However, this, in fact, is what is trying to be accomplished, in this action. A recovery can only be had by the appellant for procuring endorsements and the collection of the funds and payment for the same. If he fails to perform any acts or if he fails to receive any endorsements or accomplish any results, then no recovery can be had. All is dependent upon the actual labor and work performed by this appellant and results accomplished. Such was the intention of the parties. (DB, pp. 18–19)

The agreement, defendant continued, was a unilateral contract that specified the terms on which Wood would be compensated for business that he brought in. Wood was seeking compensation for business that he had not brought in, and it would be unjust to require Lucy to pay Wood for business he did not obtain.

The contract upon which this action is based was simply one by which the value of the appellant's services was to be measured and for which he was to be compensated. It was an agreement wherein the respondent bound herself to pay to this appellant fifty per cent (50%) of any moneys received by her for placing endorsements procured by this appellant. The action is not instituted for services rendered by this appellant, but it is one to recover for services rendered by others. It is conceded that no part of the services for which he desires to recover under this contract were rendered by him, nor the endorsements obtained by him. (DB, p. 20)

[Wood] seeks a recovery in this case and is attempting by legal means to coerce and compel this respondent to pay moneys for services which were not rendered by him, but by others and for which they have already been paid. If, under such circumstances, this Court sustains and upholds the agreement, it would in effect compel the respondent to pay twice for the same services and place this appellant in a position wherein he would not be obliged to render any services or be compelled to perform any acts of omission or commission and be paid therefor. (DB, p. 21)

Note the clear implication that Lucy paid someone else to arrange the Sears and Chalmers contracts.

Wood did not spell out his damage claim, but both parties appear to have believed that had he won, the remedy would have been disgorgement. Wood would have been entitled to half the revenue from the contracts with Sears, Chalmers, and (perhaps) others. I don't know why they would have believed this; the standard damage remedy would at least subtract out the costs Wood would have incurred had he procured these contracts. The disgorgement remedy is consistent with one theory of the contract: the contract entitled him to half Lucy's revenues regardless of who developed the business, and her breach consisted of not paying him his contractually defined share. Below, I will suggest some other damage theories consistent with alternative interpretations of the contract.

Cardozo, as we all know, held for Wood, finding that "a promise may be lacking, and yet the whole writing may be 'instinct with an obligation,' imperfectly expressed. . . . His promise to pay the defendant one-half of the profits and revenues resulting from the exclusive agency and to render accounts monthly, was a promise to use reasonable efforts to bring profits and revenues into existence." Because she was vulnerable to his decisions, he had a duty to use reasonable efforts. "Unless he gave his efforts, she could never get anything." And, again: "She was to have no right for at least a year to place her own indorsements or market her own designs except through the agency of the plaintiff. . . . We are not to suppose that one party was to be placed at the mercy of the other."[5] This argument could be turned on its head. Cardozo could have reasoned that since we are not to suppose that she would put herself at Wood's mercy, she did not in fact do so. She would only be at his mercy if it were a legally binding contract; therefore, he could just as well have concluded that there was not a legally binding contract. And if Wood's "exclusive right" in the Lucy contract was the same as his exclusive right in the Kewpie contract, Lucy again would not have been at his mercy. Indeed, even if she were "at his mercy," that need not lead to Cardozo's conclusion. To analyze the case properly it is necessary to consider three possible interpretations of Wood's exclusivity.

The Analysis

Leaving aside for the moment the precise meaning of exclusivity, what economic role does the concept play? The agent, Wood, is expected to expend energy (and time and money) drumming up business for his principal, Lucy. He must be wary of the "free rider problem." Suppose Wood works hard to develop a particular endorsement deal and then some other agent swoops in to close the deal and reap the rewards. If Wood cannot protect himself from this, and if his only compensation were contingent upon his closing the deal, he would be reluctant to put in the effort to get the deal done in the first place. If other agents feel the same way, then one plausible outcome is that none of them put in the effort and the endorsement never happens. This is not a happy outcome for the principal. One response would be for her to shield Wood from competition from other agents (or from herself). The shield could be absolute—the conventional meaning of "exclusive." Or it could be more finely tailored. The principal would recognize that there are costs and benefits arising from a weakening of the agent's exclusivity. To put it in contemporary terms, Starbucks or MacDonald's must recognize that whenever they open an outlet it adversely affects the selling effort (and the incentives) of nearby outlets. Nonetheless, even though the selling efforts of one outlet might cannibalize sales from the others, both firms find it desirable to operate numerous outlets in a given market. That does not mean that they will build indiscriminately on every street corner (although sometimes it appears that Starbucks has done so). Rather, it means that the principal's decisions on how much it should shield any individual agent from competition can be quite nuanced.

What if the agent enters into a contract with a client for, say, six months? At the end of that period, the principal could renew directly, cutting the agent out. The agent could attempt to shield itself from this possibility by maintaining a renewal right. Indeed, it could, conceivably, have the right to a share of the income from that client in perpetuity, or at least for some period beyond the term of the principal-agent agreement. Such arrangements are not uncommon. Recall (from Chapter 1) that movie producers often have a claim on earnings from a sequel, even if they are no longer involved in the project. Insurance agents have substantial property rights in their customers, allowing them to receive commissions although they are no longer soliciting business. (See Joskow 1973.) Some states provide statutory protection to a sales agent from the principal's opportunism.[6] Neither of Wood's contracts provided him with that much protection. Both contracts, if enforceable, appear to prevent the principal from cutting Wood out by contracting directly with the client at the renewal stage, but only so long as the contract remains in effect (although that might not be true under one interpretation).

Before starting this project, I had assumed that in the *Lucy* era, parties did not write "best efforts" or similar language into agreements. I believe that among contracts scholars I was not alone. The fact that Wood had a "best efforts" clause in the earlier Kewpie contract puts matters in a different light. Why imply a particular level of effort when Wood chose to exclude an express promise? What can we infer from the absence of the "best efforts" clause in Lucy's contract? Had the two contracts been otherwise identical, we could be confident that the omission was deliberate. Wood, we could reasonably conclude, modified his way of doing business in response to problems that surfaced during the Kewpie litigation. The two contracts, however, are not the same. It is possible that the hand that drafted the Lucy contract knew of neither the Kewpie language nor the Kewpie dispute. I think it more likely than not that the Lucy contract was informed by the Kewpie experience, but we will never know for sure. Assuming this to be so, the absence of "best efforts" was most likely deliberate, an attempt to get the benefits of the arrangement while shielding Wood from the potential exposure. O'Neill used the "best efforts" clause as the basis for her counterclaim, although it is possible that Wood did not know of nor anticipate the counterclaim, since O'Neill's response was not filed until May 8, about six weeks after the Lucy contract. Nonetheless, it is at least plausible that by eliminating the clause, Wood would have hoped to shield himself from a counterclaim (and the bargaining leverage inherent in a plausible counterclaim). On the basis of the Kewpie contract, I would be willing to draw the negative inference that the absence of any mention of effort in the contract was deliberate and that Cardozo was wrong to find that any level of effort was implied.

Recall that in Wood's exclusive contract with Rose O'Neill she had the right to deal directly and he had a claim to a share of the business developed by her. The interpretation of his contract with Lucy depends on whether she had the right to deal on her own, and if so, how, if at all, he should share in the revenues from the business she developed. To simplify the following discussion, I will consider three possible scenarios: (1) only Wood could place endorsements; Lucy could do nothing; (2) Lucy, like Rose

O'Neill, could also place endorsements and Wood would get 50% of all revenues regardless of who initiated the deal; (3) both could place endorsements, but Wood would only get 50% of the revenues from deals that he initiated and nothing from deals that she initiated. Cardozo, and I daresay every contracts scholar since, presumed the first scenario to be correct. None of the three, I believe, is entirely convincing. But under any of the scenarios, the "mercy" argument doesn't hold up very well.

Scenario 1.   Cardozo put a considerable amount of emphasis on the fact that, if exclusivity meant that only Wood could place endorsements, Lucy would have been at the mercy of Wood, and, therefore, he must have promised to give at least some effort. Was Lucy really at Wood's mercy? She could not, given our present assumption, go out and get endorsements on her own and still comply with the contract. But what if she did not comply? If Wood could, or did, get an injunction, then, indeed, she was at his mercy. But Wood didn't, and perhaps in that era he couldn't. His remedy was the quantity of mercy—money damages. He was asking for $50,000, and, as I noted above, his damage theory seemed to be that Lucy must disgorge. But disgorgement is inconsistent with this theory of liability. Damage remedies in the Lucy-Kewpie era were skimpier than they are today. It is not implausible that a court of that era would have found the damages from breach of an exclusive contract too speculative, so that in practice the damages would have been zero.[7] My colleague, Mel Eisenberg, suggests that a court could find in reckoning damages that Wood would have made the sales that Lucy actually arranged, and that no deduction of expenses for selling effort would have been necessary. The reason is that the court could find that there were no variable costs associated with the performance of Wood's obligation. It seems to me that, by definition, reasonable effort would entail a positive cost. But, given the loose relation between the law of remedies and economic reality, I suppose this interpretation would be possible. In any event, Lucy was at Wood's mercy on a formal level—she couldn't solicit other business and comply with the contract. But on a practical level, she was vulnerable only to the extent that she would have had to pay a price, and that price might turn out to have been quite low.

As her inability to sell on her own has been overrated, so too has his incentive to perform been underrated. What made the deal attractive for Lucy (ex ante) was not the promise of any particular level of effort. The value came from the incentive structure. True, Wood could have chosen to do nothing. But if Wood did nothing, he would get nothing. His compensation was contingent upon his effort. The sharing arrangement encouraged both parties to contribute their efforts, he to promote her name and she to produce marketable designs. The contract gave Lucy a relationship with someone who could profit by promoting her name and her clothing. If the question is whether Lucy received something valuable in exchange for her promise, the answer should be yes. So, in this scenario, one could find consideration for a contract, not from an implied level of effort, but from that which made the deal valuable to Lucy, namely, the incentive structure inherent in the deal. As a number of my contracts colleagues have told me, that is not the law; but if Cardozo is going to be innovative in stretching the doctrine, this would seem to me a plausible direction. As I note below, I no longer believe it necessary to stretch to find consideration, but if one felt compelled to do so, I do think the incentive structure argument would be the better one.

Scenario 2.   In the Kewpie contract, O'Neill was free to pursue business on her own; she had to pay the contractually determined share, 20%, to Wood if she did so. The 20% payment is the economic equivalent of a tax on O'Neill's selling effort. In Lucy's contract, there are two alternative definitions of her share. Business that she brought in could be treated like everything else, so that Wood gets 50%. Or their silence on the matter could be interpreted as meaning that her business is entirely hers, and Wood gets nothing. In this scenario, I assume the former. This scenario is consistent with the disgorgement remedy. Note first that in this scenario, on the formal level, Lucy is not at the mercy of anyone. She is perfectly free to court potential endorsees under the contract. But she would have to pay Wood half of all the revenues. That could well turn out to be greater than the damages reckoned in scenario 1. So, if we are to give any weight to Lucy's vulnerability to Wood's whims, there remains a nagging question: Is she vulnerable because she can't do it without breaching (de jure), or is she vulnerable because doing it is expensive (de facto)?

In this scenario, Wood could sit home and do nothing and still be amply rewarded by Lucy's efforts. The Kewpie contract set two separate compensation rates. Why might O'Neill have been so generous to him for business developed by her? Some of Wood's effort on her behalf might otherwise remain uncompensated if Wood makes general investments in developing

the Kewpie business and O'Neill closes the deal herself. Agents are generally concerned that after they have put in effort developing a potential
client, the principal would then do an end run and contact the client directly. Giving Wood a share of the business that O'Neill developed was one
device the Kewpie contract used to cope with this problem. The second,
and more overt, means was to put on her the burden of proof in any dispute
about who was responsible for developing a particular contract. Would the
parties go so far as to set the same compensation rate regardless of who
brought in the business (as scenario 2 would have it)? I am skeptical, but
an argument could be made for it. First, the single compensation rate eliminates the possibility of a dispute over who developed the business, since
the sharing is the same regardless. Second, while on its face the rule appears
to have very bad incentive effects, imposing a 50% tax on Lucy's effort, in
practice it might not be so bad. The high tax rate on Lucy and the belief
that her costs of finding business would generally be higher might, in effect,
convert the scenario into one in which Lucy isn't really expected to do
anything, so they might as well presume that only Wood's efforts would
generate revenue.

So, like the "mercy" argument, on a formal level (de jure) the incentive
structure doesn't provide any value to Lucy, even though in practice (de
facto) it could. As I read Cardozo, it is the formal interpretation that pushes
him toward inferring something (reasonable efforts) that would provide
consideration. In scenario 2, the formal interpretation is that she is not at
his mercy and he can get paid for doing nothing and just waiting for her
to get the business. Had Cardozo perceived scenario 2 to be the case, I do
not believe he would have searched for a rationale for finding the contract
enforceable.

Scenario 3. In this scenario, Lucy has the right to develop business on her
own and doesn't have to pay Wood anything for it. For those who put great
weight on her being at his mercy, this becomes an easy case. She is not at
his mercy either explicitly, as in scenario 1, or implicitly (with the 50%
"tax"), as in scenario 2. Lucy could pursue clients directly and presumably
could approach Wood's clients directly when their initial agreements with
Wood expired. She could not, however, use another agent to solicit clients.
This wouldn't provide much protection from her free riding on his efforts,
but it might well have been adequate. We don't know, unfortunately, how
Wood ran his business. If, for example, the endorsement business was an-

cillary to the syndication business, so that he would incur most of the costs regardless of the behavior of a particular client, this might provide him with sufficient incentives. Lucy's interpretation was even stronger: the contract was only a unilateral contract which defined Wood's rights for any business he happened to bring in. The notion that the contract would apply only if Wood actually signs a client renders "exclusive" essentially meaningless.

In Sum. The Kewpie contract provides two bases for concluding that the Lucy contract should not have been found to be enforceable. First, the existence of an explicit "best efforts" clause in a contract Wood entered into shortly before the Lucy contract, and the fact that O'Neill was using that clause against Wood in litigation at about the time he entered into the Lucy contract, casts doubts on the notion that it was necessary to imply a reasonable efforts duty. Second, giving Wood an "exclusive right" did not necessarily put Lucy at his mercy; she might have been free to seek out clients regardless of what Wood did. And, even if not free, the legal penalty for her direct solicitation of business might well have been quite modest.

2. Does It Matter?

My original presumption was that, with the commonsense meaning of "exclusive" (only Wood can get customers, and he only makes money if he does so), the agent's incentive structure provided sufficient economic value to the principal to overcome the consideration hurdle. My concern was that imposing a "best efforts" duty (whatever exactly that is) would go beyond what an agent would promise. I had in mind a talent agent who typically puts together a portfolio of clients, most of whom will spend their careers waiting tables. I am now more inclined not to stretch to find consideration. If an agent really wants to make the agreement enforceable, it would be easy enough to do so. And, given that the agent has a strong concern about the free rider problem, he would have a powerful incentive to make the consideration unambiguous. There are many ways of doing so. An agent could use an express best efforts clause (or some variant) as Wood did in the Kewpie contract. Or the agent could avoid making any commitment as to any level of effort and simply make a cash payment, promise a minimum annual royalty, or promise a cash payment. The promised payment could even be offset against future expenses so that an unsuccessful client would end up receiving nothing. If the endorser were of sufficient notoriety, the minimum payment could be substantial, as the multimillion-dollar deals of some of today's star athletes show.

I also originally presumed incorrectly that Lucy agreed to Wood's standard arrangement, which was designed for the no-name talent. Her failure to get an advance, which would have rendered the consideration issue moot, I attributed to her documented lack of business acumen.[8] Two factors lead me to believe that an advance would not have been forthcoming even for a well-informed, prominent celebrity. First, there was none in the Kewpie contract. Second, Lucy's contract notes that she had a "personal business adviser," one Abraham Merritt. Randy Bigham informs me that Merritt had been a founding member of the board of directors of Lucile Ltd.'s New York branch in 1910. According to Bigham, "Merritt, a journalist by trade, was in fact the editor of Hearst's New York Sunday American for which Lucile penned a weekly fashion page." She was also, according to Bigham, represented by Thomas Powers, who ran a wholesale fabric company and formerly had been a vaudeville agent. She might have been naive, but there is no reason to believe that her personal business advisers were as well. Rose O'Neill acknowledged in her affidavit that she also had a legal adviser, Paul Wilson. He was the trustee named in the contract, and he was authorized to act as her agent during the life of the contract; it is not clear whether he was also advising her when she was negotiating the contract, although it would be hard to imagine otherwise. So, it is most likely true that both women were well advised and that the advice did not include getting an advance.

The effect of *Wood v. Lucy* in its primary role is likely modest. Courts will reduce one category of errors (failing to find an enforceable agreement when the parties meant to have one but were careless about it) and increase a second (finding an agreement enforceable when at least one of the parties did not intend it to be so). Because it is so easy for parties to provide explicit consideration, and not too difficult for parties to make clear that they do not mean for their agreement to be enforceable, I would be surprised to find *Wood v. Lucy* having a dramatic effect in either direction. Given the modern judicial propensity to err on the side of enforceability, the rule probably does a bit more harm than good, but not much.

Lucy's mischief is in its secondary role, defining the extent of the promisor's obligation. I want to consider two aspects—the effort level required and the domain of the rule. The latter can be subdivided: First, does the rule apply if there is an explicit source of consideration? Second, does the rule apply for arrangements that fall a bit short of exclusivity?

First, what is the extent of the implied obligation? Because Wood had expressly promised nothing, the contract appeared to lack consideration. To find an enforceable contract, Cardozo needed to find something to get past that hurdle. The law does not require a whole lot; traditional doctrine holds that even a peppercorn will do. Cardozo was pretty good at finding those peppercorns, as demonstrated by some of his subsequent decisions, *De Cicco v. Schweizer* and *Allegheny College v. National Chautauqua Bank.* All Cardozo needed in order to find consideration was a peppercorn worth of effort. There is no reason to believe that when he said "reasonable efforts" he meant any level of effort greater than was necessary to find the existence of consideration.

The Restatement and the Code upped the ante, requiring "best efforts."[9] To the extent that "best efforts" means more than the minimal amount of effort necessary to provide that peppercorn, it constitutes an unnecessary extension of Cardozo's holding. The law is far from clear on the differences, if any, between the many explicit effort standards: best efforts, reasonable efforts, reasonable best efforts, commercially reasonable efforts, due diligence, and, no doubt, others. Perhaps, as is suggested by the interchangeability of best and reasonable effort in many discussions of *Wood v. Lucy,* these are all synonyms. The UCC appears to treat them as such. While §2–306(2) refers to "best efforts," the comment refers to "reasonable diligence" and "reasonable effort and due diligence." (Comment 5) However, not all courts view all levels of effort as the same. "While the phrase 'best efforts' is often used to describe the extent of the implied undertaking, this has properly been termed an 'extravagant' phrase and it should not be literally interpreted. A more accurate description of the obligation owed would be the exercise of 'due diligence,' or 'good faith.' " *(Perma Research & Development v. The Singer Company)* And again: "In the District Court and in its briefs on appeal, Emerson appeared to make the argument that Orion had an express obligation to exercise its 'best efforts.' At oral argument, Emerson clarified that it was only suggesting that Orion had an obligation to use 'reasonable efforts' or 'due diligence.' " *(Emerson Radio Corp. v. Orion Sales, Inc.)*

It is hard enough for courts to determine what is required when the contract expressly states a particular level of effort. Indeed, in a minority of jurisdictions, express best efforts clauses have been held to be too vague to be binding. Yet in those same jurisdictions, an implied best efforts clause would be enforced. I'm not making this up. (See Van Vliet 2000.) How is a court to determine what is required by an implicit efforts clause? Should it look to the interpretations of express efforts clauses? In *Bloor v. Falstaff* (analyzed in Chapter 6), for example, the court misinterpreted an express best efforts clause, holding that Falstaff's duty to promote Ballantine beer meant that it would have to do so, even if that meant losing money, as long as the losses were not "too much." Would Wood or other agents have a duty to lose some money, but not too much, in representing their principal? For an agent with a portfolio of clients, most of whom will turn out to be losers, an implied efforts clause (best or otherwise) could mean imposing a promise of a greater level of effort than the agent would have agreed to.

Of course, if the *Lucy* rule is only a gap-filler, the problem should disappear if the contract provides another source of consideration, or otherwise expressly limits the promisor's responsibility. That raises the first question about the domain of the rule: Does the rule apply if there is an explicit source of consideration? The UCC is ambiguous on this point. §2–306(2) says nothing about confining its application to cases in which there is no other source of consideration. The statute merely imposes the best efforts obligation *"unless otherwise agreed."* That could mean that any express consideration is sufficient to avoid the implied best efforts; or it could require an explicit statement that there is no promise of any particular level of effort. There is at least some case law interpreting §2–306(2) as imposing an implied duty to use best efforts regardless of the existence of adequate consideration elsewhere in the agreement. See, for example, *MDC Corp., Inc. v. John H. Harland Co.* and *Tigg Corp. v. Dow Corning Corp.*

Outside the sale of goods context, the judicial treatment has been mixed. In *Permanence Corp. v. Kennametal, Inc.*, the court refused to imply a duty of best efforts on the licensee because the licensee had paid over $100,000 in advance royalties. It stated what appears to be the majority position: "Courts have held that by imposing a substantial minimum or advance royalty payment, the licensor, in lieu of obtaining an express agreement to use best efforts, has protected himself against the possibility that the licensee will do nothing. Rather than leaving the licensor at the mercy of the licensee, the demand for a substantial up-front or advance royalty payment creates an incentive for the licensee to exploit the invention or patent."[10] (p. 102) In a similar vein, in *Emerson Radio Corp. v. Orion Sales, Inc.*, the court stated: "The courts in *HML*, *Permanence*, and *Beraha* did not blindly apply *Wood* to a situation involving an exclusive agreement and the payment of royalties but rather examined the mutual obligations and intentions of the contracting parties. They found that a substantial advance or minimum royalty payment serves to protect the licensor/supplier from the possibility of the failure of the licensee/buyer to use reasonable or best efforts, the concern in *Wood*." (p. 169) Note that both courts invoke a *substantial advance*, hardly the language of peppercorns.

Other courts have held to the contrary; see, for example, *Perma Research & Development v. The Singer Company*. This contrary position has been adopted in recent opinions in the Southern District of New York. Thus, in *Palazzetti Import/Export, Inc. v. Morson*, a furniture company granted an exclusive right to sell its products in the Boston market for ten years for which the licensee made a one-time payment of $100,000. After operating under the agreement for one year, both sides complained about the other's performance and the licensee stopped carrying the licensor's goods, whereupon the licensor sued. The jury held for the licensor. On defendant's motion for judgment as a matter of law, the court held that whether there was an implied covenant requiring that the licensee exploit the license was a question of fact and that the jury did not err in finding it so. In *New Paradigm Software Corp. v. New Era of Networks, Inc.*, a software licensee paid $2 million plus a royalty of 5% of net revenue. When it phased out the software, replacing it with a similar package, the licensor sued. The court ruled in favor of the licensee's motion for summary judgment, but it got there in a funny way. After discussing *Wood v. Lucy* and its progeny, the court concluded: "In short, the law in New York is far from clear. . . . The Court cannot rule as a matter of law that the Agreement may not contain an implicit obligation to use reasonable efforts to market the Copernicus software despite the absence of any express provision in the Agreement and despite the $2 million upfront payment." (p. 14) In a footnote it added: "Future contracting parties obviously could avoid the problem of any ambiguity in the law by including an express 'reasonable effort' provision (or conversely, by explicitly disclaiming in the contract any such requirement)." (p. 14, n.22) However, although the court extended the *Wood v. Lucy* reasonable efforts standard to protect the licensor, the licensor's joy was short-lived. The court then proceeded to find that the breach of contract claim failed because the plaintiff had failed to present any evidence of damages.[11]

The second question regarding the scope of the Lucy rule concerns the role of exclusivity: Does the rule apply when the contract falls shy of absolute exclusivity? This question goes beyond the ambiguity of the definition exemplified by the Kewpie contract. The court and drafters of the UCC were motivated by the problem of finding a ground for enforceability rather than by any interest in the underlying economic function of exclusivity. As a result they created an artificial distinction. What if the relationship were not completely exclusive? The "at the mercy" rhetoric no longer seems so compelling. Both UCC §2–306(2) and the Restatement only refer to exclusive arrangements. If the arrangement were less than exclusive, would these still apply, either in determining the existence of a promise or its content? In both *MDC* and *Tigg* the court was faced with arrangements that were not purely exclusive. Whether they were exclusive enough to come under the statute would, apparently, be a fact question. "Harland must demonstrate that . . . [the contract] puts Harland 'at the mercy of' Artistic in a particular market. Although Harland may not be able to make this showing, this court cannot decide, based on the pleadings and the text of the Agreements alone, that the Agreements do not constitute an exclusive dealing arrangement." (pp. 394–395)

Ironically, at about the same time that the UCC was being adopted, the courts, under the antitrust laws, were attacking vertical restraints of all sorts, including exclusive dealing. For reasons that need not concern us here, that was unwise policy, and the Supreme Court finally reversed itself in *Continental T.V. v. GTE Sylvania* in 1977. For a summary of the development of the per se rule against exclusive territorial restrictions in the 1950s and 1960s by a fan, see Sullivan (1977, pp. 402–406); for why this attack on vertical restraints was a bad idea, see Goldberg (1984b). The judicial hostility to vertical restraints encouraged the development of clauses that had roughly the same effect, but gave the agent a less-than-exclusive right. The agent could have a "primary area of responsibility" or it might use a "profit pass through" (if another agent sells in the territory, it must pay some fraction of its earnings to the first agent). The antitrust air was full of cries for "less restrictive alternatives." Sometimes these alternatives were adopted to avoid antitrust liability; sometimes they were adopted because the most effective distribution arrangements required less than exclusive dealing. As I noted above, principals have incentives to fine-tune the restrictions they impose on their agents. There is no good reason why the enforceability or the extent of the agent's effort obligation in these contracts should hinge on the precise manner in which the parties chose to provide assurance to the agent. It seems clear that in the 1960s the left hand of contract law did not know what the right hand of antitrust law was doing. In a stunning display of consistency, they both got it wrong.

3. Concluding Remarks

The most plausible story is, I believe, an ironic one. My suspicion is that, following his bad experience with Rose O'Neill, Wood was trying to avoid making an enforceable commitment; Lucy, on the other hand, likely assumed that her contract would be enforceable. When Lucy walked, their positions were reversed, with his lawyers arguing that there really was a contract, and hers arguing that there was not.

My colleague Marvin Chirelstein (2001, p. 212) writes:

> Much more often than not, the unexpressed intention of the parties—"what they would have wanted"—is less than obvious and can only be identified through inference and surmise. Any number of cases can be cited for this proposition, among them the well-known Cardozo [decision] in *Wood v. Lucy. . . .* Assuming [that decision is] correct, as almost everyone believes, the great strength of the Cardozo [opinion] consists not in the application of fixed and overriding rules, but in the Court's acute perception of the local factual setting and the individual aims and attitudes of the parties themselves.

He is right, I think, in describing what everyone believes. But what everyone believes ain't necessarily so.

Even if there is no factual basis for Cardozo's characterization of the Wood-Lucy contract, courts and scholars will, no doubt, carry on as if it were true. Such is the nature of precedent. Perhaps this exercise in legal archeology will at least encourage skepticism about the invocation of an implied efforts standard both for finding the existence of a contract and for determining the extent of the promisor's obligation. Further, I would hope that it would buttress the efforts of those courts that have resisted the temptation to imply a duty of any sort where the contract includes financial consideration, even if the amount be modest.

CHAPTER 3

Mutuality and the Jobber's Requirements: Middleman to the World?

An unbounded requirements contract could, if enforced, be a disaster for the seller. As Judge Easterbrook observed in *Northern Indiana Public Service Co. v. Colorado Westmoreland, Inc.* (p. 636): "a requirements contract at a price that becomes advantageous to the buyer would allow the buyer to become the middleman to the world." Farnsworth (1998, §2.15) notes that contract law has fashioned two responses to the problem. One is to find the promise illusory and the contract unenforceable. The other is to hold the seller to his promise, but impose a reasonableness limitation on the buyer's requirements. I want to propose two additional alternative ways to resolve the problem, using *Oscar Schlegel Manufacturing Co. v. Peter Cooper's Glue Factory* as the vehicle. (I will refer to this case as *Schlegel II,* and the Appellate Division opinion as *Schlegel I.*)

Schlegel is the poster child for the buyer with apparently unbounded requirements. When the price of glue almost tripled, the buyer in a fixed-price requirements contract ordered more than ten times as much glue in a three-month period as it had in the same three-month period in the previous three years. When the seller refused to fill all the orders, the buyer sued, and the New York Court of Appeals held the contract void for want of mutuality. At about the same time, a New York trial judge chose Farnsworth's second option, holding in *Moore v. American Molasses Co. of New York* that there was a valid contract, but that the seller's obligation was bounded by a reasonableness constraint. I want to suggest a somewhat counterintuitive proposition. Cooper should have been liable, regardless of whether the court found the contract enforceable. Moreover, there was no need to impose an *American Molasses* (or UCC) reasonableness limitation on the buyer's demands. On the unique facts of the case, Cooper's liability should have exceeded that limitation.

Even if the court had found the Schlegel-Cooper contract unenforceable, it could have, and probably should have, awarded damages to Schlegel in excess of those suggested by *American Molasses*. Ironically, this result stems from Cooper's attempt to be cooperative. Had it played hardball, its exposure would have (or at least should have) been less. Why? Schlegel was a jobber, a middleman, whose requirements were defined by the orders that it received from customers. Even if the contract were not an enforceable bilateral contract, the court could have found a unilateral contract, a standing order: If you, Schlegel, obtain an order, then I, Cooper, will fill that order at the stated price (9 cents per pound). Murray (2001, §40) erroneously characterizes *Schlegel* in just this way: "[In *Schlegel*] it was held that a separate and distinct bilateral contract was made every time the offeree sent an order for goods." Until Cooper withdrew the offer, Schlegel would be free to solicit business, and each time it successfully landed an order, Cooper would be obligated to perform. If Cooper was being a "nice guy," his liability would have grown. If, instead, he withdrew the offer as soon as prices rose, he would have been off the hook.

An alternative route to a similar, but not identical, result would be to acknowledge that the parties had entered into an enforceable, bilateral contract. If, when the market price rose, Cooper repudiated the contract, Schlegel would not be free to run up damages by soliciting more business. He would have a duty to mitigate, and mitigation would mean that he could not continue to solicit orders.[1] The sooner Cooper repudiated, the less his liability. If, however, Cooper had attempted to meet his obligations and failed to repudiate, damages would mount.

Cooper's problem under both these theories is that at no time in 1916 did he object to Schlegel's soliciting orders. Whether that was because he was benefiting for most of the period from Schlegel's aggressive solicitation or because he was being nice or merely naive, we do not know. Under both theories his failure to just say no would make him liable for damages for the price differential on the goods ordered by Schlegel, but not delivered.

Neither of these theories was presented to the court in full, although pieces of them were. Neither the courts nor the parties picked up on the implications of these arguments. I will elaborate on these two alternative theories of the case, but first I need to present the facts, as best they can be ascertained, and their interpretation by the various courts. Both the trial court and intermediate Appellate Division held that there was a contract and that Schlegel's requirements were made in good faith. Their version of the facts differed in some crucial aspects from that of the Court of Appeals, which, acting unanimously, reversed.

1. Background

Cooper was a producer of glue; it had been in the business for half a century at the time of the dispute. *(Peter Cooper's Glue Factory v. McMahon)* Schlegel was a jobber that, its title notwithstanding, did no manufacturing; it sold glues, shellacs, paints, and chemicals. Its salesmen would solicit orders and upon receiving one, it would inform the manufacturer, who would then deliver directly to the customer. In the contract at issue Schlegel was to take all its requirements in 1916 of a particular type of glue, Special BB Glue, from Cooper. (BB stands for bookbinder.) The parties started doing business with each other in 1910. Theirs was not a detailed contract drafted by counsel. For their initial contract, Cooper wrote: "We haven't any contract forms, but your letter and ours will constitute our agreement." (Plaintiff Brief [PB], p. 13) Subsequent contracts between them took the same form. Prior to 1915, the contracts were for Schlegel's requirements and stated an estimated quantity. In 1915, and again in 1916, no estimate was given. The 1916 contract in a letter from Cooper dated December 9, 1915, stated in its relevant part:

> Gentlemen. We are instructed by our Mr. Von Schuckmann to enter your contract for your requirements of "Special BB" glue for the year 1916, price to be 9c per lb., terms 2% 20th to 30th of month following purchase. Deliveries, to be made to you as per your orders during the year and quality same as heretofore. Glue to be packed in 500 lb. or 350 lb. barrels and 100 lb. kegs, and your special Label to be carefully pasted on top, bottom and side of each barrel or keg. *(Schlegel II,* pp. 460–461)

As Table 1 illustrates, the sales had always fallen short of the estimates, and prices had been quite stable. Why the contracts for 1915 and 1916 omitted the estimate is unclear. In their briefs, both parties gave a reason, but neither is persuasive (or even coherent). Schlegel argued: "Instead of intending to limit the amount of 'Special BB' glue, which plaintiff might obtain, the evident intent was to increase the amount as under this contract, the plaintiff was required to buy this particular kind of glue *exclusively* from the defendant. Thus, while in previous years the plaintiff had purchased also from other manufacturers, in 1916, the plaintiff purchased this

Table 1. Cooper-Schlegel contracts, 1910–1915

Contract Date	Estimate (barrels)	Actual (barrels)	Price (cents/pound)
November 1910	100	14	8
January 1912	100	63	8.25
February 1913	100	60	9
January 1914	50–75	60	9.5
March 1915	none	70	9.5

Source: 179 N.Y.S. 271, dissent, p. 279.

glue only from the defendant." (PB, p. 13) Schlegel did not say how the omission of the estimated quantity converted the agreement from nonexclusive to exclusive. Cooper's version was different, but equally unhelpful. "The cause for this change may be found, as we contend, in the fact that the plaintiff never took the full amount ordered and on account of the war and the general business conditions brought on by it, did not want to be bound to take any definite amount."[2] (Defendant Brief [DB], p. 6) Since the estimates weren't binding, this is a non sequitur.[3]

The contract language did not define "requirements." Since Schlegel was only a middleman which had no use for the glue itself, it could mean "as much as it wanted to buy." The parties agreed, however, on a more restricted definition: bona fide contracts entered into with its customers. (PB, p. 10; DB, p. 4) The Appellate Division majority stated: "This method of doing business, and the meaning of the term 'requirements' as used in the contract, were concededly well known to defendant, which had theretofore done business under the same system with the plaintiff, to which it had sold goods as far back as 1910." (*Schlegel I*, p. 845) Schlegel could not, on this interpretation, buy the glue on his own account (although, as we shall see, he did attempt to do so).

Things went fine in 1915, but some time in 1916 the market went crazy and prices soared. The parties differed on the cause. Schlegel argued that the cause was on the demand side: "The evidence shows that there was a great demand for glue in 1916, and the reasons therefor; lack of imported glue and the building up in this country of the doll, toy manufacturing and other industries since the beginning of the war, in which industries a great amount of glue was required." (PB, p. 15) "There is no contention that the glue cost the defendant more to manufacture in November, 1916, than it cost at the beginning of the year. . . . There can be no reasonable doubt that the reason why the defendant failed to make deliveries to the plaintiff was that they could get higher prices elsewhere and so profited more than by delivering to the *plaintiff*." (PB, p. 27) Cooper, on the other hand, attributed the change to the supply side. He quoted a letter from Schlegel to one of his customers: "As stated in telegram, we cannot hold this proposition open for more than 48 hours, as prices rise every day. . . . Conditions in the American Glue market are getting worse every day. The fact is, we cannot make a contract for next year at any price, because no raw materials are coming from Germany, France, or England." (DB, p. 11) From this the dissent concluded: "This shows that the plaintiff knew that the increased price was due to the scarcity, and hence high price, of raw materials, which caused an increase in the cost of manufacture." (*Schlegel I*, pp. 856–857)

The characterizations were designed to make the other side appear opportunistic. Schlegel quoted the trial judge: "Nor did any question arise as to the meaning or validity of the contract for the year 1916, until the price for this 'Special BB' glue rose so high that the contract became very valuable to the plaintiff and entailed a corresponding loss of profit to the defendant *which it could have made by selling the goods elsewhere*." (PB, pp. 14–15) Cooper countered by asserting that fulfilling the contract could have meant ruin for the seller. (DB, p. 39)

Regardless of what caused the price increase, the response was dramatic. Schlegel's orders for the first three quarters of 1916 were in the normal range, but in the last quarter there was a huge increase. Table 2 shows its monthly orders, and Table 3 compares the orders in the last three months with its orders in the previous years. In those last three months Schlegel ordered 25,000 pounds on its own account and aggressively solicited business for 1917. (Schlegel conceded that the 25,000 pounds it ordered for its own account were not for its "requirements" as a jobber, and therefore it did not ask for damages on these orders.) It also sold 18,000 pounds to a West Coast jobber. Spot market prices were being quoted in the 21–25 cent range.[4] Schlegel solicited much of the new business at prices 6–10 cents below the spot price. The defendant tried to make the gap between the spot price and the contract price look suspicious. (DB, p. 12) But given that the purchasers would not be using the glue for many months, the price could easily reflect the perception that the high spot price was an aberration and that it would be coming down.

Table 2. Schlegel monthly purchases in 1916

Month	Purchases (pounds)
January	3,500
February	4,850
March	5,500
April	2,800
May	10,350
June	4,550
July	3,050
August	6,000
September	3,100
October	29,750
November	59,300
December	37,050
Total	169,800

Source: 179 N.Y.S. 271, dissent, pp. 279–280.

As Schlegel's orders poured in, Cooper attempted to fill them. It delivered 142 barrels (of the 340 ordered). That was more than double the amount it had delivered in any previous year. In the last three months alone it delivered between 21,000 and 26,850 pounds (the evidence is conflicting).[5] Schlegel claimed (and, so far as I can tell, Cooper did not deny) that Cooper continued to accept its orders throughout 1916. "The defendant received and retained these orders and at no time did it notify the plaintiff that it would refuse to ship the glue. On the contrary, the evidence shows that the defendant's representative, Mr. Von Schuckman, with whom the original contract was made, promised repeatedly as late as the months of November and December, 1916, and said that the glue was on the way." (PB, p. 22) The majority opinion in the Appellate Division accepted this: "At no time during the receipt of these orders did the defendant repudiate the contract or disavow the same, nor did it object to, or question, the good faith of the orders." (*Schlegel I*, p. 846)

Oscar Schlegel, plaintiff's president, appears to have been less than honest in his testimony (at least according to Cooper's Brief). He testified that in the past he had purchased from Cooper 200 barrels in a year, when in fact he had never purchased more than 70. (DB, p. 8) He stated that he had always sold more than the contract called for, when in fact he never did.

Table 3. Schlegel purchases October–December 1913–1916

Date	October	November	December
1913	2,300	2,000	7,667
1914	2,422	2,900	1,450
1915	3,262	4,683	1,530
1916	29,750	59,300	37,050

Source: Defendant's Brief, p. 10.

(DB, p. 47) He claimed to have over 3,000 customers, which was a great exaggeration given that the smallest package the company sold was 100 pounds and the average sale if there were really 3,000 customers, would have been only about 12 pounds. (DB, p. 47) Still, despite Schlegel's having to recant this testimony, the trial judge, whose role it was to evaluate the credibility of the witness, found in his favor.

There was sharp disagreement on whether Schlegel had agreed to exclusivity. The Court of Appeals concluded that the contract was not exclusive. "In the instant case . . . there was no obligation on the part of the plaintiff . . . not to sell other glues in competition with it." (*Schlegel II*, p. 464) The opinion does not explain why. This position contrasts sharply with that of the Appellate Division majority: "I believe that under the contract the plaintiff was bound to order from the defendant every pound of this quality of glue which it sold to its customers and that in like manner defendant was bound to supply every pound of this quality of glue which plaintiff sold to customers and called upon the defendant to furnish." (*Schlegel I*, p. 848) Indeed, as the plaintiff observed, the trial judge had found that the agreement was exclusive.

As was pointed out in the opinion of the Trial Justice, the effect of the contract was that the plaintiff was obligated to purchase from the defendant *all* its requirements of "Special BB" glue for the year 1916. If the plaintiff instead of buying any "Special BB" glue from the defendant, purchased none at all and bought from other manufacturers such glue as it required for its customers, the defendant, unquestionably, could take this contract and point out to the plaintiff that it agreed to buy from the defendant all the "Special BB" glue, which it required and hold the plaintiff liable for damages. (PB, p. 7)

I don't really believe it. Schlegel was taking this quality of glue from five or six suppliers in 1915 (DB, p. 17), which suggests that its buying from only Cooper in 1916 might have been related to the contract-market differential, not exclusivity. Still, exclusivity was a finding of fact, and the Court of Appeals offers no discussion of why the finding failed to meet a "clearly erroneous" standard (or, for that matter, any standard at all). The defendant argued that the trial court had committed reversible error by rejecting its proposed finding that the "bookbinder's glue involved in this case possessed no special quality." (DB, p. 53) The Court of Appeals did not address this; rather, it simply asserted that the contract was not exclusive. I suspect, but cannot be certain, that the court's sub rosa rewriting of the facts reflected its disapproval of Schlegel's behavior. Exclusivity was relevant because it arguably put a constraint on Schlegel's freedom to adjust to a decline in the market price. If the deal were exclusive, Schlegel could cut back on the bookbinder glue orders it solicited, but it could not switch to other suppliers. A court would thus be more likely to find an exclusive agreement enforceable than if Schlegel would have been free to change suppliers when the market price fell below the contract price.

Had the parties taken more care at the contract formation stage, they surely could have done a better job anticipating this problem (although its magnitude would have most likely been beyond their expectations). The Appellate Division majority spelled out a number of options not taken:

> The defendant had not protected itself against any abnormal variation in price during the year nor had it fixed any limitation upon the amount of glue which it would furnish the plaintiff, if it received orders from its customers therefor. The only proviso in the contract which the defendant cared to insert was that the contract was contingent upon fires, strikes, accidents and other causes beyond the control of the parties. A rising market could have been guarded against by the defendant by inserting in the contract a clause fixing the maximum amount which the plaintiff might be entitled to receive thereunder; but instead the defendant made an absolute contract at a fixed price for the entire year to deliver as much glue as plaintiff might be able to sell to customers during that period. (*Schlegel I*, p. 847)

While *Schlegel*'s notoriety is due in part to the appearance that the buyer had acted in bad faith by aggressively soliciting new business, the trial judge and the Appellate Division majority held otherwise. The Appellate Division characterized the dramatic increase in orders by noting that "plaintiff not unnaturally sought to reap a legitimate advantage from its contract." (*Schlegel I*, p. 846) Schlegel's behavior was not in bad faith; rather, the majority asserted, "[t]he plaintiff's good faith in soliciting these orders and their validity have not been successfully attacked." (*Schlegel I*, p. 848) The dissent saw it differently: "it was not until the purpose of the plaintiff became evident under the guise of the contract, to perpetrate an evident and unconscionable fraud did the defendant refuse to be further imposed upon." (*Schlegel I*, p. 853) In its brief, the defendant also emphasized the unfairness: "These figures, found by the court as facts, at once startle one's sense of justice and fair dealing. If further analyzed they show a grasping spirit which time and human limits only prevented from bringing certain ruin on the defendant. . . . If the 'contract' is capable of such construction that one party has the other at his mercy, then certainly the court should not read something into the contract to make it an unconscionable thing." (DB, p. 39)

The Appellate Division majority held that the parties intended to enter into a binding agreement, and the seller, in effect, took the risk of price fluctuations:

> Both parties acted with full knowledge of their respective methods of doing business, and of the uncertain and fluctuating demand for glue which might come from plaintiff's customers, and which must naturally to some extent be dependent upon the market price. They entered upon this contract with their eyes open to all the conditions then existing, or which might possibly arise, and with the intention of being mutually bound thereby. (*Schlegel I*, p. 848)

Schlegel, the majority concluded, was committed to buying all its requirements of this glue only from Cooper (the contract was exclusive), and "the mere uncertainty as to the amount" did not make the contract unenforceable. (*Schlegel I*, p. 848)

The dissent and Court of Appeals disagreed. Schlegel had not agreed to carry only Cooper's BB glue, and the quantity was too uncertain. The dissent also argued that fairness and good faith imposed a limit on the jobber's requirements. "Where a contract is made by a jobber or wholesale dealer for goods that he is to sell, but for which he has no present contract of resale, and the contract is for his requirements, it must mean for his regular and ordinary business purposes." (*Schlegel I*, p. 854) That would seem to indicate that he could have found the existence of a contract, and denied Schlegel recovery for orders that went beyond his regular and ordinary business. However, neither the dissent nor the Court of Appeals held that the agreement could have been enforced, even on these restricted terms.

Both briefs cited *American Molasses*, the defense at considerable length. Before moving on, a short digression on that case is in order. The seller, American Molasses, bought and resold all the molasses from the island of Porto Rico. (Congress changed the spelling to Puerto Rico in 1932.) It entered into a series of contracts with one of its customers, Moore, for his requirements. Moore was a veterinarian who used some of the molasses for his own purposes, but the bulk of his purchases were as a middleman. Like Schlegel, Moore made his first purchases in 1911. Like Schlegel, Moore typically took orders and then had American Molasses ship directly to the customer. Like Schlegel's contract, in the first few years Moore's was for requirements, although instead of an estimate, there was a cap. And, again like Schlegel, his contract for the 1916 season (May 1915–April 1916) was for requirements with neither an estimate nor a cap. The contract price was around 10 cents a gallon, but the market price had risen to over 20 cents, the court explaining that "there was a tremendous increase in demand, because of the fact that it was discovered that molasses could be used in some way effectively in the manufacture of munitions of war." (At 444)[6]

Sales in the previous year were 842 barrels, the most in Moore's history. (There are fifty-five gallons to a barrel.) By January sales and deliveries totaled 972 barrels. (See Table 4.) On February 12, 1916, American Mo-

Table 4. Moore's purchases pre-repudiation

Date	Barrels Ordered and Delivered
May–September	21–34/month
October	198
November	167
December	222
January	163
February	127
Subtotal for Year	972

Source: 174 N.Y.S. 440, p. 445.

lasses wrote Moore notifying him that he would only be allowed a 15% increase over the preceding year and stopped delivery.

Gentlemen: We have before us one of your postal cards issued February 1st, quoting our prices on feeding molasses, the Milkmore brand at 13½ cents, and Devon brand at 12½ cents, f.o.b., New York, and stating on same that you have about 1,000 bbls. to present market. Altogether the postal card indicates an extraordinary effort to drive in business, and that this in a measure has been successful is very evident from the orders that have been coming in from you for the past week.

Now, we do not consider this fair, or consistent with the understanding that we came to, when we called your attention to this matter some time ago. You promised at that time you did not have any intention of taking undue advantage of the liberal form of our contract, and we, on the other hand, agreed to take care of your legitimate and natural requirements, governing the same by the amount of molasses you took out last year, and adding to it a normal increase of 10% to 15% for natural expansion, and increase in business.

We have just gone over our records again, and find on your contract which expired May 1, 1915, that the total amounted to 842 bbls. Up to the present, on the contract which will expire on May 1st, of this year you have withdrawn 964 bbls. This figures approximately 15%, and we consider under the circumstances, and in view of our understanding, that we can now consider this contract completed, and that we are entitled to the advance in price on any further orders based on the present market value. (*Moore v. American Molasses*, 443)

Moore ignored the repudiation and proceeded to aggressively solicit business. It quoted prices 5–7 cents below the spot price and generated orders for an additional 2,773 barrels in the last three months. (See Table 5.)

Table 5. Moore's orders post-repudiation

Month	Barrels Ordered
February	343
March	1,120
April	1,310
Total	2,773

Source: 174 N.Y.S. 440, p. 443.

The court held that Moore was not free to "speculate," but that its ability to generate requirements was limited by good faith and fair dealing. "In an executory contract, indefinite as to the quantity of goods to be furnished, there is implied good faith and fair dealing on the part of each toward the other; the contract cannot be used for a purpose which was and could not have been within the contemplation of the parties, as for speculative purposes as distinguished from the regular and ordinary business which theretofore had been carried on between the parties to the contract." (*Moore v. American Molasses*, p. 448) Moore claimed, disingenuously, that he was only ordering molasses actually required in the ordinary conduct of his business. The issue, according to the court, was "whether or not any of the molasses ordered by the plaintiff subsequent to February 12, 1916, was actually required in the business of the plaintiff to meet the reasonable, ordinary, and fair demands of the plaintiff." It concluded that the evidence "all points in the direction of an effort on the part of the plaintiff to use the contract for a purpose certainly not within the contemplation of the parties, and for such a purpose as would safely be characterized as speculating in a rising market." (*Moore v. American Molasses*, pp. 449, 450)

The question of whether there was a valid contract did not arise. Nor did the court determine whether the defendant's letter was a repudiation, and, if so, what the implications of that would be for assessing damages. It simply sorted through the post–February 16 orders to determine which of those orders were in the normal course of doing business. It concluded that 1,800 barrels, roughly two-thirds of those orders, were not acceptable, and restricted damages to the other third ordered, but not delivered. That additional third meant that American Molasses would have been required to deliver twice as much as it actually had. The damages were reckoned at 10 cents per barrel, which reflected the spot-contract differential, rather than the 3-cent differential that Moore was charging his customers.

So, if the *Schlegel* court had found that a contract existed, the defense argued that it should then follow *Moore* and hold that the huge orders in the last quarter of 1916 were obtained in bad faith and that at least some of them should be excluded when reckoning damages.

2. Alternative Analyses

I suspect that most contracts scholars and students reading these two cases instinctively feel that the plaintiffs were grasping at a large windfall, and that the decisions merely denied them that windfall (or at least some fraction of it, as in *Moore*). For Oscar Schlegel, the court's opinion would just seem to put him back at the status quo ante. Not so. Schlegel and Moore both entered into contracts with their customers and were on the hook for substantial deliveries at below market prices. Recall that in *Moore* the damages he was to receive were based on the spot market price. Thus, while the contracts of the two middlemen reflected the expected price for some time into the future (perhaps for an entire year), the damages were reckoned at the price for immediate delivery, which was substantially higher. So, for the 1,800 barrels disallowed, Moore would have been liable for damages of about 7 cents per barrel. And poor Schlegel would fare even worse, with damages of 6–10 cents per pound for virtually all of its orders in the last three months. One might respond that, hey, they did it to themselves by being piggish, and they don't deserve our sympathy. Rather than debate the morality of their aggressive solicitation of business, I want to use it as the basis for two alternative ways of analyzing the cases.

Unilateral Contract

One party in *Schlegel* stated in its brief that this was a unilateral contract. Ironically, it was the defendant: since Schlegel was under no obligation to do anything, "the contract was entirely unilateral." (DB, p. 4) Suppose that it was. The "contract" becomes, in effect, an offer which can be accepted by performance. When Schlegel places an order, it forms a bilateral contract, incorporating the terms from the "master contract" (a very slim master contract, as I noted). Until Peter Cooper retracted that offer, Schlegel was free to solicit business, and Cooper failed to retract in the contract year. Schlegel argued: "The defendant at no time repudiated or rescinded the contract in question. On the contrary it received and accepted from the plaintiff the orders for the glue in question and promised to make delivery thereof. By reason of this, plaintiff in good faith accepted orders for glue from its customers and became legally obligated to fill the same." (PB, p. 22) The Appellate Division majority made essentially the same point: "the plaintiff had a right in the absence of any notification from the defendant that it could not or would not fill all its orders to proceed legitimately in good faith to solicit orders from the trade for this quality of glue and to expect the filling of these orders by the defendant." (*Schlegel I*, p. 848) While these were arguments made in favor of the existence of a bilateral contract, they apply to the unilateral contract case as well.

Had Cooper simply told Schlegel to stop soliciting orders, as American Molasses had told Moore, any subsequent orders obtained by Schlegel would have been strictly on his own account. For at that point Cooper's standing order would no longer have been operable. But at no time in 1916 did Cooper tell Schlegel to stop. Indeed, as noted above, he continued to fill orders in the last quarter. Whether this was because for at least some of the period filling the contracts appeared profitable (ignoring the opportunity cost of selling direct), or because Cooper was honorable, naive, or a sap, we don't know. We do know that none of the players worked through the implications of finding this a unilateral contract.

Middlemen always run the risk that the customers they cultivate and develop will subsequently be "stolen" by their principals. That is the free rider problem, discussed in the previous chapter. Perhaps that is what was at stake in this case. But the rules of engagement assured that the parties never came within shouting distance of the relevant question: If a middleman is going to develop markets for a producer, what sort of protection should it have from the producer's opportunistic behavior?

A good case can be made for giving the middleman no protection, finding the letter to be a standing offer. The product was a fungible product sold to businesses; brand name was most likely unimportant, and there seem to have been an ample number of alternative suppliers. The seller, Cooper, was buying marketing services. It could have relied upon its own employed salesmen, or it could have used independents who carried and promoted its line exclusively. It did neither, since, as many other manufacturers recognized, it is often cheaper to employ someone who represents a larger line of products (possibly including those of direct competitors) who can spread the fixed costs of selling over a larger number of transactions. A fixed price to the jobber (as compared to a commission arrangement) gives the jobber the incentive to sell aggressively and to negotiate hard on price with its customers since the jobber receives 100% of the reward from aggressive price negotiation.

If market conditions were to shift, but the price Schlegel paid remained constant, Schlegel's incentives would be warped. By treating this as a unilateral contract, the seller, Cooper, could change his price, thereby keeping Schlegel's incentives roughly intact. If the market were to go down, the jobber could cut its selling effort, at least until the manufacturer repriced. And if the market were to go up, as it in fact did, the manufacturer could revise the relationship unilaterally, raising the wholesale price, still leaving the jobber with an incentive to search for business. At least it could if it were aware of what was going on in the resale market. If the jobber was not doing an adequate job, it could be terminated and replaced with no hassle.

If the jobber believed that protecting its reliance was sufficiently important and that the manufacturer's reputational constraints were not sufficient, it had a simple remedy, ex ante—it could have made the contract a bilateral one and put in some protection. Most likely, manufacturer opportunism was not a great concern for Schlegel. In normal times there were a lot of alternative glue suppliers, and most of its investment in selling would likely transfer to other clients. Moreover, since Cooper would be committed once Schlegel made a sale, Cooper could not deprive Schlegel of the benefits of a particularly successful negotiation. Schlegel might have some concern about the customer cultivated but not yet landed. That was probably not a serious concern, since if Cooper attempted to steal that customer, Schlegel could then offer to sell the customer the glue of Cooper's competitors. If Cooper unilaterally increased the wholesale price more than its competitors, Schlegel could shift its efforts to selling the competitors' glue.

The crucial points are twofold. First, almost certainly, Schlegel's reliance on the contract was negligible; it was not susceptible to opportunistic holdup. Second, if somehow protecting Schlegel's reliance were truly important, he could have written protection into an enforceable contract. His failure to do so is consistent with the conclusion that having an enforceable contract right for future deals was not of sufficient importance for Schlegel, but enforcement for deals it had already entered into was important.

Repudiation

Even if the court were to find that the parties had entered into an enforceable one-year contract, Cooper had the ability to terminate before the year was up. It could have repudiated the contract, at which point Schlegel would have been required to avoid running up damages by soliciting more orders. Indeed, Schlegel conceded this: "If the defendant had acted in good faith and instead of receiving, accepting and retaining the orders from the plaintiff for this glue and instead of promising that it would make delivery thereof and that a car load of the glue was on the way to the plaintiff, if instead of doing this it had repudiated the contract and notified the plaintiff that it would not make deliveries observance of good faith and fair dealing might possibly have required plaintiff to solicit no more orders." (PB, pp. 25–26) I am quite certain that had Cooper actually repudiated, Schlegel would have argued otherwise. Regardless, the point is correct. Schlegel had no requirements until it landed an order. Once Cooper repudiated, Schlegel was on notice not to generate more orders. Schlegel's lawyer relied on "good faith and fair dealing"; I find that too fuzzy and would prefer "failure to mitigate," but the result would be the same.

This argument could result in a remedy differing from the unilateral contract theory. With the unilateral contract, the seller could exit instantly. As soon as Cooper says no, Schlegel is without contract. With repudiation, the buyer arguably has to be given some time to adjust, so that it might be able to recover for business that it had been soliciting but had not yet landed. I would think that the period would have been exceedingly brief for Schlegel, but that would be a fact question. In *Moore v. American Molasses*, the court appeared to have recognized that the seller had repudiated, but it chose to reckon its responsibility on the basis of a projection of Moore's future reasonable selling effort, rather than on a reasonable time for Moore to adjust.

3. Concluding Remarks

If the jobber had an enforceable requirements contract for a fungible product traded in thick markets, like wheat, a very small contract-market differential would create a money pump. The buyer could, as Judge Easterbrook observed, become middleman to the world. The outcome would be less extreme in a market like that for bookbinder's glue. The middleman or his customers must weigh the costs of carrying a substantial inventory against the benefits of taking advantage of the contract-market differential. As the *Schlegel* and *American Molasses* facts suggest, that could still result in a substantial jump in "requirements," one that almost certainly was well beyond what the seller would have agreed to.

I have suggested two responses to the problem, both of which would allow the alert seller to cap its obligation while at the same time providing a decent incentive structure for the middleman. We could treat the contract as unilateral, setting terms (including price) that would be incorporated into the bilateral contracts formed when the jobber lands a customer. Or we could treat the contract as a bilateral agreement and recognize that a breach by the seller triggers a mitigation requirement for the buyer. Either route allows the parties to keep the wholesale-resale price differential (the middleman's compensation) reasonably stable, so that its incentives to solicit business and to bargain aggressively in determining the resale price are not too distorted. Given what should be its very modest reliance on the contract terms, the middleman would be content (ex ante) to allow the seller to adjust the contract price to reflect current market conditions. Intermediaries whose reliance is greater, perhaps because of brand specific promotional effort, could bargain for greater protection.

Which of the two fixes is better? My initial presumption was strongly in favor of finding the existence of a bilateral contract. I now think the cleaner solution lies in finding a unilateral contract, the terms of which would be incorporated into any sale the middleman actually made. As I suggested, the two approaches would give slightly different remedies, but the difference wouldn't be great. The important point is that either approach gives the seller the flexibility to adapt to changed market conditions while keeping the rewards to the middleman's selling effort roughly constant. And the muddled inquiry into exclusivity and good faith bounds on requirements could be avoided altogether.

CHAPTER 4

Satisfaction Clauses:
Consideration without
Good Faith

Real estate transactions routinely make the transaction contingent upon information that would be developed after the contract has been entered into. In particular, the completion of the transaction often depends upon the purchaser's satisfaction with the information. On occasion the seller wants to renege on the deal, perhaps because it has changed its mind or because a better offer has appeared. In a number of disputes, the seller has argued that the satisfaction condition rendered the promise illusory. The courts have often rescued the deal by reading a good faith requirement into the promisor's satisfaction condition. Indeed, in some instances they have done so in the face of contract language making the satisfaction a matter of the buyer's "sole judgment and discretion." (See *Horizon Corp. v. Westcor, Inc.*, p. 134, and *Resource Management Co. v. Weston Ranch and Livestock Co. Inc.*, p. 1034.)

I want to suggest an alternative rationale for enforcing these agreements, one that recognizes the economic function of the buyer's option. To do so, I will focus on a casebook favorite, *Mattei v. Hopper*, in which the sale of land for a future shopping center was subject to the buyer's satisfaction with the leases of prospective tenants. By structuring the transaction as it did, the contract gave the purchaser the incentive to produce the relevant information, and it allowed the seller to reap some of the rewards if the information turned out to be positive.

The story is a simple one. Peter Mattei, a real estate developer, entered into an agreement with Amelia Hopper to purchase a tract of land so that he might construct a shopping center on a tract adjacent to her land. The purchase price was $57,500, and Mattei was given 120 days to "examine the title and consummate the purchase." He gave a $1,000 deposit to the real estate agent. The agreement was evidenced on a form supplied by the

91

real estate agent, commonly known as a deposit receipt. The concluding paragraph of the deposit receipt provided: "Subject to Coldwell Banker & Company obtaining leases satisfactory to the purchaser." Before the 120-day period had run, Hopper notified Mattei that she would not sell her land under the agreed upon terms. He then informed her that satisfactory leases had been obtained and tendered the balance of the purchase price. She refused; he sued.

Her defense was that the satisfaction clause rendered the promise illusory. He had only promised to purchase if he were satisfied, which, she argued, committed him to nothing at all. There was no consideration and, therefore, no contract. The trial court agreed. On appeal, the California Supreme Court reversed. If there were no limits on Mattei's right to claim dissatisfaction, then there would be no contract. However, the court held, Mattei was not so free. His invocation of the clause was subject to a good faith limitation. By binding himself to go forward unless he could in good faith claim dissatisfaction with the leases, Mattei provided the requisite consideration.

Had the deal been structured a bit differently, there would have been no question of consideration or good faith. The transaction could have been conditioned on the satisfaction of some independent third party, perhaps a lender or an appraiser. (The only good faith issue would have been whether the third party's independence had been compromised by a side deal with the buyer.) Mattei could have taken an option on Hopper's land for, say, $1,000. The $1,000 would provide consideration, hence there would be a contract, and Mattei could choose not to exercise the option for any reason at all.[1] Or Mattei could have made the $1,000 deposit nonrefundable. If that were an exclusive remedy, then the situation would be identical to the option. There are two differences between the actual transaction and the $1,000 option. One is the language describing the conditions that would influence Mattei's decision to exercise the option. The other is the price. Hopper granted Mattei a four-month option with an exercise price of $57,500 and a price of $0. Is this by itself sufficient to find consideration, without resort to an implied duty to exercise his discretion in good faith?

The answer should be yes. Properly understood, the buyer's promise is valuable to the seller, even if the buyer reserved the right not to go through with the deal if he so chose. The agreement facilitates the production of information which can result in an enhanced price for the seller's asset. The apparent paradox of the sale of a valuable option at a price of zero disappears upon recognition that the agreement is in reality two intertwined transactions. In the first, the buyer purchases an option: he pays a positive price to induce the seller to take the property off the market for a period of time. In the second, the seller pays the buyer to develop some information about the commercial prospects of the property. The reasons for this second transaction are twofold. First, the seller believes that if the buyer had better information, the sales price would be higher, and, second, the buyer is the most cost-effective producer of that information. The netting of these two transactions could easily result in the buyer paying nothing. I will suggest below why a net price of zero is plausible, but not inevitable. Indeed, it is conceivable that the seller could agree to a negative price—the seller could pay the potential buyer up front or could agree to make a payment if the deal were to fall through because either the seller or the buyer decided not to consummate the transaction.

The first half of the transaction—the option—is straightforward. The second—the lockup—is less so. The seller faces two information problems. First, there is a possible information asymmetry that may cause potential buyers to fear that the seller would take advantage of the information she developed while the property was in her possession. This is a classic lemons problem. Because of their fear that they might be buying a lemon, the potential buyers might discount their bid. The seller has a number of devices, none of them free, for providing quality assurance to purchasers. She might collect and publish information; she might provide specific representations and warranties; she might make some of the sale price contingent on the future earnings from the property. Or she might choose to subsidize the production of information by one (or possibly more) potential buyer(s). Straight cash payments would not be the best way of accomplishing this, but let us put that aside for the moment. The simple point is that if the new information sufficiently enhanced the seller's credibility, the seller could receive more from the enhanced sale price of the land than it would lose from the payment to the prospective buyer. That is, the exercise price of the option is higher because the buyer and seller both know that if the property turns out to be less desirable, the buyer can walk away.

Second, given that the value of the land is uncertain and information about the value is costly to produce, the owner might not be in the best position to develop the information. The information might be on general matters of interest to most potential buyers, for example, soil conditions, traffic patterns, or the availability of potential anchor tenants. Or the information might be more specific to particular potential purchasers, for example, financing conditions or the availability of particular anchor tenants closely linked with a specific potential purchaser. If the buyer is the most efficient producer of this information, then, again, the seller might be willing to pay some of the buyer's expenses if doing so would increase the sale price by enough.

Why might sellers choose to make the payment indirectly, linking it to the option to buy, rather than simply paying cash? If the buyer's information costs are high, then the buyer must consider the real possibility that the expenditures would be for naught if the seller subsequently refused to sell. Even if the information were valuable only to the first buyer (say, the architectural plans and economic feasibility study for a unique structure), the buyer might be reluctant to incur the costs if the seller could sell to someone else or could take advantage of the buyer's sunk cost when negotiating the sale price. Potential buyers will balance the expected costs of additional information production against the expected benefits. If the seller can subsidize information production by certain buyers or otherwise increase the likelihood that the buyer would reap the rewards of its investment, it can influence the quantity and quality of the information produced. In particular, the seller must decide whether it prefers a large number of potential buyers each spending a small amount on information or a small number (perhaps one) studying the asset more intensively.

The seller might be able to use some of the information developed by the prospective buyer to its advantage in dealing with subsequent potential purchasers—in effect free riding on the first prospective buyer's efforts. If, for example, Mattei had identified some retailers with a strong interest in being anchor tenants, Hopper or a third party could approach those retailers directly. Later buyers could either use the information or draw some inferences about the content of the information from the first party's behavior. The potential purchaser must be concerned that others would free ride upon the information it produced, and, without assurances or subsidies, would likely produce too little information. Again, by providing those assurances or subsidies, the seller can influence the buyer's production of information.

Direct cash payments to the buyer would, in general, not work. Such payments would create two obvious moral hazard problems. If the seller pays for information while buyers determine how much to produce, the buyers will not bear the financial responsibility for their investment decisions; they will have an incentive to overspend. Moreover, the buyers would be reluctant to share the information with others; they would also be more inclined to tilt their information production toward information that would be of more value to them than to other possible buyers. A seller might be able to police this behavior by monitoring or by separating the production of information from the use of it (perhaps by insisting upon firewalls or by hiring information specialists who cannot benefit directly from the information generated). But if the potential buyers are indeed the best producers of information, the separation of ownership from use would defeat the purpose.

The lockup provides an opportunity for a buyer to develop the information secure in the knowledge that if the information is positive, he will be able to reap the rewards. Mattei is free to explore the matter for 120 days and, if satisfied, he can buy Hopper's property for $57,500. The option means that if the value exceeds the exercise price, all the benefits go to the buyer. If the information is negative, the buyer can refuse to exercise the option. It will, however, be out of pocket the information costs. Thus, the first moral hazard problem is resolved. The seller bears some of the information cost in the negotiated exercise price, but the buyer bears all the direct costs of information production and, therefore, has the incentive to economize. The cost of the option to the buyer is its expected expenditure on information. True, he does not promise to spend a dime on information production or to act upon any information produced. The seller's reward comes not from the buyer's explicit promise to produce information, but from the reward structure established by the bargain. This moral hazard problem explains why the net price of the two transactions often ends up being zero. Sellers do not want to overpay for the information. In effect, the net price of zero sets a limit on the amount of effort the buyer should put into the search.

The satisfaction clause suggests an all-or-nothing outcome. Either the buyer is satisfied and the option exercised, or he is not and the option expires. Good faith is obviously irrelevant in the former case; what about the latter? If we unpack that, it becomes clear that good faith adds almost nothing. Suppose that in the 120-day period after Mattei's deposit, the real estate market crashed and Mattei then chose not to exercise his option. One could argue that the nonexercise of the option because of adverse market conditions was bad faith, but that is a flimsy argument. After all, if the value of the property falls, the quality of the leases (that is, their economic value) falls too. Unless we insist that the contract meant that Mattei must be satisfied with the leases with rents determined on the date he and Hopper entered into their agreement, Mattei should be able to take into account changed market conditions when deciding whether or not to go forward with the sale. I should note that this argument depends upon the specifics of the satisfaction clause. If, for example, the buyer's obligation depended on its satisfaction with an engineer's and architect's feasibility report (as in *Omni Group, Inc. v. Seattle-First National Bank*), then a decline in the market price would not justify a decision not to exercise the option. I return to this qualification below.

If the lease information were only moderately disappointing, the buyer could make an alternative offer (perhaps waiting for the official expiration of the option). Nothing in the nature of the option precludes a subsequent sale to Mattei (or another buyer) at a new price below the exercise price. Of course, if Mattei's research gives him an informational advantage, he could exploit this advantage by acting strategically. Suppose that he finds the property worth a bit more than the exercise price. He could feign disappointment, telling Hopper that he cannot exercise his option, but that he would be willing to purchase the property at a new, lower price. Such strategic behavior might be less than admirable, but it should not trigger good faith concerns. The questionable behavior would occur only in the renegotiation of the contract, and the seller would hardly be without recourse. If the seller is suspicious, after all, she maintains the right to refuse to sell to this buyer at any price below the initial contract price; she could shop the second offer to other potential buyers who might be able to draw some inferences from the original buyer's behavior.

In both cases, Mattei's decision not to go forward with the purchase would be the result of his having already performed his part of the agreement; that is, he would have acquired information on the value of the leases and acted upon the information by choosing not to exercise his option. What if Mattei had produced no information at all? If a better offer came along, the fact that Mattei had not yet spent anything searching for information about the parcel should not destroy Mattei's option. Surely, the buyer had bought the option to act on good news, and the external offer is simply a manifestation of that good news. The only concern would be that Mattei for some reason wanted the property off the market and had no intention to either acquire information or consummate the deal. Perhaps

Mattei entered into similar agreements on a number of parcels but only intended to purchase one. Even then, there would be some likelihood that he would choose this particular parcel, so it would be unreasonable to characterize this as merely an attempt to put a parcel off the market for a period of time. There are few scenarios in which a buyer would simply tie up a property with no intention of moving forward. For one such case in which the plaintiff alleged that the defendant entered into an option-like agreement with no intention of going forward, see *Locke v. Warner Bros.* The legal response in such a case should not be "no contract"; rather, if anything, there should be a claim by the seller for fraud.

The foregoing is a somewhat convoluted path to a simple point. The seller and buyer both benefited from the agreement, regardless of whether the buyer's discretion was limited by good faith. The lockup benefited Hopper by increasing both the probability that the land would be sold by a certain date and the expected price of the asset. It benefited Mattei by giving him a conditional option and by giving him assurance that if he chose to expend resources on evaluating the property (as he most likely would, else why bother?), then he could purchase the land at the preset price if the information turned out positive. There is a bargain; both sides benefit and the seller suffers a detriment (her property is temporarily tied up).

The contract could have left Mattei's decision to his sole discretion, thereby making it a pure option. What purpose could be served by adding the satisfactory lease clause (or satisfaction with engineering studies, approval of subdivision maps, etc.)? Such clauses can be viewed as a device for conveying information to the seller about the buyer's intentions. If the seller knows that the buyer's intended use is a shopping center, that information will affect the exercise price of the option. The clause's effect is similar to a buyer's representation. Suppose, however, that Mattei had no intention of building a shopping center and that his real intent was to drill for oil (and that the land was much more valuable in that use). It could be argued that this deception should be actionable, perhaps as fraud or misrepresentation. But that is a far cry from concluding that there was no contract.

The option terminology suggests that the discretion be unbounded, but that need not be the case. The parties can, if they so choose, limit that discretion in various dimensions. They could even contract into a good faith standard, however nebulous that might be. Indeed, the default rule could be that the discretion is constrained by good faith so that the parties would have to contract around it. My concern is twofold: (a) by making the buyer's good faith a necessary element of the contract (else no consideration), the doctrine needlessly raises good faith from a default rule to a nearly mandatory rule; and (b) absent an understanding of the context, good faith does not provide a coherent constraint on the buyer's discretion.

PART III

Interpretation

In Part II, I criticized the invocation of "good faith" and "reasonable" or "best" efforts to overcome the consideration problem. My concern was not so much with the question of whether or not there was an enforceable contract. Regardless of which way the courts decided the particular cases, future parties could adapt to the decisions, and determine what hoops they must jump through to make their arrangement enforceable (or not, if they so desired). At least, they could do so if they could count on courts not to keep moving the hoops. As I suggested in my discussion of *Wood v. Lucy,* the mischief comes in the effect the implied terms have on the interpretation of the contract. In the first chapter in this part, I elaborate on that point, analyzing the perverse role of good faith in the interpretation of long-term, open-quantity contracts. I argue that the implied duty of good faith impinges on the contracting parties' balancing of discretion and reliance. The *Lucy* analysis suggested that UCC §2–306(2) was wrongheaded. The discussion here suggests that its companion, §2–306(1), is no better.

Terms like "good faith", "best efforts," "reasonable," and "material" are inevitably problematic. That does not prevent parties from using them. A typical corporate acquisition agreement, for example, will be loaded with such language. Even Otis Wood's Kewpie doll contract included an explicit best efforts term. In the second chapter, I analyze one of the very few cases involving interpretation of a best efforts clause that makes it into the Contracts casebooks—*Bloor v. Falstaff.* Once one understands the context, it turns out to be an easy case. Indeed, it might be an outlier, a rare case in which the context gives best efforts a clear meaning. Unfortunately, neither the litigators nor the judges (nor, for that matter, most commentators) could identify the context. The good news is that some elementary economic reasoning resolves this particular case; the not-so-good news is that the analysis does not help much in generalizing about the proper interpretation of best efforts clauses in other contexts.

Context was the key to analyzing *Bloor.* Context, in the form of custom, course of dealings, and trade usage, is an inherent element in contract interpretation. The UCC establishes a hierarchy in which these are subordinate to the express language of the agreement. Some courts, with encouragement from at least some contracts scholars, have given increased weight to the context. Two cases stand out as exemplars of cases in which context trumped content—*Columbia Nitrogen v. Royster Co.* and *Nanakuli v. Shell.* In the third chapter, I examine the former in depth. The results are not pretty. The trade practices were such a hodgepodge of conflicting factors that the incorporation strategy, if followed, could lead to only one conclusion: there was no enforceable contract.

In the final chapter of Part III, I try to come to grips with the battle of the forms. It seems to me that the alternative interpretive schemes—for example, the knockout rule and the last-shot rule—miss the mark. There are tremendous economies arising from the mass production of boilerplate contract terms which rational parties would not bother to read. The problem is to try to get parties when designing their forms to take their counterpart's interests into account. I propose a mechanism, dubbed the best-shot rule, which arguably induces the form designer to take the other party's interest seriously. Although the publication of this chapter was marked by a wave of indifference, I still believe that it at least frames the issue in a useful way.

CHAPTER 5

Discretion in Long-Term Open Quantity Contracts: Reining In Good Faith

Long-term contracts often promise delivery of the seller's full output, the buyer's requirements, or some variation on these. For example, an electric utility might enter into a thirty-year contract with a coal mine promising that it will take all the coal needed to supply a particular generating plant. These open quantity contracts have raised two issues. The first is whether the promise is illusory. If the utility had no duty to take any coal, a court could have found that there was no consideration and, therefore, no contract. While there was a time when full output and requirements contracts did not fare well on this ground, nowadays their validity is rarely challenged with success.

The second and more interesting question today concerns the interpretation of the quantity term. What, if anything, limits the buyer's discretion? The answer, both at common law and in UCC §2–306(1), has been "good faith." The Code's Official Comment claims that §2–306 entails "the reading of commercial background and intent into the language of any agreement." In fact, it does nothing of the sort. Rather, it often involves supplanting the parties' careful balancing of various concerns in the initial contract with a wooden, uninformed reading of the agreement. With no theory to guide them, courts have held that good faith requires that producers behave in most peculiar ways—for example, running a plant at below full capacity for the life of the contract, or operating their business to satisfy the needs of a waste remover rather than their customers.

Long-term contracts cannot completely specify in advance all the obligations of both parties over the life of the agreement. In order to adapt their relationship to changed circumstances, parties will find it necessary to give one party the discretion to respond as new information becomes available. In particular, they might find that shifting supply and demand conditions would be better met by giving one party the discretion to vary quantity. If the party with discretion were the buyer, as in a requirements contract, the seller would have two concerns. First, the buyer could use its discretion opportunistically to rewrite the contract. Second, if the seller intended to make decisions in reliance on the continued performance of the buyer, it would want a means of conveying the extent of that reliance, perhaps by setting a minimum quantity or establishing a multipart pricing regime.

My thesis is that the courts have used good faith as a blunt instrument for providing protection to one party's reliance without asking whether that party would have been willing to pay for such protection in the first place. In effect, the seller wants to confront the buyer with a price reflecting the extent of its reliance. If that price is set too high, both parties lose. It is in their joint interest to fine-tune the protection of the reliance. And, as we shall see below, they can be quite good at doing so.

A contract grants one party discretion for a reason. The reason might not always be obvious, and it might not be a very good reason. However, as in most other areas of contract law, the courts should defer to the judgment of the parties. If it turns out that the buyer has no requirements or the seller chooses to produce no output, so be it. Such a rule would encourage the parties to determine at the time of contracting how they would constrain the discretion. The invocation of good faith should be unnecessary or, at worst, it should be read narrowly to recognize one exception. If the contract linked the buyer's requirements to the needs of a particular plant, sale of the plant or the firm would terminate the requirements of the buyer, although the plant would continue to have requirements. The buyer could attempt to avoid the consequences of a bad bargain by such an opportunistic sale. Even in these situations, parties can (and do) contract to deal with just such behavior, so at most the exception would serve as a default rule to protect casual or careless contractors from themselves. Ironically, the UCC does not preclude this form of opportunism. Comment 4 places the matter outside the Article 2 scope. "When an enterprise is sold, the question may arise whether the buyer is bound by an existing output or requirements contract. That question is outside the scope of this Article, and is to be determined by other principles of law." As we shall see below, the courts have had difficulty distinguishing the buyer who no longer has requirements because it had sold its plant from the buyer who had closed the plant.

Commentators have converged on the implications of the good faith standard for open quantity contracts. According to Stacy A. Silkworth (1990, p. 236), "[c]ourts consider two related factors in deciding these cases. First, courts will uphold quantity variations if they find a valid business reason that justifies the variation. Second, courts will disallow a quantity variation and award damages where they find that the quantity determining party has attempted to manipulate the contract in light of a contract price and market price disparity." Similarly, in their treatise *Contractual Good Faith*, Steven J. Burton and Eric G. Andersen (1995, p. 57) state: "Most cases involving the obligation to perform in good faith can be synthesized using the following principle: a party performs in bad faith by using discretion in performance for reasons outside the justified expectations of the parties arising from their agreement." The problem with both formulations is that they do not provide a framework for inferring the valid business reasons (Silkworth) and reasonable expectations (Burton and Andersen) that would define the contours of good faith. Indeed, once the analytical framework is understood, it is clear that "good faith" does no work.

What follows is a tour through the case law with three different concerns in mind. First is an analysis of the decisions on the merits. Second, the decisions provide some evidence on how the parties cope with the problem of harnessing discretion. The evidence, however, is often not very good, which leads to my third concern: the quality of the evidence is poor because the courts ask the wrong questions and adduce the wrong evidence. The exercise provides further support for framing contract law questions with more attention to the underlying economics of the transaction. Paradoxically, while I look more deeply at the economics than the courts have done, the moral of the exercise is that courts should look even less. With the possible exception of the sale-of-plant cases, courts should just say yes.

1. Quantity Variation in Long-Term Contracts: An Illustrative Example

To facilitate adaptation to changed circumstances, long-term contracts typically allow one party some discretion regarding quantity—requirements and output contracts being extreme forms. Even in these, the discretion will not be unbounded. One limitation on discretion is physical. A contract, for example, would not require the seller to provide whatever quantity of widgets the buyer desires. Rather, the seller would commit to providing widgets the buyer needs for a particular purpose or to supply a particular plant. The capacity of the buyer's plant would place an outer limit on the buyer's discretion. In addition, there are numerous contractual devices for constraining discretion. The contract could set up a mechanism requiring, for example, that both parties ratify changes. Or it could give one party the power to determine output. If that party changed the quantity in a way that would adversely affect the counterparty, it would have to pay a price. For example, if Y is the party with discretion, other things being equal, the greater X's reliance, the greater the price Y would have to pay for quantity adjustments adversely affecting X. The law, as currently embodied in §2–306(2), provides a set of default rules and barriers to surmounting them. The Code exhibits a lack of faith in the ability of the contracting parties to fine-tune the protection of the counterparty's reliance. In fact, their ability to fine-tune is quite impressive—much better, I would assert, than that of courts invoking good faith after the fact. In this section, I illustrate how the reliance-flexibility trade-off varies with the context by analyzing quantity variation in contracts for a particular product during a particular period— petroleum coke before 1970. For more detail on these contracts, see Goldberg and Erickson (1987).

Petroleum coking is a process that takes the heavy residual oils left over from the initial distillation of crude oil, producing gas oil (which can be further processed into lighter, higher-valued fuels like gasoline) and petroleum coke. In 1970 there were fifty-three cokers in operation at refineries in the United States. About 15% of the crude oil refined in the United States was coked. The coke was a waste product of the refining process, bulky, and a source of pollution. If not removed promptly, the accumulation might force a refinery to shut down. However, the coke had some value, particularly to the aluminum industry. Calcining the coke made it an excellent conductor of electricity, and the calcined coke was used to make anodes for the electrolytic cell reduction of alumina to aluminum. Its value in this use was enough so that owners of calciners were willing to pay the refineries a positive price to remove the coke from their refineries. Only high quality (low sulfur) coke was calcined. Low-quality (high sulfur) coke also usually sold at a positive price, albeit a much lower one. It was used primarily for fuel in utility boilers and cement kilns.

Great Lakes Carbon Corporation (GLC) owned a dozen calciners, selling the calcined coke to end-users. GLC had storage capacity at ten different locations that could hold about an eighteen-month supply of raw coke. In the late 1950s, end-users, primarily aluminum companies, began building their own calciners. Most, but not all, of the aluminum companies' output was for internal use, although some was sold to other end users. These calciners were, for the most part, built in conjunction with new cokers.

The contracts between the refineries (cokers) and the calciners varied considerably in the way they allocated responsibility for the quantity decision, the variation reflecting the concerns of the parties. For example, when a refinery added a new coker, it wanted some assurance that the accumulation of coke would not unreasonably interfere with the operation of the refinery. But assurance is costly, so the refinery would have to weigh the benefits of additional assurance against the costs. For the GLC contracts, this weighing generally resulted in granting the refinery complete discretion to produce any quantity of coke (including zero). However, the results were dramatically different for the end user contracts.

GLC entered into ten long-term contracts with refineries that were building new cokers in 1946–1961. The cokers' capacity was less than that of GLC's calciners, which, typically, were supplied by half a dozen or more cokers. The refineries had little storage capacity, so if the coke were not removed promptly, the refinery might have to shut down its coking (and perhaps its refining) operation entirely. GLC, on the other hand, had considerable storage capacity so that it could remove coke from the refinery and store it rather than processing it immediately. Its ample storage capacity enabled GLC to adapt with ease to fluctuations in the quantity of coke produced at individual refineries. As a result, almost all the GLC contracts were full output/immediate removal contracts, with GLC bearing all the risks of quantity variation. The coker was obligated to sell only if it produced, but the decision as to whether it should produce (and if so, how much) was entirely in the hands of the refinery. A failure to remove the coke rapidly enough would constitute a breach of GLC's obligations.

It is tempting to claim that this allocation of discretion is obvious. The seller is, in effect, contracting for removal of a waste product, one accounting for less than 3% of the value of the refinery's product. Therefore, it seems logical that its production decisions would be based on the market for its product, not for its waste. However, examination of the contracts with the aluminum companies shows that this is too simple. The aluminum contracts concerned the simultaneous construction of a new coker and a new calciner. The calciners were located near the cokers, often sharing the inventory pile. Unlike GLC, the aluminum companies could not rely on multiple sources (including inventories) of coke. They were dependent on a particular refinery, just as the refineries were dependent on them for removing coke. In none of the contracts did the buyer promise to take all the coker's output. Nor did the contracts go to the opposite extreme by obligating the cokers to meet the calciner's requirements. Rather, the contracts specified a minimum quantity, granted the aluminum company some discretion in varying that quantity (up or down), and provided some mechanism to convey to the aluminum company the extent of the refinery's reliance. Thus did the parties fine-tune the protection of their respective reliance interests.

The contracts accomplished this in different ways. In one instance, the buyer agreed to pay a "standby" charge of $75,000 per month, which obligated it to pay for about 40% of the coke, whether it took any or not. In effect, if not in name, this amounted to a "take-or-pay" clause. (Take-or-pay clauses are misnamed. The buyer agrees to pay for a fixed quantity regardless of whether he in fact takes it.) In other contracts, the price per ton was higher for the first, say, 35% of the contract quantity than for the remainder. The low marginal price encouraged the buyer to take more, thereby giving some protection to the seller's reliance. One contract allowed the buyer to reduce its take if there were external evidence of a decline in the demand for its aluminum, the reduction being shared by the parties by formula. The buyer in that contract did, however, agree to pay 50% of the contract price whether or not any coke was produced (take-or-pay, again). While the mechanism varied, the basic format was the same: the aluminum company determined the quantity, but the refinery's interest was conveyed by confronting the aluminum company with a cost if it were to take less than the contract quantity.

So, although the contracts were all for the same product, petroleum coke, the allocation of discretion was dictated by the context. Where the calciners had ample storage capacity, the quantity decision was in the hands of the cokers (the pure full-output contracts). Where calciners had little storage capacity and alternative suppliers were problematic, the cokers relinquished their discretion, giving the calciner the final say. However, none of the agreements gave the buyer unbridled discretion (as would a requirements contract). The calciner's freedom to alter the quantity taken was typically circumscribed to take into account the coker's reliance. The negotiated limits on buyer discretion were different from, and far more nuanced than, those arising from the good faith standard.

2. Zero Requirements Because of Transfer

If the buyer in a requirements contract has no requirements, it should, the UCC notwithstanding, have no obligation, and an inquiry into the buyer's good faith should be irrelevant. There is one plausible exception to this rule. The basic problem is simple enough. X agrees to provide Y's requirements at a particular plant. Y then sells, leases, or otherwise disposes of the plant to Z, who continues to run the plant. Y claims to have no requirements, and Z says it is not bound by Y's contract.

In the nineteenth and early twentieth century, both English and American courts allowed that a requirements contract could be undone by a change of control. In *Drake v. Vorse,* the defendant in a requirements contract ceased doing business as an individual and entered into a partnership. The court held that he was under no obligation as an individual to take any more castings because he needed none for his business as an individual. Nor did the partnership have an obligation to take any, because it was not a party to the contract. Similarly, in *Rhodes v. Forwood,* Lord Cairns noted that a buyer could take zero requirements if the principal's colliery closed on account of low prices, strikes, etc.:

> If . . . it could not be contended that there is any provision in this contract against any of those risks, why is it to be assumed with regard to the . . . risk of the colliery owner, not selling his coal elsewhere piecemeal but selling the colliery itself to a purchaser, that there is an implied undertaking against that one risk, although it is admitted that there is no undertaking at all against any of the other risks? . . . The simple point here appears to me to be, as it is admitted that there is no express contract which has been violated, can your Lordships say that there is any implied contract which has been violated? I can find none. I cannot find any implied contract that the colliery owner would not sell his colliery entire. (p. 401)

An *American Law Reports* annotation (7 A.L.R. 498, 507 (1920)) suggested that the application of the rule was symmetrical: "where the buyer disposes of the business with reference to which he has purchased a commodity to the extent of his requirements, the seller is under no obligation to furnish such commodity to the purchaser of the business, nor is he under any obligation to furnish the same to the original buyer."

These decisions can be contrasted with another nineteenth-century case, *Wells v. Alexandre.* There, the seller agreed to furnish all the buyer's coal requirements for three steamships for one year. It did so for six months, whereupon the buyer sold the steamships, which continued to ply the same route for the remainder of the year. The new owners apparently purchased their coal elsewhere (the decision is vague on this), and the coal supplier sued the original owner. (The opinion is silent on whether they could, or did, sue the new owners.) The court held for the plaintiff:

> The fact that the defendants deemed it best to sell the steamers cannot be permitted to operate to relieve them from the obligation to take the coal which the ordinary and accustomed use of the steamers required, for the provisions of the agreement do not admit of a construction that it was to terminate in the event of a sale or other disposition of them by the defendants. (p. 143)

In effect, the court hints at what appears to be a sensible default rule: transfer of property does not terminate the obligation. Whether that really is an appropriate rule has nothing to do with variable quantity contract questions. In any event, as we shall see, parties can, and do, contract on this question. The significant point is that one can easily distinguish between the buyer who has no requirements because it had transferred the business to a successor (which does still have requirements) and the buyer who simply closes down its plant.

The courts took a wrong turn in *Diamond Alkali v. P. C. Tomson*. Diamond was an Ohio manufacturer of soda ash, caustic soda, and other related products, which were used by Tomson in its Philadelphia factory. The parties decided that it would make sense to relocate Tomson's factory adjacent to Diamond's. Diamond loaned Tomson $100,000 and sold it the land for the factory. Tomson agreed to build a plant on the site capable of taking care of its entire present business. The plant was to cost not less than $100,000. Diamond agreed to sell Tomson all of its requirements for five years. Tomson's president testified as to its reliance on the agreement:

> I think the reason for fixing a period of five years during which the Diamond Alkali Company would furnish us with our requirements, was that if we only made a yearly agreement, we would invest in a factory there, and have several hundred thousand dollars invested in it, and if anything should happen, we couldn't get our raw material, why, there would be no advantage to it. I think that was one of the reasons for it. We wanted to be sure of the supply for our manufacturing during the period of five years operating our new building. (p. 119)

The seller also relied on the contract, expanding its capacity after entering into the contract.

Tomson erected the plant in Ohio, but before it had moved its operations to Ohio, it sold its Philadelphia plant, including good will, to a third party and agreed not to enter into the business again for five years. In compliance with that agreement, it then refused to open and operate the Ohio plant. Hence, the requirements at the plant were zero. Diamond sued for equitable relief, which the court denied. However, the Court of Appeals concluded that Tomson had breached the contract, and the case was remanded to determine damages.

The agreement explicitly stated that Tomson was "not to sell, lease or enter into any contract for the operation of its manufacturing plant at Fairport [Ohio] without the consent of the Alkali Company during the continuance of this agreement." (p. 118) This term almost certainly would have prevented someone from operating the Ohio plant without using Diamond's products. It would have policed most of the ways that Tomson could have shed itself of the contract. It did not, however, deal with the situation here, in which the new factory is abandoned. The court does not tell us why the sale price of the Philadelphia facility was so attractive that the parties would be willing to turn their back on a brand new facility that had cost over $100,000 (in pre-Depression dollars) to build. It must have been a heck of a deal. The court, citing *Wells v. Alexandre*, held that the mutual intentions of the parties were that they would continue in business for five years and that Tomson, by accepting the covenant not to compete, had breached this contract.

It seems odd that a third party would offer to pay Tomson enough so that in effect it would be dynamiting its expensive new factory. I suspect that this was not the case and that the court, confused by its framing of the matter, left out a significant piece of the story. It is silent on whether anything in the contract with the third party precluded Tomson's sale of the new plant to either Diamond or another firm. Because it is likely that such a deal would be a Pareto improvement over demolition of the new factory, one suspects that resale was the likely outcome. Had it sold to another (with Diamond's approval), the requirements contract should have remained alive—Diamond could have insisted on that as a condition for granting its approval. Had it sold to Diamond, the question would be moot. The court's resolution was probably not the final step. Most likely, it merely defined the starting point for bargaining over the disposition of the new plant.

That is all speculation on my part. The significant points are two. First, there is a huge distinction between the case in which the requirements of the physical facility cease, and the case in which the buyer transfers ownership of the facility, but the facility continues in operation. Second, the contract gave Tomson the discretion to adapt to changed circumstances; had Diamond wanted more protection of its reliance, it could have insisted upon minimum payments (for example, a take-or-pay provision). It chose not to because it believed that Tomson's self-interest provided adequate protection for its reliance. The likelihood was very low that Tomson would find that the most profitable use of a brand new factory would be to close it. There is no reason to rewrite that contract to give Diamond more protection than it had bargained for.

The issues in *Diamond Alkali* were somewhat obscured by the lack of information regarding the future use of the new plant. *Central States Power & Light v. United States Zinc Co.*, which concerned a three-year contract supplying natural gas to a smelter, presented a simpler problem. The gas supplier would have to incur a considerable relation-specific investment, constructing a pipeline to the smelter. It appears from the decision that the costs of that pipeline would be covered by the expected future gas sales. The smelter required about 6.5 million cubic feet of gas per day. The contract called for a fixed quantity of 3 million cubic feet. However, if the buyer's total requirements did not reach 3 million, its obligation would be capped by its total requirements. The buyer had no obligation to resell (or store) gas it could not use. If it operated at more than 50% capacity, it either had to find other suppliers or buy gas from Central States at a price (and other terms) to be negotiated.

Nine months after signing the contract, after failing to renegotiate a more favorable price, the buyer dismantled the plant and discontinued its operation. The gas supplier sued, claiming that the buyer had implicitly promised to stay in business and to continue to have requirements. The majority, relying in part on *Wells* and *Diamond Alkali,* agreed. The buyer "owning an established business had the implied obligation to continue it in the usual manner, and accept during the time fixed the gas required to so conduct it." (p. 834) The court in effect turned a contract in which the parties had limited the buyer's discretion in a way that protected it from having to be a reseller of gas it could not use, into a take-or-pay contract in which the buyer promised to pay whether it took the gas or not. The dissent highlighted the distinction between this case and *Wells*:

I think the [buyer] was entitled to a directed verdict. The parties agreed upon a partial supply of gas needed for a particular smelter described in the contract. If that smelter burned any gas, appellee must purchase it of appellant, up to the specified amount. That is a fair and valid contract. Vendee could not escape its obligation by selling the smelter; as long as the smelter required gas, the obligation remained. But does the obligation remain if the smelter is destroyed by fire, or is razed by a tornado, or is dismantled because of the collapse of business? In such events, no gas is required for the smelter, and there was no agreement to buy gas not required. It matters not whether the dismantling occurred in a year, or a month, or a day. That is the contract the parties made. (p. 836)

Tri-state Generation & Transmission Ass'n, Inc. v. Shoshone River Power, Inc. illustrates how a party might opportunistically sell its business in an effort to get out from under an onerous requirements contract. Tri-state, a generation and transmission (G&T) cooperative, provided electricity to twenty-five distribution cooperatives including Shoshone. Part of Tri-state's financing came from the Rural Electrification Administration (REA), which required as a condition of its loans that its G&T borrowers get requirements contracts of matching maturity. Shoshone's original contract was of thirty-three years duration, and the most recent modification had extended the life to forty-three years. The requirements contracts between Tri-state and its member distribution cooperatives were meant to be security for the loans. However, there was no minimum payment. Shoshone had over 1,000 members to whom it supplied electricity. The arrangement worked fine for decades, but in the mid-1980s when fuel prices collapsed, Tri-state's prices remained high. Pacific Power & Light Company offered to supply Shoshone and other distribution cooperatives at prices substantially below Tri-state's. To take advantage of Pacific's low prices, Shoshone agreed to sell to Pacific its assets, which consisted of the power-delivery subscriptions of its members and, to a lesser extent, its poles and power lines. That is, Shoshone's members would continue to have electricity requirements, but Shoshone would not. The members would be supplied by Pacific, not Tri-state.

Tri-state attempted to enjoin the asset sale. The court denied specific performance, but found that Shoshone's action was a breach of the contract and awarded damages. The majority held that "as a matter of law . . . when there are sufficient members in Shoshone's system requiring electric power, a sale of Shoshone's assets or member subscriptions to Pacific cannot qualify as a good faith reduction or elimination of requirements." (p. 1360) The dissent, which would have remanded for a new trial on liability, noted that the seller could have achieved greater protection of its reliance by including a take-or-pay clause in the contract. It also remarked on the lack of provisions preventing the sale of the business or making the contract binding on the buyer's successors or assigns. In effect, the court came up with a plausible default rule—the requirements are defined by the physical assets, not by the identity of the contracting party. The moral is blurred, however, by a convoluted opinion that relies extensively on *Diamond Alkali* and *Central States,* failing to recognize that in both these cases the facilities would not remain in operation.

For a decision suggesting the default rule that the agreement should survive the sale of the asset, see *Proctor v. Union Coal Co.* In that case, the court states, "The construction [of the contract] that the defendant could terminate the plaintiff's rights at any time by a sale of the premises, would leave the plaintiff wholly at the mercy [of the defendant]. . . . It is not to be presumed that the parties intended so unreasonable an agreement, in the absence of language expressing such intention." (p. 660) I am not insisting that this default rule is the right one. So long as the barriers to contracting around this default rule are low, it should not much matter. My point is that the cases in which the party sells the underlying asset are analytically different from those in which the party closes down the plant or drastically reduces its requirements.

3. Reduced Requirements

Most commentators agree that the law, both pre- and post-Code, treated increases and decreases asymmetrically. A dispute continues over whether the "unreasonably disproportionate" language of the UCC applies on the downside. The preference for asymmetric treatment stems from the recognition that there is less opportunity for the quantity-determining party to take advantage of price variations by decreasing its requirements. A requirements buyer could increase its purchases without limit (if the contract placed no limit) to take advantage of a rising market, but it could only cut its requirements to zero to take advantage of a market price decline.

The Code puts considerable emphasis on the role of quantity estimates and prior dealings between the parties in imposing extracontractual limits on the quantity-determining party's discretion. Even under the Code, however, a buyer could in "good faith," substantially cut back or even eliminate its requirements. But "good faith" is interpreted, heaven knows why, to mean that the firm can shut down for lack of orders, but not to curtail losses. (Comment 2) In effect, the Code interpretation implies a take-or-pay obligation, with that obligation determined ex post by the court. No attempt is made to relate the standard to any economic context. Why would businesses want this default rule, especially if it is difficult to contract around? A simpler starting point would be a default rule that gives complete flexibility on the downside.

The case cited in the UCC comments for the proposition that a firm can drastically reduce its requirements in good faith is *Southwest Natural Gas Co. v. Oklahoma Portland Cement Co.* A cement company had a fifteen-year requirements contract for provision of all its natural gas needs. It subsequently redesigned its boilers so that they would utilize the waste heat of the kilns, and this resulted in a substantial decrease in the amount of gas needed to power the boilers. The gas company's attempt to enjoin the use of waste heat as a violation of the contract was denied. The result was surely correct, but it was softened by the court's language:

> The term of the contract here involved was 15 years. That was longer than the ordinary life of certain of the appliances and equipment in the cement plant. It is a reasonable assumption that the parties contemplated that whenever it became necessary to renew worn-out equipment the Cement Company would install modern equipment in its place. Certainly, the parties did not contemplate that the contract should obligate the Cement Company to replace worn-out equipment with a like type of equipment that had become obsolete in the cement manufacturing industry, or not to utilize fully, modern equipment when installed. We are of the opinion that the Cement Company had the right to install modern equipment whenever it was necessary to replace worn-out equipment so long as in so doing it acted bona fide.
>
> The boiler plant of the Cement Company became worn out in 1933. To replace it the Cement Company installed a modern boiler system similar to the types generally used in other cement manufacturing plants. In the improved plant a new or different fuel was not substituted for gas, but a more efficient and economical utilization of gas was effected, so that the heat resulting from the combustion of the gas in the kilns was used both to heat the product in the kilns, and the boilers. . . . In so improving its

plant, the Cement Company acted in good faith and in the exercise of prudent business judgment. This it had the right to do. (p. 633)

"Bona fide," "good faith," and "prudent business judgment" presumably impose some constraints on the buyer. But what are the constraints? If the relative price of an alternative fuel fell, could the cement company switch? Would that be "imprudent"?

The most plausible explanation for the structure of the fifteen-year contract is that the cement company needed assurance of a continued supply, and that replacement of Southwest by another supplier would have been difficult. Southwest, on the other hand, likely supplied a number of customers and had only modest relation-specific investments. If that were indeed the case, then we would expect that the contract would give the buyer considerable assurance of supply and the flexibility to alter the amount taken as circumstances change. That does not, of course, mean that the gas company need grant it unlimited discretion. Possibly, it might want to confront the cement company with an additional cost when it contemplated a change to a less gas-intensive technology if relative prices or technology changed. But why rely on an after-the-fact review by a court or jury guided by such loose language as "good faith" or "prudent business judgment"? The parties could have fine-tuned the gas company's protection in a number of ways. The simplest would be to impose a minimum quantity, perhaps in the form of a take-or-pay arrangement. Or the gas company could be given a right to revise or terminate following the occurrence of certain events, such as a change in relative prices of a certain magnitude, a reduction in quantity beyond a certain point, or a finding by an arbitrator that the technology has changed. Such protection was likely unnecessary, because I doubt that the gas company had any need to protect its reliance. But why, absent explicit language, should there be any presumption that the buyer was promising to adapt inefficiently as new information became available?

In *Northern Indiana Public Service Co. v. Colorado Westmoreland, Inc.*, Judge Easterbrook, sitting by designation, held in favor of a public utility purchaser which had substantially reduced its coal requirements. Northern Indiana Public Service Co. (NIPSCO) entered into long-term contracts with Colorado Westmoreland Inc. (CWI) in 1977. The contracts were renegotiated in 1980 and again in 1982. The dispute concerned NIPSCO's performance under the last contract. That contract was for its coal requirements at a particular generating facility. The contract included both estimated re-quirements (about 1 million tons per year) and a maximum annual obli-gation by the seller (1.25 million tons). In finding for the utility, Judge Easterbrook provided elaborate detail on the nature of the transaction and its negotiating history.

The contract was one of two NIPSCO contracts for low-sulfur western coal. The other was with Carbon County Coal Company. After fuel prices collapsed in the early 1980s, NIPSCO sought declaratory judgments re-garding both contracts. It sought, and failed, to be excused from the Carbon County contract, a fixed quantity contract with an indexed price well above the current market price. (See *Northern Indiana Public Service Co. v. Carbon County Coal Co.*) In the CWI contract dispute, NIPSCO sought a declaratory judgment that, despite a substantial reduction in requirements, the contract was still in force. In addition to these two contracts, NIPSCO was supplied by an unspecified number of high-sulfur Midwestern coal companies with less expensive coal. NIPSCO had eleven coal-fired generating units. The CWI contract was for the requirements of one particular unit, Schahfer 15. To simplify the story somewhat, when determining which units to operate, NIPSCO had to balance the costs of generating at those units and the reli-ability of the system; it also had to take into account directives from the regulatory commission (economy purchase orders) and the possibility that the commission would not allow it to recover all of its costs. As a conse-quence, NIPSCO started using more high-sulfur and less low-sulfur coal. In addition, hard times in the steel industry—a major determinant of the de-mand for NIPSCO's power—led to a scaling back of power needs. So, despite the contract estimate of approximately 1 million tons of coal per year, re-quirements in 1983–1985 ranged from 573,000 tons to 713,000 tons.

CWI argued that a quantity reduction of this magnitude was not in good faith, citing Comment 3 of UCC §2–306. Judge Easterbrook rejected the argument on four grounds: (a) NIPSCO acted in commercial good faith; (b) the variance from the estimate was only 45%; (c) the parties dickered over the boundaries on the requirements and the court should not read language into the agreement which the parties explicitly chose not to include; and (d) the restrictions in the statute are asymmetric, applying only to buyers who attempt to unduly increase their requirements.

The most interesting aspect of the opinion for my purposes is the rich description of the contractual alternatives considered by the parties before they settled on the final language. CWI initially proposed a minimum-take contract. Alternatively, CWI suggested a 900,000-ton "walk away" provision. If NIPSCO ordered less than 900,000 tons in any year, CWI would have the option of declining to fill the orders and canceling the contract. With such a contract, if NIPSCO were concerned about protecting its long-term supply of coal, then it might place orders just to keep the agreement alive. In effect, by purchasing coal that it did not need today, NIPSCO would be renewing its option to purchase coal tomorrow. If NIPSCO did not exercise the option, then CWI had an option to terminate the deal. The risk of termination would have been one of the costs that NIPSCO would have to consider when deciding whether it should order coal that it did not need today. However, all this was moot as NIPSCO rejected both the minimum-take and the walk away provision. NIPSCO proposed a clause that would define the parameters of its discretion:

> [1] Nothing contained in this Agreement shall be construed to require the use of coal for generation of electrical energy or to prohibit Buyer from utilizing any and all other or substitute sources of energy as may become available; [2] nor shall anything in this Agreement be construed to require the purchase of more coal than needed for the operation of Buyer's Schahfer Unit 15; [3] nor shall anything in this Agreement be construed to cause Buyer to operate Schahfer Unit 15 to any greater extent than Buyer in its sole discretion deems prudent, either as to hours of operation or as to load carried on said Schahfer Unit 15; [4] nor shall anything in this Agreement be construed to prevent Buyer from operating any and all of its generating stations, including Schahfer Unit 15, and utilizing other sources of power supply in the most efficient, economical, and prudent manner for the production and supply of electrical energy for Buyer's Customers. (p. 633)

In the course of the negotiations both the first and third clause were eliminated. The first deletion means that the generating unit could not be shifted to an alternative fuel without CWI's permission. The second deletion is harder to explain because the language of the next clause seems to allow NIPSCO to justify its decisions on roughly the same grounds. Judge Easterbrook concluded that deleting the clause allowed CWI to protect itself against irrational changes in requirements. (p. 615) Nonetheless, it is clear that the contract would, with one exception, allow the buyer to adapt to changed circumstances by varying its requirements in a way that it reasonably perceived to be in its long-term economic interest without having to get permission from, consult with, or pay CWI. The exception, as noted, was a change in the relative price of fuels.

Again, it should be emphasized that this allocation of decision making was hardly inevitable. Indeed, in its contract with Carbon County, NIPSCO opted for a very different arrangement in which it sacrificed its quantity flexibility. Carbon County had only one customer, and the mine was developed only after the contract had been entered into, so there was an obvious interest in protecting the seller's reliance. On the other hand, CWI's mine was already developed and the Schahfer unit built when the parties entered into this requirements contract. It is not clear from the opinion whether CWI had other customers (although its proposed "walk away" term suggests strongly that it did). CWI needed less protection of its reliance than did Carbon County and therefore was more willing to give NIPSCO control of the quantity decision. Judge Easterbrook did not allow the fine-tuning of the parties to be trumped by the wooden standards of the UCC.

Judge Easterbrook's decision, which places the contract in its commercial context, contrasts with three New York cases that require a firm to continue in operation, despite the lack of an explicit promise to do so. *Feld v. Henry S. Levy & Sons, Inc.*, the leading New York case, illustrates how the good faith implication complicates a simple case and undoes a sensible allocation of decision making. Levy & Sons operated a wholesale bread baking business. As part of its operations, it generated considerable waste product in the form of stale or imperfectly appearing loaves. One option for disposing of this material was to convert it into bread crumbs by removing the labels, processing the loaves through two grinders, toasting the product in an oven, and bagging it. Levy & Sons purchased the oven and entered into a one-year evergreen (automatically renewed) contract with the Crushed Toast Company, which agreed to purchase "all bread crumbs produced by the Seller in its factory at 115 Thames Street, Brooklyn, New York" (p. 321) at a price of 6 cents per pound. Either party could cancel on six months' notice. The Crushed Toast Company was required to deliver a "faithful performance bond," presumably to provide assurance to Levy of timely removal of the waste. In the first eleven months, Levy delivered about $30,000 worth of bread crumbs. Apparently the operation was not profitable for Levy. It attempted to renegotiate the contract price up to 7 cents, but was rebuffed. One month before the end of the first year, Levy dismantled the toasting oven and ceased production of bread crumbs. The waste was then sold to animal food manufacturers. Dismantling the oven did not amount to termination of the agreement since Levy was required to give six months' notice; had it reinstalled the oven, it would still have been obliged to deliver the crumbs to Feld. Feld sued for breach, arguing that Levy could not in good faith reduce its output to zero.

The New York Supreme Court denied both parties' motions for summary judgment. The Appellate Division affirmed over a strong dissent, which would have (properly) granted Levy's motion for summary judgment. The Court of Appeals affirmed unanimously, rejecting the dissenters' argument that the language was clear and unambiguous and that there could be no inference that Levy had promised to continue to produce bread crumbs to sell to plaintiff. The court first noted that output contracts were not unenforceable because the seller was required to conduct his business in good faith. The seller was not free to decide whether he should produce any bread crumbs. "The seller's duty to remain in crumb production is a matter calling for close scrutiny of its motives." (p. 323) That scrutiny would require data on "the actual cost of the finished bread crumbs to defendant, statements as to the profits derived or the losses sustained, or data specifying the net or gross return realized from the animal food transactions." (p. 323) Moreover, "[s]ince bread crumbs were but a part of defendant's enterprise and since there was a contractual right of cancellation, good faith required continued production until cancellation, even if there be no profit. In circumstances such as these and without more, defendant would be justified, in good faith, in ceasing production of the single item prior to cancellation only if its losses from continuance would be more than trivial, which, overall, is a question of fact." (p. 323)

The court failed to recognize that, in its own statement of the facts, it had already provided the relevant economic data. The contract price was 6 cents per pound, and Levy's actions (dismantling the oven) indicate that this amount would not even cover the variable costs; it was cheaper to shut the project down. However, Levy indicated that a price of 7 cents per pound would have been sufficient to warrant its continued operation of the toaster oven. So, the fight is over one penny. The court gives no hint as to how the information would help answer the question it has posed. Further, it glosses over the question of why Levy's termination of an operation that does not cover variable costs would be in bad faith. Given the incoherence of the question, the elusiveness of the answer is hardly surprising.

That this was an output contract rather than a requirements contract matters not. It can be viewed as a requirements contract for a service—

waste removal. The deformed loaves and day-old bread were waste products that happened, by chance, to have a positive market value for various uses. Suppose instead that they were of no value and that Levy had entered into a contract to have all its trash hauled away at a price of, say, 3 cents a pound. The only difference is that the net flow of cash now would be from Levy to Feld. Can one seriously argue that Levy has a duty to stay in business to produce garbage for Feld to haul away? Yet that is precisely what the court has done.

It is conceivable that a producer would, under certain circumstances, promise to produce a specific level of a waste product. That, recall, was what the oil refineries promised to the aluminum companies who were building calciners in reliance upon the refineries' coke output.[1] The contrast between the GLC and aluminum contracts suggests the conditions under which the parties might want to give substantial protection to the trash remover's reliance interest. Those conditions are certainly not met in *Feld v. Levy*. The facts are spotty, but a reasonable inference is that the Crushed Toast Company was in existence prior to the formation of this contract, that it had other suppliers, and that toasted bread crumbs could be held in inventory at less expense and for a greater period of time than unsold loaves of bread. Hence its willingness to subject itself both to Levy's discretion in determining the bread crumb production and to post a faithful performance bond. Levy was the party that had carefully protected its reliance because it had purchased an oven for making bread crumbs and had a clear need to assure the removal of unsold loaves. So, its dismantling the oven should have been sufficient to end the inquiry. Instead the court, under the banner of good faith, encouraged a fruitless inquiry into the costs and revenues associated with the two alternative ways of disposing of the waste. (For another waste removal case in which the buyer was required to furnish a surety company performance bond, see *Neofotistos v. Harvard Brewing Co.*)

A half century earlier, the New York Court of Appeals mishandled a similar case. In *Wigand v. Bachmann-Bechtel Brewing Co.*, the defendant, a brewer, entered into an agreement in which it agreed to sell to the plaintiff all the "wet grains" produced at its brewery for a five-year period, or until 500,000 barrels of beer had been brewed. Wet grains were a waste product of the brewing process, which would be dried and sold as cattle feed. Wigand would, under the contract, install a plant for drying the grains in Bachmann-Bechtel's brewery. It had in previous years installed such plants in other breweries. The cost of installation was $6,050, borne entirely by

Wigand. At the end of the five years (or after the 500,000 barrels had been produced), title to the drying plant would be transferred to the brewer. Wigand's compensation would come entirely in the form of a favorable price for the wet grains of 6 cents per barrel of beer. In addition, Wigand advanced about $5,000 to the brewer for modifications of the brewery so that the drying plant could be installed. That was to be paid back at $250 per month to be offset against Wigand's payments for wet grains. The contract included an excuse clause broader than the typical *force majeure* clause:

> Should the party of the first part hereto be prevented from operating its brewery by reason of strikes, break downs in machinery, or for any reason whether beyond its control or otherwise, then and in that event this contract and the performance thereof by the party of the first part shall stand in abeyance until the brewery of the party of the first part shall again be in operation. (p. 619)

In the first twenty-one months the brewery produced 158,000 barrels of beer and both parties complied with the contract. Then the brewer sold its beer business (but not the physical plant) to another brewer. It covenanted with the purchaser that it would not operate its brewery for two years. It complied with the covenant and, for reasons unstated, did not reopen the brewery even after the two years had expired. Wigand sued and ultimately prevailed, although the Court of Appeals rejected the jury verdict of $8,500 and remanded for a new trial.

The court put great weight on Wigand's reliance on the brewery's continued operation in concluding that the brewery had breached the implied covenant of good faith and fair dealing.

> The mutual promises in the contract, many of which we have stated, are such that a voluntary and intentional failure to perform by the defendant would be inequitable and unjust. The large expenditure by the plaintiff for machinery which he placed in the defendant's plant for which pay could only be obtained by him through a continuance of the business; the furnishing by him of $5,000 to the defendant, only to be returned by deductions from the purchase price of the wet grains received; the necessity of expenditures to keep the plant in repair and for insurance as stated for the full period of five years, are important facts to be considered in determining what was meant by the defendant when it promised to sell to the plaintiff "all of the wet brewery grains produced from the brewing at its brewery" as in the contract provided. (p. 619)

In *Feld,* the seller had made the significant relation-specific investment—the toasting oven. Here, the relation-specific investments (over $6,000 in pre–World War I dollars) were made by the buyer. Recoupment depended on the continued operation of the brewery. Wigand could have reduced its reliance by phasing its compensation differently. Failing that, it might have forced the brewery to take this reliance into account when making decisions on how much beer to produce or whether to produce beer at all. It could, for example, have insisted that if the brewery were shut down, the brewer would have to purchase the drying plant for a fraction of the $6,050 related to the length of time the drying plant had operated. Instead it relied, not unreasonably, on the seller's self-interest. Under most circumstances the brewer would find operating the brewery more attractive than mothballing or destroying it. But in those rare cases (as the present) where the brewery seems to be worth more dead than alive, Wigand's reliance remains unprotected, at least until the court comes in and trumps the agreement. It is possible that the brewery might agree ex ante that it would have to pay a fee to the waste removal firm if it chose to go out of business to cover at least some of Wigand's reliance costs. But is it likely? Other suppliers, notably workers, also relied on continued operation of the brewery and presumably received nothing. The court simply found an implausible duty to produce waste, imposing a particular vision of the balance between discretion and reliance other than the one designed by the parties.

In yet another tail-wags-dog opinion, *407 E. 61st Garage, Inc. v. Savoy Fifth Ave. Corp.,* the New York Court of Appeals held that a Manhattan hotel should remain in operation for the benefit of a parking garage (or pay the consequences). The Savoy Hilton entered into a five-year contract with the parking garage, promising to use reasonable efforts to enable the garage to have "the exclusive right and privilege of storing the motor vehicles of [the hotel's] guests, tenants and patrons." The garage agreed to pay the hotel 10% of the transient storage charges incurred by the hotel guests. Thus, the garage paid a fee for the hotel's encouraging patronage. The garage was about one-half mile from the hotel. (Only in New York!) Savoy purchased the hotel (which was over thirty years old) shortly before it entered into the contract. Less than two years after entering into the agreement, Savoy demolished the hotel. There was some dispute over the reason. The owner claimed that it was losing money on the hotel and that there was no hope of making it profitable. The plaintiff claimed that the real reason for demolition was that the land had a higher and better use—namely, construction of a fifty-story office building (the General Motors Building just south of Central Park). The plaintiff made much of the motive in his affidavit and briefs, but the claims of both sides come down to the same point: like the Bachmann-Bechtel brewery, the hotel was worth more dead than alive.

The parking garage sued for damages for lost profits during the last three years of the agreement. The garage did not attempt to obtain an injunction that would have given it the right to hold out for a piece of the increased value of the office building. A *New York Times* article, introduced by the plaintiff, identified two tenants, a coffee shop and a flower shop, that did have the right to throw a monkey wrench into the planned conversion. The two threatened to remain in business if their terms were not met, and Savoy, in turn, threatened to raze the hotel around them and construct the office building on the remainder of the site. See Robbins (1965).

Judge Breitel, speaking for a unanimous Court of Appeals, reversed summary judgment for the hotel and remanded. While this was not a variable quantity contract, the New York Supreme Court classified it as a requirements contract and granted summary judgment to the hotel because there was no evidence of bad faith. The Court of Appeals held that "the agreement between the garage and Savoy is not a 'requirements' contract, but is akin to the grant of a license or franchise by Savoy to the garage." (The court then went on to note that categorization was not particularly helpful in analyzing the case.) The court framed the question in a neutral way: "The real issue in this case is . . . whether this agreement imports an implication that Savoy was obligated to remain in the hotel business, or, better, had undertaken indefeasible obligations for the full term." It recognized "the incongruity of an enterprise, as large as a metropolitan hotel, being obligated to 'continue in the hotel business' merely because of various relatively minor incidental service contracts, such as that involved here." (p. 41) Nonetheless, the court asserted a default rule: when the promisee relies upon the promisor's continued activity, a promise to remain in business will be implied. Savoy could avoid this result in two ways. Ex ante, Savoy could have included an express term in the contract that would terminate the agreement if the hotel went out of business. Ex post, Savoy could invoke custom or usage in the industry to show that incidental service contracts are terminable on the hotel's going out of business.

So, the net result is a default rule, which could be overcome by explicit contract language or by demonstrating that people in the industry knew (or should have known) that the default rule does not apply here. The court did not explain why the default rule should give complete protection to the garage's reliance with no concern for the hotel's discretion. Nor did it indicate how one should give content to the custom and usage standard. Whose custom and usage? Hotels'? Parking garages'? Hotels dealing with parking garages? In Manhattan? Would the custom and usage depend on whether the garage owner relied upon the contract in building the garage, whether the hotel customers constituted 100% (or 50% or 5%) of the expected revenues of the garage? The garage's interest in protecting its reliance depends crucially on these matters. Under most circumstances, the garage would require only modest, if any, protection of its reliance; indeed, the most plausible scenario is that the multiyear agreement was designed to protect the reliance of the hotel, which was concerned about the consequences of not having a convenient parking garage nearby.

Suppose that instead of closing, the Savoy had changed its business strategy. Perhaps it chose to remodel and offer fewer, and larger, rooms. Would it have to compensate the garage during the remodeling period or for the lower number of potential patrons? Could it introduce a subsidized airport shuttle service, which would result in a smaller number of patrons with cars to be parked? Could it close the hotel restaurant for lunches or on Monday evenings? Would it have to clear its advertising budgets with the parking garage? Would we expect a hotel to require approval from (or to promise payment to) a parking garage as it adapts its business decisions to changing circumstances? If the court does not mean to hold the hotel responsible for these decisions, how does one draw the line between these and the decision to tear the hotel down? Must these all be fact questions relying on proof of custom and usage? It makes little sense to have a fact-sensitive default rule where the facts are so elusive.

The three preceding cases are like shooting fish in a barrel, at least when one is properly armed. *Empire Gas Corp. v. American Bakeries Co. (Empire III)* presents a more difficult problem. After entering into a requirements contract, the buyer, American Bakeries, changed its mind and had no requirements for the life of the contract. The seller, Empire Gas, sued and won a jury verdict in excess of $3 million. On appeal, Judge Posner upheld the verdict. Although the contract concerned potential sales of more than $5 million and was between firms with combined sales in 1980 of around $1 billion, the agreement was prepared by two laymen without, it appears, any assistance from counsel. (*Empire I*, p. 271)

American Bakeries was a distributor of bakery goods in different parts of the country, operating a large fleet of trucks. Concern over the energy crisis of the late 1970s sparked interest in the possibility of converting part of its fleet to the use of propane gas. It entered into a four-year requirements contract with Empire for provision of conversion units (approximately 3,000, "more or less, depending upon requirements of Buyer") and propane motor fuel. The units would give the trucks the capability of running on either fuel. Empire did not manufacture conversion units; it would purchase them elsewhere and supply them to American. The contract fixed the price for the conversion units ($750 apiece), but did not give the brand or specifications. Empire had at least five brands of conversion equipment in inventory, and the court opinions suggest that delivery of any of these would have been appropriate at the contract price. According to Judge Posner, Empire was not in the business of marketing conversion equipment; its primary concern was sale of propane. "Empire Gas does not manufacture conversion equipment, but supplies it essentially as an accommodation to the customers for its propane, the major part of its business." (p. 1336) American agreed to take its requirements of propane from Empire at roughly the market price. The pricing term was a loosely worded "meeting competition" clause:

> In consideration of providing propane dispensing equipment, American Bakeries Company agrees to purchase propane motor fuel solely from Empire Gas Corporation at all locations where Empire Gas has supplied carburetion and dispensing equipment as long as Empire Gas Corporation remains in a reasonably competitive price posture with other major suppliers. Buyer may elect to call for price negotiations at which time seller will have the opportunity to alter buyer's price to buyer's satisfaction. (*Empire II*, p. 2)

The court, focusing only on the quantity term, ignored the open-ended nature of the price term, which it could easily have found too vague to make the agreement enforceable. In addition, "Empire promised to provide [American] with propane dispensing equipment, including a 1,000 gallon tank at no charge at all locations where Empire supplied . . . dispensing services." (*Empire II*, p. 8)

After the parties signed the agreement, American advised Empire that it was having financial difficulties. For over a year American failed to take any conversion units or propane, but informed Empire that it intended to honor the contract. Finally, Empire sent an invoice for the purchase of 3,000 conversion units, which it claimed to be holding in inventory. American refused to accept conversion units or to pay for them, and Empire sued for lost profits on both the conversion units and the propane. The jury concluded that, but for the breach, Empire would have sold 2,242 conversion units (an exactitude suggesting capriciousness) to American. The jury also concluded that Empire had lost profits on conversion unit sales of about $600,000, roughly 36% per unit, and that the lost profits from the foregone propane sales were $2.6 million.

Judge Posner suggested that, on the basis of the negotiating history, the contract could have been interpreted as one for a fixed quantity of conversion units. The reason for this conclusion is unclear because he also noted that American rejected Empire's standard contract, which called for a minimum number of conversion units per month. Regardless, the parties concurred that the agreement should be classified as a requirements contract and therefore that it fell under UCC §2–306.

In interpreting UCC §2–306, Judge Posner adopted the majority position holding that a reduction in requirements was constrained only by the buyer's good faith, not by the "unreasonably disproportionate" proviso. American would have been acting in bad faith had it purchased conversion units or propane from competitors, he held, although it is not clear why one would choose to characterize this as "bad faith" rather than as a flat-out breach. However, it would not have been acting in bad faith "if it had a business reason for deciding not to convert that was independent of the terms of the contract or any other aspect of its relationship with Empire Gas, such as a drop in the demand for its bakery products that led it to reduce or abandon its fleet of delivery trucks." (p. 1339) If American simply changed its mind without a reason, this presented a more difficult case. The requirements contract could plausibly be characterized as giving American an option, but that, Posner concluded, was not the law.

Good faith, according to Judge Posner, puts a burden on the buyer to give a valid business reason (other than "I changed my mind") for the failure to take any goods. American did not give any reason and, apparently, could not. Ergo, its action must have been in bad faith.

The essential ingredient of good faith in the case of the buyer's reducing his estimated requirements is that he not merely have had second thoughts about the terms of the contract and want to get out of it. Whether the buyer has any greater obligation is unclear, but need not be decided here. Once it is decided (as we have) that a buyer cannot arbitrarily declare his requirements to be zero, this becomes an easy case, because American Bakeries has never given any reason for its change of heart. (pp. 1340–1341)

The dissent disagreed: "The majority thus transforms the seller's theoretical burden of proof on bad faith (unarticulated to the jury) into an actual presumption of the buyer's bad faith (articulated post-trial)." (*Empire III*, p. 1343, Kanne, Circuit J. dissenting). Judge Kanne would have reversed and remanded because Empire had not met the burden of proving bad faith, or, alternatively, because, if an unreasonably disproportionate reduction in requirements creates a presumption of bad faith to be rebutted by buyer's proof of good faith, this was not the rule under which the trial was conducted.

The contract differs from others discussed in this chapter in that it was a two-stage requirements contract. American agreed to buy all its propane requirements from Empire; it would only have propane requirements if it had conversion units, and these too it promised to buy only from Empire. It is useful to analyze the contract in two stages, beginning with the propane stage. Had American installed the conversion units, its requirements would have depended on overall fuel needs (the demand for its products) and on the relative cost of fuels. If gasoline prices had fallen relative to propane, American could have reduced its requirements to zero. That was precisely the flexibility it had bargained for. It was crystal clear to both parties that the only reason to go through with this contract was to have vehicles that could use either fuel and to allow Empire to choose the most efficient. If the two fuels were very close substitutes, we should anticipate that fairly minor fluctuations in relative prices would have resulted in dramatic shifts in American's requirements. That is how Judge Posner interpreted the agreement, citing the position taken by Empire's expert witness:

> American Bakeries objects violently to the assumption made by Empire Gas's expert witness that the vehicles converted by American Bakeries, had it honored what Empire Gas contends were its obligations under the contract, would have run 100% on propane. The conversion units would have been dual units, which permit the driver by a flick of a switch in the engine to run his vehicle on either gasoline or propane. But since the parties agree that the price of propane was lower than that of gasoline throughout the entire contract period, a driver would have switched his conversion unit to gasoline only when he was low on propane and too far away from a propane station to reach it before he ran out. This factor was not big

enough to upset the expert witness's calculations significantly. (*Empire III*, pp. 1341–1342)

Empire could have demanded some limits on American's discretion to protect its reliance. It is hard to imagine that much protection would have been necessary, given the meeting competition clause and the fact that Empire had a large number of propane customers at most locations. Not surprisingly, the contract provided no explicit protection (e.g., minimum purchases of propane); Empire bore the risk that the relative price of propane would rise and that American would purchase gasoline instead.

The requirements for conversion units would also be sensitive to the relative prices of propane and gasoline—not the day-to-day fluctuations that would have determined propane requirements, but the long-term expected costs of the alternative fuels. If, in time, American learned that the future price of propane was expected to be relatively high, then the requirements contract would give it the flexibility to adapt to the new information by discontinuing installation of the conversion units. The seller could have constrained the buyer's discretion by, in effect, imposing a cost if the buyer were to reduce its purchases. It could have done so by providing for a specific minimum, or an installation schedule, or a flat payment to be offset against future purchases. American had, recall, rejected Empire's initial proposal, which would have required installation of a minimum number of units. The parties' failure to include protection of Empire's reliance in their agreement was no accident; it reflected the low value of that protection.

If, because of a shift in relative prices, American concluded that it would no longer be profitable to purchase additional conversion units, then it could cut back or eliminate its requirements. That is the efficient response and, unless an aggressive definition of good faith were interposed, that would be the outcome. The point is twofold. The parties could have explicitly limited the buyer's discretion to adapt to changed circumstances, but chose not to. Further, it is doubtful that the courts, using an open-ended standard like good faith, could provide a default rule better than the zero-protection rule—if the contract is silent, the seller imposes no fee to protect its reliance and the buyer has absolute discretion to cut back or eliminate requirements.

There was no evidence that relative prices had changed. Indeed, Judge Posner noted that propane prices stayed below those of gasoline for the entire period. The facts are unclear, but the only changed circumstances appear to be either that American's financial condition deteriorated or that it simply got cold feet. Posner's opinion holds that cold feet are not enough, although the relative price change most likely would have been. In that sense, his interpretation is far more respective of the contract language than the *Feld* or *Wigand* courts. But that does present a puzzle. Why would the seller be willing to bear the risk of relative price changes, but not the lesser risk of the buyer changing his mind?

Unlike most of the other contracts discussed in this chapter, the underlying business sense of the contract is not clear. American did not enter into this agreement to assure a supply of conversion units. The units were produced by a number of suppliers, with Empire acting only as an intermediary. It could easily have found such units on the open market. That part of the agreement was most likely ancillary to the fuel requirements contract. It is not obvious why American would want to take all its fuel requirements from Empire. Perhaps Empire used the tied sale to circumvent price controls, charging an above market price on the conversion units, although there is no evidence of this in the opinion. Perhaps American was desperate to line up any fuel sources in that era of shortages and rationing. Perhaps it would have been vulnerable to short-term inventory fluctuations and it was buying assurance of a continuous supply of propane. On this Judge Posner is silent. Indeed, his only invocation of reliance is with regard to the *seller's reliance* on the estimated requirements. (*Empire III*, p. 1340) Given that Empire sold propane to a large number of accounts, its reliance on any particular one was likely trivial; its failure to protect its reliance in the contract is consistent with this.

The lost profits remedy provided a ludicrously high level of protection for Empire's reliance. The high measure of damages could conceivably arise from the tie-in alluded to above; however, once again there is no evidence that this was the case. Leaving that possibility aside, the damages are the markups on commodities that Empire bought and sold in competitive markets. Empire stocked and resold conversion units made by others. The contract was for sale of a commodity, propane, at roughly the market price (given the meeting competition clause). The jury found, in effect, that American agreed to pay for 30% of the estimated 3,000 conversion units whether it took them or not. That outcome, as Judge Posner observed, was due at least in part to American's litigation strategy. American attacked Empire's damage estimates but did not present its own. "American Bakeries gambled . . . [;] we will not relieve it of the consequences of its risky strategy." (*Empire III*, p. 1342) The court was unwilling to use the damage assessment to make any inferences about the plausible contract structure. The seller could not have wanted nearly so much protection of its reliance.

Ironically, in an earlier decision, *Lake River Corp. v. Carborundum Co.*, Judge Posner held a minimum guarantee clause to be an unenforceable penalty, although the penalty was no worse than the one imposed by the *Empire Gas* jury. Lake River had installed a bagging system for $89,000, in reliance on its contract with Carborundum. Had the buyer breached immediately, it would have owed $533,000, which Posner found an unreasonably high penalty. In *Empire Gas*, Empire's reliance expenditures were $0 and the damages in the millions thanks to the "lost profits" formulation. Illinois law might well require both outcomes. I think one could come to the opposite (and preferable) result under existing law,[2] but it would certainly require fewer contortions if the Code were revised to deal with the problems cleanly.

4. Large Quantity Increases in Long-Term Contracts

The notion that one party might take undue advantage of a favorable market-contract price differential in a requirements or output contract is at the core of the Code's concern about unreasonably disproportionate demands. In long-term contracts, the parties generally include boundaries on the quantity-determining party's discretion. Courts invoking good faith sometimes disregard these boundaries. In this section, I discuss three cases in which the courts did just that, paring back the buyer's requirements. I conclude with an analysis of a case in which the court found for a seller in an output contract, despite a huge increase in output.

In both *City of Lakeland, Florida v. Union Oil Co. of California* and *Orange and Rockland Utilities, Inc. v. Amerada Hess Corp.*, the purchaser of fuel oil substantially increased its requirements following an increase in the market price. The increased requirements were due both to substitution of oil for gas and increased wholesale sales. In both instances the courts disallowed the full increase, although the courts differed in their treatment of the two. In each case the buyer's requirements were limited by the capacity of its plant, and the court held, implicitly, that good faith required that the buyer run its plant at below full capacity.

The City of Lakeland, Florida, owned power plants that could be fired by burning natural gas, Bunker "C" oil, or a mixture of the two. It entered into a ten-year contract for the primary fuel, natural gas, in 1960. That contract, not at issue here, specified a minimum amount of gas the City must take. However, it also gave the City a right to terminate if Bunker "C" oil became available at a more favorable price that the gas company refused to match. The fuels were interchangeable, but they differed in their method of delivery. Oil is transported by carrier and stored in on-site tanks; gas is received from transmission lines with no on-site storage. Difficulties in transmission or increased consumption might result in interruption of gas supply, particularly in cold weather.

In 1968 the City entered into a contract with Union Oil for provision of Bunker "C" as a standby or alternate fuel. The contract price was $2.28 or the going market price plus specified transportation costs (which at the time of first delivery was $2.16), whichever was lower. It was a five-year contract with Lakeland having the option to terminate every year. If the supply of natural gas was interrupted, the City could take all its fuel requirements from Union Oil. Moreover, if the contract price of oil fell below that of natural gas, the buyer could take 100% of its fuel requirements from Union Oil.

In the first three years, the share of oil increased from 20% to 40% to 56%. In the third year, in May 1970, the City entered into a new gas contract, which set a fixed price for gas of 3.3 cents per therm (equivalent to about $2.08 per barrel of oil) plus an escalation factor based on the market price of oil. So long as the market price of oil was less than $2.47, gas remained the cheaper fuel. Rising oil prices in late 1970 brought the adjusted gas price above that, and the City shifted a substantial amount of its purchases to oil. When the City notified Union in June 1971 that it had elected to continue the agreement for the fourth year, Union responded that it would no longer be willing to sell at the contract price. The City sued for injunctive relief and damages. Union Oil argued that the agreement was not valid because the City's promise was illusory. Natural gas and oil are, Union argued, the same commodity, so the City was at liberty to buy the same commodity from others (the gas company) if it so desired.

There can be no doubt, under the literal terms of the contract . . . that the City is free to purchase as much or as little Bunker "C" oil as it may want from Union, i.e., "capriciously desire." Hence, the prime question is whether the City is also at liberty to purchase the same article or commodity from other suppliers as well. Union insists that it is, arguing that gas and oil are "apples and apples," that both are fuels subject to interchangeable or even simultaneous use. As a result, because the agreement also permits the City to purchase natural gas in any amount it desires, Union would conclude that the contract contains no promise at all sufficient to supply a valid consideration. (p. 764)

The court dismissed this argument, noting that the agreement "expressly contemplated the possibility of a conversion from gas to oil as the primary fuel," and denying that interchangeability rendered gas and oil the same commodity. Because oil was a different commodity, if the City elected to take any oil at all, it was bound to take it from Union. That was sufficient to dispel the illusory nature of the promise and permit the court to find consideration.

Union Oil also argued that if this were a valid contract, then the City had abused its discretion by increasing its purchases in a matter not contemplated by the parties. It had converted fuel oil from a standby fuel to the primary fuel and had increased its overall demand for fuel oil by increasing its wholesale sales to Tampa Electric, a public utility. The court dismissed the former argument, noting that the contract was quite specific in allowing the buyer to do so. It accepted the latter, however, pointing out that initial sales to Tampa had been less than 1% of electricity production, but that they had grown to over 13% by 1971.

> The simple fact is that Union entered into an agreement which later proved to be improvident, from its point of view, when the market price of oil advanced to unforeseen heights. The City, on the other hand, realized a concomitant advantage; and that is precisely what the business and the law of contracts is all about. This is not to say, however, that the City may add insult to injury by taking undue advantage of its favorable contract and increase its wholesale exchange of energy with a neighboring system. Such increases must be regarded as beyond the contemplation of the parties and the scope of the contract, and must be taken into account as a limiting factor in determining the damages to be awarded to the City. (p. 768)

The only contractual limit on Lakeland's requirements was its generating capacity, known to both parties at the time of contracting. If Lakeland had shifted to using fuel oil for 100% of its internal needs, that would have been acceptable, according to the court. However, that would not have fully utilized Lakeland's capacity. The court appears to conclude that the existing level of underutilization was an implied term in the contract; increased utilization in response to the favorable price somehow "added insult to injury." The court provides no hint as to why, in the absence of any explicit language, the requirements should be bounded by the existing level of capacity utilization rather than the more natural actual generating capacity.

Orange and Rockland is oft-cited as an example of a buyer unreasonably expanding its requirements in response to an increase in the market price. Properly framed, this is an easy case. The parties entered into a ten-year contract in December 1969 in which Amerada Hess agreed to supply O&R's requirements for fuel oil No. 6 for its Lovett generating plant in Tompkin's Cove, New York. (The facts are taken from this decision and a prior dispute between the parties in which Hess was enjoined from terminating the contract, *O&R I.*) The contract required Hess to lease a parcel of land from O&R and erect storage facilities to which it would deliver the fuel oil. The price for the first five years was $2.14 per barrel, subject to escalation for cost-related factors. The price for the second term would be renegotiated. If the parties failed to reach agreement, the contract would terminate. The quantity clause specified estimated annual sales for the five years. It was expected that the primary fuel at the plant would be gas; projections were for gas to account for about 60% of the Btu's generated by the plant. However, the contract stated: "[nothing] herein shall preclude the use by Buyer of . . . natural gas in such quantities as may be or become available." (*O&R II*, p. 816)

Five months after the contract was signed, the price of fuel oil began to rise. By March 1971 it had more than doubled. O&R increased its fuel oil requirements by over 60% in 1970 and continued to order quantities that were more than double the contractual estimates. In April 1971, Hess unilaterally attempted to raise the price by 97.7 cents per barrel and threatened to terminate deliveries if O&R declined. O&R obtained a preliminary injunction enjoining Hess from ceasing delivery of the fuel oil. Apparently, this did not prevent Hess from limiting its sales to the contract estimates. O&R purchased additional fuel oil at the market price and sued Hess for the difference for fuel oil purchased through September 1973. (Hess's obligation terminated prematurely because of an environmental regulation that went into effect in October 1973. Ironically, the huge run up in oil prices began almost exactly when the contract terminated.) The trial judge, sitting without a jury, held for Hess, and the Appellate Division affirmed. O&R's requirements, said both courts, were not incurred in good faith. They were, as a matter of law, unreasonably disproportionate.

O&R could not (and did not) take oil under the contract and resell it at the higher market price. It could only demand fuel oil to supply the needs of the Lovett plant. Its requirements increased over the estimated needs for two reasons. First, it increased its sales to the New York Power Pool, in effect sharing with other utilities the benefits of its below-market price. Second, it substituted oil for gas at the Lovett plant. The court was not impressed:

> The former factor is tantamount to making the other utilities in the state silent partners to the contract . . . while the latter factor amounts to a unilateral and arbitrary change in the conditions prevailing at the time of the contract so as to take advantage of market conditions at the seller's expense. . . . Hess was therefore justified in 1970 in refusing to meet plaintiff's demands, by reason of the fact that plaintiff's "requirements" were not incurred in good faith. (*O&R II*, p. 820)

Again, the court uses "good faith" to impose a quantity ceiling short of the plant's capacity. The contract placed a clear limit on O&R's maximum demand—the capacity of the Lovett generating plant. It should surprise no one in the industry that if the relative prices of oil and gas change, the buyer would react in the appropriate manner. Nor was the existence of the New York Power Pool a deep secret. O&R's requirements depended only in part on the electricity demand of their direct customers. The contract gave O&R flexibility both in its choice of fuel and in its dealings with the power pool.

If Hess wanted to place tighter limits on O&R's discretion, it would have been easy to do so. It could have included a quantity maximum short of the plant's capacity, tied its supply obligation to the market price, or constrained O&R's ability to take advantage of the relative price of fuels. Recall that interfuel substitutability was specifically bargained over in the NIPSCO-CWI dispute. To be sure, Hess did not anticipate the price increase in 1970 (let alone the much larger increase after October 1973), but that risk was allocated to Hess in the contract. By interposing the "unreasonably disproportionate" standard, the courts deprived O&R of the flexibility it had bargained for, converting the contract into a (nearly) fixed-quantity contract.

As in *Lakeland*, the court implicitly ruled that the seller had promised to run its plant at less than full capacity for the life of the agreement, never asking why on earth a party would make such an odd promise.

In neither *Lakeland* nor *Orange & Rockland* did the seller increase its requirements by expanding its plant. Nor, under the contracts, could they, a point missed by Judge Easterbrook in his implicit approval of the two decisions in his *NIPSCO* opinion. The physical limits of the plant were the only constraints on their discretion. The contracts could have imposed further limits on interfuel substitution, sales to non–end-users (Tampa Electric and the New York Power Pool), or total sales. Or they could have set price as a function of annual power sales (perhaps allowing for renegotiation of the price for all sales above a certain level). Apparently, they felt these additional constraints unnecessary. In fact, the *Lakeland* contract explicitly rejected limits on interfuel substitution. In both instances the court rewrote the contract, placing additional constraints on the seller's discretion.

A much earlier case, *Loudenback Fertilizer Co. v. Tennessee Phosphate Co.*, posed a slight variation on these cases. Loudenback entered into a five-year requirements contract to purchase rocks in order to make fertilizer, with a 3,000 ton annual maximum. In the first two years it ordered none. After a doubling of the market price of rocks in the third year, it ordered 3,000 tons, which the seller refused to deliver. The court sustained the seller's demurrer, saying that the buyer's failure to take any rocks in the first two years was a breach of the agreement. Burton and Andersen (1995, pp. 47–49) approve that result, arguing that it was based on the buyer's opportunistic demand for the maximum, not its failure to take in the first two years.

Why did the buyer take no rocks in the first two years? The rocks were an input into an intermediate product, namely, acidulated rocks. In the first two years it was cheaper to buy acidulated rocks directly rather than to make them by combining seller's rocks with sulfuric acid, because, the buyer claimed, there had been a large increase in the price of sulfuric acid. In the third year, however, with acidulated rock prices up and sulfuric acid prices down, it was cheaper to make them. In both *Lakeland* and *O&R*, the increased quantity demand came in response to a fall in the relative price vis-à-vis a substitute. In *Loudenback*, it came in response to a fall in the relative cost of a product produced internally versus that same product already "assembled." Perhaps the parties did not mean to give the buyer the discretion to respond to such price changes. Or perhaps one could argue that the requirements contract covered both the raw material and the assembled product (although the court does not come close to saying that). The minimal statement of the facts gives no indication of why either party would want a multiyear contract, or why the quantity discretion was given to the buyer. Absent any facts, the most natural interpretation would seem to be that the buyer agreed to buy between zero and 3,000 tons per year, with the actual quantity depending on the overall demand for its fertilizer and the relative costs of make versus buy. Rather than sustaining the seller's demurrer, the court should have granted summary judgment to the buyer (perhaps leaving the window open for some narrow defenses).

In *Lenape Resources Corp. v. Tennessee Gas Pipeline Co.*, a closely divided court upheld a buyer's claim despite a huge increase in the quantity it demanded. The dispute involved a long-term take-or-pay contract—the Gas Purchase Agreement (GPA)—entered into in 1979. It was typical of gas contracts entered into at that time, by pipelines in general and Tennessee in particular, in both the length and the commitment to a high take-or-pay option. The contract did have one unusual feature, as we shall soon see. Market conditions changed dramatically shortly afterward, leading to industrywide renegotiation and litigation. One court noted:

> In the 1980s . . . conflicting forces increased the gas supply, yet decreased demand, thereby leading to a sharp decline in sales and market price. Thus, pursuant to their long term take-or-pay contracts, pipelines were required to buy gas at a cost significantly above the market price at which they could later sell it. Confronted with the prospect of bankruptcy, many pipelines refused to either take or pay for gas, despite their contractual commitments. Producers recognized that instability among the pipelines would ultimately be detrimental to their own interests by causing massive dislocation within the industry. Resultingly, most pipelines and producers agreed to reform their contracts and settle their disputes. (*Williamson v. Elf Aquitaine, Inc.*, pp. 549–552)

In 1983 and again in 1985–1986, Tennessee informed its producers that it would refuse to honor its take-or-pay obligations. Not all the producers caved in graciously. Settlements of some of Tennessee's litigation are described in *Mandell v. Hamman Oil & Refining Co.* and *Williamson v. Elf Aquitaine, Inc.*[3] Lenape did acquiesce initially because, as the Court of Appeals noted, although "Lenape recognized as early as 1983 that it could file suit against Tennessee for breach of the GPA . . . it made a business decision 'to let the big boys fight that battle' rather than to file suit." (*Tenn. Gas Pipeline*

Co. v. Lenape Resources Corp., p. 304) However, in response to a 1989 suit against it by its lessors for breach of the implied covenant to develop its leases, Lenape developed new wells, dramatically increasing its production and thereby precipitating this litigation.

The GPA reflected Tennessee's weak bargaining position in 1979. The trial court found, and both the majority and dissent agreed, that "[w]hen the parties negotiated the GPA in 1978 and 1979, and executed it on January 16, 1979, Buyer needed and wanted to obtain under long term commitment or dedication as much gas as possible, and the parties intended that the GPA not limit, for any reason, the volume of the committed reserves or amount of gas to be delivered therefrom to Buyer by Seller(s) over the 20-year term of the GPA." (*Lenape*, p. 580) Tennessee agreed to take, on a take-or-pay basis, 85% of Lenape's delivery capacity (defined as the amount of gas that could efficiently be withdrawn from the wells) of the defined gas reserves in a particular field. The decision as to the development of the fields was left exclusively in Lenape's hands. The contract specifically reserved the seller's right "[t]o operate its property free from any control by Buyer in such a manner as Seller, in its sole discretion, may deem advisable, including without limitation, the right, but never the obligation, to drill new wells, to repair and rework old wells, and to plug any well or surrender any lease or portion thereof." (*Tenn. Gas Pipeline*, p. 293 n.4)

Production in the first twelve years was modest, with annual payments never exceeding $300,000. Following the development of the new wells, there was a huge increase in production. In 1993 Tennessee paid, under protest, $89 million. It sought a declaratory judgment that the increased production was in bad faith and unreasonably disproportionate to prior production. Alternatively, it argued that if the contract were not governed by UCC §2–306, then the agreement was void and unenforceable for lack of mutuality.

The trial court's decision for Lenape was reversed by the Court of Appeals; the Texas Supreme Court in a 5–4 vote reversed that decision. There was considerable disagreement as to whether the GPA was an output contract subject to §2–306. The majority's ostensible ground for concluding that it was outside §2–306 was that the section applies "only when a contract does not unambiguously specify the quantity of the output of the seller or the requirements of the buyer." (*Lenape*, p. 570) This, however, fails to distinguish the GPA from other carefully crafted agreements delineating the limits of the quantity-determining party's discretion. More to the point, the majority noted that §2–306 is a gap filler and the contract language clearly filled the gap. (*Lenape*, p. 570) The real question should have been whether the clear language of the GPA could be trumped by the imposition of a fact finder's notion of good faith.

It is illuminating to compare the differing views of what a good faith test would entail. The majority catalogued the difficulties:

> Instead of defining Tennessee's take-or-pay obligations in terms of a fixed percentage of Sellers' delivery capacity, Tennessee would have us read the GPA as requiring Tennessee to purchase only a portion of gas that may be tendered as reasonably proportionate to any normal or otherwise compa-rable prior output. The quantity of gas which Tennessee must either take or pay for would depend on a number of indeterminate variables: prior output; *normal* prior output; *comparable* prior output; proportionality to ei-ther normal or comparable prior output; and *reasonableness* of the propor-tionality. Reading these factors into Tennessee's take-or-pay obligations, any increase in production and delivery capacity would be measured after the fact by these variables, thus injecting uncertainty into the parties' ob-ligations under the GPA. (*Lenape*, p. 571)

According to the dissent, "The basic test for good faith here is whether and to what extent the Sellers would have increased the quantity of gas proffered had the contract price equaled the market price, *i.e.*, was there a valid business reason for the increased quantity independent of price?" (*Lenape*, p. 582) That is, the seller enters into a long-term agreement giving it complete flexibility to develop its business in response to all new circum-stances save the inability of the contract price to track market conditions. It is hard to understand why that should be a mandatory rule, especially because there are so many devices available for linking the contract and market price. The dissent goes on to link the "unreasonable disproportion" standard to the parties' expectations at the time of contracting:

> But whether the magnitude of the disproportion here is unreasonable under section 2.306 depends on the expectations of the parties when the contract was executed and whether such an increase in output could have been reasonably forecast or anticipated. *Orange and Rockland.* Objective in-dicia of the parties' reasonable expectations at that time may also be con-

sidered, including the size and capabilities of the pipe lines and other facilities, the history of the area, the nature of the formation, local industry
practices, reserve and deliverability estimates and so forth. (*Lenape*, p. 583)

The evidence on expectations and trade practice would be confined to
conditions in 1979 at the time of contract execution. There is no question
that when the contract was executed, Tennessee was not concerned about
the possibility that Lenape would have too much delivery capacity. Tennessee might not have anticipated an expansion of this magnitude, but it
surely hoped for one. It was scrambling for gas sources, and the more the
merrier. Granting Lenape complete discretion in this dimension seemed
costless at the time. That turned out to be a big mistake. But that mutual
misjudgment should not empower the court to rewrite the contract.

Tennessee compounded its mistake by failing to renegotiate limits on
Lenape's discretion in the six-year window before the suit by Lenape's lessors forced it to expand its capacity. Lenape did not take full advantage of
its windfall for years, and it would not have been very expensive for Tennessee to buy its way out. It chose not to do so, and as a result the price
of a buyout rose dramatically. It is conceivable that had the parties engi-
neered a buyout, Lenape could still have been sued successfully by its lessors for its failure to develop the leases. If so, it, not Tennessee, would have
been the big loser.

Lenape's relationship with its lessors was likely the proximate cause of
the huge expansion of delivery capacity. However, that should not matter.
Suppose that Lenape owned the properties outright. When the gas market
collapsed, the contract gave Lenape a valuable right. It could threaten to
develop a gas field for which it was assured above-market prices. If the
market conditions did not warrant the development, this was at least a
threat point in its dealings with Tennessee. Lenape's taking a hard line
might be less appealing than if it could say credibly, "The lessors made me
do it." Still, there is no reason for the courts to take sides in the renegotiation between two sophisticated hard-nosed bargainers. Invocation of good
faith would just tilt the subsequent bargaining in Tennessee's favor.

In *Lenape*, the seller of gas dramatically increased its output. *Northern
Natural Gas Co. v. Conoco, Inc.*, presented an interesting twist. Northern, a
pipeline, had contracts to purchase natural gas from a number of suppliers
and a contract to supply all of that gas to Conoco. Northern was to deliver
gas "in keeping with all the quantity and other provisions of the various

gas purchase contracts in effect from time to time." However, after the deregulation of the gas market, Northern managed to buy itself out of all its contracts to buy gas, so its gas purchases and sales dropped from 3 billion cubic feet per day in the mid-1980s to zero in 1994. Hence, it had no gas under contract and, therefore, had no obligation to deliver to Conoco. Conoco sued, arguing that Northern could not avoid its obligation by canceling contracts with its suppliers, and a jury awarded it $20 million for lost processing profits. That result was overturned, however, with the court finding that the contract did not require that Northern buy any gas and, therefore, that it had no obligation to deliver any gas to Conoco. Still, Conoco won half a loaf, with a unanimous Supreme Court remanding on the question of whether Northern's cancellation of its contracts was in good faith.

> Nothing requires the seller in an output contract to have any output, and nothing requires the buyer in a requirements contract to have requirements. On the other hand, parties to output/requirements contracts are required to exercise good faith in determining outputs or requirements, as well as accept the concomitant risk that their counterparts to the contract may make good faith variations, even to the extent of liquidating or discontinuing the business. . . . We agree with Conoco that a party who seeks to avoid performance of an output contract by having no output—or of a requirements contract by having no requirements—may not do so in bad faith. Accordingly, we affirm the court of appeals' judgment remanding this cause for a new trial for Conoco to attempt to prove that Northern canceled its gas purchase contracts without a valid business reason and in bad faith. (*Northern*, pp. 608–609)

The *Lenape* majority's skepticism about defining a good faith response to the dramatic changes in the natural gas market seems to have evaporated in the three years between the two decisions. If Northern's closing out its unprofitable contracts with suppliers was a valid business reason for having no gas to deliver to Conoco, as the court held, what could be bad faith? That, apparently, is a jury question, although there is no hint as to how a juror could possibly answer it.

5. Concluding Remarks

One might object to the preceding discussion by invoking the circularity problem. The backdrop against which these contracts were written, either the common law or the Code, included "good faith." If the parties drafted their agreements against that backdrop, then, it could be argued, they have incorporated the present understanding of the law into the contract. If the parties expected courts to apply the Code's good faith standard, then a failure to do so would amount to a rewriting of the agreement. Putting a "rational expectations" spin on things, when they entered into the agreement, the parties could have anticipated what the courts ultimately did. The implied limitation, the argument goes, was part of the deal. Without a theoretical framework there is no particular reason to prefer one interpretation to another. The theoretical framework proposed here allows us to break the circle and to reject the notion that the parties intended to incorporate the Code's good faith standard.

The relevant theory is hardly esoteric. The core notion is that in long-term agreements, adaptation to changed circumstances is often best achieved by granting one party considerable discretion in determining quantity. The discretion will not be unbounded; the contracts will typically relate the quantity to a physical constraint, such as the capacity of a particular plant of the buyer or seller. Moreover, the contracts will often go further than that. If the opposite party is vulnerable to quantity variation, it will want to convey the contours of its reliance by, in effect, confronting the decision maker with a price reflecting the extent of its reliance.

In some instances, such as the Great Lakes Carbon (GLC) petroleum coke contracts, the contract allows the seller to operate the plant at any level at all without taking into account any adverse effects on the counterparty. This is not an accident, because GLC's ability to hold a large inventory meant that its reliance costs would be very low. Likewise, Levy relied on Feld to remove the day-old bread, but Feld, who apparently was selling bread crumbs long before Levy bought his toaster oven, did not need a promise that Levy would continue to produce bread crumbs; Levy's self-interest (it had bought a toaster oven that appeared to have no other economic use) provided sufficient protection of Feld's reliance. The buyer's reliance in *Wigand* and *Diamond Alkali* was considerably greater than in *Levy*, because the buyer owned capital assets the value of which depended crucially on the continued operation of the plant. In both instances, the buyer's protection was the penalty (lost revenue) that the seller would incur from closing an otherwise viable facility—an entire factory, rather than a mere toaster oven.

The other party's self-interest is not always enough. The preceding discussion has provided numerous examples of devices that constrain the exercise of discretion. For one, by incorporating flexible pricing, the contracts could decrease the rewards to opportunistic behavior by the quantity-determining party. The meeting competition clause in the Empire Gas contract provides an example. Many of the petroleum coke contracts had indexed prices and maximum-minimum prices, so that if the contract price were too far out of line, it would have to be renegotiated. (Goldberg and Erickson 1987, pp. 389, 394)

Two-part pricing is another example. If the per unit price for small quantities is high, then so long as the buyer is likely to require an amount above that minimum, the seller will have some assurance that it will receive enough compensation to make its initial investment worth while. This device was common in the petroleum coke contracts of the aluminum companies. Alternatively, the buyer could be required to make a fixed payment. Two-part pricing would mean that if the buyer's demand fell off dramatically, the seller could end up bearing all the risk. The seller might insist upon more assurance so that even if the buyer took nothing, the seller would still receive some compensation. There are numerous devices for reaching this outcome: take-or-pay, minimum quantity, standby charges, or liquidated damages (and variations on these) all set the marginal price at zero for low quantities. The options considered in the NIPSCO-CWI negotiations, as described above, indicate the range of choices and the ability of serious commercial parties to tailor their contracts to their own needs. The contrast between NIPSCO's contract with CWI and Carbon County is another indication of the ability of parties to tailor the contracts.

The tailoring need not always be wise, either ex ante or ex post. But the important point is that the parties have an incentive to take their reliance interest into account, and, because protecting reliance can be costly, they have a further incentive to economize by not insisting upon too much protection. There is no reason to believe that a court, using a theoretically ungrounded good faith standard, could do better.

CHAPTER 6

In Search of Best Efforts:
Reinterpreting *Bloor v. Falstaff*

When contracting parties cannot quite define their obligations, they often resort to placeholder language, like "best efforts." They
(and their counsel) likely have little idea of what they might mean, but, so
long as they avoid litigation, it will not matter much. But "best efforts"
clauses are on occasion litigated, and courts must read content into them.
In *Bloor v. Falstaff,* a casebook favorite, the court held that Falstaff's lack-
luster promotional efforts for Ballantine beer violated its best efforts covenant. So far as I can tell, no commentators have questioned this outcome.
Indeed, some commentators have found Falstaff's behavior so egregious as
to provide not much of a test of the boundaries of "best efforts." Farnsworth
(1984, p. 11), for example, says, "Unfortunately, its decision did relatively
little to add precision to the meaning of 'best efforts,' since Kalmanovitz [of
Falstaff] fell so far short of the mark."

"Best efforts" can only be defined contextually. However, neither Judge
Brieant at trial nor Judge Friendly on appeal attempted to place the contract
in its business context. Had they framed the problem properly, the outcome
would have been different. Falstaff was not contracting to be a distributor
for another beer producer, the remarks of numerous commentators notwithstanding.[1] The fact that some of Ballantine's compensation was contingent upon Falstaff's selling effort makes it appear similar to a distribution
agreement, but the purpose of the contingent compensation was quite different, and that should have been taken into account when interpreting
the contract. Thus, while I am sympathetic to the Goetz-Scott (1981,
pp. 1120–1123) argument that the contract should be interpreted to max-
imize expected joint profits, I disagree with their application of it to this
case (which, in effect, treats the deal as if it were a distribution arrangement).

The essential feature of the contract is that Ballantine was exiting the beer business and was making a one-shot sale of some of its assets to Falstaff. That purpose is crucial for understanding the role of this "best efforts" clause. The buyer of an asset is naturally concerned about the asset's quality. There are numerous devices for assuring the buyer that it is not purchasing a "lemon." The satisfaction clauses in real estate transactions (Chapter 4) are one example. The seller could provide extensive representations and warranties, the buyer could incur significant due diligence expenses, or the seller could make a portion of its compensation contingent upon the quality of the asset. The royalty arrangement in this transaction, essentially an "earnout," served precisely this role. Profits or, in this case, gross sales serve as a "meter," an imperfect measure of the quality of the asset. Because an earnout alters the buyer's incentive structure, the seller must limit the buyer's ability to take advantage of the meter's imperfections. The best efforts clause can best be understood as an attempt to cope with that problem. The question the court should have asked was: Did Falstaff opportunistically redirect revenues away from the meter (Ballantine's sales)? And the facts make clear that Falstaff did not.

In Section 1, I summarize the facts and the two opinions. In Section 2, I explore the role of the contingent compensation in the sale of an asset and apply that analysis to the facts of *Bloor*. In Section 3, I speculate on how a court might properly frame the question absent help from counsel. Even if courts choose not to be so proactive, the implicit argument is that litigators can (and should) frame their arguments in a more transactionally sensitive way.

1. The Background

The Facts

Ballantine, a regional brewery selling low-priced beer primarily in the New York area, was sold to Investors Funding Corporation (IFC), a real estate firm, in 1969. IFC lost a considerable amount of money with Ballantine, and left the beer business in 1972. It kept the brewery (eventually selling it for non–beer making purposes),[2] selling off the remainder of the business to Falstaff, a larger regional brewery that had no presence in the New York market. The parties had explored the deal for a few months, but the final negotiations involved a marathon session of three days with no breaks for meals, characterized by one of the participants as "negotiation-by-endurance." Judge Brieant scolded the parties for their method, but acknowledged that "it was the manner chosen by the parties for their own purposes, and they must each accept the consequences. . . . They should have conducted themselves in a more mature fashion. Had they done so, at least some of the later disputes and difficulties could have been anticipated and avoided." (*Bloor* I, p. 276, n.11)

Falstaff paid $4 million plus a royalty of 50 cents per barrel for six years. Ballantine's sales in the IFC years were about 2.2 million barrels per year, well below the 1964 peak of 4.4 million barrels. (Plaintiff Exhibit [PX] 9 at A1618) Had Falstaff maintained Ballantine's sales volume, the royalty payment would have been over $1 million per year. For acquisition purposes, the rule of thumb in the beer business at that time was to value the target at about $4 per barrel, which would have put a value on Ballantine of about $8.5–$9 million. (Falstaff's Ralph Weir's Dep. at A1576) Falstaff agreed to use "best efforts" to promote and maintain a high volume of sales and further agreed to pay a cash sum in the event of a substantial discontinuance of distribution under the Ballantine brand name. The terms will be discussed in more detail below.

Falstaff's strategy was to enter the New York market, selling beer from its Cranston, Rhode Island, brewery, under both the Ballantine and Falstaff labels. Falstaff was a premium beer, Ballantine a low-priced beer, although, in fact, the beer in the two containers was identical. Falstaff expected that buying the Ballantine assets would help it in three ways. First, Ballantine had a trademark that was potentially valuable, especially in the New York area. Second, it had an existing distribution network in the New York area (it was servicing some 25,000 accounts); Falstaff would not have to assemble one to sell Ballantine and could use that network to develop the market for Falstaff. Third, consolidating production in the Cranston facility and closing Ballantine's Newark brewery, which had been operating at less than 50% capacity, would increase the capacity utilization rate, thereby decreasing average production costs.

The record is mixed as to the appropriate weighting of these components. In his letter to the Justice Department immediately following the acquisition, Falstaff's outside counsel described the purpose:

You requested that I confirm Falstaff's purpose in acquiring the Ballantine brands and the steps which will be taken to produce and market Ballantine beer and ale. The primary purpose of the acquisition is to utilize the excess productive capacity of Falstaff's seven plants.

A further purpose of the acquisition (though not a major one) is that opportunity is afforded to introduce Falstaff beer on a premium price level in the New York metropolitan market. Any such introduction would necessarily be low-keyed, since Falstaff does not have the resources to support any other kind of entry into this market. (PX 23 at A1677–1679.)

A Falstaff internal document written at the very beginning of the process put much more weight on using the acquisition to facilitate Falstaff's entrance into the New York market:

> Let us further assume that, since Ballantine is a declining brand, that Falstaff will not support and promote the brand, but, rather, cut advertising and promotion expenses to the bone and expect a rapid decline in sales of approximately 20% per year. Let us assume further that Falstaff uses the direct distribution system set up by Ballantine in the 5 boroughs and Northern New Jersey to promote Falstaff at a premium price. Since this is a large market, the market entry costs will be high. . . . In other words, the Ballantine distribution system will increase its distribution of Falstaff to offset the loss of volume for Ballantine such that the plants continue to produce at the capacity level the same as when Ballantine production was initiated.

> Thus, under these assumptions, it does not seem worthwhile to purchase Ballantine except for the entry to the N.Y. markets. (Falstaff internal document entitled "Opportunistic Approach to Ballantine," PX 9 at A1616, A1618–1619, dated September 1, 1971)

In any event, it did not work out. Falstaff continued to promote Ballantine at about the same level as IFC had, but sales kept falling and red ink spilling. Falstaff claimed losses in 1972 through 1975 of $22 million on its Ballantine operations. In 1975 Paul Kalmanovitz acquired effective control of Falstaff and dramatically changed its operations. Kalmanovitz arrived in America penniless in his mid-twenties and built a fortune in beer and real estate estimated at $250 million (enough to earn him a spot on the *Forbes* 400 list) at the time of his death in 1987. (See Folkart 1987, p. 28.) His treatment of Ballantine was consistent with his treatment of the other beer labels he acquired. "Kalmanovitz's reputation as a cost-cutter was so dreaded that employees at Falstaff Brewing's St. Louis headquarters flew the flag upside down and at half-mast when they learned that [he] had taken it over in 1975. 'He went through Falstaff like Grant went through Richmond—he took no hostages,' recalls [his successor]." (Lubove 1995, p. 46) In particular, Kalmanovitz cut the Ballantine advertising budget nearly 90%, cut sales personnel, and closed or phased out four of the six distribution centers. Ballantine's sales plummeted. Some of the decline was attributable to the general sales decrease of regional beers, but Ballantine's sales fell faster than the sales of similarly situated beers.

In the meantime, IFC went into bankruptcy. Bloor, the trustee in bankruptcy for IFC, filed suit against Falstaff, claiming, among other things, that Kalmanovitz's change of direction in 1975 violated Falstaff's best efforts obligation or, alternatively, amounted to a substantial discontinuance. There were some side issues related to the fact that some of Ballantine's pre-transaction sales volume was generated by illegal marketing practices, most of which were widespread in the industry, but the core of the dispute remained the best efforts and substantial discontinuance questions.

The Contract

Falstaff purchased the "Ballantine Assets" which were defined in Clause 1 of the contract. (The complete contract is available as PX 1 at A1584–A1616. In each instance Falstaff would acquire Ballantine's "right, title, and interest," with the specific items defined in separate exhibits.) These included (a) the "Proprietary Rights," Ballantine's brand names, trademarks, trade names, and copyrights; (b) Ballantine's distribution network, including contracts, orders agreements, commitments, supply and requirements contracts, and collective bargaining agreements relating to the sale and delivery of its malt alcoholic beverage directly to retail sellers; (c) most of Ballantine's accounts receivable; and (d) miscellaneous items including the existing inventory and supplies, vehicles, cooperage, returnable cases and bottles, and similar items. Falstaff paid $4 million in cash in three installments, the last payment on the date of closing. In addition, Falstaff would pay a royalty of 50 cents per barrel:

> on the 7th day of each month, commencing May 7, 1972, and terminating April 7, 1978 (the "Royalty Period"), a sum in cash computed at the rate

of $.50 per barrel for each barrel of 31 U.S. gallons sold by the Buyer during the preceding calendar month under any of the Proprietary Rights, as royalties in respect of the use of such Proprietary Rights. (Clause 2(a)(v))

In addition, the clause included a liquidated damages clause that would have come into effect if Falstaff substantially discontinued distribution of Ballantine.

[I]f during the Royalty Period the Buyer substantially discontinues the distribution of beer under the brand name "Ballantine" . . . it will pay to the Seller a cash sum equal to the years and fraction thereof remaining in the Royalty Period times $1,100,000, payable in equal monthly installments on the first day of each month commencing with the first month following the month in which such discontinuation occurs. (Clause 2(a)(v))

The clause at the center of the litigation, which included a rather embarrassing typographical error, read as follows: "Certain Other Covenants of Buyer. (a) After the Closing Date the Seller [sic!] will use its best efforts to promote and maintain a high volume of sales under the Proprietary Rights." (Clause 8(a))

This was not the only appearance of "best efforts" in the agreement. It appeared six other times. Falstaff agreed to use its best efforts to keep confidential nonpublic information about the seller. The seller agreed that if any of its contracts were not assignable, it would use its best efforts to obtain consent of third parties. Falstaff agreed to use its best efforts to collect the seller's receivables (a contractually defined subset of the receivables). The buyer also promised to use best efforts to collect the *buyer's* receivables. This is not as odd as it first appears, since the seller had some financial stake in the buyer's receivables. Falstaff also agreed to use best efforts to retain as its own employees Ballantine's sales, marketing, clerical, and administrative personnel. The casual usage of the phrase in these varied contexts does suggest a certain lack of care about its content.

The contract provided virtually no assurance as to the quality of the assets. "Ballantine Assets will be sold by the seller hereunder 'as is' and . . . the Seller makes no representations or warranties of any kind with respect to the description, condition, merchantability or fitness for any particular purpose of any of the Ballantine Assets." (Clause 16)

At the closing Falstaff was to pay cash for 75% of Ballantine's receivables. In addition, it would pay to IFC 75% of all receivables collected beyond that, subject to a ceiling of $7,125,000. There was some concern over the receivables since in Pennsylvania it was unlawful for beer to be sold on credit, and at least one large receivable (Pflaumer) was from Pennsylvania. (*Bloor I*, pp. 274–275) The treatment of receivables, as we shall see, turned out to have some significance, since IFC claimed (and Judge Brieant agreed) that Falstaff's payment for the receivables was part of the horse-trading involving the critical terms in the contract.

The contract included what amounts to an acceleration clause, requiring Falstaff to pay immediately all money due under the royalty clause in the event of its bankruptcy. The language is unclear, but I believe the clause means that the $1.1 million per year liquidated damages would be due, not the uncertain expected value of the sum of future royalty payments. Falstaff also agreed to pledge to IFC the proprietary rights (the trademarks) as security for the royalty payments. If, however, such a pledge would be in violation of any of Falstaff's preexisting agreements, Falstaff would "in good faith attempt to obtain . . . any consents to such pledge which may be required; and if any required consent is unobtainable or obtainable only upon conditions detrimental to [Falstaff], such pledge will not be deliverable as aforesaid. In such event, [Falstaff] will furnish [IFC] with such evidence as it may reasonably request to ascertain the reasons therefor." Falstaff agreed not to transfer the proprietary rights during the royalty period without IFC's written consent.

The Decisions

Trial was held without a jury. Falstaff argued that best efforts "must include consideration of Falstaff's own allegedly precarious financial position. Plaintiff, on the contrary, cited substantial precedent holding that financial difficulty and economic hardship do not excuse performance of a contract, and argued for the application of an objective standard, that of the 'average, prudent comparable' brewer." (*Bloor I*, p. 266) Judge Brieant cited, with approval, precedent which would not excuse performance even in the face of financial difficulty or economic hardship. But he did not go this far. Falstaff did not have to spend itself into bankruptcy to meet its contractual obligation, but it did have to meet the prudent comparable brewer standard, "and this it failed to do." (*Bloor I*, p. 267)

Judge Brieant presented a litany of things Falstaff did (or did not do) in failing to meet its best efforts obligation. He cited Falstaff's closing of four of its retail distribution centers, including the North Bergen facility, which, he said, had been losing about $2.2 million annually distributing Falstaff and Ballantine products. He criticized Falstaff's shifting from a distribution system that sold to a large number of retail accounts to one selling to a small number of wholesale accounts, in particular the assignment of the New York market to a particular distributor (Fatato) and Falstaff's failure to accept a different one (Molyneux). "Mr. Kalmanovitz as a traditional businessman expressed at trial his contempt for 'studies' and 'projections.' Consequently, in making the decisions to close the North Bergen facility and to appoint Mr. Fatato distributor in the New York City area, no effort was made to ascertain in advance the effect on Ballantine sales." (*Bloor I*, p. 269) The judge also criticized Falstaff's severe "cutback of personnel in distribution, sales, marketing, administrative and warehousing areas. It virtually eliminated its promotion and advertising of Ballantine Beer and closed its advertising department." He quoted, and implicitly criticized, Kalmanovitz's description of his marketing strategy:

> We sell beer and you pay for it. . . . We sell beer, f.o.b. the brewery. You come and get it.
>
> Our responsibility is to give good product and you got responsibility to pay for it. That's it. That's the substance of my arrangement. It's working. (*Bloor I*, p. 270)

Falstaff had not, the court held, treated Ballantine equally. Even if they had, the court held, that would not have been enough.

> Falstaff's relationship to Ballantine is essentially different from its relationship to its own products. In the latter case, it may promote, continue or discontinue its products as it wills, subject to its duty to shareholders; in the former case it is bound by a contractual duty to the promisee. As the court said in a case cited by the defendant here: " '[B]est energies' meant such effort as in the exercise of sound judgment would be likely to produce the most profitable results to the promisee in view of the nature of the business and the extent of the territory over which it was to be conducted." (*Bloor I*, pp. 270–271, quoting *Randall v. Peerless Motor Car Co.*, p. 226)

Moreover, he suggested, Falstaff's incentives favored promoting Falstaff at the expense of Ballantine:

> Some of this apparent callousness towards Ballantine sales is undoubtedly caused by the fact that even though the liquid in a can of Ballantine Beer

and in a can of Falstaff Beer is identical, and accordingly costs exactly the same amount to produce, sale of Falstaff Beer produces a greater profit for Falstaff. In part this is the result of the fact that Falstaff is a "premium" beer and nets Falstaff about $4.20 more a barrel than does Ballantine, even before the $.50 Ballantine royalty is subtracted from the latter. (*Bloor I*, pp. 269–270)

A price differential of around 13% is not trivial. However, we should recognize that brewers engage in a form of (legal) price discrimination by targeting different groups with beers priced accordingly. There is no reason to believe that Falstaff could sell its brand to the "price beer" market reached by the Ballantine brand and maintain the price differential.

Judge Brieant did side with Falstaff in rejecting Bloor's claim that Falstaff's behavior amounted to substantial discontinuance of Ballantine. Falstaff had continued to distribute beer under the Ballantine name and had introduced Ballantine in other markets. While Ballantine's sales had dropped dramatically, the court found that

[a] very significant part of this decline is attributable . . . to the general decline of the market share of the smaller brewers, and to other causes unconnected with Falstaff's closing of the North Bergen facility. The remaining decline is regarded as "insubstantial" under the contract. It is clear from the royalty rate established in the contract itself that the liquidated damages clause was included to cover situations approaching the total cessation of Ballantine production, rather than situations involving gradual but significant declines in sales. (*Bloor I*, p. 266)

Damages were calculated by subtracting Ballantine's actual sales from the sales that would have been made had Falstaff used its best efforts (as determined by the court). The court accepted the expert witness's estimate, which was based on the assumption that Ballantine's sales would have followed the same trend as two other small New York labels, Schaefer and Rheingold. After some modest adjustments, primarily to exclude Ballantine sales that were the product of illegal activities, the judge concluded that the royalties lost by Ballantine were approximately $630,000. Falstaff had withheld royalties during the litigation, and these too were awarded, bringing the final judgment to about $1.3 million.

Falstaff appealed the best efforts ruling, and Bloor appealed the rejection of the substantial discontinuance claim. Judge Friendly, speaking for a unanimous court, affirmed. He restated Judge Brieant's conclusion, soft-ening it a bit. Brieant's decision might have been interpreted as requiring Falstaff to continue promoting Ballantine regardless of the financial con-sequences. Friendly made clear, however, that "best efforts" did not mean that Falstaff must go to these lengths. But it did have a special duty to promote Ballantine beer sales.

> While [the best efforts] clause clearly required Falstaff to treat the Ballan-tine brands as well as its own, it does not follow that it required no more. With respect to its own brands, management was entirely free to exercise its business judgment as to how to maximize profit even if this meant serious loss in volume. Because of the obligation it had assumed under the sales contract, its situation with respect to the Ballantine brands was quite different. The royalty of $.50 a barrel on sales was an essential part of the purchase price. Even without the best efforts clause Falstaff would have been bound to make a good faith effort to see that substantial sales of Ballantine products were made, unless it discontinued under clause 2(a)(v) with consequent liability for liquidated damages. . . . Clause 8 imposed an added obligation to use "best efforts to promote and maintain a high volume of sales. . . ." Although we agree that even this did not require Falstaff to spend itself into bankruptcy to promote the sales of Ballantine products, it did prevent the application to them of Kalmanovitz' philosophy of emphasizing profit über alles without fair consideration of the effect on Ballantine volume. Plaintiff was not obliged to show just what steps Falstaff could reasonably have taken to maintain a high volume for Ballantine products. It was sufficient to show that Falstaff simply didn't care about Ballantine's volume and was content to allow this to plummet so long as that course was best for Falstaff's overall profit picture, an inference which the judge permissibly drew. The burden then shifted to Falstaff to prove there was nothing significant it could have done to promote Ballantine sales that would not have been financially disastrous. (*Bloor II*, pp. 614–615)

2. The Deal

Judges Friendly and Brieant take it as axiomatic that the contract required Falstaff to trade off its profits for Ballantine's sales. Conspicuous by its ab-sence in their decisions is any analysis of why the contract included the royalty arrangement and the best efforts covenant. That is not entirely the fault of the judges, as the record was completely silent on this point. The context dictates how "best efforts" should have been interpreted. We are left with the somewhat peculiar spectacle of a court giving meaning to a context-sensitive phrase with no guidance as to the context. Had the court recognized that the royalty was, in effect, an "earnout," ancillary to the one-shot sale of some of Ballantine's assets to Falstaff, the outcome would have (or, at least, should have) been different.

An earnout makes part of the payment for an asset contingent upon some measure of future performance. Often it is a function of profits; here, it is a function of sales. Most corporate acquisitions do not involve earnouts. In 1998, of the over 9,000 acquisitions, only 153 included an earnout.[3] They would make little sense in the sale of a public corporation with numerous shareholders where the seller ceases to exist as an entity. Here, where the seller is a private entity that survives the transaction, it is more likely that the parties would choose to use an earnout. Earnouts rarely show up in appellate litigation; a Lexis search found only forty-two cases. That might not adequately indicate the frequency with which they generate disputes. I suspect, based in part on my consulting experience, that the disputes are far more common, but that they arise in arbitrations, not litigation.

IFC was, essentially, selling two assets—Ballantine's brand name (the proprietary rights) and its distribution network. IFC's purpose was simple: it wanted to sell at the highest price. That should be obvious, but the court's failure to recognize this basic point is the core of the problem. The fewer post-sale restrictions on any asset, the more a buyer would be willing to pay. Any constraint on Falstaff's exploitation of the assets would, other things being equal, reduce the amount it would be willing to pay. Falstaff's pursuit of "profit über alles," ex post, redounds to IFC's benefit, ex ante. So, any restriction, like the best efforts clause, immediately raises a red flag: how might the particular restriction raise the value of the Ballantine assets, ex ante?

The Earnout

Falstaff could have purchased the Ballantine assets outright rather than spreading the compensation over six years and making the payment contingent upon Ballantine sales. Why did they choose the latter course? There are three plausible reasons for using an earnout: (1) the seller is also filling the role of financier; (2) the seller is providing a bond for a promise not to engage in post-sale activities that would adversely affect the value of the assets to the buyer; and (3) the parties are responding to information asymmetry. In this instance, the third is most plausible.

Ballantine was, in effect, making a six-year loan to Falstaff. The security arrangements and acceleration clause discussed above are manifestations of this. A loan would make sense only if Falstaff could get terms at least as favorable from IFC as from alternative sources. If restrictions in its existing capital structure—debt covenants and the like—constrained Falstaff, spreading the payments over time might have been a simple way of financing the transaction without violating the constraints. A Falstaff planning document entitled "Ballantine Observations" hinted at some of the financing considerations:

4. Falstaff's financing of this purchase—What form would it take—would it take external financing, stock issue, additional long-term debt, what is the availability of any of the forms of financing and what would it cost and what restrictions would it place upon our operations.
5. The present debt agreements
   a. Do they allow this type of acquisition and when must these insurance companies be notified that we are considering such action.
6. The stockholder approval—What would be the mechanics here—what is the timing of such notification and what are the consequences of our announcing such to the stockholders in light of our present earnings situation and that of the last few years. (PX 14 at A1624–1625, dated January 8, 1972)

While spreading the payments over time might be a perfectly sensible way to finance the project, financing considerations cannot explain why the payments were contingent upon *Ballantine sales.* Something more is necessary to explain why IFC in its role as financier would choose to take neither a fixed return nor an equity position in Falstaff.

Earnouts are sometimes used to discourage the seller's management from engaging in post-sale actions detrimental to the buyer. Ballantine's managers would provide a bond to Falstaff to assure that they would not reduce the value of the Ballantine trademark by their future actions. Suppose that the top management of Ballantine had developed some good will with the beer market. The value of the brand name they were selling would be impaired if they could subsequently reenter and compete against Ballantine. A promise not to compete would, if enforceable, make the Ballantine assets more valuable. Giving these managers an interest in Ballantine's future sales or profits could substitute for, or complement, the noncompete covenant. The problem with this explanation in this instance is that a promise not to compete, or any variant thereon, would have been worthless. The outgoing Ballantine executives had no competence in the beer industry or expectation of staying in the beer industry, and Falstaff knew that. Judge Brieant accurately characterized IFC's competence in the beer business:

> Mr. Donald Orenstein was Executive Vice-President of Investors Funding Corporation and of P. Ballantine & Sons at the time the negotiations with Falstaff took place. He testified at trial to the IFC management's complete lack of experience in the brewing industry. His own career began with IFC as a clerk, and ultimately he became President of IFC Realty Service. He stated at trial his views on IFC's acquisition of Ballantine (Tr. p. 124): "Q. When did it become apparent to you that Investors Funding should sell P. Ballantine & Company? A. The second day that I arrived at P. Ballantine, in '69. He (Mr. Jerome Dansker, Chairman of the Board of IFC) bought it on a Thursday; I told him Friday to sell it." (*Bloor I*, p. 263, n.6)

Thus, the most likely story is that the earnout was a response to the problem of asymmetric information, the lemons problem. In sales of complex assets the seller typically has more information than the prospective buyer. If buyers cannot distinguish good assets from bad, then they are likely to be suspicious of any particular asset and to reduce their offer price accordingly. If the seller believes his asset to be sound, then conveying that information to the buyer can result in a higher net price. The parties have an incentive to economize on the joint production of information. By accepting some of its compensation in a contingent form, the seller provides some assurance to the buyer of the quality of the asset. Instead of insisting upon elaborate representations and warranties or engaging in extensive due diligence, Falstaff bought the Ballantine assets "as is" with over half the expected cost contingent upon future sales.

The parties want an arrangement which maximizes the value to the buyer ex ante. But producing information and assurance is not costless. The process of maximizing the value of the asset can reduce the size of the joint pie. That would obviously be true if the parties had spent months negotiating elaborate representations and warranties and/or engaging in a due diligence investigation. In this instance the parties avoided these costs using the royalty payment instead. It, too, is not costless. Earnouts, generally, have a number of value-reducing features. They do not track value perfectly; they can distort incentives; and they are not strategy-proof—that is, the buyer can operate the business in a way that exploits the mechanism. For example, if an earnout were based on profits in the first three years, the buyer could make investment decisions that shift profits from the third to the fourth year. Anticipation of these costs will reduce the final price of the asset. If the best efforts clause means anything, its role would be to prevent the buyer from taking undue advantage of the earnout.

Falstaff bought the Ballantine trademarks in order to exploit them. As Falstaff's CEO at the time of the transaction, Robert Colson, testified:

> The intention when we went into this deal was to use our best efforts, and that's exactly what it says there. We were going to go out and do our best efforts to promote the brand, or why would we have bought the brand? You don't buy something with the intention that you're going to abandon it. If you did, then you spend a lot of time wasting your time. (Colson's Test. at 1099)

Conceivably, Falstaff could have bought the Ballantine brand name with the intention of eliminating Ballantine as a competitor. However, since Falstaff was not in the New York market and the two beers were targeted at different customers, this would not have been a concern of the parties. During the life of the earnout, Falstaff could have combined with another brewer with a significant presence in the New York market, so the best efforts clause could possibly be viewed as protecting against that contingency, although I doubt it.

The royalty acts as a tax (roughly 2%) on sales. (Ballantine's 1970 price was $26.60 per barrel and the royalty rate was 50 cents per barrel. (PX 9 at 1618)) The "tax" could induce Falstaff to market a somewhat smaller amount of Ballantine product than it would have but for the royalty. So "best efforts" might possibly mean that Falstaff should push its sales effort a bit beyond the point that would otherwise be optimal. The distortion of incentives, which in this instance is quite minor, is a common problem in contingent compensation arrangements (franchise fees, percentage leases, oil and gas royalties, and so forth), and "best efforts" is just one of the devices for dealing with the problem.

The most likely function of the royalty was to police diversion. Falstaff bought two sets of assets: the proprietary rights and the distribution network. But the earnout was related only to the value of the former. Ballantine's owners had some reason for concern on this score. Falstaff was, after all, attempting to break into the New York market to sell its own brand, and Ballantine's owners were aware of this possibility. "There was an expression of concern stated by somebody on the Ballantine side that possibly Falstaff would use the Ballantine distribution system to come into the New York area, and then for reasons of its own, it might be possible . . . that Falstaff would concentrate on the sales of Falstaff, and either abandon or let the Ballantine beer sales diminish." (Melvin Carro (of Falstaff) Test. at A1074–1075) Had Falstaff simply jettisoned the Ballantine brand entirely and used the distribution network to distribute Falstaff beer instead, Falstaff would not simply be *maximizing* the value of the asset (the distribution network)—it would be *diverting* payment for that asset. The royalty arrangement would fail completely in its purpose. More generally, to the extent that Falstaff could use the distribution network to sell Falstaff rather than Ballantine, the royalty would not track the value of the asset.

A "best efforts" requirement is one contractual device for protecting against this sort of diversion. But the context suggests how the clause should be read. "Best efforts" in this context means that Falstaff agreed that in its pursuit of "profit über alles" it would not opportunistically divert sales from Ballantine (the sales of which were to track asset value) to Falstaff. Did Falstaff use the network to divert more sales than the parties should reasonably have expected? That might be a difficult question to answer for some fact patterns, but for the facts of this case the answer is easy and negative. When Kalmanovitz took charge he dismantled the distribution system. The evidence Judge Brieant relied on to document what he believed to be Falstaff's lack of best efforts supports the conclusion that Falstaff did not exploit a loophole in the earnout. Falstaff did not divert resources to the more profitable brand; it simply terminated (or at least drastically pared) a project that did not work.

So, we are left with three possible meanings of "best efforts" in the context of this transaction. First, it could be aimed at preventing Falstaff from abandoning the brand following a merger with a brewer with a significant presence in the New York market. Second, it might have been an attempt to correct Falstaff's incentives, which were a bit distorted by the royalty "tax." Third, and the most plausible, it could have been an attempt to limit diversion of revenue away from the device chosen to provide assurance of that value. None provides a basis for concluding that Falstaff's pursuit of profit "über alles," by revising its Ballantine marketing strategy and dismantling much of the Ballantine distribution network, violated its obligation to Ballantine.

This is a simple and, I believe, compelling story. There is only one problem with it. It is not the story told by the witnesses or counsel. That does not make it wrong, but it does raise the question of how a court is supposed to figure it out, and, if it does, how the court should respond. That problem is compounded by the "substantial discontinuance" proviso, which can be explained, but the explanation is neither so simple nor compelling. After attempting to make some sense of the proviso, I will return to the problem of decision making by an ill-informed court.

Substantial Discontinuance

It is common to couple royalty payment schemes with minimum payment obligations. Such arrangements are common in publishing and movies (talent receive royalties or a percentage of the gross to be offset against a bargained-for fixed fee), licensing agreements, franchising, and shopping center and other retail leases. It is tempting to assume that such arrangements would make sense in the sale of an asset, as in the present case. Indeed, my initial presumption was that the "substantial discontinuance" clause was a poorly drafted attempt to create a minimum obligation. However, I was wrong. The minimum does not add anything useful for the sale of an asset where the seller, like Ballantine, has no interest in, or effect upon, the outcomes other than the receipt of its compensation.

Up to the minimum, the effective tax rate created by the earnout is zero. Incentives still are distorted at the margin, but a high minimum means that at least over a broad range, the buyer's incentives are not distorted. But the higher the minimum, the weaker the quality assurance provided by the royalty. A high minimum undercuts the quality assurance function since the purchaser must pay regardless of quality. So, while a minimum annual payment might help correct the tax distortion of the per barrel royalty, it does so only by undercutting the purpose.

Ballantine asked for a minimum guarantee, but Falstaff refused. Ballantine's Orenstein testified:

Falstaff was never willing to give us a guarantee of a million one. They said they would use their best efforts . . . they didn't give us really, what we wanted. We wanted a million one guarantee, that if for any reason the sales dropped below fifty cents a barrel times two million two . . . we would be guaranteed at least, a million one, and that's not in the contract.

Q: It did not get in there?

A: No. We traded that off. It did not get in there. (Orenstein's Dep. at A1465–1466)

Although the contract did not include a minimum guarantee, it did include liquidated damages of $1.1 million per year (the same amount Ballantine had been asking as the minimum) in the event of Falstaff's substantial discontinuance of Ballantine. If this proviso were included as part of the quality assurance mechanism, as I first thought, it makes no sense. In effect, it says: if the assets are really terrible so that they are unusable, then Falstaff pays Ballantine $1.1 million per year for the duration; if, on the other hand, they are only pretty bad, Falstaff pays less. That is a perverse result, which I thought could only be explained by poor drafting.

However, the clause makes more sense if it is viewed as being independent of the quality of the proprietary rights and instead concerns diversion of revenues. Falstaff says, in effect: we agree that we will not cheat you by diverting receipts from the metering device (Ballantine sales) and profiting by the use of the other valuable asset we have purchased, your distribution network; if we have done too much diversion, we agree to pay a penalty (although the law does not permit us to call it that).[4] The trigger for the penalty would not be the *quantity* of Ballantine sold nationally. Rather, it would be the *percentage* of Ballantine being sold through the old Ballantine network.

But this mechanism had one big hole. What if the network itself turned out to be of little or no value? Falstaff had bought not one lemon, but two. Falstaff essentially abandoned the network, but continued to exploit the proprietary rights as best it could. If the proviso's purpose was to thwart massive diversion of revenues, there was no diversion. Falstaff bore the direct risk of the distribution network being a lemon; it seems unlikely that ex ante the parties would have wanted Falstaff to post an additional bond against that prospect. But—and this must be emphasized—it is most likely that neither party expected the distribution network to be worth so little, and the contract reflected their failure to anticipate this possibility.

3. So, What's a Poor Court to Do?

The parties did not give the court much assistance in framing the case. This is, I believe, less a matter of the peculiar way in which facts percolate up through the judicial system than of genuine confusion. Orenstein's testimony on the origins of the controversial terms is indicative:

> In substance what happened is that we just couldn't get together on those three items. It was the accounts receivables, the best efforts, and . . . the words substantial discontinuance. What does that really mean? How does one determine that? Can't we put in a formula? No, we won't give you a formula; we don't want to attach ourselves to anything. That's Colson's exact words. We told him, How can we make a deal not knowing where we're going? He said, Well, you have to believe that we're experts in the beer business for so many years; you're not selling to us just to collect a million one, you're going to look to us to collect much more, and we'll be able to increase the sales.
>
> I said, Well, if that's the way you feel, why don't you write it? He said, No, he's not prepared to do that. They have certain standards under which they do deals, and that's one of them. They didn't want to put it in writing, but that's how we came to the receivable. I said, If that's the feeling, give me something. Take my receivables. He said, Maybe we'll do that. That's how the next dialogue started. They then recessed. . . .
>
> I told [my colleagues] that the substantial discontinuance thing bothers me. What does that mean? Should we put in a percentage? Do you think we should try for a percentage? Then we all collectively said, in our minds, 30 percent would be considered a substantial discontinuance. I went back and mentioned that figure and they laughed. There was no way they would do it. (Orenstein's Test. at A1473–1474)

Bloor's lawyers asked various witnesses what best efforts meant to them and whether the term meant more than good faith, a sterile inquiry designed to wrench damning statements out of the mouths of unwary witnesses. But neither side ever framed the question in terms of the underlying purpose of the transaction: sale of an asset of uncertain value. Counsel never even hinted at the possibility that the dismantling of the Ballantine distribution network should count in favor of Falstaff, instead of counting against it. The courts accepted the parties' terms of debate.

This was not inevitable. A court with a confident understanding of what the deal was about could easily have framed the best efforts question properly and disposed of it cleanly. From the contractual context, the plausible meanings of best efforts were narrowly circumscribed, and under those meanings, Falstaff had satisfied its obligation. The substantial discontinuance proviso presented a somewhat more difficult problem. Still, the most plausible explanation is policing diversion. Given the purpose of the transaction, we should conclude that shutting down the distribution network completely would not constitute a substantial discontinuance.

I am not suggesting that courts should ignore contract language and attempt to determine the parties' true intent. Rather, I am suggesting that when contract language is context sensitive, the court should use that context in interpreting the contract. The emphasis should not be on what these parties meant, but on what reasonable people in this situation should have meant. So, even if Orenstein's testimony regarding the origins of the substantial discontinuance was accurate and the best efforts language was lifted from a form book with the parties giving it no mind, that should not matter in interpreting the agreement. We ought not, in Judge Easterbrook's colorful phrase, invite "a tour through Walters' cranium with Walters as the guide." (*Skycom Corp. v. Telstar Corp.*, p. 814)

The starting point should be this: a rational seller would not want the buyer to promise to use the asset sub-optimally. It makes little sense to have an interpretative strategy that presumed such an irrational policy. An interpretation of a contract that begins with the presumption that the seller intended to restrict the buyer's subsequent use of the asset is bound to fail unless there is an understanding of the possible gains from tying the buyer's hands.

4. Concluding Remarks

Generally speaking, giving content to an amorphous concept like "best efforts" is extremely difficult. Even in this contract, in which "best efforts" was invoked seven times and "good faith" once, it is hard to determine how a court should respond to claims that particular best efforts obligations had not been met. How, for example, should one deal with a complaint that Falstaff had failed to meet its best efforts obligation to maintain as its own employees Ballantine's sales, marketing, clerical, and administrative personnel? Ironically, while the problem is generally difficult or intractable, in the one case that has filtered down to the casebook level, the problem turns out to be an easy one. The context—a one-shot sale of assets—delimits the feasible meanings of "best efforts," and that leads to a simple conclusion: the courts got it wrong.

Again, I must emphasize, I am not asking courts to ferret out the true intent of the parties. People do often enter into foolish deals, and it would be disastrous for courts to continually second-guess their choices. But where the language is inherently ambiguous, the court should not impose an irrational agreement on the parties. The peculiar feature of *Bloor* is that the way the controversy was framed made the irrational seem natural to the litigators, the courts, and the commentators. When the irrational seems natural, it is time to rethink how we got there and to seek a better alternative.

CHAPTER 7

Columbia Nitrogen v. Royster:
Do as They Say, Not as They Do

Columbia Nitrogen v. Royster is one of the Terrible Twosome—the other being *Nanakuli v. Shell*—in which the courts invoked custom and usage to rewrite contracts that were plain on their face. In both decisions, the trade usage was the nonenforcement of specific contract terms regarding price or quantity. *Nanakuli* found a trade practice of "price protection," meaning that a clause that said the price would be the posted price at the time of delivery really meant either that price or the price when the contract was entered into, whichever was lower. *Columbia Nitrogen* held that despite the fact that the contract set both a fixed price (subject to indexing) and a minimum quantity, the buyer was not necessarily bound by either. What it was bound to do remained a secret. My late colleague, Allan Farnsworth, told me that the decision made Milton Handler (who won the antitrust claim for the losing side) apoplectic. And well it should have.

There is considerable debate on how course of dealing and custom and usage should be taken into account in contract interpretation, especially given the UCC's warm embrace of the concepts. Throughout this book, I argue that interpretation can be enhanced by an understanding of the context of a transaction. But that does not mean that anything that might be labeled a course of dealing or a custom should be incorporated into the contract. The danger of a *Nanakuli–Columbia Nitrogen* interpretative strategy is that parties will be frustrated in trying to devise the terms of their agreement, and they will have little confidence in their ability to predict the outcomes if their disputes do end up in litigation.

It is well known that parties often adapt their agreements to changing circumstances without recourse to the formal contract. The analytic response to this has taken two paths. One, which is embodied in the two decisions, is to elevate the informal adjustments at time X or place Y into a contractual term in contract Z. This might be done by a liberal invocation of waiver, by invoking course of dealing, or custom and usage or various excuse doctrines. The court infers what parties really meant by looking at what they, or others, did in circumstances that might be characterized as similar.

The opposite strategy, toward which I lean, is to recognize that contracts are enforced by a mix of formal (legal) and informal sanctions (including, specifically, reputation). Parties routinely ignore the formal law, adapting to changing circumstances in ways that need not be consistent with their formal agreement. However, the informal sanctions will sometimes not be sufficient. To put it somewhat crudely, if the short-run gains of "cheating" exceed the long-run gains of cooperating, the informal sanctions can break down. The role of the formal law, in this view, is to provide an anchor. If the litigation outcome is relatively certain, it provides a clear base point for negotiating a settlement. There is an interplay between the informal rules of an ongoing relationship and the rule of law that parties might invoke in the "end-game." Variations on this argument abound; see, for example, Macaulay (1963), Scott (2003), Bernstein (1999), and Klein (1980).

One argument favoring liberal incorporation of trade practices is that it could reduce ex ante drafting costs. Parties do not have to protect themselves from all manner of bad outcomes at the drafting stage if they expect things to work out okay in the litigation phase. (See Kraus and Walt 2000.) That is surely correct for some contextual facts. One of my primary complaints in this book is that courts seem rather oblivious to the economic context when interpreting contracts. The problem in both *Columbia Nitrogen* and *Nanakuli* is that the courts invoked context with no analytical framework other than a vague notion that in these cases it was appropriate for the parties to share the pain.

The record of the case includes a substantial joint appendix which provides a considerable amount of useful material. It does not provide enough information to explain why the written contract took the form that it did. Nor does it provide a coherent picture of what the trade practice—the commercial context—was. An examination of that record does exemplify the type of mischief unleashed by the court's freewheeling interpretative strategy. With no analytical grounding, the defense was free to advance a number of logically inconsistent arguments and the court was ill-equipped to sort them out.

1. Background

Royster had been in the fertilizer business since 1885. It was a seller of mixed fertilizer that was not vertically integrated backward into the raw materials. Its president testified: "Royster is not truly basically in any of the three plant foods. We do not mine phosphate rock. We purchase phosphate rock, and we process it into high grade phosphate. We do not make ammonia, which is the basis of the nitrogen in fertilizer, and we do not mine potash." (Appendix, p. 328) In 1966, it built a phosphate plant in Florida, which, in order to achieve scale economies, had a productive capacity greater than its captive needs.

On May 8, 1967, Royster entered into a three-year contract with Columbia Nitrogen to remove at least some of its excess production. (The record is silent on whether there were any other contract customers.) In 1962, Columbia, a subsidiary of PPG Industries, had acquired Bradley & Baker, a national brokerage firm. Columbia did not use the fertilizer itself; it resold the fertilizer to customers primarily in the Midwest and Southwest. Columbia also was a seller of some of the fertilizer components, in particular nitrogen, and Royster was one of its regular customers. Royster's purchases from Columbia were of interest both because the amounts purchased frequently diverged from the contract terms, allowing Columbia to claim that the course of dealing between the two firms indicated that they did not take the price and quantity terms of their agreements seriously, and because Columbia could allege that Royster linked the nitrogen purchases with the fertilizer sales and that this reciprocal dealing violated the antitrust laws.

The relevant terms of the CNC-Royster contract are reproduced in the published opinion. The contract was to run from July 1, 1967, to June 30, 1970, and would be renewed automatically for an additional year unless either party gave ninety-day notice of cancellation. The contract specified a minimum annual tonnage of three products: 15,000 tons for both diammonium phosphate 18–46–0 (DAP) and granular triple superphosphate 0–46–0 (granular) and 1,000 tons of run-of-pile triple superphosphate 0–46–0. The seller promised to meet the buyer's requirements beyond the minimum, subject to two provisos. First, the seller could not be required to ship more than 15% of any annual product minimum in any one calendar month. More importantly, the seller agreed "to provide additional quantities beyond the minimum specified tonnage . . . provided Seller has capacity and ability to provide such additional quantities." (Appendix, p. 8) The contract did not indicate how that "capacity and ability" would be determined. If a third party came along and offered a higher price, could Royster sell its remaining phosphate to that buyer and then claim it had no more to sell to Columbia? I think so, as long as Royster met the annual minimum. The original contract proposed by Royster differed in that it set minimum tonnages of 20,000 and maxima of 25,000 for the two major products. (Run-of-pile was not included.) (Appendix, p. 379) The price was fixed at $61.25 per ton, $40.90 per ton, and $0.86 per unit for the three products. These prices were subject to escalation, up or down, based on the change in price of raw materials (sulfur and rock phosphate) and labor.

Columbia's previous contract had been with American Agricultural Chemical Co. (Agrico), which was later purchased by Continental Oil. The Agrico deal was a two-year evergreen agreement, which was allowed to terminate on June 30, 1967. Like the proposed Royster contract, it had minimum and maximum tonnages. And, like the proposed Royster contract, it did not explicitly state which party had discretion within that range, although I presume that the buyer would have the discretion. That did not matter, since a CNC [Columbia Nitrogen Corp.] executive testified that "we never took anywhere near that tonnage." (Appendix, p. 267) The price was also indexed, albeit using different factors than those in the Royster contract. The prices were adjusted upward, as per contract, in June and August 1965. (Appendix, pp. 387–389) In April 1967, CNC entered into a second contract with Agrico's successor, Continental Oil, for the same time period as the Royster contract. The prices were about 5% higher than the Royster contract and quantities were much reduced, being only about 10% of the previous contract. These appear to be CNC's only supply contracts in effect at the time the dispute arose. In response to the question "Did you think the over-all business effect of having two suppliers of phosphates was desirable?" a CNC executive responded, "There is some merit in having more than one source of supply." (Appendix, pp. 268–269)

Two weeks after signing the contract, Columbia sent Royster a blanket purchase order. This would be of no moment, except for the fact that when the deal went sour fifteen months later, Columbia claimed that the purchase order either supplanted or modified the original contract.

Almost immediately after the contract was formed, the market deteriorated. A CNC executive testified that "a large cost of phosphate is involved in the cost of sulphur, which is the primary raw material for phosphate manufacture. During this particular period sulphur prices went unexpectedly high. In fact, historically high, while phosphate prices themselves went down, historically down." (Appendix, p. 126) By September the price of DAP had fallen to $58.45, and by spring the price had fallen to the $48–49 range. (Appendix, p. 135) CNC complained that it was unable to resell the fertilizer at a profit. Royster made a partial accommodation by not escalating the contract price in response to the increased sulphur price. After about a year of trying to work things out, during which time CNC had taken only 1,598 tons of DAP and 343 tons of granular (Appendix, p. 5), Royster gave CNC an ultimatum: take the fertilizer or be in breach. On September 20, 1968, Royster notified CNC that it had arranged to sell the fertilizer to a third party, Mobil, at a much reduced price ($43 for DAP and $29 for granular) if CNC refused to honor its contract. (Appendix, p. 6) CNC denied that it had any contractual obligation, and shortly thereafter this action commenced.

CNC put forth six defenses and a counterclaim. While course of dealing (#4) and custom of the trade (#5) were the decision's ticket into the casebooks, CNC's main emphasis was on the notion that the purchase order amended the contract (#1) and the antitrust counterclaim, both of which turned out to be losing arguments. In the following section I will describe CNC's other arguments to set the stage for the analysis of what turned out to be the winning argument.

2. CNC's Other Defenses

One strategy for arguing cases is to throw in as many arguments as one can, whether or not they are consistent, and hope that at least one sticks. ("My client didn't do it and it was self-defense.") That evidence adduced to support one argument undermines another should, one would hope, police this sort of argumentation. Two striking features of the *Columbia Nitrogen* litigation are the defendant's vigorous presentation of a number of mutually contradictory arguments and the passive response by plaintiff and judges alike.

The Purchase Order Removed CNC's Obligation

CNC claimed that the purchase order issued on May 19 amended and supplemented the original contract. On the back of the form, paragraph 8 said:

"Purchaser reserves the right at any time to change this order, in any particular with respect to goods not theretofore shipped thereunder. If any such change shall increase Seller's cost of performance, Seller shall immediately notify Purchaser thereof and an equitable adjustment in the price shall be made by written amendment to this order." (Appendix, p. 20) CNC counsel's interpretation was that the "purchase order which was agreed to by the plaintiff left the defendant with the option to order, or not order, to do anything." (Appendix, p. 27)

The trial judge rejected this argument:

> My observation from simply off the top of my head is that when parties get into a negotiation that affidavits supplied to me indicate that the top officials, eight belonging to your people and some thirteen of the Royster people, including the Presidents of the organizations, if they get together and conclude an arrangement and then for a week afterward for there to be summarily received a purchase order which talks about that period that the contract covers, shipping instruction, invoicing instruction, and then to argue that because on the reverse side it says "purchaser reserves the right anytime to change this order in any particular ground with respect to goods," this in substance cancels out the negotiations that required the thirteen and eight top people of these two companies—it just doesn't strike a very responsive note with me. I am rather of the opinion, being an old waybill sorter for the Seaboard Airline Railroad, that what is contemplated on the reverse side of this is that this is the form usually used for a purchase order of some particular quantity of goods. (Appendix, p. 30)

That position seems obviously correct, and the Court of Appeals agreed. (p. 11) The only reason to think this defense not entirely ludicrous is that the issue had specifically been covered in Columbia Nitrogen's contracts with its other supplier, Agrico. In both the 1964 and 1967 contracts, this ploy was explicitly rejected: "This document constitutes the full understanding between the parties and no amendment modification or release from any provision hereof shall be effective unless in writing signed by both parties and specifically stating it is an amendment to this contract. No modification shall be effected by the acknowledgement or acceptance of purchase order forms containing different conditions." (Appendix, pp. 397, 406) The defense did not call this clause to the court's attention. Nonetheless, it makes little sense to have a default rule that allows the buyer to play "gotcha" by sneaking new terms into a long-term contract on the back of a purchase form.

Lack of Mutuality

The May 8 contract lacked mutuality and was therefore unenforceable, said CNC, because Royster had the option of nonperformance if CNC defaulted, but CNC had no such option if Royster defaulted. This defense, I should note first, presumes that the contract does not include the purchase order amendment. Ironically, the lacking mutuality claim would be more plausible if the purchase order were incorporated in, or superseded, the initial agreement. If CNC could "do anything," it could also do nothing. A court could easily find "I will if I want to" provides insufficient consideration to form a valid contract. Regardless, the basic claim is wrong. If Royster breached, CNC's obligation would be at an end; that is the standard default rule, and any failure to make the rule explicit is irrelevant. CNC abandoned this defense, so we need not consider it further.

The Contract Was Not Take-or-Pay

Despite the May 8 contract's explicit language, CNC argued that "it was clearly understood and agreed that the entire arrangement between plaintiff and defendant was that defendant would sell plaintiff's products in the area of the United States where they are principally used on a 'best efforts' basis and that the arrangement was not a 'take-or-pay' arrangement. . . . [Therefore] this defendant is not obligated to the plaintiff in any amount of money for its decision not to purchase products from plaintiff." (Appendix, p. 38) This defense has three prongs: CNC's obligation was only to use its best efforts to sell Royster's phosphates; purchasers for resale are different from purchasers for use; and the obligation depends on whether the contract was take-or-pay. As we shall see in the next section, these arguments fit awkwardly with the custom, usage, and course of dealing arguments since there was no evidence on whether any of the other transactions forming the background norms were for sales to resellers or had take-or-pay provisions.

The contract had a no-oral-modification clause: "No verbal understanding will be recognized by either party hereto; this contract expresses all the terms and conditions of the agreement." (Appendix, p. 11) That clause would seem to preclude the notion that there was an agreement that CNC was obligated to take only what it could sell, using its best efforts; CNC did not push very hard on this point. It put more effort into the other two prongs, especially the not-a-take-or-pay prong. It argued that in the negotiations it had rejected a penalty clause of $10 per ton, and this had transformed the contract: "[T]he elimination of such penalty clause changed the character of the contract from what the trade called a 'take-or-pay' contract to one which would be handled flexibly in accord with usage in the trade and course of dealing." (CNC Brief, p. 38) No doubt, had the $10 penalty remained in the contract, CNC's counsel would have claimed that it was an unlawful penalty clause; litigators, unlike mere mortals, are not constrained by good faith.

CNC's argument implies that take-or-pay contracts would be unaffected by custom and usage, a point to which I return in the next section. A CNC executive elaborated on the significance of the distinction:

Q: In other words, I think you testified that you recommended that the contract, as submitted by Royster which contained a $10.00 per ton penalty clause should Columbia Nitrogen fail to purchase, that you recommended that clause be deleted?

A: Yes, sir.

Q: Do you know whether or not the clause was, in fact, deleted?

A: Yes, sir, it was.

Q: Did the deletion of that clause, in your mind, make a different type of contract between Columbia and Royster?

A: Yes. As far as I was concerned, it altered the intent of the contract completely because it ceased to be a take or pay, in effect, contract.

Q: What is a take or pay contract?

A: You either take the product or you pay for what you do not take, or you pay a penalty for failure to take.

Q: State whether or not the deletion of the $10.00 penalty clause changed the contract in any way?

A: There was then no statement in the contract, as far as I was concerned, and based upon experience in the industry, which would then compel Columbia Nitrogen to take the tonnage involved in the contract. (Appendix, pp. 133–134)

Most contracts are not take-or-pay. In the run-of-the-mill case, does the buyer have an option to perform with no liability if it chooses not? Hardly.

The standard remedy would be the contract-market differential, perhaps with incidentals and consequential damages thrown in. In a true take-or-pay, the contract would require that CNC pay the entire contract price for the minimum "take." That would have been about six times the proposed $10 penalty. So, while the penalty and the take-or-pay both pre-specify the buyer's minimum obligation, they do so in different ways. The failure to pre-specify just means that the default contract remedy rules would apply. It should have had no effect on the underlying obligation.

Contract Procured by Misrepresentation

CNC claimed that the contract was procured by misrepresentation and was therefore null and void. What was the misrepresentation?

> Plaintiff . . . pressed defendant to enter into the contract in question for a period of three years. Normal fertilizer contracts are entered into on a year-to-year basis. Plaintiff represented to defendant that the three year term was necessary as a trade method to hold the market prices up on plaintiff's phosphate products and defendant thereupon entered into the said contract for the three year term.
>
> After the contract was entered into, the President of plaintiff informed a former Vice President of defendant that the contract sued upon was one of several contracts which had enabled plaintiff to procure its permanent long-term financing on its multi-million dollar facility at Royster, Florida, this apparently being the true reason for plaintiff's insistence upon a long-term contract. (Appendix, p. 44)

The rationale that CNC allegedly fell for was, in effect, that this contract is really different and we really need firm prices over the next three years because we are constructing a multimillion dollar plant and will have a substantial amount of phosphates we will have to sell. That by itself should undercut the notion that the contract incorporated the customs and usage of the other contracts. If Royster had told CNC that it needed a three-year agreement because the circumstances were really different than other fertilizer sales, then why could CNC conclude that the usual trade practices would be incorporated? It also undercuts the notion that CNC would believe that, two weeks after entering into this contract, Royster would accept an amendment giving CNC the option to do nothing.

The meaning of the claimed misrepresentation is not entirely clear. It seems to be only that Royster needs a three-year contract with a firm price. But the contract it finally entered into was indexed in both directions, so it appears to have given up on the firmness of the price. Regardless, since the alleged misrepresentation states *no reason* why Royster would want the three years, it is consistent with *any reason,* including the "true reason" alleged by CNC. The law regarding pre-contract misrepresentation is not crystal clear, but it certainly does not require parties to state every reason they might have for entering into a deal.

The Reciprocity Counterclaim

CNC alleged that Royster used its purchasing power in the nitrogen market to induce CNC to enter into the contract:

> By using the extensive economic leverage of plaintiff's purchasing power in the nitrogen fertilizer products market to coerce defendant into a three-year contract to buy for resale phosphate fertilizer products from plaintiff at a price too high to permit defendant to resell in competition with plaintiff's own price offers to other buyers of such phosphate products, with the result that defendant was eliminated as a competitor of plaintiff in the sale of such phosphate products. (Appendix, p. 48)

Note first that the "too high" price was in fact below the price in CNC's concurrent Agrico contract. The price was too high only after market conditions changed. Note second that the "elimination of competition" resulted in Royster selling phosphates to Mobil at a price that CNC claimed was too low; see the next subsection. An odd use of Royster's alleged power.

Antitrust law regarding trade practices was pretty confused in the mid-1960s. The notion that reciprocity might be a violation had some plausibility at the time. A substantial portion of the record, the jury charge, and the opinions (trial and appellate) relate to the counterclaim despite the fact that it was utter nonsense. This is not the place to go into an antitrust analysis. Suffice it to say that the industry was not concentrated, the firms were both small players, and the amounts at issue were a tiny portion of the market. The ironic aspect of the counterclaim is that CNC's own executive made clear that the reciprocity was a recognized trade practice:

Q: Mr. Baker, I believe you made reference to the practice of trading or exchanging products in this industry. Would you explain to the jury exactly how it works.

A: Well it's been common practice in the fertilizer industry for quite a few years to sell your product by exchanging with another supplier of a product that you need in your own operation. This was a widespread practice. All companies, large companies to my knowledge did this sort of thing; and it was a form of reciprocity practiced by most companies, so called "You scratch my back; I'll scratch yours for you." (Appendix, p. 246)

Royster's Cover Was Inadequate

Royster covered by selling over 30,000 tons of fertilizer to Mobil at prices of $43 (DAP) and $29 (granular). CNC complained that Royster could have done better and therefore that its damages were overstated. It noted that Royster's published price list that October had DAP at $60 and granular at $43. "This was coupled with evidence that Royster was shipping the same product to other customers at the higher list prices during the same period of time in which it was shipping to Mobil at the low sales price." (CNC Brief, at p. 44) This argument is inconsistent with the claims that the market price had fallen so far that CNC's contractual obligation would have to be adjusted. Perhaps CNC meant to argue that the current market price was above the Mobil prices but still well below the list prices and that the shipments at the list prices were under contracts negotiated at an earlier date. That argument would present a problem for CNC since it suggests that others in the trade did not adjust prices downward in a weak market, contrary to its claim that such adjustments would be part of the custom and usage of the trade.

Royster claimed that, given the large amount of product it had to dispose of, the Mobil contract was the most effective way of doing so:

Well sir, there is only two ways that you can get rid of a product when you are in this kind of trouble. One, you can just advertise to the world that you have a depressed merchandise, and almost have the equivalent of a fire sale, and I think all of us know what a fire sale means, that you are not going to get anywhere near the value of the product. Or else you can try to find someone who uses this product, who has the capacity to store some of it, put it in some of their storage and relieve you of your inventory problem, and not make it wholesale knowledge that there is some tonnage that is going to be disposed of because of litigation or something of this nature. (Appendix, pp. 82–83)

Nothing in the record helps in assessing the validity of CNC's claim that Royster's effort was inadequate. Nor, for our purposes, is it necessary to do so. For what it is worth, the Court of Appeals thought that the trial judge's instructions to the jury regarding the cover transaction needed to be beefed up: "On retrial, therefore, the instruction explaining this section of the code should mention Royster's duty to realize as high a price as possible under all the circumstances." (At 13) My concern is not with the measurement of damages, but with the interplay between CNC's defense (the market price fell too much) and its liability (but not *that* much).

Putting It Together

Columbia Nitrogen's argument thus far, stripped to its essentials, is as follows: (a) there was no contract; (b) the (non)contract was amended by a purchase order to give CNC the right to cancel whenever it wanted; and (c) CNC was induced to enter into this arrangement (contract? noncontract?) by Royster's misrepresentation and abuse of its economic leverage. Columbia Nitrogen did not appear to feel the need to explain why anyone would bother to fool or coerce it into entering such a benign (or nonexistent) relationship. And it gets worse once we add in CNC's two other defenses discussed in the next section: the contract incorporated custom and usage and course of dealings. If CNC had the discretion it claimed was customary, then where is the misrepresentation?

3. Custom and Usage, Course of Dealing

Despite the primacy of CNC's "purchase order" defense and the inordinate amount of effort devoted to the reciprocity counterclaim, the crux of the case is the custom and usage defense. The trial judge refused to allow the introduction of evidence showing that industry participants did not take the price and quantity terms of their contracts seriously. He did, however, permit the testimony to be given out of earshot of the jury, so that the evidence was available on the record on appeal. In this section, I first summarize the judicial response to the defense. This will be followed by a sampling of some of the evidence and a critical analysis of the Appeals Court's conclusion.

In its brief, Columbia Nitrogen argued:

In the fertilizer industry . . . buyers and sellers of agricultural chemicals traditionally enter into what appear on their face to be firm or binding contracts but are not regarded or enforced as to their precise quantities and prices. The entire sales and distribution structure in the fertilizer industry is based upon confidence that a buyer will be kept competitive in the market place and will be given relief in either price or tonnages when he would otherwise suffer serious losses for reasons over which neither party has any control. (CNC Brief, pp. 26–27)

It added a more elaborate statement of the usage:

But the trade custom and course of dealing on which CNC relies go no further than to require a renegotiation of the tonnages or prices upon the occurrence of a condition subsequent—a concept not at all new to the law and one that had long been applied as between these two experienced "merchants." The practice embodied in both the trade usage and the parties' course of dealings and course of performance is nothing but a re-opening clause something like those common in labor contracts. It becomes operable upon the event of a drastic, unpredictable and uncontrollable change in marketing conditions and is designed to stabilize contractual relationships in the fertilizer industry[,] not to eviscerate them. (CNC Brief, pp. 33–34)

The trial judge would have none of it:

I feel like somebody said about a member of the vestry of my church. It may well apply to me in this case. I certainly may be wrong, but I am not in any doubt. So I will have to leave that matter with the Court of Appeals.

My feeling about the situation is that there is no question in the law of contracts that parties may reform or may choose a course with reference to a contract already entered into. And if it is a mutually agreeable change, it is perfectly all right.

The other people who have testified, including Mr. Worthey, have all used the language as they talk that these were mutually agreed upon. Well, I haven't any argument that parties can mutually agree to anything. But it is the unilateral assertion that I find wrong in this case. This is a perfectly plain, unambiguous contract stating tons, stating price, stating delivery information, providing for variations in the price as reflected in raw materials. If these parties wanted to enter into any ambiguous proposition where they could change it at will with the unilateral wish of one when the other one didn't agree to it, they should have said so. (Appendix, pp. 244–245)

CNC's counsel responded to this by linking the contract to the aforementioned clause in the purchase order.

[T]he District Court again made the basic mistake of referring to the May 8 document alone as being plain and unambiguous, but most important the Court put its finger on a basic error which it had committed at pretrial as follows:

"If these parties wanted to enter into any ambiguous proposition where they could change it at will with the unilateral wish of one when the other didn't agree to it, *they should have said so.*" (Emphasis in original.)

This is exactly what the parties did by underscoring their understanding with the exchange of the purchase order. (Appendix, p. 9)

The Court of Appeals reversed and remanded. Even though it rejected the purchase order argument (and therefore CNC's argument that it had "said so"), it accepted the custom and usage defense. Custom and trade usage reflects "the reality of the marketplace and avoids the overly legalistic interpretations which the Code seeks to abolish." (p. 10) The evidence in question, it claimed, could reasonably be construed as consistent with the express terms of the agreement. Among the reasons for this conclusion, the court found:

1. There was silence about adjusting prices and quantities to reflect a declining market.
2. The quantity language of the contract spoke of "products supplied under contract," rather than of "products" or "products purchased under contract," and this language, it claims, is consistent with the proffered testimony. (I have no idea what this means. Probably nothing.)
3. The default clause only referred to the buyer's failure to pay; in the negotiations CNC rejected Royster's liquidated damages proposal and Royster rejected CNC's meeting competition proposal. This left a gap that could not be filled by the Code's default damage rules because the issue was not damages, but the existence of a default.
4. CNC's interpretation did not give CNC a unilateral right to modify the contract, contrary to Royster's claim.
5. The no-oral-modification clause did not preclude supplementing the language of the written agreement with custom and trade usage.

6. [T]he contract does not expressly state that course of dealing and usage of trade cannot be used to explain or supplement the written contract." (p. 9)

The court did not go so far as to identify the content of this newly constructed contract. That task would, apparently, be left to a jury. This is just as well, since the contract the court created did not really exist. That is, it was so vague that had it been written explicitly, it would be hard to imagine that any court would find it enforceable.

To start, even if one wants to give considerable weight to custom and usage, relying on it is problematic when the situation is unprecedented and the industry is in flux. As previously noted, shortly after the contract was entered into, sulfur (input) prices soared and phosphate (output) prices tumbled. If, as a CNC executive testified, these price changes were indeed historic, there is no reason to believe that the past industry responses to smaller changes would be an indicator of the appropriate response to such a historic change. In fact, in the years immediately preceding the formation of this contract, the price of phosphate was firm and high. (Appendix, p. 89) How are we to infer the trade custom of responding to a falling market when the observed behavior occurred in a rising one?

Moreover, the industry itself had been transformed in the years immediately preceding the formation of this contract by a series of mergers, with small companies being taken over by larger ones, primarily oil companies. Royster's president testified:

Now, this business has changed greatly since 1960. Prior to the Second World War Royster was considered a large fertilizer company because you had many small fertilizer companies all over the country. And then in the 60's a dramatic thing happened. The oil companies and the big industrial and chemical companies moved in, and sulfur companies moved into the fertilizer business on the assumption that . . . the only way we are going to save the world was with fertilizer. But you don't want to hear about that. They moved in and they had vast resources which had never been known in the fertilizer industry before.

Between the years 1963 and 1968 4,300,000,000 dollars was poured into the fertilizer industry in this country and in Canada. And you had companies, the smaller companies, or the old line companies were all taken over by the oil companies. You had Mobil Oil Company which took over V-C. Continental took over A. A. Borden took over Smith-Douglass. City Service took over Tennessee Corporation. U.S. Phosphoric on down the line. Columbia Nitrogen took over Bradley and Baker. They took over some of the smaller companies. A couple in Georgia and one in South Carolina I believe. And this put these industrial giants into basic position because they poured all the necessary funds in that were needed to get themselves basic in two or three of the basic materials. (Appendix, pp. 328–329)

Must we assume that the past sins of the children must be visited on their adopting parents? More generally, how do we determine whose trade usage is to count when the makeup of the trade changes drastically? The court ignored this; there was no discussion of who would constitute the trade or whether the new participants adopted the same practices as the old.

Suppose that the industry makeup had remained unchanged. Trade usage still could not produce a coherent, enforceable contract. The court never asked whether the Columbia Nitrogen–Royster written contract bore any resemblance to the written contracts of others that it used to infer the trade practice. Could the court have meant to say that regardless of what words are on the paper, all fertilizer contracts are alike? Since it took no notice of the content of the other written contracts in its interpretative effort, that seems to be the inevitable result. So, for example, if all the other contracts were for one year and this one was for three years, then one might at least question whether the trade response to the others should carry over to this agreement as well. No evidence was taken directly on this point, although there is sufficient evidence sprinkled over the record to suggest that there was considerable variation in the content of the written agreements and that the Columbia-Royster agreement was an outlier. The term of the Columbia-Royster contract was three years, longer than most; the usual contract was for one year, although a CNC executive noted that some were for four, five, or six months. (Appendix, p. 154) Recall that CNC claimed it was misled into entering into the three-year contract; that at least suggests that this contract was special. Is the trade usage totally independent of the contract length? If not, how is a court to determine which contracts are close enough to the one being litigated, especially if their content is not made available to the court?

Columbia Nitrogen argued that the fact that it was a reseller rather than an end-user affected the integration of custom into the agreement:

Q: Is there any difference, or has there been in your experience, any difference in the application of this custom as concerns the resale contract?

A: Yes, to the extent that if the product is being used for manufacturing purposes by the buyer, the buyer can more accurately anticipate and forecast his requirements, because he has control over it to a certain extent. But on resale products, the buyer has no control whatsoever. He is subject to the whims of his buyers, subsequently. (Appendix, p. 105)

I suppose this means that the custom in general was not to take the price/quantity language very seriously and, specifically when the contract was for resale, to take it even less seriously. Does the distinction matter? If some sales to end-users did not involve quantity adjustment, should that count against CNC in interpreting this contract?

As noted above, CNC and the Court of Appeals emphasized that CNC had rejected Royster's take-or-pay (or penalty clause) proposition. That suggests that if Royster had succeeded in getting that language into the written contract, the outcome would have been different. Otherwise, why tell us? Unless Royster's proposal was completely out of the blue, it seems likely that at least some contracts in this industry were take-or-pay. Again, since the content of the other contracts was not in evidence, neither we nor the court have any knowledge regarding the existence of take-or-pay or of its interplay with usage.

Royster claimed that some fertilizer contracts included "meet and release" clauses and that one had been specifically rejected in the course of negotiation.

In fact, the only term which CNC requested but did *not* succeed in obtaining was a "price reduction" or "meet and release" clause, a provision found in some fertilizer contracts, which would have allowed CNC to demand during the contract term that Royster meet lower prices offered by competing sellers or release CNC from the contract. Such provision—which would have shifted the risk of a decline in prices from the buyer to the seller—was unacceptable to Royster and, by agreement of the parties, was not inserted in the contract. This rejection is highly significant in view of CNC's contention that evidence should have been admitted to prove an alleged usage of trade or course of dealing identical to the rejected clause. (Royster Brief, pp. 5–6)

As in the take-or-pay case, the same question arises: Would trade usage apply equally to contracts with and without such clauses?

The CNC-Royster contract was for a fixed minimum. What if the "data base" for inferring custom and usage contained requirements contracts? The court had no way of knowing the extent of such contracts. Should performance under those contracts be irrelevant in inferring custom and usage? Should it count only if the custom and usage appeared compatible with the custom and usage under fixed quantity contracts? Conversely, in interpreting a requirements contract, should the courts rely on the performance of the fixed quantity agreements? There was only one isolated reference to requirements contracts in the record, and that suggested that the parties did not take the language too seriously (or that they didn't know what they were talking about):

> Well, requirements contracts were often done in the industry, although many buyers in the last few years, I would say, have swung away from requirements contracts so they could have an open source of supply. But there have been instances I know where buyers have had requirements contracts with as many as three suppliers, a contract with three suppliers for their requirements.
>
> *Q.* What would this mean?
> *A.* This would mean that the one or two of these three suppliers would just be without a customer where he thought he—if he didn't know the customer he may have thought he had one.
> *Q.* In your experience in the fertilizer industry did you find this situation to prevail generally or not with regard to requirements?
> *A.* As far as my experience is concerned, and the part of the industry I was in, I would say it was more or less a general occurrence.
> *Q.* Would that apply as well to contracts for fixed amounts at fixed prices—
> *A.* Yes. (Appendix, p. 170)

The upshot of this discussion is that the more heterogeneous the written contract language, the more difficult it is to infer from observed behavior the existence of a custom that could be plugged into any or all of the heterogeneous contracts. How much heterogeneity there was, we do not know. Nor did the court. Nor could a court find out. At least some contract language would have overcome custom, but the court says nothing about that beyond acknowledging that an explicit disclaimer would trump custom. A possible response to this line of argument is: The fact that contracts were modified even if they had take-or-pay, penalty, or requirements clauses suggests how powerful the practice was; the court takes no position regarding interpretation of contracts *with* those clauses, but only on those *lacking* the clauses. That sort of argument might be persuasive to some (not me) if the response to changed circumstances was uniform, regardless of the written contract language. But in disputing Royster's cover contracts, CNC rejects that possibility. There appear to be some contracts in which Royster continued to charge a high contract price. Recall CNC's claim that the cover sale to Mobil was inadequate because Royster was receiving higher prices elsewhere.

CNC put considerable weight on the course of dealings between the parties. There had previously been only a handful of sales by Royster to CNC, but Royster had purchased a number of products from CNC over the years. CNC introduced evidence showing that in twenty-six of forty such contracts in 1962 through 1968, Royster revised its obligation downward for price, quantity, or both. (CNC Brief, pp. 28–30) It did not present any evidence on the actual contract language, although it is clear that forty contracts over a six-year period should have a structure quite different from a three-year contract. CNC presented no evidence on market conditions or on whether Royster made any concessions to CNC in conjunction with these revisions. Nor is there any indication of why the contracts were consistently too optimistic, especially in a period of prosperity in the fertilizer industry. The record evidence of prosperity is only indirect. The record indicates that the price of phosphates was high, not the price of nitrogen (which Royster was buying). I confess to finding these data a bit fishy, but the court was surely bound to accept them as true. What should we make of this? Is the moral that adjustment is to be made: (a) when the market declines? (b) when the buyer wants it? (c) when Royster wants it? (d) whenever either party asks for it? (e) whatever spin a lay jury decides to put upon it? The price differentials in the contracts in which Royster was a buyer are unknown. Are we to infer that CNC's "condition subsequent" had been met, or was that immaterial? Do the magnitudes matter? The average sale in the twenty-six contracts was less than $100,000 and the total dollar amount forgiven was around $500,000, roughly the same as the damages claimed by Royster for the first year of the single disputed contract. (CNC Brief, p. 30)

To this point I have assumed that there was a custom that could be identified and read into the written contract to produce a coherent contract.

Let us now turn to the content. The custom, I claim, was so ill-defined as to preclude the finding of an enforceable contract. In its reply brief, CNC characterized the trade usage as follows:

> [I]t has been the custom and usage in the fertilizer industry that contracts have been in the main gentlemen's agreements, are projections of the buyer's best estimate of anticipated needs, are flexible, the result of a loose contractual science and are adjusted depending on changes in the market place, the state of the market being the main determining factor. . . . The effect of said usage is that a buyer is kept competitive in the market place by either reduction to market price or relief from tonnage requirements. (Appendix, pp. 6–7)

A CNC executive testified on the trade practice, but also suggested that the language was in the *written* agreements:

Q: Referring to the contracts which were for fixed tonnages and for fixed prices, state whether or not there has been a custom in the trade, to your knowledge, under those contracts, if there was a market price decline?

A: Well, the contract would state, *it was in the contract,* that if the seller could show that he was able to purchase reasonable quantities of a similar product at a lower price, the seller had the option of either meeting the price or withdrawing from the contract.

Q: Was this without exception? Did all contracts have the phraseology?

A: To the best of my knowledge, yes, sir.

Q: So, from that point, in the event you had a decline in market price below any particular contract price, state whether or not there would be a custom as to adjustment of the price between buyer and seller?

A: As time went on and the market did change, it became the custom to protect your account if you wished to retain the business, and you met the lower price. (Emphasis added) (Appendix, p. 131)

What would trigger an adjustment? The preceding statement describes a "meet and release" clause—any market price below the contract price would be the trigger. In its brief, however, CNC suggested that a mere price differential would not be enough. There was an unwritten "condition subsequent" that would allow for readjustment for "a drastic, unpredictable and uncontrollable change." The Court of Appeals appears to have adopted something short of this position, restricting the usage to a "declining" market. (pp. 9–10) The evidence presented was only qualitative; it never indicated how much prices would have to change. Indeed, there was no evidence restricting the change to declining prices. If the market price had risen, would a gentlemanly buyer adjust the price upward? The evidence did not condition the custom on the state of the market.

There is no hint in the record as to why the bailout should be asymmetric. Yet the characterization of the custom by both CNC and the Court of Appeals relates only to a market decline. Perhaps they would recognize a second custom for adjusting the contract in a rising market. One cannot invoke the relative ability to absorb risk, since Royster was a buyer in the contracts illustrating the course of dealing, and a seller here. Regardless, the trigger for the obligation to adjust is defined in an extremely fuzzy manner. That, by itself, might render the court-created contract a nullity. But it gets worse. Even if we accept that the trigger is well enough defined, the response is not.

What would happen if the market declined? According to CNC's witnesses, virtually anything. One claimed that the buyer could take only as much as it chose to. "Generally speaking if a buyer did not take what he anticipated he would take there was no effort made to coerce him to take it." (Appendix, p. 111) Another suggested that there were a number of alternative responses, including spreading the obligation out over a number of years:

> Now, this could happen a number of ways. If you had to take 50,000 tons of product in two years, you might be relieved to take 50,000 tons in three or four years; or you [might] be allowed to pay a somewhat lower price and keep the 50,000 tons. There are various ways you can do it in terms of price changes or changes in duration of the contract or tonnage changes themselves. So it is hard to really know how these things are handled, you know, in a general rule; but there are flexibles in more than one way. (Appendix, pp. 126–127)

Another testified to an even mushier rule:

> Some of your bigger customers where say contracts were signed on a personal level between the vice-president of one company and the buyer or vice-president of the seller who may have had a long experience of mutual relationship in the industry and stated his problem that he either could or could not live with his contract and was there any way they could com-

promise on a new pricing or tonnage. This usually was either made somewhere in an amicable type of atmosphere where the two people said, all
right, I'll do this, you do that. It usually was a compromise of some sort.
(Appendix, p. 157)

If we try to write down the contract that the Court of Appeals has recognized, what do we get? Columbia Nitrogen agrees to take a fixed amount
of fertilizer at a fixed price for three years. If, however, the market price
falls by enough, CNC can ask Royster to modify the price and/or quantity
term. If Royster refuses, then. . . . To paraphrase Gertrude Stein, there is no
"then" there. This is too vague to be an enforceable contract. The court has
managed to transform a perfectly reasonable contract into an unenforceable
gentleman's agreement. Well, maybe it would be enforceable if we hold
that Royster must bargain in good faith. The fact question for the jury, then,
would be the adequacy of the process: Did Royster try hard enough to work
something out? This seems like a pretty dubious path. Even CNC, in its
throw-everything-against-the-wall approach, didn't dare suggest that
Royster had breached their agreement.

A Columbia Nitrogen executive did suggest, probably inadvertently, that
the written word mattered:

Q: Mr. Baker, if this had been your old family partnership that was doing
business with Royster and you were the senior partner at that time, in
the summer of '68, would you have lived up to this contract for your
firm?
A: I wouldn't have had such a contract. That is an academic question, sir.
(Appendix, p. 109)

Well, if the court's interpretation was right, why not?

4. Why This Contract?

There was no discussion of why the parties entered into the contractual
relationship and how this might influence the interpretation of the contract.
A few isolated tidbits in the record shed some light. It seems at least plausible that the length of the contract reflected Royster's concerns about constructing a large new plant that would produce more fertilizer than it
needed for its own use.

To achieve economies of scale, Royster built its plant with a capacity greater than its own captive needs. It was necessary that it find an outlet for the additional phosphate products. As a CNC executive testified: "Well, there was numerous things that was discussed. But relating to the phosphate, the question was brought out that, right out in the open, that they had this surplus phosphate to move. They were going to have to move it for the operation to be successful. They knew that we were sellers in the market." (Appendix, p. 252) Fertilizer is low value, bulky stuff. If it is not removed in timely manner, Royster might find that it would have to curtail production. Other things being equal, the less storage capacity available, the more valuable is the promise of prompt removal. While Royster did indicate that removal was a potential problem, the inventory constraint was not particularly tight. (Appendix, p. 81; Royster Brief, p. 7) In the first thirteen months Columbia took only about 10% of its contractual obligation, and Royster indicated that it still had enough storage space to take two to three more months of production before the storage constraint would force it to suspend production.

Nothing in the record indicated that finding another buyer would be a particularly onerous task, given adequate time. The possibility that inventory accumulation might eventually cause a plant shutdown might be significant, but the record is inadequate. Not only was the inventory constraint fairly loose, but it appears that the fertilizer was the primary output of the plant. This was not an instance in which the failure to remove a waste product meant that production of the primary product might cease, as would be the case with petroleum coke at an oil refinery or stale loaves of bread in a bakery. If market conditions for phosphate fertilizers turned out to be so bad that inventory accumulated for fifteen months, a temporary shutdown might well turn out to be the best response.

Suppose that Royster's ability to hold inventory was drastically reduced, say to one month's accumulation. The written contract would have looked very different. It would likely have been a real take-or-pay contract with a very high take. If the inventory constraint were loosened somewhat, a penalty less than the contract price (like the proposed $10 penalty) might become appropriate. That penalty would, in general, be greater than money damages (although in the actual case measured damages might have exceeded the $10 penalty). The lesser penalty is consistent with Royster having only modest reliance on CNC's taking the fertilizer.

Perhaps the best evidence in the record as to the value to Royster of the three-year contract (and it's not very good evidence) is CNC's statement that Royster's lenders wanted (needed) the commitment. The lenders' only concern would be the downside risk—sales below cost and/or sales below the minimum quantity. These are precisely the conditions for which CNC claimed it had the right to deviate from the written contract. So, if the bankers did indeed care, the contract they would have approved would surely not be the one alleged by CNC.

Of course, we don't know what that alleged contract was or, indeed, whether it was a contract at all. That said, there are two rationales for finding that CNC's obligation in the event of a market price decline was ameliorated. The first is "fairness"—sharing the pain. That raises the symmetry issue: why is there no pain-sharing in an up market? Or is there? Further, if the parties are expected to negotiate a fair outcome, what is the baseline for the negotiations? Fairness is, after all, relative, not absolute. On the assumption that, for at least some contracts, the law would honor the price/quantity choices in the written document, there is nothing in the record to suggest why this industry would choose the pain-sharing option.

There is a possible efficiency rationale, although it does not follow from the custom/usage/course of dealing interpretation. As the case was presented, the issue appears to be who bears the loss if the market price changes, and CNC argues that it should be the seller. If that is all that is at stake, there is no obvious reason to favor buyers rather than sellers. The buyer's loss is the seller's gain and vice versa. But perhaps this is not a zero-sum situation. CNC's task was *distribution* of fertilizer already produced. Royster's was *producing* it. If the market were to deteriorate, as it in fact did, the cost-effective response might well be to curtail production. If that were indeed the case, then the effects of a market change would not be symmetric and it is possible that the contract would allow the buyer to reduce its take. That said, there is no indication that this would be true for this particular contract. It appears that Royster continued to produce fertilizer in the year preceding the contract termination. Moreover, that explanation would be inconsistent with the custom and usage/course of dealing argument, which puts no weight on the seller's role as producer.

One of the potential risks with an open-ended commitment to a reseller, especially one that has more than one source of supply, is that it will take advantage of contract-market differentials, buying a lot (and adding to inventory) when the market price exceeds the contract price, and curtailing purchases (and running down inventory) when the contract price exceeds the market price. The Royster and Agrico contracts illustrate two different ways of capping the seller's obligation. The maximum annual quantity (Agrico and Royster's draft contract) gave the buyer discretion to determine how much it would take up to that limit. The Royster-CNC contract gave CNC the right to ask for any quantity above the minimum and Royster the discretion to decide whether or not it should acquiesce. Royster was obligated to sell, and CNC to buy, the contractual minimum. If either wanted to do less, it had to get the permission of the other. The only thing that the evidence on trade usage showed was that the permission was often forthcoming. Each had a valuable option. It could reduce the other party's obligation and, perhaps, extract something in exchange. Sometimes there was a clear quid pro quo, other times, apparently not. The forgiving party in the latter cases could be investing in reputation or merely enjoying the glow of being a good guy. Taking the written contract seriously made the option more valuable—it gave the party the right to say no.

So, the record does not provide a lot of help in explaining why the parties entered into a three-year minimum quantity contract. It is likely that Royster was more concerned about assuring removal of product than CNC was about assuring supply, but the evidence supporting even that modest statement is thin. What is clear is that the written agreement gave Royster a valuable option. It was that option that the court's opinion undermined.

5. Concluding Remarks

The case settled on June 27, 1972; the terms of the settlement were confidential. Counsel for CNC informed me that the parties continued to do business with each other during the trial and stipulated that the continuance would not be admissible as evidence. My understanding is that CNC continued to buy from Royster post-settlement.

Academic commentary on *Columbia Nitrogen* typically has the Court of Appeals saying that custom and usage/course of dealing showed that express price and quantity terms in the written contract were only fair estimates. (See, for example, Scott 2000, p. 855.) Actually, the court said a little less than that. It held that the trial judge improperly excluded such evidence and remanded. A jury, not the court, would have to determine whether the context altered the written agreement and, if so, how.

If the case on remand had gone to trial, new evidence would have been necessary to ascertain the content of this new contract. Would the custom and usage apply as a condition subsequent only "operable upon the event of a drastic, unpredictable and uncontrollable change," as CNC argued in one of its briefs? (CNC Brief, pp. 33–34) Or does it always apply—could one party insist upon revision if the market price deviated from the contract price by only 1%? Would it apply only for middleman purchasers? Would it apply symmetrically in up as well as down markets? Would it trump penalty, take-or-pay, or requirements clauses? What language, if any, could shield the written terms from the jury's second-guessing?

If the jury can somehow figure out the answer to those questions, what is it to do then? Does it put the warring parties into a locked room and let them out only after they have resolved their dispute? Does it propose or mandate a specific compromise? To what factors does it look in determining whether a contract has been breached and, if so, how it should be remedied?

Indeed, given that the trade practice seems to be that no one takes the written contract seriously, the cleanest resolution of the entire mess would be to declare that there was no contract and therefore CNC owed Royster nothing. If the written contract simply said, "Here are a bunch of estimates of sales and a suggested price, but we will work out both the quantity and price when the time comes," a court would likely throw that out as too vague to be an enforceable agreement. That contract would never reach the jury, yet that seems to be the shape of the contract the court has asked the jury to define.

Fans of *Columbia Nitrogen* treat the case as an enlightened court unearthing the true meaning of an agreement. John Murray (1986, p. 1382, n.260), for example, praises the decision. "One of the better illustrations of a sophisticated judicial understanding of the major modifications of contract law appears in *Columbia Nitrogen Corp. v. Royster Co.* . . . The opinion evidences a clear understanding of the importance of trade usage and prior course of dealing in effecting the parties' factual bargain. It suggests a precocious understanding of the Code parol evidence rule and the necessity of repudiating the 'plain meaning' rule of interpretation. The court is well aware of the anti-technical nature of Article 2 . . . and even displays an early sophistication with respect to 2–207." The real story is darker. Instead, we have the court's ratification of a cynical attempt by CNC's counsel to undo, by whatever means necessary, what had turned out to be a bad bargain. In the process it converted a straightforward agreement into an incoherent mess.

It is not clear to me that anyone other than contracts professors takes

Columbia Nitrogen seriously. So far as I can tell, courts still seem to take price and quantity language as defining the obligations even if parties routinely deviate from the written language. The governance of contractual relationships by two complementary systems—legal enforcement with a rather strict set of rules and social enforcement with informal norms—seems a pretty workable system. The attempt to infer the former from the latter, if not closely cabined, can easily undo the former or hamstring the latter. That is the potential cost of *Columbia Nitrogen.*

CHAPTER 8

The "Battle of the Forms": Fairness, Efficiency, and the Best-Shot Rule

Typically, after the parties agree to a sale, the buyer sends a purchase order with one set of boilerplate terms on the reverse side, and the seller responds with an acknowledgment and invoice with another set of boilerplate terms. Do they have a contract? If so, on what terms? This so-called battle of the forms has given rise to a great outpouring of scholarship and a legislative solution (UCC §2–207) widely perceived as inartfully drafted and generally unsatisfactory. In particular, the Code solution has been criticized because it attempts to solve both the formation and interpretation problems with one rule. The Uniform Commercial Code has recently been revised, although adoption seems unlikely. In the new Code, the two issues have been disentangled. While the revisers' separation of the two issues is laudable, their execution leaves something to be desired. They have failed to address what I perceive to be the primary problem: when designing their forms, the parties have insufficient incentive to take their counterparties' concerns into account.

Most of the commentary fails to recognize the incentive question as a problem. One significant exception is the Baird-Weisberg (1982) analysis, which concludes that the old common law rule—the "mirror-image" rule—induces the parties "to adapt the terms in their forms to the needs and abilities of buyers and sellers in their particular market." (p. 1223) That argument fails for reasons that I spell out in section 1. My proposed solution entails two notions seldom associated with economists: fairness and the Golden Rule ("Do unto others as you would have them do unto you"). I suggest that when interpreting a contract with inconsistent forms, courts should choose the fairer of the two to determine the governing contract terms. I explain in Section 2 why this leads to convergence between the terms of buyers and sellers, how it can be operationalized, and what the golden rule has to do with it.

In a modern economy, there are tremendous advantages to the mass production of contracts in which the inessential terms are boilerplate in forms that go largely unread. Fine tuning contracts to take into account the precise needs of the parties will often be impractical, or at least costly. There is a trade-off between obtaining the scale economies of standard forms and customizing the language to the particular needs of the parties.

The Code provides a set of default terms that will be read into all transactions with inconsistent standard terms. To avoid this outcome, the parties would have to sacrifice the economies of the standard form and particularize the transaction, by adopting master agreements, bargaining over the specific terms, or otherwise manifesting assent to those terms. If the Code default rules are generally thought desirable, then this resolution of the trade-off is not particularly onerous. Indeed, Murray (1994), one of the current law's more vocal critics, proposed an even stronger rule: The Code's terms are a desirable starting point, and if a seller wants to propose deviant terms—for example, warranty disclaimers, limitations or exclusions of various damages such as consequential damages, and arbitration clauses—then the burden is on the seller to prove the buyer's assent to the deviant terms.

I have less faith in the Code default rules. If parties had the time to bargain intelligently over these rules, I believe that they would generally choose not to compensate consequential damages, or that they would at least limit such damages to a modest multiple of the contract price. I spell out my reasons for that in Chapters 13 and 14. Of course, I might just be wrong. Nevertheless, this predilection leads me to a somewhat different resolution of the trade-off that would permit the parties to contract out of the default rules while at the same time obtaining the economies of standardization. It would induce parties to take the concerns of their potential counterparties seriously when it matters—when legal resources are being concentrated on the problem. I must emphasize that the solution is an imperfect one and that its purpose is to salvage some of the benefits of standardization and the mass production of forms while still giving the parties at least some incentive to get it right.

1. Of Mirror Images, First Shots, Last Shots, Etc.

If a seller has promised to deliver goods at a particular price and the market price subsequently rises, that seller has an incentive to find a reason not to perform. Discrepant language in the forms of buyer and seller could provide such a reason. Because the terms are not identical, the parties have failed to agree; there is no contract, and the seller can walk away without legal liability. The "mirror-image" rule, which, taken literally, requires that the terms of the offer and acceptance be identical, facilitates the opportunistic invocation of nonidentical language in forms to avoid performance of an onerous contract. In practice, courts have adopted a number of doctrines to soften that rule. See Farnsworth (2004, §3.21) and Baird and Weisberg (1982, p. 1222). The Code has made it less likely that a party could use nonidentical forms to escape a bad deal. I presume that the existence question has been resolved and focus on determination of content. The seller delivered goods, the buyer accepted them, and then a dispute arose. Their behavior indicates that they had a contract, but the content of that contract is unclear since the parties had forms with inconsistent language.

Under the mirror-image rule, the dickered terms (price, quantity, etc.) and the terms of the buyer's purchase order constitute an offer. If the seller returns an acknowledgment form with identical terms, those terms define the contract. If, however, the seller's boilerplate terms differ, then a court could find an acceptance with insubstantial differences (hence, the buyer's terms prevail), an acceptance with suggested modifications (the buyer's terms would again prevail, since the buyer's silence is interpreted as rejection of the proffered modifications), or a counteroffer. If it is a counteroffer and the buyer accepts the goods without objecting to the seller's terms, then the contract is defined by the seller's terms. The parties have an incentive to jockey for position so that theirs is the last shot. The key feature of the mirror image rule is that only one party can be deemed the offeror, and the offeror's terms control. In practice, the commentary suggests that the last shot is typically fired by the seller. (See Farnsworth 2004, §3.21a.)

The UCC §2–207 changed this rule, although there was considerable dispute as to what was put in its place. That dispute has been resolved in the revised Code with the adoption of the "knockout" rule, which had already become the majority rule. If the parties' boilerplate terms conflict, the discrepant terms knock each other out and the Code term is substituted. If, as the commentators argue, the gap fillers are skewed in favor of buyers, then UCC §2–207 tends to impose buyers' terms. See Farnsworth (2004, §3.21a) and Baird and Weisberg (1982). Sellers could try to avoid this outcome by including language in their forms which expressly limits the acceptance to the terms of their offer, although courts have not been inclined to give these expressions much weight. See, for example, *Diamond Fruit*

Growers, Inc. v. Krack Corp., in which the court disregarded such a statement even though the parties had actually discussed the particular term, a disclaimer of liability, and the seller had rejected the buyer's efforts to remove that term from their contract.

The knockout rule produces some anomalous results, knocking out terms that would yield the same result in a particular case and replacing them with a default rule yielding a different outcome. Thus, consider the following from an early draft of the revised Code:

> Suppose the standard form records of both parties contained arbitration clauses which differ in material ways. For example, Buyer's clause might agree to arbitrate "all disputes arising out of or relating to" the contract and Seller's clause might agree to arbitrate only disputes "involving breach of warranty claims." Here the terms vary. Under §2–207(a)(2) neither clause becomes part of the contract. The "knock out rule" is in effect. The parties are left with the usual default rules.
>
> On the other hand, if the form records contained arbitration clauses which agreed in substance, the parties must arbitrate to the extent of that agreement. (November 1, 1996, Draft, Illustration E(4), p. 32)

If the dispute related to a breach of warranty claim, both forms would have resulted in arbitration, but the net result of the knockout rule is that the default rule—no arbitration—would apply. The Code revisers stated quite clearly that the question of whether the terms vary sufficiently must be answered prior to asking whether their variation would be relevant to the particular dispute. A court could, perhaps, determine that since either clause would have required arbitration, the clauses are not sufficiently different for this particular purpose. That sensible result is at odds with the revisers' language.

When drafting boilerplate language under the knockout rule, the parties have no incentive to take the interests of their opposites into account. As Murray (1986, p. 1373) suggests, the forms "are designed by their drafters to use the latest weaponry in a surreptitious fashion to win the battle of the forms." If the party is lucky, its terms will govern; if unlucky, the worst that can happen is that the Code default rules will govern. There is no cost to a seller (or a buyer) from adding increasingly one-sided terms to its standard forms, save the possibility that someone will actually read the fine print and refuse to transact on the objectionable terms.

While the costs of producing a one-sided form are low, are there any benefits? If the Code default rules will prevail, why would a seller even bother to produce a self-serving form that courts would ignore when interpreting the contract? The answer is that in some subset of transactions, the seller's terms might prevail. Litigation might take place in a jurisdiction that does not follow the knockout rule. Or the buyer might fail to return a form, either because it does not issue forms for such transactions at all or because its delivery of the form was not timely—performance preceded dispatch of the form. (See, e.g., *Harlow Jones, Inc. v. Advance Steel Co.*) In such a case, there is no battle, and the seller's form would govern. Or the court might accept the expressly conditional language in one of the forms and convert the form into a counteroffer accepted by performance with the original offeror's form being read out of the transaction. (See, e.g., *Salt River Project Agricultural Improvement and Power District v. Westinghouse Electric Corp.*) Seller's counsel would be rewarded, not for bringing the parties closer together, but for producing creative language which increased the likelihood that its terms, rather than the Code's default rules, would define the contract.

The problem with the knockout rule is that it fails to induce the parties to provide an honest indication of their willingness to deviate from the Code terms, unless they are willing to forego the convenience of exchanging mass-produced, unread forms. As Baird and Weisberg (1982, p. 1256) argue: "A standard that allows a court to substitute general off-the-rack terms for fine print cannot at the same time give the parties an incentive to draft forms in their mutual interest. The more the off-the-rack terms control, the less the fine print matters, both to the courts and to the parties themselves." In describing the virtues of a return to the mirror-image rule, Baird and Weisberg argue that it would overcome this nonrevelation problem: "Under the mirror-image rule . . . each party, in designing its form for a particular type of transaction, has an incentive to hypothesize the terms that the parties would have settled upon had they dickered over them." (p. 1257) Nonreaders of forms would be protected by the efforts of the few who read them. Market discipline, they suggest, would prevent the seller from making its form too one-sided. The seller would recognize that at least some buyers would be careful enough to read the forms and that if the forms were too biased in the seller's favor, the buyer would walk away. "Indeed, the mirror-image rule, compared to other possible approaches, takes maximum advantage of these market forces. It makes printed forms matter more by encouraging or even forcing parties receiving documents to read them more carefully. The rule thereby encourages parties sending documents to make them attractive to their intended recipients." (p. 1255)

I am skeptical. First, suppose that some buyers actually would be induced to read the sellers' mass-produced documents more carefully. It is far from clear that inducing such behavior would be socially useful. Maintaining lawyers on the loading docks is not cheap. The advantage of standardized transactions is that the lawyering is concentrated on the drafting of documents and the costs spread over a large number of similar transactions. These benefits are dissipated if the rules induce some parties to expend resources scrutinizing boilerplate language. Thus, even if the Baird-Weisberg marginal buyer's scrutiny does police the seller's self-serving drafting (which it probably does not), it does so by sacrificing some of the economies of standardization. Second, suppose that a buyer does read the form and finds a term it does not like. What happens next? The parties could negotiate over the contested term, taking the transaction out of the battle of forms context. Or the buyer could accept the terms on the presumption (or perhaps even the salesman's assurance) that the offensive terms would not apply to this transaction (the terms are only there to deal with the bad guys). In neither case does the seller who accedes to the concerns of the reluctant buyer find it necessary to change the language in the form. The marginal buyers who care enough can be accommodated while the basic form remains unchanged. Baird and Weisberg must rely on buyers who would find the terms offensive enough to refuse, yet still not worth fighting over.

Third, and most important, if the Baird-Weisberg argument is correct, it should be symmetric. If the marginal buyer could police seller's terms under the mirror-image rule, then the marginal seller could just as easily influence the buyer's terms under the knockout rule. The results should be the same neutral, mutually beneficial terms under either rule. There is no reason to believe that the occasional scrutiny given to buyer's forms by sellers would be any less efficacious. Indeed, rational sellers need not even bother with forms incorporating their boilerplate. Buyers would design their forms to be attractive to sellers. If the seller's language were identical to the buyer's, it would be redundant. If not, the knockout rule applies and the parties are stuck with the Code default rules. But if sellers really believed that the Baird-Weisberg market mechanism worked, they would find that by producing a document they risked undoing the buyer's terms—presumably sellers would prefer the buyer's "attractive" terms to the Code's default rules. Rational sellers would, therefore, issue no forms. There would be no battle, the buyer's form would govern, and sellers would be content. Not credible.

The Baird-Weisberg market discipline stems from the seller's concern that some fraction of his potential customers will read the form, and if it is unreasonable, go elsewhere. They ignore the converse. There are a lot of potential buyers who will rationally choose not to subject the boilerplate to intense, or even casual, scrutiny. Some sellers will, à la Baird and Weisberg, temper their terms for fear of losing a deal. Others will presume that the random buyer they run into will not have read the form and that by stacking the deck the seller can perhaps gain more from the nonreaders than it loses to the readers. The rational buyer who does not carefully parse sellers' forms might plausibly believe that the seller has chosen the self-serving form route. That is, after all, what sellers believe buyers would do under the knockout rule. If they believe that, one plausible response is to draft defensively, which is cheaper than reading defensively. It is not inevitable that the noncooperative strategy would dominate. But that seems the more plausible outcome of a game in which players expect only a small fraction of their counterparts to read the terms of their forms.

In sum, competition between either buyers or sellers on the terms of their standardized forms is unlikely to induce either party to eschew self-serving language in their forms under either the mirror image or knockout rule. The lawyer drafts language in a vacuum with virtually no incentive to consider the concerns of the other side. What is needed is a mechanism that would bring the counterparties' concerns to the lawyer's attention at the moment at which the standardized form is being produced.

2. The Best-Shot Rule

Suppose two parties are trying to determine the price of an asset one is attempting to sell to the other. One possible device is final offer arbitration. Each side proposes a price and a third party chooses one or the other. It does not compromise—it only has the two alternatives. The seller recognizes that if it gets too greedy, the probability that the arbitrator will choose its price declines. Likewise, the buyer. Each must temper its final offer lest it end up with the other party's bid setting the price. If we can imagine the possible bids as being located along a line with the high numbers on the right, the seller would want to move as far to the right as possible and the buyer to the left. However, they are drawn by the decision rule toward the center.

My proposed mechanism is a variation on final-offer arbitration. When confronted with two nonconforming forms, the court must choose only one to govern the transaction. Which one? The one that it perceives to be the fairer of the two (the one closest to the "center"). The court looks neither to the first shot nor the last shot; it looks to the *best shot*. Leaving aside for the moment the question of how we determine fairness, this has the same basic structure as final-offer arbitration. If either side tries to tilt its offer too much in its own favor, it risks having its entire set of terms disregarded. Each side has an incentive to move toward the center. The only difference is that when everything is measured in a single unit—dollars—it is easier to ascertain where the center is.

While it might seem paradoxical to have the court's treatment of an arbitration clause turn on the respective treatment in the two forms of unrelated terms, say, the disclaimer of consequential damages, the all-or-nothing approach is essential. The more terms considered at the same time, the easier it will be to judge the overall reasonableness of the package. Moreover, when drafting, a seller will have an incentive to make trade-offs between terms depending on which it perceives to be the most important. If limitations on the warranty period are extremely important to a seller, then it can include them, but give up on some other features; if they are sufficiently important, of course, they can be lifted out of the boilerplate entirely.

Operationalizing fairness will not be easy. If the Code's default terms were taken as prima facie fair, then this proposal might have minimal impact. If, as many claim, the Code rules favor buyers, the buyers would never have an incentive to move toward the sellers; indeed, they might be induced to take an even more extreme position.

But we can do better. One source of evidence on fairness is the behavior of the parties. Specifically, as noted earlier, I propose that the courts give serious weight to the Golden Rule. That is, since firms are often both buyers and sellers, the standard forms the parties use when they are on the other side of transactions should be taken as evidence of what they perceive to be fair. If a firm's forms disclaimed liability when it acted as a seller, but rejected disclaimers when it acted as a buyer, this should weigh heavily against the firm when determining whether its form or its counterpart's would win. Thus, lawyers drafting standardized forms for a client would, in effect, be bargaining with an informed party—themselves. It is easy to add a consequential damage disclaimer to a form if your client is always a seller selling to anonymous future buyers who can't talk back and will not bother to read the form. If the client is also a buyer and the clause would prevent it from recovering, then the lawyer has to weigh the merits of the disclaimer at the one point in time when it actually makes sense for the lawyer to give the problem careful attention.

Implementation of the Golden Rule presents a number of difficulties. Most importantly, it might result in a one-size-fits-all approach. It might turn out, for instance, that under the circumstances a particular firm should have very different terms when it is a seller rather than a buyer. Yet it might be difficult to make that argument credible in the litigation context. Of course, that is precisely the problem with the Code's default rules. If the Golden Rule does result in a single standard, at least that standard would be generated by counsel with a direct stake in the outcome rather than by drafters of a statute. Sympathetic interpretation should give counsel drafting forms some leeway to vary terms depending on context. Firms might maintain a portfolio of forms and match them to particular contexts.

Of course, that will raise another set of problems. If a firm has, say, half a dozen different purchase orders, which should be used when applying the Golden Rule? Should the court look to the most used form (by number of transactions or by dollar value)? Should it look to all, and, if so, what weights should be attached to the different forms? Will sellers have incentives to produce purchase orders for litigation purposes only? Should the seller in one division or subsidiary be constrained by the purchase orders from its corporate relatives?

It is conceivable that problems of this sort will overwhelm the Golden Rule, but I think not. A seller might be able to convince a court that the only purchase order in its portfolio that limits consequential damages is indeed the only one relevant to this particular transaction. But that will not be an easy argument to make. The Golden Rule in essence requires litigants to justify deviations between the standardized form at issue in the particular dispute with the form or forms it would use when on the opposite side of the transaction.

At first blush, it would appear that the best shot rule would be more expensive to litigate and would provide less certain outcomes. If the terms of the two forms are clearly at odds, and if neither form made assent conditional, then the knockout rule easily wins on the certainty issue. Neither contract governs, and the Code's default rules apply (unless course of dealing or trade practice suggests otherwise). I will suggest below that the knockout rule's superiority with regard to litigation costs, even under these ideal conditions, is less clear. For the moment I want to focus on certainty, because in some circumstances the knockout rule both increases uncertainty and leads to a result that neither party desired at the formation stage. Recall the arbitration illustration discussed above. Under a best shot rule, the dispute would clearly be arbitrable. Under the knockout rule, a court would have to determine whether the two "arbitration clauses . . . agreed in substance." Both parties wanted arbitration at the formation stage; under the knockout rule, one party might have the ability to renege if it can show a large enough difference in the terms.

Similar problems might arise with regard to liability limitations. Consider the following clauses:

Seller: No claim of any kind, whether as to products (or materials) delivered or for non-delivery of products, and whether or not based on negligence, shall be greater in amount than the purchase price of the products in respect of which damages are claimed; and failure to give notice of claim within ninety (90) days from date of delivery, shall constitute a waiver by Buyer of all claims in respect of such products. No change or expense incident to any claims will be allowed unless approved by an authorized representative of Seller. Products shall not be returned to Seller without Seller's prior permission, and then only in the manner prescribed by Seller. The remedy hereby provided shall be the exclusive and sole remedy of Buyer, and in no event shall either party be liable for special, indirect or consequential damages, whether or not caused by or resulting from the negligence of such party.

Buyer: A) Should any goods, other than equipment, fail to conform with the express warranties, Seller's sole liability and Buyer's sole remedies shall be as follows: Seller shall replace the non-conforming goods promptly following Buyer's notification or, at Buyer's option, refund the purchase price. Seller also shall reimburse Buyer for any costs incurred by Buyer to remove, store, transport or dispose of non-conforming goods. Seller shall, however, have no liability under this Paragraph A if Buyer fails to notify Seller of non-conformance (i) within 90 days after date of delivery; or (ii) if the non-conformance is not reasonably discoverable within that time, then within 90 days after date on which the non-conformance was or should have been discovered.

B) All equipment shall conform with the express warranties and for 12 months from date of installation but no more than 18 months from date of shipment. Seller shall repair or replace any non-conforming equipment promptly after Buyer's notification or, at Buyer's option refund the purchase price. Seller shall also reimburse Buyer for (i) any costs incurred by Buyer to remove, store, transport or dispose of non-conforming equipment and to install repaired or replaced equipment, and (ii) any resulting costs incurred by Buyer for the standby charges of Buyer's other contractors up to a maximum of the Order value.

C) To the extent permitted by law, neither party shall be liable to the other for any special, consequential or punitive damages, even if caused by negligence, willful misconduct or breach of contract.

The terms do not differ by much; is the difference large enough so that the buyer could claim that the terms knock each other out so that it might recover consequential damages? Variations on these clauses would make it even harder for the damage limitation to survive the knockout rule despite the obvious intent of buyers to forego the Code's default remedies. Interestingly, both terms are DuPont's. Thomas McCarthy, DuPont's corporate counsel and chair of the American Bar Association's Task Force on the Article 2 Revision, graciously provided me with DuPont's standard forms. Contrary to the conventional wisdom, DuPont did not stack the deck in its favor; it would likely be content as a seller living with its purchase form and as a buyer with its standard conditions of sale. The warranty terms also were similar, with enough variation that a court could choose to knock out both:

Seller: Seller warrants that the products (or materials) delivered hereunder meet Seller's standard specifications for the products or such other specifications as may have been expressly agreed to herein. Buyer assumes all risk and liability resulting from use of the products delivered hereunder, whether used singly or in combination with other products.

Buyer: Seller warrants good materials and workmanship, merchantability, and compliance with the following with respect to any goods sold hereunder: Seller's product literature and all referenced or attached specifications, drawings, samples and information.

For many cases, to be sure, the knockout rule will be clear (the terms conflict, therefore go directly to the default rules) compared to the fairness test of the best-shot rule. The more predictable the rule, other things being equal, the less costly it would be to litigate. Other things are not equal, however. If the best shot rule works properly, the forms of the parties should be less divergent. The stakes should, therefore, be smaller. The smaller the stakes, the less parties should be willing to spend on litigating a dispute. This second factor is probably not enough to offset the first, although I suggest below a slight variation on this theme that makes complete offset more likely.

The certainty of the knockout rule is undermined if a party can interject uncertainty with regard to the assent. It is not at all obvious that the conspicuousness of the conditional assent clause would be any less fuzzy than the fairness of the form. Under the best-shot rule, a court would not have to agonize over whether language in one party's form making assent conditional were sufficiently conspicuous. Such a clause would be lumped with the rest in a fairness inquiry and would, most likely, count against the drafter. This does not, of course, preclude a party from making assent conditional; it just means that it would have to be done out in the open.

Forms drafted by trade associations for commodities like grains and coffee are drafted in a forum that enables buyers and sellers (often the same people) to weigh the merits of the boilerplate terms; my understanding is that they typically do not allow recovery for consequential damages. That provides at least some indirect evidence that the best-shot rule would result in parties limiting consequential damages. Under the knockout rule (modified or not) those damages would likely be recoverable. The best-shot rule could, therefore, have two dampening effects on litigation costs: the stakes would be smaller and the costs of ascertaining the consequential damages could be avoided. Economizing on litigation costs is a legitimate concern of parties structuring their contractual relations. To the extent that the best-shot rule enables them to fine-tune their agreements, it would permit them to avoid default rules that might result in increased litigation costs. It is, therefore, hardly inevitable that the best-shot rule would be more expensive to litigate than the alternatives.

If the cost of litigation were really a high-priority item for the Code's drafters, they could, as the preceding paragraph suggests, have dealt with it more directly by choosing default rules that were less litigation-prone. Their proposal reflects a choice. Altering the default rules by standard form language will be very difficult. If sellers do not like this, they will have to sacrifice the advantages of the standard form. The best-shot rule, unlike the Code (present or revised), gives at least some attention to the crucial question: How might we obtain the benefits of mass production of boilerplate terms while giving the parties the incentive to draft with the concerns of their counterparty in mind.

PART IV

Remedies

Contract remedies should be viewed as a subset of contract interpretation. That is, it often will be helpful (and sometimes dispositive) to ask: What remedies would reasonable people have included in their contract? Or the converse might even be more revealing: Could reasonable people possibly have meant to impose this remedy? Would a buyer agree that in the event that it cancels an order it would be liable for 75% of the contract price? Would a middleman grant a seller an option to sell goods at the contract price if the market price had fallen? Would a provider of a service give unlimited insurance against consequential damages to a buyer? The remedy should be viewed as one term in the contract, and when considering various outcomes we should ask which of the alternative constructions would make the most sense. I do not, of course, propose that courts do so on a case by case basis; rather, the principle should guide the legal interpretation. As Oliver Wendell Holmes wrote a century ago:

> [A]s the contract is by mutual consent, the parties themselves, expressly or by implication, fix the rule by which the damages are to be measured. . . . If a contract is broken . . . [w]e have to consider . . . what the plaintiff would have been entitled to recover in that case, and that depends on what liability the defendant fairly may be supposed to have assumed consciously, or to have warranted the plaintiff reasonably to suppose that it assumed, when the contract was made. (*Globe Refining Company v. Landa Cotton Oil Company*, p. 541)

I confess to some surprise that this rather innocuous formulation should be viewed as controversial, or even discredited. Thus, Farnsworth (2004, §12.14) observed: "The underlying concept of damages as somehow based on agreement between the parties has not prevailed, however. The 'tacit agreement' test has been generally rejected as overly restrictive and doctrinally unsound, and it is explicitly condemned in the comments to the Uniform Commercial Code." The decoupling of damage measurement from the economic sense of the agreement has produced some unfortunate doctrine.

In previous chapters, especially Chapter 5, I have emphasized the notion that one party to a contract will often be given the discretion to adapt as new information becomes available, and that the contract will sometimes confront that party with a price reflecting the interests of the other party. The deliberate termination of an agreement is a special case of this adaptive change, and contract remedies can be viewed as default rules for determining a price for the exercise of the termination option. The standard refrain is that contract remedies should protect the injured party's expectation interest by putting it in as good a position as if the contract had been performed. This framing of the problem seems natural, but it is the wrong question. Once we reframe the matter as one of contractual design, the tripartite classification of expectation, reliance, and restitution, drilled into first-year law students, loses much of its charm. Is being made whole something the injured party would have wanted, ex ante? Sometimes yes, sometimes no.

My discontent with the rhetoric of the expectation remedy is not entirely idiosyncratic. Scott and Triantis (2004) arrive at the same conclusion by a somewhat different route. My conjecture is that the roots of the casual acceptance of the expectation remedy can be traced to a number of sources. The first is that for the paradigmatic contract case of a commodity purchase in which one party refuses to go forward because the market price has changed, the expectation remedy—the contract-market differential—is the right remedy. Moreover, the rhetoric of making the victim whole is consistent with the damage remedy in tort (although Issacharoff and Witt (2004) suggest that in practice the tort remedy doesn't work quite that way). The mischief comes when we start deviating from the simple commodity contract. To some degree, the potential problems were cabined by doctrines that made it difficult to go much beyond the contract-market differential, for example, certainty and foreseeability. As these doctrinal constraints have been relaxed, the problems with the expectations rhetoric have become apparent.

A strong argument can be made for protecting what I label the narrow expectation interest, the contract-market differential. I develop that argument in the context of a specific question: Why enforce a purely executory contract on which no one has relied? The answer: to protect property in price. I expand on this somewhat cryptic phrase and develop its implications in Chapter 10. Some courts and commentators have been confused by an apparent conflict in the UCC. If a middleman charges a fixed fee for its services and the seller breaches after the market price soars, what should the middleman's damages be? The market-contract differential would appear to overcompensate, since the middleman expected to receive only the fixed fee. In Chapter 11, I show why, properly understood, the appearance is deceiving, there is no conflict, and the market-contract differential is indeed the proper remedy.

The expectation interest concerns more than the market-contract differential. Here is where trouble arises. I focus on two categories of damages: the lost profits of the so-called lost-volume seller and consequential damages. In the former (Chapter 12), the debate concerns whether a buyer's cancellation of an order would result in the seller selling one less unit, thereby losing the "profit" it would have earned on that additional unit. Regardless of whether or not the answer is yes, it is logically separable from the question of what the appropriate remedy should be. I argue that conflating the two questions has been a mistake.

Holding a seller liable for consequential damages is equivalent to making it an insurer, but without the insurer's tools for dealing with the problems of adverse selection and moral hazard. Since in the long run sellers must cover their costs, buyers as a group pay for that insurance. That makes me skeptical about whether buyers would be willing to pay for including a consequential damages remedy in their contracts. My impression is that doctrine has been evolving in the wrong direction, liberalizing the conditions that would allow a buyer to recover consequentials and raising the barriers to contractual limitations on the remedy. Chapter 13 is a brief note introducing the topic. In Chapter 14, I come at the issue of consequential damages from an oblique angle, considering the liability in contract or tort of inspectors, surveyors, weighers, certifiers, and similar intermediaries for unworkmanlike or negligent performance. If faulty weighing resulted in a buyer getting too little, the default rule is restitution—the seller must compensate the buyer; however, parties typically contract around the default, and courts usually uphold their agreement. The intermediaries often contract out of liability as well; however, courts generally reject their damage limitations, although they will sometimes find another doctrinal hook to reject the claim.

A recurring debate in the literature on contract remedies concerns the relative virtues of damages versus specific performance. I don't intend to take on the whole question. Instead I will focus on a single case that highlights a ground for granting specific performance that has not, as far as I know, been articulated. I will open Part IV with analysis of *Campbell Soup v. Wentz,* a case that was decided, wrongly, on the ground of unconscionability. The court held that but for the unconscionable clause it would have granted specific performance because of the uniqueness of the subject matter. I will show that the uniqueness argument, which appears plausible on its face, fails. I propose an alternative rationale for awarding specific performance, one that recognizes that under a full output contract the grower has an incentive to cheat.

CHAPTER 9

Campbell v. Wentz:
The Case of the Walking Carrots

The prominence of *Campbell v. Wentz* stems from the eminence of its author (Herbert Goodrich, a former director of the American Law Institute) and its invocation in the *Restatements* (§208, Illustration 1 and §364, Illustration 5), the *UCC* (§302, Comment 1), and *Williams v. Walker Thomas,* one of the great casebook favorites. In a nutshell, Judge Goodrich ruled that the uniqueness of the subject matter of the contract, Chantenay red-cored carrots, would have justified granting Campbell's request for specific performance. However, the harshness of Campbell's standard form contract rendered it unconscionable and, therefore, a court of equity need not enforce the agreement. I want to make two points. First, the unconscionability finding is based on a misunderstanding of the contract. Second, while the stated basis for specific performance was the uniqueness of the carrots, that is not the essential reason that Campbell (and other canners and packers) want specific performance; indeed, as the defendants observed, Campbell's behavior was inconsistent with that explanation. Instead, I believe their concern is with the enforceability of a full output contract—what might be labeled the "walking carrot" problem.

The Campbell Soup Company had contracts with growers of eleven different types of vegetables in seventeen different states. (Campbell Petition for Rehearing, p. 5) It bought some of its needs on the spot market, and some in fixed price contracts at the beginning of the growing season. The record does not indicate the breakdown between contract and open market purchases in a normal year. In the 1947–48 season, in which there was a severe shortage, only one third of the carrots were contract carrots. Campbell's contracts were similar to those of other food processors. The manager of Campbell's agricultural department testified:

207

Q: And do you familiarize yourself, or are you familiar with the type of contracts that other canning houses use, like Phillips, and Hurff and Heinz and so forth?

A: I am.

Q: Can you tell us whether the provisions of the Campbell Soup contract, particularly with respect to the agreement of the grower not to sell the contracted vegetables to anyone else than Campbell Soup Company is common to contracts used by these other canners?

A: To the best of my knowledge it is. (Appendix to Campbell Brief, p. 79a)

However, the trial judge was not interested in looking at any other contracts than the one at issue: "If it is a valid contract, I do not care what the policy of the other companies is. I have to interpret this contract." (Appendix to Campbell Brief, p. 89a)

The dispute arose in one of these seasonal contracts. Campbell would buy the entire crop of the grower (up to a maximum per acre). For at least some of the produce, including the carrots at issue in this case, Campbell provided the seeds to the farmers or, in the case of tomatoes, plants. It normally purchased about 30 million pounds of Chantenay carrots in a season. (Campbell Brief, p. 17) In June 1947 it entered into a full output, fixed-price contract with the Wentz brothers for all the Chantenay red cored carrots grown on fifteen acres of their farm in the growing season of 1947–48. Campbell reserved the right to refuse carrots in excess of twelve tons per acre. So, the Wentz carrots would account for a bit over 1% of its expected Chantenay carrot purchases. The Wentz farm was 500–600 acres, and the Wentzes had been selling tomatoes to Campbell for a decade; on two previous occasions they had contracted to sell carrots to Campbell. It appears that the Wentzes, like other growers, went back and forth between selling under contract and selling to the spot market. It should be noted that tomatoes were a more significant input for Campbell. Its capacity for handling tomatoes during the two month packing season was more than 250,000 ⅝-bushel baskets of tomatoes per day. (*Campbell Soup Co. v. Diehm*, p. 212)

The contract price for carrots to be delivered in January 1948 was $30 per ton. Bad weather reduced the size of the crop and, according to the court, Chantenay red-cored carrots were selling for at least $90 per ton and were virtually unobtainable, a statement which, to economists, is like fingernails on the blackboard. This sort of shortage was not unusual—four years earlier carrot prices had jumped to $60 per ton. (Appendix to Campbell Brief, p. 70a) The Wentz brothers harvested approximately 100 tons of carrots, but refused to deliver at the contract price. Instead they sold sixty-two tons to Lojeski, a neighboring farmer. (In the previous year, when the Wentz brothers did not have a Campbell contract, they sold all their carrots to Lojeski.) Lojeski resold fifty-eight tons on the open market, about half to Campbell. Campbell, suspecting it was buying its own contract carrots, refused to buy more from Lojeski and sued to enjoin Wentz and Lojeski to prevent further sales to others and to compel specific performance of the contract.

The trial court denied specific performance, concluding that Campbell had failed to establish that the contract carrots were unique. Recognizing that the carrots were a perishable commodity and that lifting its temporary restraining order might make an appeal moot, the court gave the defendants an option. Either they could post a bond ($5,000 for Wentz and $600 for Lojeski, which works out to almost $150 per ton for the carrots remaining with Wentz) or they could sell the remaining carrots to Campbell at the prevailing market price, with $30 per ton going to Wentz and the remainder to be paid into the court awaiting a determination on appeal as to whether Campbell was entitled to specific performance. Of course, if the Appellate Court were to find (as it did) that Campbell was not entitled to injunctive relief, then Campbell could still collect money damages; the damages during the period in which Wentz was required to sell to Campbell would be the contract-market differential, which was what Campbell had been paying into the court. If Lojeski could have sold the carrots elsewhere, then Campbell would have argued for a different remedy, which I will get to shortly. But given the perishability of carrots, the court's stopgap measure assured that Campbell would receive the carrots, so that the only damages would be the market-contract differential.

On appeal, Judge Goodrich found that the carrots were unique. He cited the lower court's finding of fact (#19) that at the time of the trial it was "virtually impossible to obtain Chantenay carrots in the open market." The Chantenay carrot was distinguishable from other carrots in terms of its shape (easier to process), color, and texture. Chantenay carrots were used in fifteen of Campbell's twenty-one soup varieties. "The preservation of uniformity in appearance in a food article marketed throughout the country and sold under the manufacturer's name is a matter of considerable commercial significance and one which is properly considered in determining whether a substitute ingredient is just as good as the original." (*Campbell v. Wentz*, p. 82) That conclusion would have justified his granting specific performance.

However, he declined to do so, finding the contract unconscionable. While Judge Goodrich noted a few clauses that might have been some cause for concern, the clause he found harshest was the force majeure clause, in particular the last two sentences:

> Grower shall not be obligated to deliver any Carrots which he is unable to harvest or deliver, nor shall Campbell be obligated to receive or pay for any Carrots which it is unable to inspect, grade, receive, handle, use or pack at or ship in processed form from its plants in Camden (1) because of any circumstance beyond the control of Grower or Campbell, as the case may be, or (2) because of any labor disturbance, work stoppage, slowdown, or strike involving any of Campbell's employees. Campbell shall not be liable for any delay in receiving Carrots due to any of the above contingencies. *During periods when Campbell is unable to receive Grower's Carrots, Grower may with Campbell's written consent, dispose of his Carrots elsewhere. Grower may not, however, sell or otherwise dispose of any Carrots which he is unable to deliver to Campbell.* (Emphasis added) (*Campbell v. Wentz*, p. 83)

This last the judge characterized as "carrying a good joke too far." That's the extent of his analysis. Properly understood, it's not that funny. If, because of force majeure conditions, Campbell is temporarily prevented from taking the carrots, Campbell does not want to allow those carrots to disappear. When the force majeure condition ends, Campbell might be able to accept the carrots, processing them at a higher rate. As long as Campbell believes that it might be able to use the carrots, it requires that the grower keep them available. When it finally determines that it cannot use them, it gives to the grower its written consent to resell elsewhere. Does the contract require that it give this consent? No. Does good business judgment? Yes. Perhaps the grower might suffer a bit while waiting as the carrots deteriorate. But Campbell wants the flexibility to gain access to the carrots in the event that the business disruption proves temporary, and it must pay for that flexibility in the initial price. If the gains from Campbell's flexibility outweigh the expected costs of the grower's being stuck with unsold carrots, then giving Campbell the option would be the efficient and sensible thing to do.

With its full output contracts, Campbell shifts some of its inventory risks to the growers. If Campbell waits too long under the force majeure clause, the carrots rot in the farmer's field. In fact, I suspect that the farmers were more concerned about being stuck with rotting carrots from a different Campbell decision. Campbell could reject carrots on quality grounds (notably "excessive dirt") when the contract price exceeded the market price. Wentz and two of his witnesses made this point. (Opportunism works both ways: there was some evidence that when the market price exceeded the contract price, a grower would deliberately turn in dirty carrots, have them rejected, and then sell them at a premium in the open market.) (Appendix to Campbell Brief, p. 122a) Campbell denied that it behaved this way and asserted that the percentage of carrots rejected remained fairly constant in good times and bad. The scant record provides no data on this, but suppose that the growers' claim is true. Campbell cannot costlessly shift the risk of rotting carrots—it has to pay the growers to bear it. Growers know that a fraction of their crop will be unsaleable; that is captured in the price. If the growers are the superior risk bearers, then ex ante they should be happy to bear the costs (and ex post we would expect them to be quite grumpy). My guess is that the cost to growers of bearing this risk would be extremely low.

Was the "unconscionable" clause essential to Campbell? Hardly. Right after the decision Campbell redrafted its standard contract, eliminating the offending clause and a few others cited by Judge Goodrich (but probably not, I would guess, the offending behavior). With the contract thus sanitized, courts had no trouble granting Campbell and others specific performance in similar circumstances. *American Law Reports* notes that the courts' willingness to grant specific performance to processors is the one factor distinguishing the legal treatment of grower-processor contracts from other contracts for the sale of goods: "[P]erhaps this is one instance where the nature of the contractual relationship between a grower and a purchasing processor, packer, or canner has brought about a set of rules and principles especially applicable to such relationship, with a tendency in favor of granting equitable relief because of such factors as the perishable character of the property involved, the peculiar needs of the processor, packer, or canner, and the shortness of growing seasons." (Lind 1963, 732 §27)

A few years after *Wentz*, Campbell sought specific performance against some farmers (and brokers) for delivery of tomatoes after the market price rose from $30 per ton to $50. *(Campbell Soup Co. v. Diehm)* The court rejected the unconscionability argument, noting that the offending terms had been removed. It went on at some length about the importance of performance:

> The Campbell Soup Company's production of these tomato products is in accordance with a carefully devised schedule, based upon a steady flow of tomatoes of certain kinds and qualities. The Campbell Soup Company, in order to secure the desired quantity of tomatoes at fixed prices and in a steady flow of the desired qualities, necessary to assure uniformity of quality and price in the finished product, contracts with . . . growers in Pennsylvania, Delaware and Maryland, and . . . New Jersey. These contracts are entered into in March of each year immediately prior to the planting season, and five months prior to the tomato canning season.
>
> At or about the same time that contracts are made with the tomato growers . . . the Campbell Soup Company plans for its Fall production on the basis of the estimated contract crop. It orders the necessary tin plate for containers, the necessary labels for the containers, cases for the containers, and makes arrangements with the Continental Canning Company for the rental of sufficient machinery to handle the canning. It also makes its contract with the Labor Unions for the necessary supply of labor, [and] purchases the other ingredients to be mixed with the tomato products in the quantities necessary to meet the estimated needs. Contracts are let for advertisement, based on a percentage of the estimated amount of tomatoes to be canned. The Campbell Soup Company also enters into contracts at this time with dealers all over the world, at set prices for the sale to said dealers of well over half of its estimated production of canned tomato products.
>
> Contracts are entered into . . . with farmers in widely diversified areas with a view to avoiding regional crop failures and also so as to make the flow of tomatoes to the canning plant more evenly distributed over the seven or eight week canning period. (*Campbell v. Diehm,* pp. 212–213)

Campbell's extensive reliance on its many full output contracts, the court suggested, would subject it to losses substantially greater than the contract-market price differential. Indeed, the defendants argued that if the damages were measured by the price difference, the case would not have met the jurisdictional minimum. The court rejected this argument:

The theory would be tenable if the actions herein were for specific performance of sales contracts, since the rule is that in an action for specific performance alone the actual value of the property involved is the correct measure of the amount in controversy. But it is plain that the injunctive actions herein involve much more than simple specific performances of sales contracts. They involve a carefully planned system of doing business which has been placed in jeopardy by the conduct of the defendants.

The rights that the plaintiffs are endeavoring to protect in the present injunctive actions consist of a plan of doing business and a vast system of manufacture . . . which are being attacked by the conduct of all of the defendants. Obviously, the value of these rights by far exceeds the jurisdictional requisite. (*Campbell v. Diehm*, p. 214)

When I first encountered *Campbell v. Wentz*, I thought it obvious that the consequential damages arising from seller's breach would be substantially greater than the contract-market differential and that the consequential damages were the commercial manifestation of "uniqueness." Perhaps they would have to shut down the cannery; or they might have to use inferior inputs, perhaps risking their brand name. The price-differential remedy would undercompensate, consequential damages would be hard to prove (was the brand name degraded because Wentz breached?), and even if you could prove the damages, the grower would not have sufficient resources to cover the losses.[1] Moreover, it would be hard to disentangle the effects of this single breach from that of the other suppliers who reneged. Campbell did not rely specifically on a single supplier—it relied on dozens of growers to get it enough carrots or tomatoes for the season.

My initial instincts were wrong. In fact, the last argument can be turned around. Campbell's reliance was not on the individual grower (who accounted for less than 3% of the carrots it intended to use). It was on the group of growers. This generalized reliance is quite different from the specific reliance of the coal mine located adjacent to a power plant and far from any rail lines, or from the shipper who puts his goods into the hands of a negligent carrier. Here, and in other grower/processor cases, the processor's problem arises even if the goods were entirely fungible. In a raft of decisions following the disastrous cotton harvest of 1973, the courts routinely granted specific performance to buyers (often intermediaries), while, in effect, conceding that the cotton was essentially fungible.

The present actions are the result of an unprecedented rise in the price of domestic cotton from approximately $.30 per pound to $.80 or $.90 per pound between the spring and the fall of 1973. This has been the fastest rise and to the highest price known in more than a century. Suits for specific performance of cotton contracts have been brought throughout the southeastern part of the United States.

A great deal of time could be spent in discussing whether cotton as a commodity is so unique as to be the proper subject of an action for specific performance. Numerous District Court decisions in the last few months seem to indicate that cotton contracts may be specifically enforced at the present time due to the unusual interdependency of the various persons handling cotton from the time of its planting, through its sale, manufacture and delivery to the ultimate consumer." (*Carolinas Cotton Growers Association, Inc. v. Arnette*, p. 66)[2]

Or, as another court put it: "The cotton in question is unique and irreplaceable because of the scarcity of cotton described." (*Mitchell-Huntley Cotton Co., Inc. v. Waldrep*, p. 1219)

Even if we were to recognize the notion of reliance on a group of suppliers, there is no reason to believe that the consequential damages would exceed the market price. This might seem counterintuitive at first, but it is quite straightforward. In a period of shortage, the market price reflects the willingness to pay of the marginal customer. Who wants Wentz's carrots the most? Campbell. How much is it willing to pay? Enough to avoid the consequential damages. The market price does not understate Campbell's injury. (Indeed, if anything it overstates the harm since Campbell's demand for carrots is downward sloping, a nicety we can ignore). Perhaps someone else who values the carrots less will come into possession of them and choose to use them rather than resell to Campbell. But, by and large, we should expect Campbell to outbid the others if the consequences of a shortfall of carrots (or tomatoes) are as severe as the courts suggest. The buyer's concern is not uniqueness. It is just that there are too few carrots.

Consequential damages are, therefore, a red herring on two counts. The damages arise not because this particular contract was breached, but because there is too little to go around. One could quibble with this, and argue that it is appropriate to assign at least some of the consequential damages to the breach of this particular contract. But the second point is devastating: the so-called consequential damages are captured in the market price.

In a rather remarkable statement, defendants' counsel made essentially this claim:

> Finally, it appears from the evidence that at least part of the carrots in dispute were offered to plaintiff by Lojeski, and were refused on the ground that they were contract carrots. Furthermore, it appears that the carrots remaining at the Wentz brothers' farm were available to Lojeski at the same price he had paid for the first 124,000 pounds, and that Lojeski was perfectly willing to sell these carrots also to plaintiff. The only thing that stood in the way of delivery of the carrots to plaintiff was its own refusal to accept delivery under Lojeski's terms. And yet, plaintiff now comes into court to invoke the extraordinary remedy of preliminary injunction to compel delivery under the contract terms, asserting its remedy at law is inadequate!
>
> The meaning of such an assertion is difficult to understand, since it is apparent that the only difference between delivery under Lojeski's terms and delivery under the contract terms is that delivery under the latter would be at a lower price. The dispute thus resolves itself into a controversy over the amount of money to be paid by plaintiff for the carrots, and, if the higher price were paid, the amount of money recoverable by plaintiff for alleged breach of contract. . . . It is obvious that plaintiff could have been made whole by an action at law, and that the invocation of injunctive relief was entirely unnecessary. (Lojeski Brief, pp. 12–13)

To paraphrase: Campbell could have mitigated by buying the contract carrots from Lojeski at the contract price and then come back to sue Wentz for the difference. If it would have suffered irreparable harm from nondelivery of the carrots, then why on earth would it reject those carrots just because they were being offered by Lojeski? As the defendants noted: "With one breath the Plaintiff contends that it will suffer irreparable injury if it fails to receive these carrots and at the same time it refuses to buy the very same carrots involved here." (Wentz Brief, p. 5) The defendants are right: uniqueness has nothing to do with it. That raises an obvious question: Why breach—what's in it for Wentz? If the damage remedy works so well, the net effect is that Campbell pays the contract price and Wentz receives only the contract price. I will suggest two explanations: (1) the litigation process is costly and imperfect; (2) carrots walk.

If the processor's recourse is to law rather than equity, it has to take into account the vagaries of the legal system. (The two remedies are not mutually exclusive—pursuing specific performance gives the plaintiff a first bite at the apple and an indicator of how a case for damages might fare.) The processor might find compromise cheaper than pursuing a remedy, especially if damages are hard to measure, litigation is expensive, the defendant can manufacture some plausible defense, or a jury might find the farmers to be worthy of their sympathy. For example, in the cotton cases, the growers threw out a number of defenses: vagueness; fraud; unconscionability; variable quantity contracts lack mutuality; the contracts are illegal gambling contracts; and contracts for sale of goods not yet produced are unenforceable. Also, the injunction gives the goods to the processor today; the damage remedy gives the cash to the processor some time in the future. In the interim the defendant has time to lose it or hide it. Recall that while Campbell's motion was on appeal, the trial court required that the cash be held by the court. Once it lost, the lifting of the injunction terminated the court's control of the funds.

These arguments are not context-specific. One could just as easily make them with regard to a contract to deliver widgets. Perhaps, as Alan Schwartz (1979) and others have argued, the widget contract does warrant specific performance. The grower/processor contracts are not out of step—everybody else is. Is there something about the grower/processor contract that makes specific performance relatively more attractive? The answer, I believe, lies in the fact that these are fixed-price contracts for all the goods (up to a defined maximum) grown on specific acreage. The concern is that the produce will migrate depending on the contract-market differential.

The contract recognizes this problem in a number of places. The defined maximum is responsive to this problem. Suppose that there had been a bumper crop of Chantenay carrots. The surplus of carrots would have pushed the market price down. The Wentzes could take advantage of this situation by buying carrots at the market price, sneaking them onto their property, and then selling them to Campbell at the higher contract price. The maximum of twelve tons per acre limits Campbell's vulnerability to this ploy. Similarly, if the grower entered into a contract with Campbell, it could not enter into a contract with any other canner for the same commodity. Thus, even though only 15 acres of the Wentzes' 500+ acres were under contract to Campbell, the Wentzes could not grow carrots for anyone else. A Campbell manager testified:

If a man has more than one contract, or a contract with more than one canner, it would be almost impossible to trace where the vegetables would go. Speaking of carrots, and being specific, if there were two contracts on the farm, we would not be able to know which ones were coming to us and which ones were going to the other canners. It is merely a protection, knowing where those carrots will go. We permit the farmer to grow as many carrots as he wishes, but we simply state that they should come to us, and other canners do the same.

Q: So it is largely a matter of policing the contract, or enforcing the provisions of the contract, in order to give you some method of checking on the behavior of the grower under the contract that the provision is inserted? (Appendix to Campbell Brief, p. 88a)

Campbell made the argument more tersely in its brief: "As a practical matter, if carrots were grown by the grower upon a part of his acreage not covered by the contract, it would be impossible for Campbell Soup Company to determine whether it were receiving all of the carrots to which it would be entitled from the specified acreage, or that the growers were not including carrots from other acres." (p. 23)

If the market price exceeded the contract price, as in the actual case, the carrots can walk in the opposite direction. Wentz would take the carrots to Lojeski, perhaps under cover of night, and tell Campbell that its output was particularly disappointing this season. The court in one of the cotton cases recognized this problem: "When the cotton produced by Defendants was picked and ginned, it could be stored by them in places unknown to Plaintiff and disposed of so as to put it beyond the reach of Plaintiff." (*Mitchell-Huntley*, p. 1219) There was some evidence in the *Wentz* record of this having happened in the past—Campbell had refused to enter into a contract with Lojeski because in previous seasons he had sold some of his contract carrots to other processors. (Appendix to Campbell Brief, pp. 83a–84a) To enforce a damage remedy, Campbell would have to determine Wentz's actual output. Campbell could, out of its own pocket, attempt to police the illicit movements of its contract produce, ex ante, or track the movements, ex post. Or it could let the government do it. The specific performance remedy enables it to do precisely that.

Is that enough reason to overcome the presumption against injunctive relief? My inclination would be to say yes, but reasonable people could easily disagree. This is a very different question than whether a particular type of carrot or tomato or cotton is unique. If "uniqueness" were really the issue, then surely Goodrich was wrong, Campbell's subsequent revision *(Diehm)* should have been unavailing, and the cotton cases were ludicrous. The carrots (and tomatoes and cotton) are not unique. Indeed, the problem arises precisely *because* the produce is not unique. The relevant distinction in the processor-grower cases should not be uniqueness; rather, it should be whether the contract was an "output" contract. So, if Campbell had entered into a fixed-quantity contract for Chantenay carrots, the remedy should be damages, and the "uniqueness" of the carrots should only be relevant for fine-tuning the money damages if Campbell covered with a different type of carrot.

The argument that the buyer would suffer substantial consequential damages in excess of the market price differential is a tempting one—it fooled me. But a little bit of simple economic reasoning revealed its fundamental flaw. A little more suggested what was really at stake: enforcement of a full output contract. By trying to force the argument into the uniqueness box, Campbell and Judge Goodrich and authors of casebooks and treatises have obscured the central issue and have failed to identify one motive—policing cheating in a full output contract—for pursuing (and, perhaps, granting) injunctive relief.

CHAPTER 10

Expectation Damages and Property in the Price

I want to propose a rationale for enforcing the narrow expectation interest, the contract-market differential. My explanation concerns the production of market information. Specifically, I argue that the production of information about the future course of prices is costly, and by early contracting the parties can economize on those costs.

With an executory commodity contract, the promisee can avoid the costs arising from untimely contracting. Entering into a contract too close to the performance date can raise costs. Thus, if a buyer of wheat in Buffalo waits until he needs the wheat before entering into the contract, he might find that there is little wheat of the proper quality on hand at that time. Timely contracting avoids the costs associated with last-minute search. That, however, does not explain why the contract price would be fixed months before performance; the parties could have set the price at the spot market price at the moment of performance. Indeed, such contracts are not uncommon. In any event, if the seller's breach were early enough so that the buyer could cover without incurring these additional costs, this argument would not provide grounds for enforcing the agreement; nor does it provide a reason for compensating the buyer with the contract-market differential. We are still left with the question: Why would the parties find it worthwhile to contract on April 1 to fix the price for a June 1 delivery?

To simplify the following discussion, assume a purely executory commodity contract. Assume further that the commodity is traded in a thick market (ex ante and ex post) so that the promisee could always cover by buying (or selling) at the current market price. A commodity's future price is uncertain, and there exist potential rewards to people for obtaining information as to what the prices will be. That is, if X knows a lot about the market and Y is relatively ignorant, X should get the better of the deal. The greater the information advantage, the better X does. The closer we are to the performance date, the more information will exist about factors that might affect the price. The traders will each have an incentive to expend resources to gather and evaluate that information. By making their contract early, the parties reduce the incentive to expend resources on this activity, thereby economizing on their joint search costs. Early contracting enables them to avoid excessive searching for price information.

Analytically, this is a "rent-seeking" problem. There is a rather complicated economic literature on rent-seeking, but the basic point is a simple one. The efforts of one party influence the efficacy of the efforts of the other. For example, if one fisherman increases his effort, this will have an adverse effect on the costs of others in the same fishery. Absent any coordination, they will exploit the fishery inefficiently. In the present context, the contracting parties expend resources to improve their information about the future course of prices. If one party has better information, it will get the better of the bargain. Knowing this, the parties' incentive is to spend until the marginal benefit just equals the marginal cost (given their assumption about the level of their counterparty's spending). The higher the level of spending by the two, the less sensitive the result to one party's outspending the other. So, we should expect that if Y spent nothing and X spent $10,000, X should gain a considerable bargaining advantage; but there would be less advantage if Y spent $90,000 and X $100,000.

Varying the time between contract formation and contract performance has two offsetting effects. On the one hand, the longer the period between contract formation and the date of performance, the greater the dispersion of price estimates. Hence, the reward for acquiring information should be higher; the earlier the contract date, the greater the incentive to spend resources in pursuit of information. On the other hand, the earlier the contract date, the less likely an incremental investment in pursuit of information will be valuable. Expenditures on weather patterns two months from now might prove very useful in projecting future prices, but attempts to produce two-year projections would be fruitless. This factor would lead to a reduction of expenditures on information gathering as the length of time between the contract date and performance date increases.

Thus, there are both benefits and costs from increasing the length of time between the performance date of the contract and the time at which the parties enter into the contract. The problem the parties face is determining the optimal lead time. Absent enforceable contracts, they would be unable to attain that lead time, since the party disadvantaged by a price change in the interval between contract execution and performance would have no reason to honor the original agreement. If the law does enforce these executory contracts, parties will be able to contract in a timely fashion, thereby enabling them to avoid the waste inherent in the search for price information.

This argument is not novel. It is a variant on Kitch's (1977) claim that American patent law, by defining property rights in an invention at an early stage of development, reduces the amount of wasteful research. I do not mean to imply that businesspeople make calculations about the optimal time for entering into a contract, or even that they pose the problem in this way. It is reasonable to presume, however, that market forces would sort this out, penalizing those who contract too early or too late and rewarding those who contract in a timely manner. The contract-market differential remedy enables the market to perform that function. In effect, enforcement allows the parties to assert a "property right" in the price, just as a patent allows the patentee to assert a property right in an idea.

The notion that enforcement of the executory contract enables people to economize on price search costs goes a long way toward illuminating some of the problems arising in the area of contract damages. In particular, the idea that the parties were attempting to establish a property right in the price suggests that damage measures should be designed to protect that interest. Suppose that on April 1, Able enters into a contract to sell a commodity to Baker at a price of $2.00 per bushel for delivery at Baker's plant on June 1. Five days later, Able changes his mind and says he wants to withdraw the promise. Baker, in the meanwhile, has done nothing in reliance upon the existence of this particular contract. The damages should be the market price–contract price differential, but which market price? Suppose that on April 5, the spot price for the commodity was $3.00 per pound and that on June 1 it had fallen to $2.50 per pound. Should either of these be taken as the market price? In the ideal case, the answer is no. The relevant price is the price on April 5 for goods to be delivered on June 1 to Baker's plant. That is the market price at the time of breach for what had been promised: delivery at a particular time and place. That damage remedy preserves Baker's property in the price. Damage measurement, at least for this component of damages, is an asset valuation problem. We ask, What would the seller have to pay at the time of breach to get a new contract to provide the same quantities at the same time and location at the same price? For some commodities there is a sufficiently thick market so that the value of the contract is easily determined. Futures contracts are an example. The contract is for wheat meeting certain specifications to be delivered at a certain location and a certain date. Most real-world situations fall short of this, and compromises will have to be made. But these should be guided by the basic principle: the price we are trying to replicate is the price at the time of breach for performance at the relevant time and place.

To illustrate application of this concept and the types of compromises that might have to be made, we can consider a few examples where the measurement problem gets progressively harder. In the ideal situation, post-breach price movements should be irrelevant, but in less than ideal conditions they might have to be taken into account. If the buyer in a long-term contract covered by entering into a similar contract for the remainder of the contracting period, then the price differential between the original contract price and the cover price would be the remedy. That is what the court should have found, but did not, in the venerable case of *Missouri Furnace Co. v. Cochran*. The seller was to deliver a fixed quantity of coke at a price of $1.20 per ton every day for a year. After the first month, the spot price soared to over $4.00 per ton and the seller breached. The buyer covered by entering into a contract for the remainder of the year at a price of $4.00. By May the spot price began to fall, and it remained relatively low for the rest of the year. Missouri Furnace sued for the difference between the contract price and the price of its cover transaction—a little more than $80,000. The defendant countered, arguing that the relevant damages were the spot price of coal at each delivery date, roughly $22,000. The court held for the defendant. The time of breach, the court held, was the moment at which the defendant failed to perform; each day was a new failure and a new time of breach.

This case long stood for the proposition that cover was not a remedy for a contract breach. Even today cover is treated as an *alternative remedy* to the contract-market differential rather than as *evidence* of that differential. Tom Jackson (1978, pp. 76–78) did an excellent job debunking *Missouri Furnace*. If Missouri Furnace had known that the court would impose this remedy, covering as it did would have been an unprofitable strategy. Covering with a forward contract at a fixed price would mean that if spot prices had risen in the interim, Missouri Furnace's damages would be limited to the difference between the initial contract price and the single cover contract. That damage remedy would "make the plaintiff whole." If the spot prices fell, however, all the benefit would accrue to Cochran. The asymmetric payoffs make covering in this manner a negative value proposition.

The symmetry would be restored if the cover contract were for daily deliveries of the same quantity, but with the price being the spot price on the date of delivery. Contracts in which the price will be a market price or posted price at time of delivery are not uncommon. But that is not the contract these parties entered into. Theirs was a contract for delivery throughout the year at a price determined at the beginning of the year. Had they wanted to enter into a variable price contract, they could have chosen to enter into such an agreement in the first place. In effect, the court's remedy transformed the contract into something completely different. In some contexts, the transformation could be justified on the ground of convenience. That factor cut the other way in *Missouri Furnace*. The replacement contract was available, and it was a better measure of the contract-market differential at the moment of breach than were daily purchases on the spot market.

A slightly more complicated case arose in *Compania Naviera Asiatic v. The Burmah Oil Co.*, which concerned a seven-year charter on a ship. Before performance of the charter began, the Yom Kippur War disrupted the international shipping market; the market price of shipping doubled and the owner breached, chartering the ship to someone else for one year. In subsequent years a glut developed in the ship charter market, so that the annual price of a charter fell considerably below the initial charter rate. The breaching owner attempted to introduce evidence on the subsequent course of prices. However, market information on the value of a seven-year charter at the time of breach was probably available, and it would have provided a better picture of the damages than would annual charter rates in the remaining period. In such circumstances the court should refuse to allow the breacher to introduce evidence on the subsequent decline in price. The determination of when it is appropriate to take subsequent events into account will not always be easy, but it will be easier if the courts have a theoretical framework to guide them.

While it might not be clear precisely where the line should be drawn, *Laredo Hides Co. Inc. v. H & H Meat Products Co., Inc.* provides a good example from the other side of that line. The seller breached in the third month of a ten-month full output contract to provide hides. The ideal damage measure would be the amount that would be paid at the time of the breach in an arm's length transaction for the right to receive the producer's output at the contractually specified price for the remaining seven months. However, you can't just look that up in the papers. If the buyer covered by purchasing in the spot market for the remainder of the contract period, the comparisons between those prices (weighted by the monthly output) and the contract prices would be the damages as reckoned under UCC §2–712. If the spot market price had changed substantially after the breach in a way not anticipated at the time of the breach, these cover prices would not reflect accurately the true contract-market differential at the time of the breach. However, they are likely the best that a court could do. The variable quantity and odd remaining term make it very difficult for a finder of fact to approximate the "true price."

The preceding discussion started with a simple commodity contract in which the parties set a single price and their task was to minimize information costs by varying the timing of their contracting. If we start at the opposite extreme, a long-term supply contract in which there is considerable relation-specific investment and great uncertainty about future supply and demand conditions, then the analysis looks quite different. The contract most likely will not entail a single price; rather, it will include a price adjustment mechanism. And the remedy will look quite different. But those differences should not obscure the fact that the parties (and the law) are trying to resolve the same problems; the context dictates different solutions.

What would happen if one party were dissatisfied with the price in the twelfth year of a thirty-year, variable price, take-or-pay contract for delivery of coal from a particular mine? The ideal remedy for a breach would be the value at the time of the breach of the remaining eighteen years. Given that price and quantity for the duration are both uncertain, and given that there likely are no quoted prices for this unique asset, it would be extremely difficult to ascertain that value. Rather than having the finder of fact put a value on the remainder, courts will often resort to the specific performance remedy. The court does not have to engage in the futile exercise of valuing the contract today. Nor does it have to wait eighteen years to look at the actual trajectory of prices and quantity. Specific performance does not, of course, mean that the parties would be bound together for the duration. The court merely directs the parties to perform the contract or negotiate their own damages remedy in the form of a buyout. The remedy, in effect, gives the nonbreaching party the option to terminate, with the price to be determined by negotiation away from the status quo.

CHAPTER 11

The Middleman's Damages:
Lost Profits or the
Contract-Market Differential

Suppose that X sells to a middleman Y who has a contract to resell to Z. The resale contract might be for a fixed fee, back-to-back, or cost-plus. In any of these cases, the middleman has eliminated its price risk. If the contracts are performed, it receives a fixed amount regardless of what might happen to the market price. Suppose also that prior to the date of performance, the market price increases substantially, and the seller refuses to deliver. If Y sues for damages, some courts have held that Y was limited to its commission, while others have given Y the contract-market differential. Farnsworth (2004, §12.12) refers to this as "a particularly vexing problem." Properly framed, it is not that hard, but a lot of serious contracts scholars have failed to understand the problem. For the better part of a decade, for example, the draft revision of the UCC took the position that allowing recovery for the contract-market price differential would overcompensate the middleman. (The history of the aborted UCC revision is recounted in numerous places; see Ben-Shahar and Bernstein 2000, pp. 1910–1911.) This despite convincing scholarship to the contrary. (See, for example, Scott 1990, Clark 1997, and Matthews 1997.) While that mistake was undone in the final version of the revision, it is instructive to work through how they managed to get it so wrong. It provides a nice illustration of the value of framing the problem in terms of protecting the property in the price.

Part of the problem is that it is possible to read the UCC as presenting two conflicting rules. One, §1–106, states that "the aggrieved party may be put in as good a position as if the other party had fully performed," while the other, §2–713, states that the measure of damages for nondelivery by the seller is "the difference between the market price . . . and the contract price." The most persistent advocate of the primacy of §1–106 is Roy Ryden

Anderson (2001, p. 833), who characterizes the reasoning of those courts favoring §2–713 as bordering on the absurd. See also White and Summers (1995, p. 394). If the middleman's two contracts are read together, the two sections appear to be in conflict, since full performance would result in the middleman receiving a modest amount, substantially less than the contract-market differential. If the contract between the middleman and the seller is viewed in isolation, however, the inconsistency disappears. And that is how it should be. Privity matters. If the middleman were simply a broker, the seller's breach would result in liability to the final buyer for the contract-market differential. The middleman's recovery, if any, would be limited by the terms of its contract with one or both of the principals. But in these cases the middleman is not a broker. It takes the role of a principal in two separate, albeit related, transactions. It would have a claim against the seller, and the ultimate buyer would have a claim against it.

The confusion seems to arise when the buyer fails to pursue its claim against the middleman and the middleman's recovery of the price differential from the seller is not offset against the buyer's recovery. The key to understanding these cases is that the middleman's contract with the buyer is none of the seller's business. The seller should be indifferent as to whether the middleman is acting as a broker or a principal; the consequences for the seller should be identical regardless. The contract sets a price for future delivery, and the contract-market differential protects that price. If the middleman acts as a broker, the damage award goes directly to the buyer; if the middleman acts as a principal, the award goes to it, and it is potentially liable to the buyer under the second contract.

In this chapter I discuss two cases in which courts faced this problem, *Allied Canners & Packers, Inc. v. Victor Packing Co.* and *Tongish v. Thomas*. Both involved a sale to a middleman and a substantial increase in price. In the former, the court held that, on the specific facts of this case, §1–106 trumped §2–713, and it limited recovery to the expected commission. The mirror image of *Allied* is presented in *Nobs Chemical, U.S.A., Inc. v. Koppers Co., Inc.*, in which the buyer breached following a dramatic price decline. The seller/middleman secured a release from its supplier and then sued for the contract-market differential. The court took the same path as the *Allied* court, limiting the damages to the middleman's buy-sell spread. In *Tongish*, the trial court took the same position, but it was reversed and the middleman was allowed to recover the contract-market differential. (For other decisions reaching this outcome, see *Texpar Energy, Inc. v. Murphy Oil USA,*

Inc. and *KGM Harvesting Co. v. Fresh Network.*) While American law is in a somewhat confused state, I should note that the English got it right over a century ago in *Rodocanachi, Sons & Co. v. Milburn Brothers.*

1. Allied Canners

The facts are a little complicated because the contracts are embedded in a regulatory framework. A federal marketing order established the Raisin Administrative Committee (RAC), which was intended to keep prices up by regulating the flow of raisins to the domestic market. The RAC does so by taking surplus raisins out of the domestic market, allowing these to be sold only outside the Western Hemisphere. The result is a two-tiered market of "free" raisins that can be sold anywhere and "reserve" raisins that can only be sold abroad. In good times, a substantial amount of raisins will be diverted to the reserve category in order to support high domestic prices. If the price of free raisins is greater than that of reserve raisins, there are incentives for packers to engage in arbitrage, buying reserve raisins and then reselling them in the domestic market. To prevent this, the RAC sells only to member packers. The packer must file an application to purchase the raisins. It must include the name of the foreign buyer or exporter (who in turn must provide the name of the foreign importer). The identity of the exporter's ultimate purchasers is not revealed to the packer/seller. The information does not assure that the reserve raisins will not reappear in the domestic market, but it gives the RAC quite a bit of control.

Victor was a packer and a member of RAC. Allied, an exporter, was not eligible for membership. In early September 1976, free raisins were selling for about 43 cents per pound. (*Sun Maid Raisin Growers of California v. Victor Packing Co.*, p. 794) Victor could buy reserve raisins from RAC at the quoted price of 22 cents per pound. It entered into a contract to sell reserve raisins to Allied, which had contracts to sell ten containers (375,000 pounds) in Japan at 29.75 cents; Allied would get a discount of 4%, which would net it roughly $4,400.

Heavy rains on the night of September 9 severely damaged the raisin crop, destroying perhaps 50% of the new crop. (*Sun Maid*, p. 794) The next day, the RAC withdrew its offer to release reserve raisins to members who had not made the appropriate application and deposit as of 8:30 A.M. Victor had not yet filed and was unsuccessful in persuading the RAC to release raisins to it. The diversion of raisins from reserve to free had some damping effect on prices in the free market; however, those prices still soared to over 80 cents per pound. (The parties stipulated to a market price of 87 cents.)

Victor conceded that it had breached, and Allied chose not to cover. One of the Japanese buyers agreed to rescind the contract for three containers; no reason was given in the opinion. The other buyer, Shoei Foods, demanded delivery of the remaining seven containers. Some commentators have asserted that Allied was excused from delivering raisins to its buyers under a force majeure clause in those contracts; see Ben-Shahar and Bernstein (2000, p. 1908) and Clark (1997, p. 826). They were wrong. Allied said that Shoei would hold off suing it until the Allied-Victor litigation was resolved. Apparently, the statute of limitations expired without Shoei ever bringing suit, and there is no indication that Allied paid any damages to Shoei.

The trial court treated Allied as a broker and awarded it the lost "commission" of $4,400. The Court of Appeal rejected the broker label, but then concluded that the contract-market differential would overcompensate Allied. The court took into account circumstances specific to this case: (a) the seller knew that the buyer had a resale contract (a requirement of the RAC); (b) the buyer had not been able to show that it would be liable in damages on its forward contracts; and (c) there was no bad faith on the part of seller—it had not resold to another at a higher price.

All three factors should, of course, be irrelevant. The buyer locked in a price in this contract, and that is all the court should have looked at. It might have felt sorry for Victor, which had done no wrong (although Victor could have saved itself from being in this situation had it made the appropriate deposit with the RAC before September 10). But Victor, apparently, did not even attempt to argue that it should be excused in any way. The court linked the two contracts and concluded that the 4% discount was all that Allied was entitled to.

Allied's counsel did not help matters. It raised a "loss of reputation" claim, arguing that Allied "had suffered additional consequential damages through the loss of the entire account."[1] The first response to this should be: So what? The second is to recognize that it is just counsel's attempt to jump through the hoops set by the courts. If court and counsel understood the problem, such nonsense would never see the light of day. Allied's damage claim is further evidence of its misframing of the case. It wanted the contract-market differential as damages: 87 cents − 29.75 cents = 57.25 cents. Multiplying that by the 375,000 pounds gives damages of roughly

$215,000. But Allied was asking for only about $150,000. The difference is accounted for by the fact that it was not asking for any compensation for the three containers sold to the buyer who had rescinded the contract (70% of $215,000 is $150,000). Thus, it was not arguing that the price differential per se was the appropriate remedy. Rather, it was suggesting that its compensation should be based on its potential liability to Shoei. Indeed, the court noted that "when the trial court asked [Allied's president] whether in the event that damages of $150,281 were awarded, he would consider that to be his company's own money . . . [h]e replied that he would not." (At 915) Coupling this with the claim that the statute of limitations precluded Shoei's recovery from Allied, it would not be unreasonable for a court to limit Allied's compensation. But even if that is the right answer, it is to the wrong question. If the question were properly presented, Victor should have been liable for the full $215,000. It failed to deliver ten containers of raisins; the failure was not excused; and the contract-market differential was 57.25 cents per pound. The disposition of the Japanese claims against Allied was neither here nor there.

The Second Circuit made a similar error in *Internatio, Inc. v. M. S. Taimyr*. The plaintiff had purchased coffee beans for about 81 cents per pound and resold them to M&M Mars at about 92 cents. When they arrived, the price had risen to $2.01. Some of the beans were lost in transit, and the question arose at which price the lost beans should be valued. The trial court opted for the higher price, but was reversed. The court held that if Mars had insisted upon delivery or had sued, then the plaintiff could have recovered at the higher price. But, since there was no evidence that Mars had held the plaintiff liable for damages, "the market value measure is not applicable here because it would result in a recovery greater than the loss suffered." (p. 50) As in *Allied*, the court was confused by the fact that the two contracts were related, and it lumped them together when assessing the harm to the plaintiff.

2. Tongish

Tongish, a grower of sunflower seeds, entered into a contract with the Decatur Coop Association (Coop) in which he promised to deliver all the output from his 160 acre plot (later reduced to 116.8 acres) to a particular processor, Bambino. Bambino was one of the two processors to whom the Coop sold sunflowers. The form contract the Coop signed with Tongish was titled Confectionary Sunflower Seed Grower Contract with Decatur Coop to Be Processed by Bambino Bean & Seed, Inc. (Tongish Brief) The Coop had a separate oral contract with Bambino. The price depended on the size of the seeds—13 cents per pound for large and 8 cents for small. Bad weather caused prices to soar. Tongish complained (perhaps legitimately) about the Coop's assessment of the quality of its seeds. It then sold its output at an average price of 20 cents per pound to Danny Thomas. Thomas paid for about half the seeds; its refusal to pay for the remainder is unexplained, although it appears that it was in response to a complaint from the Coop. Tongish sued Thomas, who paid the balance into court and was dismissed from the action. Meanwhile, the Coop intervened, seeking damages for the breach.

The trial court found that Tongish had breached. The Coop asked for the contract-market differential, about $5,000, but the trial court reckoned that its only loss was the foregone handling charges, 55 cents per hundred pounds, or $455. In correspondence, Tongish's lawyer informed me that Bambino was insolvent and that if Tongish had performed and the Coop had delivered the seeds to Bambino, the net result would have been that the Coop would have paid Tongish and not recovered from Bambino. Tongish, if this version of facts is correct, did the Coop a favor. However, the Court of Appeals properly reversed on the damage measure, and its opinion was upheld by the Kansas Supreme Court.

The Tongish-Coop contract specifies the handling charge of 55 cents per 100 pounds if the seeds came through its elevator and 15 cents per 100 pounds if they went directly from the farm to the processor. Since the trial court used the 55 cents fee, it is reasonable to infer that in the normal course of events, the sunflowers would be sent to the Coop's elevator for storage. The contract (a form contract provided by Decatur Coop) set a modest daily fee for storage (½ cent per hundred pounds per day). The seeds would then be commingled with the seeds of other growers and ultimately sent on to the buyer. The contract price included transport to the buyer.

There is some conflict as to whether Coop would have been liable to Bambino for failure to deliver on its contract. Tongish claims (almost certainly incorrectly) that it would not be liable at all: "Coop was locked into its profit; while it forward contracted with Bambino, it had no obligation to deliver any sunflowers unless they were actually delivered to it; the contract was an acreage contract and not a contract for a specific quantity." (Tongish Brief, p. 5) Coop claimed otherwise:

The Coop owed sunflowers to its buyer who demanded the sunflowers be supplied and failed to pay for sunflowers already delivered. The Coop, per testimony, could not realistically cover due to high prices and very tight supplies of a commodity normally sold on forward contract, and without the sunflowers it had no way to protect itself from its defaulting buyer [*sic*]. (Supplemental Brief of Coop, p. 6).

And further:

The only evidence concerning Bambino's interest in the Tongish sunflowers was that when informed of the failure to deliver to the Coop, Bambino advised the Coop that Coop would either have to supply the sunflowers or take a reduction in money. (Supplemental Brief of Coop, p. 8)

"Reduction in money" could mean contract-market differential, but I doubt it. Given that the Coop was asking for the contract-market differential, the fact that the lawyers chose not to use that phrase suggests that Bambino was suggesting some lesser amount.

The Kansas court distinguished *Tongish* from *Allied*, suggesting that Victor's behavior was more justifiable, since it had no raisins to sell, while Tongish resold the sunflower seeds at a higher price. However, the court did not rely on the blameworthiness of the breaching seller. It canvassed the law review literature and concluded that those arguing for the contract-market differential had a better case. It concluded that "[w]hile application of the rule may not reflect the actual loss to a buyer, it encourages a more efficient market and discourages the breach of contracts." (At 817)

The second half of that sentence, recognizing the property in price to be protected, is fine. The first embodies the confusion that stems from linking the two contracts to arrive at the injured party's expected net gain. The Coop was a principal in two contracts, and not a broker. That is a big difference; brokers do not bear counterparty risk; principals do. The Coop raised the counterparty risk point in passing in its reply brief: "while the Coop had locked in the price it was still exposed to failure of the seller to bring in the grain, failure to receive grain of the standard set, or failure by the Coop's buyer to complete the purchase from the Coop or pay the Coop for grain received." (Reply Brief, p. 2) Ironically, because of Bambino's bankruptcy, that last risk turned out to be real. The crucial point is that Tongish had made an early commitment to deliver sunflowers at specified prices. Enforcing its obligation with the contract-market differential measure of damages makes such an early commitment possible. Whether Tongish is liable to an intermediary or the final purchaser depends on whether the intermediary assumes the role of a counterparty (and accepts the associated risks) or acts merely as a broker. Either way, Tongish should be liable to someone for the contract-market differential. If the middleman acted only as a broker, the buyer would have a claim. If the middleman were the principal in two related contracts, it would have a claim for the contract-market differential against the seller and exposure for the same to the buyer.

3. Concluding Remarks

There have only been a handful of middleman cases that have made it to reported decisions. The importance is not in the specific problem, but in the broader point regarding the protection of the narrow expectation interest. There are three easy paths to the proper outcome in these cases. The *Allied* court found none, the *Tongish* court one. The first is to respect privity and the allocation of counterparty risk. There is no reason for the court to treat the middleman as a broker when the contractual arrangement specifically rejects that. How, or whether, parties deal with the price risks of a particular contract in the remainder of their business is irrelevant. The second, as the *Tongish* court put it, is to encourage a more efficient market. Allowing sellers to back out of forward contracts when the market price exceeds the contract price discourages forward contracting. Finally, the *Allied* court could have considered the nature of the contract it was constructing if it granted the commission-only damage remedy. The seller receives a "put option" (the right, but not the obligation, to sell) with the contract price being the exercise price and the price of that option being the middleman's commission. Middlemen who willingly write such contracts do not survive long. There is no good reason to impose such a contract on them.

CHAPTER 12

An Economic Analysis of the Lost-Volume Retail Seller

Suppose that a customer agrees to buy a boat, but before it is delivered, he reneges. The dealer subsequently resells the boat to another customer at the same price. Has the seller suffered damages (aside from incidental damages) and, if so, should he be compensated? This question, dubbed the lost-volume seller problem, has generated considerable confusion for courts and commentators alike. It has been the subject of considerable legal analysis, usually in the context of explicating §2–708(2) of the UCC. The right answer should be: yes, there was a loss which in the retail context is roughly the gross margin (the retail-wholesale differential); and no, the seller should not be compensated. The conflation of the two questions has led to much of the confusion over this problem.

The option notion is particularly useful in this context. When placing an order, the buyer gets an option; the lost-volume remedy, in effect, sets the price of that option as the gross margin. That is, the buyer implicitly agrees to pay the gross margin whether or not it chooses to go ahead with the purchase; if it does go forward, it pays the remainder. There is, however, no reason to believe that the price of an option would bear any resemblance to the seller's lost profits. A more sensible default rule would be to set the option price (that is, the damage remedy) at zero and facilitate the explicit determination of an option price in the form of liquidated damages or a nonrefundable deposit. Scott and Triantis (2004, pp. 1482–1484) make a similar argument.

I will use the case of *Neri v. Retail Marine Corp.* as a vehicle for analysis. Professors Goetz and Scott (1979, p. 332) summarize the *Neri* facts and decision concisely:

Retail Marine, a dealer in marine equipment and supplies, contracted to sell a new boat to Neri for $12,500. Marine then ordered and received the boat from its supplier. Six days after the agreement Neri repudiated the contract. Four months later Marine sold the boat to another buyer for the same price. When Neri sued to recover his downpayment, Marine counterclaimed for lost profits of $2,500 under U.C.C. 2–708(2), arguing that absent Neri's default it would have earned two profits rather than one. The New York Court of Appeals sustained Marine's lost-volume claim, holding that "the conclusion is clear from the record—indeed with mathematical certainty—that [market damages are] inadequate to put the seller in as good a position as performance . . . and hence . . . the seller is entitled to its [profit]." The court categorized Retail Marine's situation as that of a dealer with an "inexhaustible" supply of boats; consequently, the second buyer did not replace the first.

Assume initially that once Neri has placed his order, he is legally bound to take the boat for his own or to arrange for its resale to another buyer. In Calabresi-Melamed (1972) terminology, Neri's placement of the order gives Marine an entitlement protected by a property rule. Conceivably, Neri could sit outside Marine's showroom and try to convince potential buyers to purchase his boat rather than the dealer's boat. Obviously, this is costly to Neri, but it would be feasible. Alternatively, Neri could pay a retailer to resell the boat for him. If Neri could choose from a number of equally attractive dealers, he would pay a fair market price for the reselling service. Whether that price is 1%, 10%, or 20% of retail price depends upon the anticipated costs of retailing. Thus, even if Neri has access to a competitive market of resellers, he could find disposing of the boat a very expensive proposition. Neri's situation is complicated if the initial seller—Marine—is better situated than others to resell the boat. This would be so, for example, if Neri's purchase and resale converts the boat from a new to a used one and results in instant depreciation of, say, 20%.

When ordering his boat, Neri has a choice from a number of boat retailers, some of whom carry brands that he prefers. After he has placed the order with one, however, that dealer has an advantage that it could exploit in bargaining to determine the price of reselling. Suppose that the retailer could demand specific performance. That would serve as a backdrop for bargaining to determine the price of the reselling services. The price would depend upon such considerations as Neri's vulnerability to Marine's opportunism (the costs of the next best alternative), Marine's interest in maintaining customer good will, the costs of using the legal system (the status quo determines whether one party must invoke the costly legal system), the existence and amount of any down payment, and the like.

Alternatively, Marine's entitlement could be protected only by a liability rule (damages rather than specific performance). This is the more customary rule for breach of contract. What are Marine's damages? A reasonable approximation would be the competitive price for the service of re-negotiating the sale of a new boat. This damage rule would not permit the retailer to take advantage of his unique ex post situation in the post-breach bargaining. The competitive price of the reselling service is, roughly, the gross margin (retail minus wholesale price) of the dealer. This measure of damages is precisely what the drafters of the UCC had in mind under §2–708(2):

> The provision of this section permitting recovery of expected profit including reasonable overhead where the standard measure of damages is inadequate . . . [is] designed to eliminate the unfair and economically wasteful results arising under the older law when fixed price articles were involved. This section permits the recovery of lost profits in all appropriate cases, which would include all standard priced goods. The normal measure there would be list price less cost to the dealer or list price less manufacturing cost to the manufacturer. (§2–708, Comment 2)

It would appear, then, that the arguments of the proponents of the lost-profit notion are vindicated. This conclusion, however, would be premature. The following section considers other aspects of the economics of retailing and relates them to the damages problem.

1. The Economics of Retailing and Lost Profits

Why would a manufacturer choose not to sell directly to consumers? The simple answer is that it would cost too much. Retailers provide services to manufacturers and customers, reducing the costs of distributing the goods. The retailer's revenue minus the costs of goods sold will compensate for the costs of retailing, including a normal rate of return on the retailer's investment. While it would be possible for a retailer to sell retailing services separately (for example, by charging an admission fee or by selling a catalogue), the typical retailer's compensation is directly tied to the sale of its output. The gross margin is set high enough so that the costs will be covered by sales revenue. Thus, regardless of which customers use the retail services, the retailer's compensation comes solely from the buyers of his goods. If Mr. Jones buys, he pays for the product and for a share of the retailing services; if Mr. Smith does not buy, he pays nothing for the retailing services, regardless of how much selling effort was exerted on his behalf. If Mr. Neri orders a boat and then reneges, should he bear any of the costs of retailing in the absence of specific contract language on this point? If we were to hold him liable for lost profits, then the answer would be yes.

A Fish Story

A retailer can influence his sales volume by his price or his selling effort. To simplify the discussion, assume that price is fixed. Selling effort includes a broad mix of activities, some of which are specific to the particular transaction and some of which are spread over the entire customer base: advertising, maintaining high ratios of inventory or salespeople to sales, locating in places that generate a high volume of foot traffic, maintaining elegant facilities, providing high-quality service departments, developing high levels of consumer good will, and so forth. Diminishing returns to selling effort reflect the increased difficulty of reaching additional customers. For example, an advertisement targeted to an audience within a one mile radius of a boat dealership is likely to result in a larger percentage of recipients responding to the ad than would one aimed at customers within a 100 mile radius. With the retail and wholesale prices fixed, the profit-maximizing firm sets marginal selling costs equal to the gross margin.

Suppose that one customer, Neri, breaches. What are the effects on the dealer's sales and costs? The seller, Marine, loses the sale, and his costs are reduced roughly by the wholesale price of the boat—his loss from the breach is, approximately, the gross margin. Goetz and Scott (1979, pp. 333–335), however, argued either that another sale would replace the Neri sale, or that Marine's cost saving would be the marginal cost, which is equal to the retail price. (In a competitive industry, price equals marginal cost.) Hence, there would be no lost profit. The difference between the approaches lies in the interpretations of the marginal cost concept. Marginal cost should not relate to actual output, ex post, as Goetz and Scott's analysis implies; rather, it concerns planned output, ex ante.

An analogy is helpful. Think of the customers as fish and the retailer as a fisherman. The fisherman makes decisions on boat size, crew, equipment, et cetera, on the basis of the relationship between these inputs and expected catch. For a given combination of inputs (a given level of expenditure on fishing or retailing), on a normal day the fisherman might anticipate a catch of, say, 1,000 pounds. On a good day he might land 2,000 pounds, and on a bad day he might do no more than drown a lot of worms. The fisherman's optimal level and mix of expenditures depend upon the distribution of expected outcomes and their relationship to the input mix. There is no unique marginal cost concept in this formulation. But if we had to have a single, summary marginal cost measure, it would almost surely be the cost of increasing the *expected* catch by one pound. Thus, if on a particular day, a fish is hooked and then on the way back to port it falls back into the sea, the fisherman loses the revenue from that fish and avoids virtually no costs— the ex post marginal costs are roughly zero. The fish that got away, like Neri, constitutes a net loss of revenue for the business.

This analogy captures the notion that the lost-profits proponents were trying to convey—the typical retailer can expand sales in the short run with little cost beyond the wholesale price in the sense that, if he has a lucky month, then he could fill the additional orders. Commentators, however, have used awkward terminology, such as an ability to "supply all probable customers" and the "seller has an unlimited supply of goods," to describe this concept.

The Price of Options

By now the reader should be convinced that the breach does impose a loss upon the retailer and that the gross margin is an approximation of the magnitude of that loss. So what? That does not tell us what the remedy should be. When Neri orders the boat, he can be viewed as purchasing an option. If the boat is delivered, he pays the contract price, which, of course, includes a share of the overall costs of retailing. If between the contract date and the delivery date Neri changes his mind, the option is canceled (i.e., the contract is breached). Neri would then pay the price of the option. What would be a reasonable measure of the value of the option? The remedy embodied in §708(2) says that the option price is the retailer's profit, the gross margin. If one has doubts that reasonable customers know or ought to know the extent of their commitment when making an option contract, then one should be uncomfortable about assessing the customer for lost-profit damages. Most buyers of boats and cars probably would be shocked to learn that the price of their option exceeds 15% of the retail price. And rightly so. The gross margin bears no relation to either the value of the option to the buyer or the cost of offering the option to the seller.

While it is true that the cancellation would mean that the seller loses the gross margin on this particular sale, in the long run cancellations are just a cost of doing business. The rate of cancellations would affect the seller's long-run costs by its impact on the firm's inventory policy. It can use the price of the option to influence the rate of cancellations, and, thereby, its costs. The cost to the seller of writing the option and the value of the option to the buyer will both vary depending on market conditions. In normal times, I would expect that the option price for most consumer transactions not involving customization would be close to zero. In a tight market, consumers would be willing to pay a positive price for the option. Note that this is just the opposite of what the lost-volume measure would yield. When the seller has the capacity to deal with lots of potential buyers, the damages are the full gross margin, but when the market is so tight that the retailer could not sell any more units, there is no lost volume, and under the lost volume measure the damages fall toward zero. Ironically, the tighter the market, the less likely the finding of lost-volume profits. The option price falls as the market tightens, a perverse result.

The option as designed by the parties is likely to take the form of a nonrefundable deposit. First, it is cheap to arrange, given that the parties are already entering into a contract. Second, it provides evidence that the customer has been apprised of the extent of his liability in the event that he fails to take delivery. Third, it forces the customer to value explicitly the option he purchases. Conversely, it induces the seller to state ex ante the price it is willing to put on that option. Finally, a policy of finding no damages in the absence of a nonrefundable deposit has low enforcement costs. Other things being equal, a policy of leaving the losses where they lie is very attractive.

A nonrefundable deposit is, in effect, a prepaid penalty, and this could run afoul of contract law's historic distaste for contractual penalties, and specifically §2–718(2)(b). ("Where the seller justifiably withholds delivery of goods because of buyer's breach, the buyer is entitled to restitution of any amount by which the sum of his payments exceeds . . . twenty per cent of the value of the total performance for which the buyer is obligated under the contract or $500, whichever is smaller.") The justification for the law's hostility has come under increased attack, and I join the critics. Regardless, the combination of the no-penalty-clause rule and the lost-volume rule produces a bizarre result. We will not permit the consumer to negotiate a specific penalty (or option price), but we will hit him with a penalty of unknown (but probably greater) magnitude in the name of preserving the seller's expectations.

The *Neri* contract did utilize a deposit, and its fate was interesting. Neri's initial deposit was only $40, but when the dealer arranged for "immediate delivery on the basis of a firm sale" the deposit was increased to $4,250, even though the dealer's margin turned out to be only around $2,500. On the back of the contract, in small print, the following term appeared: "If the within agreement is cancelled by mutual consent, the seller shall retain the deposit paid hereunder, whether paid in cash or other consideration, as liquidated damages." In his complaint, the plaintiff alleged, "The said provision of the contract appeared on the reverse side in fine print and is fraud." The trial court judge did not agree, but did rule that "[t]he liquidated damage clause . . . does not apply to the instant case since the contract was not cancelled by the mutual consent of the parties. Accordingly an assessment of damages must be had, at which time it may be determined whether the plaintiffs are entitled to the return of any portion of the down payment previously made." This ruling was not appealed. Consequently, the magnitude of the deposit was not a relevant factor in the determination of damages. The court only allowed Marine to keep the $2,579, expected profit plus an additional $674 for incidental expenses of storage, upkeep, finance charges, and insurance.

2. The Lost-Volume Business Buyer

The lost-volume expectation remedy has been applied in the manufacturing context as well. I should note first that there can be no pretense that the difference between the seller's cost and the price bears any relation to selling costs. So, if the remedy were an attempt to replicate selling costs (not, I hasten to add, a good idea), it would fail on that score.

The contract created by the courts invoking the lost-volume damage measure looks like this: the buyer purchases an option, the price being the seller's lost profits as determined ex post by the courts. The option allows it to buy the goods at the contract price minus the option price. The option price for the commercial customer is the difference between the contract price and the court-determined but-for costs. The price of that option is a number that no buyer should know at the time of contracting, since it depends on determining the seller's but-for costs, confidential information zealously guarded by sellers. More importantly, the buyer should not care. The damage remedy bears no relation to the parties' needs. There are, as I have made clear throughout this book, lots of good reasons for parties to establish an option price (or penalty) to increase the likelihood that a buyer would perform. The lost-volume remedy sets the price independent of any possible function.

The penalty imposed by the lost-volume profit remedy bears no relation to the option value. Its perverseness can be illustrated nicely by three decisions. In all three, there was no indication that market conditions had deteriorated prior to the buyer's cancellation. Consider first *Teradyne, Inc. v. Teledyne Industries, Inc.,* in which the court accepted the lost-volume measure without question, the only issue being whether some subset of costs were truly but-for costs. Because most of the contract price reflected a high level of research and development spending, the incremental production costs were only about 25% of the contract price. By awarding lost-volume profits, the courts created a ludicrous contract, regardless of how the appeals court dealt with the particular cost component. The buyer, in effect, was presumed to pay $75,000 for an option to buy a transistor test system for an additional $25,000. There are few circumstances that would require such a high option price. One would be a partial offset to a binding price ceiling (the high takes in take-or-pay contracts for natural gas prior to deregulation would be an example; see Hubbard and Weiner 1991). Another would be protection of substantial seller reliance (see Chapter 5), but, of course, that would be inconsistent with the notion that the seller could easily resell the goods.

Next, consider *Davis v. Diasonics,* a casebook favorite. After canceling an order for an MRI unit with a price of around $1.3 million, the buyer asked for the return of its $300,000 deposit. Both sides conceded that §2–718(2)(b) would require that Diasonics refund all but $500. (Why Diasonics was willing to concede this point I do not know.) In response, the seller counterclaimed for its lost-volume profits, winning a jury verdict of about $450,000. Had Davis let sleeping dogs lie, it would have saved a substantial amount of money and years of costly litigation. The court's analysis was confined to whether Diasonics could have produced and sold an additional unit and whether it could have done so profitably. It never asked why the contract included a substantial deposit or why the implied option price would be 50% greater than the deposit.

A weak justification for the lost-volume remedy and a rationale for parties not contracting out of it is that it serves as a device for enforcing agreements that otherwise might not survive the hurdles put up by the law of contracts. Given the uncertainty about enforcement of liquidated damages clauses in general and, in particular, the threat of a breaching buyer's invocation of §2–718(2)(b), the seller has a hammer to discourage a buyer's avoidance of the liquidated damages. Two wrongs make a right. The cleaner way to deal with this matter would be to repeal §2–718(2)(b) and to relax the presumption against penalty clauses. Until that is done, the threat of a counterclaim for lost-volume profits will be a powerful deterrent to attempts to recover the deposit. That is a pretty lame justification.

A liquidated damages clause was the focus of the third case, *Rodriguez v. Learjet*. Lear sold an airplane for future delivery with the contract calling for a series of progress payments when certain milestones were reached. The buyer made the first payment of $250,000, canceled the order, and then asked for the return of the payment. The §2–718(2)(b) issue was not raised. The buyer's claim was that the liquidated damages clause was not enforceable because it acted as a penalty. The clause in question read as follows:

> Learjet may terminate this Agreement as a result of the Buyer's . . . failure to make any progress payment when due. . . . If this Agreement is terminated by Learjet for any reason stipulated in the previous sentence Learjet shall retain all payments theretofore made by the Buyer as liquidated damages and not as a penalty and the parties shall thenceforth be released from all further obligations hereunder. Such damages include, but are not limited to, loss of profit on this sale, direct and indirect costs incurred as a result of disruption in production, training expense advance and selling expenses in effecting resale of the Airplane.

Lear sold the jet to another customer for a "profit" of $1,887,464. Here is where it gets weird. To show that the liquidated damages were not unreasonable, the court considered Lear's argument that it was a lost-volume seller. It found that Lear was and that the lost-volume profits were the $1.8 million profit that it received in the subsequent sale. The court went through the *Diasonics* exercise, finding that Lear had the capacity to produce an additional airplane and that it would have been profitable to do so. So, had Lear been greedy (at least in the short term) it could have argued that the clause was unenforceable and taken the $1.8 million instead. To its credit, it was more concerned about establishing the legality of its standard system of progress payments than about making a one-time killing. Rather than simply recognizing that the progress payments established a series of options for the buyer, the court was forced to ask a bunch of foolish questions. Only by accident did it come up with the proper outcome.

CHAPTER 13

Consequential Damages

For want of a nail the shoe was lost.
For want of a shoe the horse was lost.
For want of a horse the rider was lost.
For want of a rider the battle was lost.
For want of a battle the kingdom was lost.
And all for the want of a horseshoe nail.

So, if the contract was for that nail and the seller failed to deliver, making the buyer whole would, I suppose, mean that the damage remedy would be the monetary equivalent of a kingdom. Fortunately, the law does not go quite that far. The consequential damages are recoverable only if they were "foreseeable." The fountainhead of the foreseeability limitation is, of course, *Hadley v. Baxendale*. As almost everyone who has studied contracts knows, the carrier delayed, the shaft was delivered five days late, and Hadley claimed damages for his lost profits for those five days. The court denied recovery because the carrier had no reason to know how significant the delivery was for the operation of Hadley's mill. Had the carrier been informed, or perhaps even if it had reason to know, it would have been responsible for the damages. The standard interpretations of *Hadley* emphasize the knowledge issue. A promisor faces a potential adverse selection problem if it is unable to identify customers who might suffer large consequential damages. If the promisor had known of the special circumstances, it could have taken more care, charged a higher price, or refused to take on the responsibilities.

While much attention has been given to the adverse selection problem, moral hazard has received relatively little attention. The probability of the provider's failure is under its control, but the magnitude of the damages is not. In tort language, Hadley's vulnerability to Baxendale's failure constituted a "thin skull," but the thinness was not inexorable. The possibility that Hadley could have held a larger inventory of shafts (an input) has been widely recognized. Less attention has been given to other ways in which the costs of the failure could have been limited by Hadley's efforts. It could have held a larger inventory of flour (the output). After the shaft was delivered and the mill again operating, Hadley could have made up for some of the lost output by running at a higher level of output than he otherwise would have. (In effect, that entails having a larger inventory of productive capacity—another input—than Hadley might otherwise carry.) Indeed, there is no reason that Hadley should have held the inventory of inputs or outputs only at this location. Hadley could have increased its output from another factory (it could have been diversified).

The modern trend has been to liberalize the rules regarding the recovery of consequential damages. At the same time, it appears that the barriers to contracting out of liability have risen. Both trends, I believe, are unfortunate. My impression is that scholarly writing in this area has been at too general a level. In the next chapter, I risk erring in the other direction, going to a level that could be viewed as too particular. I focus on a narrow class of problems, faulty performance by a specialist firm for weighing, inspecting, or certifying quality. The narrow focus allows us to explore some subtle points regarding the interplay among incentives, liability, disclaimers, and insurance.

CHAPTER 14

A Reexamination of *Glanzer v. Shepard:* Surveyors on the Tort-Contract Boundary

In international commodity transactions, intermediary certifiers of quantity and quality play a crucial role. Sometimes they err. When they do so, the aggrieved party can pursue remedies against the counterparty or against the intermediary, either in contract or tort. The Restatement of Restitution (§20 (buyer overpaid); §39 (buyer underpaid)) provides for compensation by the counterparty. The remedy against the intermediary has depended, at least in part, on whether the plaintiff was in privity. Even absent privity, the aggrieved party could possibly recover in tort (or perhaps as a third-party beneficiary). So held Cardozo in the leading New York case *Glanzer v. Shepard.* Cardozo was confronted with the claim of a buyer of beans (Glanzer) against a public weigher (Shepard) who had negligently weighed the beans, the buyer having paid for 5% more beans than it received. Cardozo found for the plaintiff, despite the fact that the weigher had been engaged by the seller.

Glanzer's prominence stems in large part from its juxtaposition with another Cardozo opinion, *Ultramares Corp. v. Touche, Niven & Co.* In *Ultramares,* Cardozo held that an accountant would not be liable to an indeterminate class that might have relied upon the accountant's findings even though they had no contract. He distinguished *Ultramares* from *Glanzer* by noting that although Glanzer had had no contract with Shepard, his reliance on Shepard was obvious. In *Ultramares,* however, there were a potentially large number of people who might have made unfortunate decisions in reliance upon the accountant's faulty work; the accountant could not be expected to take the potential problems of this ill-defined class into account when performing, and he therefore held the accountant not liable for negligence.

Although Glanzer and Shepard had no contract, it would not have been difficult for them to allocate the risk of negligent weighing explicitly, either in their respective contracts with the seller or by contracting with each other. The costs of liability for certifiers of quantity or quality are ultimately borne by the parties. It is predictable that measurement errors will occur. Buyers and sellers must determine how much effort should go into reducing the incidence of errors, given that error reduction has both costs and benefits. Thus, buyers and sellers have an incentive to economize by assigning the consequences for such errors to the party that can most efficiently bear them.

So it is a bit misleading to view *Glanzer* as a matter of tort. It is one piece of a default rule for the contractual triad, the first piece being recovery from the counterparty. Its bite depends on the damage measure and the ease with which the parties can contract around the default rule. American courts, it turns out, have been rather liberal in allowing the principals to contract around the default rule (although not so liberal as their British counterparts), but less so for the intermediaries.

Public weighers are members of a broader category of surveyors who provide independent certification of quantity, quality, cleanliness, readiness, and so forth. In *Glanzer,* damages were easily measured as the product of the contract price and the difference between the measured and "true" weight. For other surveyors, the damage issue is more complicated. Suppose, for example, that a cargo of oil satisfied the contractual standard of a sulfur content less than 1.5%. If the certifier negligently found the content to be 1.52%, the buyer could reject the shipment as nonconforming, and the seller would have to resell either to this buyer or to a new one at a lower price. The certifier could be held liable for the entire price difference or some lesser amount. The Restatement (Second) of Contracts (§351 f) allows the court to limit the magnitude of the certifier's liability in certain circumstances, although the parameters of that default rule are ill-defined. Relying in part on *Glanzer,* the Second Circuit appears to have rejected that limitation in *International Ore & Fertilizer Corp. v. SGS Control Services* (*Interore II*), holding the certifier liable for the seller's entire loss.

This chapter is organized as follows. In Section 1, I review the *Glanzer* litigation, with special emphasis on how the court suppressed many of the significant facts. In Section 2, I then turn to the first piece of the default rule—restitution by the principals. Parties appear to routinely contract around the remedy, making the word of the intermediary "final and binding," and those clauses are generally (but not always) upheld. In Section 3, I explore the courts' general hostility to intermediaries' attempts to limit their liability by contract. In Section 4, I consider the judiciary's sporadic efforts to place extra-contractual limits on intermediaries' liability. In Section 5, I examine the surveyors' response.

1. The *Glanzer* Proceedings

The dispute arose over the sale of about 100 tons of Caballero beans from Chile by an importer, Bech, Van Siclen & Co., to a New York bean merchant, Glanzer Brothers. That agreement was not put in evidence, and there is some confusion as to when it was entered into—the Complaint (Record, pp. 5–6) alleging February 18, 1918, while Glanzer's uncontradicted testimony put the contract date in June. (Record, p. 23) Though the parties failed to place the Bech-Glanzer contract in the record, they did enter the invoice, dated August 13, 1918. (Plaintiff Exhibit [PX] 2, at 95–96) The beans were shipped from Chile in May and arrived in New York in late July. Bech then sent an engagement letter to Core & Herbert (a weighing firm in which Shepard was a partner) directing them to weigh the beans:

> These beans have been sold to Glanzer Bros. . . . and arrangements have been made for them to take delivery first thing Tuesday morning, July 23rd.
>
> Kindly communicate with Glanzer Bros. on Monday afternoon, to see if it will be in order for your weighers to be on the pier first thing Tuesday morning to weigh these beans. (PX 10, p. 105)

Core & Herbert determined that the 905 bags weighed 228,380 pounds. Since that was in excess of the amount contracted for, the parties agreed that seventeen bags would remain with the seller. These bags were weighed, and their weight was subtracted from the total, so that on net, Glanzer received 888 bags, which, according to the Core & Herbert weight certificates, weighed 224,086 pounds. On the basis of the weight certificates, Glanzer paid the contract price of 10.5 cents per pound to Bech, and the beans were then stored in a bonded warehouse. Glanzer sold the beans over the next five months, the last, and largest, transaction taking place at the end of January 1919. For each of these transactions, the beans were again weighed by Core & Herbert; after the last weighing, it was clear to Glanzer that the weight of the beans it had sold was about 5% less than the weight of the (same) beans it had bought.

Glanzer then sued Shepard for the difference, $1,262.26. After a two-day trial, Judge Peter Schmuck gave a directed verdict for the plaintiff. The Supreme Court, Appellate Term, reversed unanimously, finding that the defendant owed no duty to the plaintiff to weigh the beans accurately; if the plaintiffs were to have any remedy, the Court held that it should be against the seller, Bech. This opinion was then unanimously reversed at Appellate Division, and Cardozo, writing for the Court of Appeals, affirmed.

Cardozo found that the weigher had a duty "imposed by law," so that it was unnecessary to deal with the issue of privity:

> We think the law imposes a duty toward buyer as well as seller in the situation here disclosed. The plaintiffs' use of the certificates was not an indirect or collateral consequence of the action of the weighers. It was a consequence which, to the weighers' knowledge, was the end and aim of the transaction. Bech, Van Siclen & Co. ordered, but Glanzer Brothers were to use. The defendants held themselves out to the public as skilled and careful in their calling. They knew that the beans had been sold, and that on the faith of their certificate payment would be made. They sent a copy to the plaintiffs for the very purpose of inducing action. All this they admit. In such circumstances, assumption of the task of weighing was the assumption of a duty to weigh carefully for the benefit of all whose conduct was to be governed. (pp. 275–276)

The defendants, he held, "weighed and certified at the order of one with the very end and aim of shaping the conduct of another. Diligence was owing, not only to him who ordered, but to him also who relied." (p. 277)

No direct evidence of the weigher's negligence was introduced. If the weights were off by 5% and if the defendant could not present a plausible alternative explanation of the discrepancy, the court would presume negligence. The plaintiff introduced testimony from a federal customs agent and two bean merchants suggesting that shrinkage could not have been greater than .5% in a year. (Record at 30–31, 34, 38) Glanzer also testified (in a somewhat disjointed way) that the original bill of lading—which was not in evidence—was for about 12,000 fewer pounds than the weighing certificates:

> Mr. Shepard was sitting at his desk. I showed him all the papers. He carefully looked at them. . . . I said, "Here is a bill of lading which reads for itself; it shows the shipper has never shipped so much goods at all; where did you get it from? You have given us a weighing certificate nearly 12,000

pounds over; where did you get the goods from? The bill of lading reads there was never shipped that much." (pp. 41–42)

Glanzer further testified that he had another conversation with another employee of Core & Herbert:

He said, . . . "We have weighed the goods and that settles it. We don't know anything about it. For instance," he says, "the man was in a hurry to ship these goods, and he probably gave him five or six or seven thousand pounds too much," and I says, "For the lord's sake, is it possible that a shipper would ship five or six thousand more pounds than he should; where is the steamship? They would demand freight charges for it if they would, and they have showed a bill of lading only for 101,000 kilos." (p. 43)

The defendant did propose three alternative explanations: (1) there was more shrinkage in these beans than would generally have been the case because green (not dried) beans had been shipped; (2) the bags were not in very good shape and some beans were lost; and (3) the batch of beans weighed on arrival in August was different from the batch weighed on resale in January. The last argument was buttressed by the fact that the weight certificates in August rightly identified the ship carrying the beans as the *Panama*, while the January weight certificates erroneously identified the ship as the *Totten Maru*, a Japanese ship that had almost certainly never been to Chile. The trial judge apparently did not believe that these explanations deserved jury consideration (and given the evasiveness of the defense witnesses, he was most likely right).

No evidence was offered on the amount that Bech paid the weighers, nor did Cardozo comment on the absence of this evidence. This omission was rather odd, since only a few years later, in *H. R. Moch Co. v. Rensselaer Water Co.*, he was quite willing to infer that the rates charged by the negligent water company were so low that it could not have intended to bear the risk of liability.

The normal remedy for the buyer in this case would have been restitution from the seller. Indeed, the Restatement (First) of Restitution uses a variation on *Glanzer* as an example of a case in which restitution is the proper remedy. "A agrees to deliver to B 10,000 bushels of wheat at sixty cents per bushel, the wheat to be measured by a third person. By mistake of the third person B receives 11,000 bushels. A is entitled to restitution of 1000 bushels or the value." (Restatement of Restitution §39 illus. 4) The record was not entirely clear regarding Glanzer's claim vis-à-vis Bech. Glanzer did pay Bech; that much was certain. (Mr. Hasselriis, of Bech, testified: "Q. Were you paid for those beans by Glanzer Brothers? A. I should say so." (Record, p. 64)) There was no evidence as to whether Glanzer had attempted to recover the overpayment. Defense counsel asked Mr. Hasselriis, "Was any demand ever made on you for the return of any of that money?" Plaintiff's objection to the question was sustained. (Record, p. 64) One can infer that Bech never disgorged. The defense, in its opening statement, said that it would show that the sellers "were a large concern and were responsible," but Judge Schmuck (Record, p. 16) upheld an objection to such testimony being admitted. The defense did, however, raise the argument in its brief:

> According to plaintiff's own story, through a mistake in fact, they have overpaid [Bech] $1,262.31. Apparently [Bech] still holds this money and the plaintiffs have never demanded the same back or sued for its return. If the plaintiff's story is correct, the payment to [Bech] was a plain payment in mistake of fact, and recoverable. Plaintiffs have not shown why they have never demanded or sued for recovery from [Bech] or that [Bech] was insolvent. In fact, defendants offered to show [Bech] was solvent, but this was ruled out. (Defendant's Brief, p. 25)

The apparent lack of an effort to pursue redress against Bech remains a puzzle. It is possible that Bech was, indeed, insolvent. It also is conceivable that an importer might be beyond the reach of American courts, although the fact that a Bech executive testified for the defense casts doubt on that. It also is possible that the Bech-Glanzer contract precluded Glanzer's recovery. According to the Complaint, the initial contract said "goods to be weighed by an official weigher, and to be paid for in accordance with the weight sheets to be furnished by said official weigher." (Record, p. 6) It is not clear, however, whether the Core & Herbert weights would be "final and binding." As we shall see, many contracts do include such language, and courts generally enforce the agreements even if the weigher had erred. The unfortunate omission of this contract from the trial record prevents us from ascertaining whether the buyer and seller had allocated the risk of weigher error between themselves.

If the default rule were that the weigher would be held liable for negligence, then the weigher could either accept the rule and set a price for its

service that incorporates the implicit insurance of accuracy, or it could contract out of liability. It could, that is, if the law did not constrain the
weigher's freedom to do so. If public weighers were regulated entities, it is
possible that the price of their services would be fixed by law or that their
ability to alter contract terms would be restricted in some way. Indeed, if
one looks in standard legal references like *Corpus Juris Secundum*, there is
ample evidence that in some instances, parties identified as public weighers
were subjected to considerable public regulation, including fixed maximum
prices. (94 C.J.S. *Weights and Measures* § 6; see also 79 Am. Jur. 2d *Weights
and Measures* §§ 5, 6, 13, 19, 20, 21, 22) Public weighers like Core & Herbert
(Shepard) were almost certainly not subject to governmental regulation,
but the trial court was decidedly unhelpful on this matter. Thus, Shepard's
lawyer asked of him:

By what right are you a weigher?
Do you have any license to do weighing?
From whom do you get your license?
Who are the proper authorities to license you? (Record, pp. 45–46)

The plaintiff's objection to all these questions was sustained. Shepard's
deposition testimony is a bit more helpful:

A: Our firm is known as City weighers.
Q: State how appointed.
A: Business has been handed down for a long time.
Q: Is there a license issued to you?
A: There is a general agreement amongst the merchants that a disin-
terested party should do their weighing.
Q: There is no formal license issued to you, is there?
A: By the Exchange.
Q: By the Exchange you mean Coffee Exchange?
A: By the various Exchanges and their different rules. (Record, pp. 84–
85)

In its reply brief, the defense asserted that the public weighers were in
no way regulated by any government:

There is no such thing in law as an official weigher. We have examined
both federal and local laws as well as city charter and can find nowhere
any official or public weigher. It is entirely a private enterprise. The defendants do not claim otherwise.

If the plaintiffs had claimed that they were members of an exchange licensing the defendants, and claimed the benefit of the exchange rules, and had brought an action thereon, the case might be different, but no such claim was made, nor is there any proof [of] . . . any rule making the defendants liable. (Defendant's Reply Brief, p. 6)

That language is not entirely unambiguous, but a plausible interpretation is that if the beans in question had been coffee beans, the public weigher would have been subject to the rules of the Coffee Exchange, a private organization with an elaborate set of rules governing transactions. However, since Glanzer's beans were not traded on any exchange, the only rules governing the parties and the public weighers were those of New York contract law. Apparently, the court was not inclined to infer commercial practice by looking at the manner in which the formal exchanges regulated the relationship between weighers and merchants.

Because damages were reckoned by looking to the contract price, there was almost no effort to introduce evidence on changing market conditions. If there had been a substantial price decline, it would not be terribly surprising to find Glanzer looking for some way to mitigate the losses arising from a bad deal. The defense, in its attempt to show that the beans might have been shipped green and therefore might have been subject to greater shrinkage, attempted to elicit testimony that beans were in great demand in June, but less so in July and August. However, the only testimony was that the demand was high in June and remained high until the first of the year (a month before Glanzer discovered the weighing error). (Record, p. 35) This seems plausible, since the contract had been entered into while the war was still on and the bad news was revealed two months after the Armistice; one might reasonably expect that the market price had collapsed in the interim. Surprisingly, the facts do not bear this out. Prices did not budge following the war's end.

To sum up, processing the facts through the legal system left a number of large holes. We do not have the underlying contracts. We do not know whether the seller would have been legally obligated to make restitution. Nor do we know whether Shepard had attempted to contractually limit his liability in any way. Indeed, we do not even know for certain whether Shepard's behavior and responsibilities were delimited in any way by regulations of the state or of any commodity exchange, although we can be reasonably confident on this score. Cardozo's ambiguities are, in

large part, a manifestation of the raw materials with which he was provided.

2. Resisting Restitution

The Restatement of Restitution rule sounds simple enough. If, because the
weigher had erred, Glanzer ended up with fewer beans than it had bargained for, then the seller should make him whole. Yet traders usually undo
that result. Their contracts make the surveyor's certificate final and binding.
And with good reason. A typical clause for an international petroleum
product contract reads:

> The quantity and quality of the Oil shall be determined by an independent
> inspector at the discharge port, such independent inspector shall be ap-
> pointed jointly and the cost of his services shall be shared equally by the
> parties. All determinations as to quantity and quality made in accordance
> with the provisions of this Section . . . shall be conclusive and binding upon
> both parties. (*Cities Serv. Co. v. Derby & Co.*, p. 493)

Notice, in passing, that the inspector is hired *jointly*, so that the privity question disappears. Neither buyer nor seller would be a third party like Glanzer.
    The virtues of final and binding clauses were nicely laid out by the plain-
tiff in a suit against a surveyor:

> Even when done erroneously, [the measurements] still were binding and
> either party had the right to act thereon. If this were not so, the Inspection
> clause in the contracts would be meaningless. Oil traders, and others who
> deal in the sale of commodities, need quick, definitive, prompt and binding
> results or else there would be chaos. Buyers would shop around for results
> showing cargoes to be non-conforming and sellers would do the converse.
> (*Vitol Trading S.A., Inc. v. SGS Control Services, Inc.*, Plaintiff's Brief, pp. 36–
> 37)

In upholding a similar clause involving a domestic corn shipment, Judge
Wisdom noted that

> where an inspection by a third party is stipulated, it supersedes the buyer's
> right to inspect. . . . The obvious purpose of that inspection at origin was
> to establish a certain, reliable, and objective standard at a fixed place and
> time to give the transaction certainty. It would serve little use to have this

inspection, if the buyer were free to accept or reject the shipment after its arrival on the basis of its own inspection at destination. (*Bartlett & Co., Grain v. Merchants Co.*, 506)

"To allow a mere mistake or error in decision of an umpire to nullify his decision," Wisdom concluded, "would make the chosen means of avoiding litigation—breed litigation." (p. 508) In the absence of fraud, bad faith, or such gross mistake as amounts to fraud, the inspector's decision will be upheld. *Bartlett* is the rule in most American jurisdictions. (See Tan, 7 *A.L.R. 3d* 555, and cases collected there.) That qualification leaves a window for overcoming final and binding clauses. American courts have proved more willing to exploit that opening than their British counterparts. Thus, the British court accepted the surveyor's certificate on quality (asphaltine content), despite the disappointed buyer's claim that the surveyor had not actually measured the content but had simply asked another oil company (which apparently had been in possession of the cargo prior to the disputed transaction). *(Coastal (Bermuda) Ltd. v. Esso Petroleum Co., Ltd.)*

That final and binding clause might not have survived in an American court. A surveyor's certificate could be overridden if the error could support an inference of "fraud, bad faith or gross error." In one of the few litigated cases, this turned out to be a very low hurdle. In *Cities Service Co. v. Derby & Co.*, Judge Kram's finding of bad faith was based both on her conclusion that the inspector's testing methods did not comply with the industry standard and on the magnitude of the error. In an earlier decision, *Amoco Oil Co. v. H. Grunewald & Co.*, the court had upheld a final and binding clause, holding that an error of 1.7% was not sufficient to conclude that there had been bad faith or gross error. She rejected the defendant's argument that an error of 2.4% should likewise be insufficient. "However, defendant's argument ignores that in the *Amoco* case the damages sought totaled $42,181.80, while here damages of $374,225.26 are sought. The magnitude of the loss here clearly is much greater than in *Amoco*. As a result, this Court finds it sufficient to justify such an inference of fraud, bad faith or gross error." (p. 503) In a few other instances, courts and arbitration panels have followed *Cities Service* in rejecting a final and binding clause. Nonetheless, American courts in general have been kinder to these clauses than they have been to the disclaimers of the intermediary certifiers. To these I now turn.

3. Disclaimers by Intermediaries

Even if surveyors do perform in a substandard manner, they could avoid legal responsibility by including disclaimers or exculpatory clauses in their initial contracts. At least they could do so if courts were willing to enforce such clauses. However, there is hostility to the surveyor disclaiming liability for negligence that does not carry over to the corresponding disclaimer by the seller. The different legal treatment of final and binding clauses and surveyor's liability limitations or disclaimers is intriguing. A final and binding clause is, after all, a disclaimer of liability: X promises to deliver to Z goods of a certain quantity and quality as certified by Y. If, in fact, X delivers less than was certified by Y, it is not X's problem.

Courts will honor some disclaimers, but it is not something one should be confident about. Since the validity of a disclaimer is questionable even when it appears in the contract between the surveyor and its customer (even a commercially sophisticated customer), the validity is even more problematic in *Glanzer*-type situations. The aggrieved party had not, after all, agreed to the liability limitation. The general suspicion of liability limitations, coupled with the lack of privity, makes avoiding the *Glanzer* rule a tricky problem.

In *Plata American Trading, Inc. v. Lancashire*, the purchaser of tallow paid for 501 tons as per the bill of lading, but received only 375 tons because of fraud on the part of the seller. Payment was made "relying upon the weight certificate." (p. 48) (The opinion is silent as to whether there was a "final and binding" clause.) The quantity was to be measured as the tallow flowed from shore tanks to the ship. However, some of it was diverted back to the storage tanks after measurement, never reaching the ship. The court did not mention any suit against the seller, the perpetrator of the fraud, I suspect because the seller was judgment proof. The purchaser attempted to recover from the ship, the marine underwriter, and the cargo inspector. The action against the first two failed. Against the third, it was successful. Citing *Ultramares* and *Glanzer*, the court stated, "Marco diverted tallow from one of his tanks to another and it seems to me that Martin [the cargo inspector] negligently—grossly so—lent himself to the scheme. . . . When Martin was retained by Marco he was told that the shipment was for the account of Plata and his certificate recites that it was Plata that had delivered to it 501 tons. Martin's liability seems to me to be plain." (p. 49)

It is not clear from the opinion why the court labeled Martin's negligence "gross" or whether that label mattered. In *Glanzer,* it was not necessary to prove gross negligence, and it is unlikely that the court was attempting to raise the standard of proof, although gross negligence was one of the exceptions under *Ultramares.* From my perspective, the most interesting piece of the opinion was the dog that did not bark. Nowhere did the court mention the possibility that Martin, the inspector, had attempted in any way to disclaim liability. The court continued to enforce *Glanzer,* and nearly four decades later, there is no hint that there was any attempt to contract around the *Glanzer* rule.

The apparent silence could simply result from the court's ignoring the liability limitation—that appears to be what happened in some petroleum product disputes, as we shall see below. More likely, there was no disclaimer. This is speculative, but there are some pretty good reasons for reaching this conclusion. First, weighers at this time were typically small firms that would not be plausible deep pockets. Second, the losses from a weigher's error were not likely to result in significant dollar amounts. Disclaimers would be more likely today when surveyors (at least some of them) have become billion-dollar companies and when small errors could result in claims in excess of $100,000. In fact, as we shall see, even where the surveyors are deep pockets and their exposure significant, the contracts do not all have disclaimers. But before getting to those, let us consider two classes of contracts that feature disclaimers and the courts' general indifference to them.

Consider first the treatment of the surveyors' close cousins, classification societies. Ship classification societies provide a variety of services to owners of ships. Hull and protection and indemnity (P&I) insurers will refuse to insure a ship if it does not have the appropriate certification from a classification society. Sales of vessels, charter arrangements, and contracts with cargo owners are often contingent upon the society certifying that the vessel meets a certain quality standard (that it is "in class"). There are a handful of cases in which classification societies have been sued for performing their service in a negligent or unworkmanlike manner. If the classification society errs, a ship might sink, resulting in huge damage claims. Although the courts have rejected their contractual disclaimers, the classification societies have defeated claims against them on other grounds.

In *Great American Insurance Co. v. Bureau Veritas,* a ship sank with the loss of the entire cargo and the lives of eleven crew members. The owner, the charterer, and their respective insurance companies settled claims against them and then sought indemnification and subrogation from Bureau Veritas, the ship's classification society. Although Judge Tyler he found in favor of the classification society, he ignored its disclaimer of liability, asserting that it "is overbroad and unenforceable as contrary to public policy." (p. 1010, n.6) In another case involving a claim against a classification society for a more modest loss, *Sundance Cruises Corp. v. American Bureau of Shipping*, the court denied the defense's motion for summary judgment because the non-prominence of the clauses in the contract "raise[s] a question of fact as to the actual intention of the parties. Moreover, we are inclined, without the benefit of trial testimony as to the parties' intention, to agree with Judge Tyler's dictum." (p. 378) One wonders what sort of trial testimony would help resolve this question.

Disclaimers did not survive in cases in which the surveyor's alleged negligence resulted in a cargo being lost. In *Royal Embassy of Saudi Arabia v. S.S. Ioannis Martinos*, the surveyor certified that cargo was properly stowed on board. In the course of the voyage, eighty-seven containers stored on deck, with a value in excess of $8 million, were lost at sea, and the surveying firm was among those sued for the loss. The magistrate refused to grant summary judgment to the surveyor, despite the disclaimers that appeared on the Certificates of Readiness. "[The surveyor] makes no warranty of any kind, either express or implied, including warranty of workmanlike service, respecting its work or services, and is not an insurer of cargo or other property or of the ship . . . and disclaims all legal responsibility for any loss, damage, personal injury or death resulting from any act, default, omission, negligence, error or breach of any said warranties." Exculpatory clauses would be honored, said the magistrate, so long as they do not increase the likelihood that negligence will occur. Concluding that enforcement of the clause would increase that likelihood, the magistrate held the disclaimer void as against public policy. (pp. 788–789) In a similar case, *Bosnor, S.A. de C.V. v. Tug L. A. Barrios*, the marine surveyor was one of many defendants in a comparative fault proceeding following the loss of a cargo worth over $1 million. The survey report included this standard clause:

The surveyor agrees to use best efforts in behalf of those for whom this survey is made, however, this report is issued subject to the conditions that it is understood and agreed that neither this office nor any surveyor thereof will have any liability for any inaccuracy, errors or omissions, whether due to negligence or otherwise, in excess of the actual charge made for this survey, and that use of this report shall be construed to be an acceptance of the foregoing. (p. 781)

The court, however, could find no evidence that the plaintiffs had "agreed to this limited liability clause. Clauses that purport to limit a party's legal responsibility are strictly construed and to be given legal effect must clearly express the intent of all parties whose liability is altered by the agreement." (p. 781)

Limitations on liability are commonly used in petroleum transactions. In *Global Petroleum Corp. v. Torco Oil Co.*, the court recognized that the surveyor, Saybolt, had attempted to limit liability, but still denied Saybolt's motion for partial summary judgment.

> The basis for Saybolt's motion is straightforward. Saybolt, since at least 1983, has published a booklet entitled "Price Schedules and Terms, Conditions and Limitations of Services" (the "price booklet"). They claim that it has been their regular business practice since that time to send copies of this booklet to all of its regular customers and that it is customary for all independent testing laboratories to do so. Further, Saybolt maintains that it is industry custom for there to be no formal written agreement between testing labs and their customers and for those customers to rely on information in the price booklet. In addition, Saybolt includes a notice in bold letters at the bottom of each of its invoices directing the reader to "Refer to our price list for terms, conditions and limitations of our services." (*Global I*, p. 1)

The terms, conditions, and limitations included the following:

> (a) Neither E.W. SAYBOLT & CO., INC. nor any of its employees, agents or sub-contractors shall be liable for any loss or damage arising out of E.W. SAYBOLT & CO., INC.'s performance or non-performance, whether by way of negligence or breach of contract, or otherwise, in any amount greater than twice the amount billed to the customer for the work leading to the claim of the customer. Said remedy shall be the sole and exclusive remedy against E.W. SAYBOLT & CO., INC. arising out of its work.

> (c) E.W. SAYBOLT & CO., INC. reports are submitted in writing and are for our customers only. Our customers are considered to be only those entities being billed for our services. Acquisition of an E.W. SAYBOLT & CO., INC.

report by other than our customer does not constitute a representation of
E.W. SAYBOLT & CO., INC. as to the accuracy of the contents thereof.

(d) In no event shall E.W. SAYBOLT & CO., INC., its employees, agents
or sub-contractors be responsible for consequential or special damages of
any kind or in any amount. (*Global I*, pp. 1–2)

Hence, Saybolt, and probably the other inspectors, had for some period
of time expressly limited their liability for *Glanzer*-type damages. These
terms and conditions were incorporated into the contract by the notice on
the invoices. Or at least they would be as long as the principals did not
have inconsistent language in their documents. In a battle of the forms, the
disclaimer would likely lose.

In support of its motion, Saybolt produced an affidavit from someone
who had worked in the petroleum testing industry for over thirty years,
stating that he has

> personal knowledge that it is customary in the petroleum testing industry
> for the parties to an agreement with an independent testing laboratory to
> refer to the independent testing laboratory's schedule of services, prices,
> terms and conditions in determining the terms and conditions between the
> independent testing laboratory and the customer. (*Global I*, p. 2)

However, the plaintiff's vice president filed an affidavit in which he
claimed that "he has been involved in 'hundreds of transactions' and has
retained the services of independent testing laboratories, including third
party defendant Saybolt on 'hundreds of occasions'; that he knows of the
custom of the industry in retaining testing laboratories, and that it is 'not
customary for a buyer and seller to refer to the testing laboratory's schedule
. . . in determining the terms and conditions.' " (*Global II*, p. 141535) That
apparently was enough to produce a triable issue of fact.

Despite the fact that Saybolt claimed to make its liability limitations
known to all customers, three cases concerning alleged negligence on Saybolt's part were decided without reference to the disclaimers. In *Marathon
International Petroleum Supply Co. v. I.T.I. Shipping, S.A.*, the court ruled that
had Saybolt's negligence caused the loss, it would have been liable, citing
Glanzer and *Plata*. Saybolt avoided liability, however, because its negligence
did not cause the harm. In *Coastal (Bermuda) Ltd. v. E. W. Saybolt & Co.*,
Saybolt again avoided liability by showing that it was not negligent. In
Anschutz Petroleum Marketing Co. v. E. W. Saybolt & Co., Saybolt failed in an

attempt to bring in a third-party defendant to reduce its liability by indemnity or contribution. The court took no position on whether Saybolt had, in fact, breached its obligation.

In only one instance, *Conoco v. Tank Barge Interstate*, did the court both mention the disclaimer and honor it. Saybolt's negligence "did not rise to the level of gross negligence and certainly not to the level of reckless, wanton, or indifferent misconduct which would negate its limitation of liability." (p. 3) Saybolt's limitation of liability as set forth in the standard terms and conditions in its 1986 schedule of services and prices limited liability to "[t]wice the amount billed to the customer leading to the claim of the customer." Since the fee for tank inspection was $200, Saybolt's liability was limited to $400.

The uneven treatment of the Saybolt liability limitation is partly due to the courts' general hostility to disclaimers. It also reflects the manner in which Saybolt, and others, have attempted to incorporate the limitations into their contracts. Did the principals agree to incorporate the clause from the price list? A court could easily find that they had not. One anonymous industry source told me that after receiving the price lists, some oil traders send back letters rejecting the disclaimers. This suggests that rather than confronting the matter directly, the parties have chosen instead to jockey for position in the battle of the forms. While the principals are quite at ease with final and binding clauses, there seems to be a lot more resistance to the surveyors' disclaimers. I will explore some of the reasons for that in Section 5. First, however, I will examine the judicial treatment of damages in the absence of a contractual limitation on liability.

4. Extra-Contractual Limits on Surveyor Liability

If Glanzer's beans were misweighed, the potential liability would be easily ascertainable as the product of the contract price and the shortfall. Other failures by the surveyor intermediaries can have much more significant consequences. If a classification society messes up, people can die; ships and cargoes can be lost. Less dramatic, but still substantial, losses can result if the intermediary's failure enables the buyer to reject a cargo. A minor error in measuring quality could result in a million-dollar loss for the seller. If the surveyor's contract includes no liability limitation, or if the court chooses to ignore one, there remains the question: What is the extent of the surveyor's liability?

The Restatement (Second) of Contracts, §351f., suggests that the surveyor's liability might be limited if the losses are grossly disproportionate to the price charged for the service.

> There are unusual instances in which it appears from the circumstances either that the parties assumed that one of them would not bear the risk of a particular loss or that although there was no such assumption, it would be unjust to put the risk on that party. One such circumstance is an extreme disproportion between the loss and the price charged by the party whose liability for that loss is in question. The fact that the price is relatively small suggests that it was not intended to cover the risk of such liability.

The Ship Classification Cases

While rejecting their contractual disclaimers, the courts have invariably shielded the ship classification societies from liability, either by invoking the disproportionate liability exception, or by suggesting that it is impractical for the societies to serve as insurers. In *Great American Insurance,* Judge Tyler held that the defendant's acts were neither negligent nor unworkmanlike (no fault) and that even if they had been at fault, the owner and charterer were fully informed of the defects. (There was intervening fault, or alternatively, there was no reliance.) The finding of no fault made it unnecessary to deal with the general question of subjecting classification societies to liability for substandard performance. Although the issue had not been briefed, Tyler suggested that it would be unwise to hold the classification society liable, noting that liability would convert the classification society into a de facto insurer.

> [T]his right of action would have the effect of making the classification society an absolute insurer of any vessel it surveys and certifies. Not only is this liability not commensurate with the amount of control that a classification society has over a vessel; it is also not in accord with the intent of the parties, the fees charged or the service performed. Further, by making classification societies the effective insurers of nearly all seagoing vessels, insurance companies such as those here involved, might be putting themselves out of business, a result they certainly did not contemplate by bringing this suit. (p. 1012)

In *Sundance Cruises Corp. v. American Bureau of Shipping,* the Bureau issued a safety certificate for a vessel, such certificates being required if a vessel is to obtain hull insurance and to operate in international trade. Fifteen days after the certificate was issued, the ship sank. The owner sought compensatory damages of $64 million and punitive damages of $200 million. The court granted the defendant's motion for summary judgment.

> [T]he disparity between the $85,000 contract price paid and the more than $64 million in damages claimed supported our conclusion that in issuing the certificates defendant had no intention of guaranteeing the vessel's seaworthiness or becoming the shipowner's insurer. . . . [W]e inferred that the fees defendant charged here are comparable to those that any other of the classification societies nominated by the Bahamas to issue statutory safety certificates on its behalf would have charged. It thus appeared to us that accepted classification society practice with respect to fees indicates that such societies do not assume the risk of acting as insurer. (p. 376)

Thus, as in *Great American Insurance*, the court relied in part on an inference from the magnitude of the fees to conclude that the classification society could not have meant to act as an insurer.

We are left, then, with the odd picture of a court inferring the content of a contract, while at the same time rejecting the explicit language (the disclaimers) of the contract. What makes that rejection especially odd is that the *Sundance* court emphatically rejected two of the primary grounds for not enforcing exculpatory clauses—buyer naivete and seller market power. The plaintiff was a large, sophisticated business entity with the capacity to negotiate terms for itself, and the ship certification business itself is highly competitive. "[T]he Agreement into which plaintiff ultimately entered could not be found to be the result of anything but arms-length bargaining." (p. 383) Granted that, what function could be served by substituting the inference from the apparent inadequacy of an $85,000 fee for explicit contract language?

The House of Lords came to the same result without invoking disproportionate liability, relying instead on intuitions about the interaction between liability and insurance in *Marc Rich & Co. AG v. Bishop Rock Marine Co. Ltd. (The Nicholas H)*. It would be wasteful, the Lords suggested, for the society to act as an insurer. After the ship went down, the cargo owners collected $500,000 from the shipowner, the statutory maximum (a tonnage limitation), and then sued the classification society for the balance of their claim, $5.7 million. Assuming for purposes of the litigation that the society had been careless and that the consequences of the lack of care had been foreseeable, the Lords held that the shipowners had a nondelegable contractual duty to the cargo and that it would not be "fair, just, and reasonable" to impose through tort a duty of care upon the classification society. The owner's contractual duty was circumscribed by an elaborate set of legal rules (the Hague Rules on tonnage limitations) that "create an intricate blend of responsibilities and liabilities, rights and immunities, limitations on the amount of damages recoverable, time bars, evidential provisions, indemnities and liberties"; holding the defendant liable "would add an identical or virtually identical duty owed by the classification society to that owed by the shipowners, but without any of these balancing factors, which are internationally recognised and accepted." (p. 238)

Lord Steyn for the majority suggested that imposing liability might have unfortunate effects on the classification society's incentives.

> [T]he question is whether . . . classification societies . . . would be able to carry out their functions as efficiently if they become the ready alternative target of cargo owners, who already have contractual claims against shipowners. . . . In my judgment there must be some apprehension that the classification societies would adopt, to the detriment of their traditional role, a more defensive position.
>
> If such a duty is recognised, there is a risk that classification societies might be unwilling from time to time to survey the very vessels which most urgently require independent examination. It will also divert men and resources from the prime function of classification societies, namely to save life and ships at sea. (p. 241)

He further suggested that the costs of liability would ultimately be passed on to shipowners, either in higher fees for classification services (to cover increased insurance costs) or in indemnification arrangements, which, in effect, would allow an end run around the statutory limitations on recovery against the owner. Allowing a claim of this sort would, he claimed, add considerable deadweight costs to the process of settling claims between cargo and ship.

> At present, the system of settling cargo claims against shipowners is a relatively simple one. The claims are settled between the two sets of insurers. If the claims are not settled, they are resolved in arbitration or court proceedings. If a duty is held to exist in this case as between the classification society and cargo owners, classification societies will become potential de-

fendants in many cases. An extra layer of insurance will become involved. The settlement process will inevitably become more complicated and expensive. Arbitration proceedings and court proceedings will often involve an additional party. And often-similar issues will have to be canvassed in separate proceedings since the classification societies will not be bound by arbitration clauses in the contracts of carriage. (p. 241)

In dissent, Lord Lloyd of Berwick questioned the majority's arguments regarding insurance. There was, he noted, no evidence on the costs of insurance or on whether the costs would be passed on. (p. 222) Regarding the claim that liability would entail a wasteful extra layer of insurance, he argued that traditionally, courts have treated the availability of insurance as irrelevant. Even if it were to be given some weight, in this particular case no evidence had been introduced. He continued:

> [T]he court should be wary of expressing any view on the insurance position without any evidence on the point, and should not speculate as to the effect, if any, of an extra layer of insurance on the cost of settling claims. For what it may be worth, I would for my part doubt whether it would make much difference. More generally, I suspect that a decision in favour of the cargo owners would be welcomed by members of the shipping community at large, who are increasingly concerned by the proliferation of sub-standard classification societies. (p. 229)

The Surveyor Cases

The disproportionate liability question arose in two cases involving SGS, one of the major surveyors. In the first, *Vitol Trading S.A. v. SGS Control Services*, it was merely *dictum*, as the court decided the case on other grounds. In the second, in *International Ore & Fertilizer Corp. v. SGS Control Services (Interore)*, the Court of Appeals reversed the trial court's finding on the issue despite the fact that the issue had not even been argued by the plaintiff.

Vitol sold naphtha to Sun Oil; SGS was jointly hired to test the cargo contents to assure that the shipment met the specifications. The market value of the cargo was about $11 million, and when SGS's tests showed that the cargo failed to meet specifications, Sun rejected the cargo. It then purchased the same cargo from Vitol at distress prices. Vitol sued SGS for its losses (around $475,000), which consisted primarily of the price differential. The plaintiff's brief included a strong hint that there had been no disclaimers:

> SGS argues that Vitol's loss was not foreseeable because SGS's inspection fee was so low. There is no case law to the effect that the liability of a provider of services is somewhat limited by the amount charged. . . . If SGS wanted to limit liability it simply could have inserted such a provision in its rates and tariffs so that a potential customer would have knowledge of any limitation before deciding whether to utilize such services. (Plaintiff's Brief, p. 40)

SGS, the court found, had breached its duty of workmanlike performance. However, since the facts suggested that Vitol had tendered nonconforming cargo, the breach did not cause the harm. Vitol's remedy was, therefore, limited to return of its share of the fee SGS had received for performing the particular test—$220. But what if SGS's failure had caused Vitol's loss? In *dicta*, the court suggested that Vitol would not have been entitled to recover for these special damages. Given the modest compensation, it was not reasonable to infer that SGS had assumed this risk.

> This enormous disparity between the fee SGS charged Vitol and the damage liability SGS allegedly assumed is persuasive evidence that assumption of that risk was not within SGS's contemplation at the time it agreed to perform the testing. . . . If, as a rational economic actor, SGS intended to assume that risk, plainly it would have charged substantially more for its testing services. Or it might have turned down Vitol's request altogether rather than risking so large a liability for a pittance. (p. 81)

The court cited the Restatement (Second) of Contracts, §351: "The fact that price [charged] is relatively small suggests that it was not intended to cover the risk of such liability." (p. 81) Judge Cardamone, writing for the panel, also attempted to distinguish the case from *Glanzer* by arguing that the public weigher had had more notice of the consequences of its error than had SGS. In his concurrence, Judge Pratt disputed this, arguing that SGS's knowledge of the Sun-Vitol contract put it squarely within the *Glanzer* exception. The third member of the panel, Judge Feinberg, felt it unnecessary to choose sides.

Ironically, the evidence of the disparity was not introduced at trial. In papers filed after the decision, the plaintiff observed: "[T]here is no proof as to what SGS charged because SGS did not submit any during the trial as its charges and fees were not in issue at any time. The only part of the record that contains any mention of the fees is in SGS' Answer." The $220 fee was the charge for a single test, which had been performed negligently (by a subcontractor); the charges for the entire SGS service were $13,556.36, half of which was assessed to Vitol and half to Sun. (Plaintiff's Petition for Rehearing at 12) That, arguably, is not a pittance.

Petroleum shipments are large enough so that even fairly modest errors in the measurement of quantity can translate into significant dollar amounts. Nonetheless, as in *Vitol*, the surveyors' significant exposure comes from cases where the error allows the buyer to reject delivery. That was also the case in *Interore*. The underlying transaction was a $4 million contract for the sale of fertilizer by Interore to buyers in New Zealand. Part of the cargo was picked up in Sweden, and the remainder in Florida. The contract required Interore to secure the services of a "hold inspector" to certify that the ship's hold was clean prior to loading. SGS, which had provided such a service to Interore hundreds of times in the past, agreed to do so for $50 per hold, $150 in total. (SGS performed other services, supervising the loading and chemical analysis of the fertilizer, for an additional $1,860. (*Interore I*, p. 252) The inspection failed to detect some barley left over from a prior voyage. When the cargo arrived in New Zealand, it was contaminated with barley, and the Ministry of Agriculture denied it entry. The cargo was ultimately rejected and resold in Europe for less than the contract price. While the contamination was the ostensible ground for rejection, the buyer's refusal to accept the fertilizer was more likely based on the facts that the market price for fertilizer had fallen considerably prior to delivery and that New Zealand's currency had been devalued. There was some testimony from those in the trade that rejection of a contaminated cargo of fertilizer was unprecedented, the normal remedy being a price adjustment. (Defendant's Brief, pp. 42–43.) However, the court did not find this significant.

The seller brought suit in the United States against SGS for its failure to perform its inspection in a workmanlike manner. It did not sue the Swedish inspector (another SGS company), even though the holds loaded in Sweden also had been contaminated (perhaps because the Swedish inspector included a liability limitation in its contract). The seller's suit against SGS was a small piece of the litigation pie, with the primary litigation taking place in New Zealand involving the buyer, seller, vessel, and cargo insurers.[1] The buyer, East Coast, ultimately paid $400,000 to Interore to settle the New

Zealand claim. However, the parties designated the settlement as pertaining only to the Swedish portion of the cargo, thereby allowing Interore to pursue its claim for the American damages against SGS. (Plaintiff's Brief, pp. 34–35)

Unlike its Swedish counterpart, SGS did not attempt to disclaim liability. The following legend, in capital letters, appeared at the bottom of its Certificate of Readiness, a preprinted form: "All inspections are carried out to the best of our knowledge and ability and our responsibility is limited to the exercise of reasonable care." (*Interore I*, p. 254) The court interpreted this to mean that the service was to be performed in a workmanlike manner. The defense, in its post-trial motions, did not attempt to deny that SGS would be responsible for negligent performance; rather, it attempted to show that the performance was reasonable, even though the outcome was unfortunate. "Plaintiff knew from extensive prior experience what the inspections they requested would entail. If they wished to alter the nature or scope of the duties to be performed under the inspection contract they were free to do so at any time." (Defendant's Post-Trial Brief, p. 4) After cataloguing a number of things that SGS could have done, the defense argued, "[A]ll of these services could have been arranged . . . and all of these would have found the barley. None of them would have been performed at the price or within the parameters of the service that had previously been routinely requested by and performed for plaintiff." (Defendant's Post-Trial Brief, p. 4) The argument failed, with the court holding the performance inadequate. That left the question of damages.

Citing the Restatement (Second) of Contracts §351, Comment f, and *Vitol*, the trial court held that it would be unreasonable to hold SGS liable for the consequential damages. The informal nature of the dealings, including absence of a detailed written contract, indicated that there had been no careful attempt to allocate risks. Because of the extreme disparity between the loss and the price charged—the contract was for $150 and the damages requested were $2.4 million—the court inferred that the parties had not meant to allocate this risk to SGS. Since this was a bifurcated trial with damages to be determined later, the $2.4 million figure's relationship to "the damages" is looser than usual. In the damage phase of the trial, the damage was reckoned at $480,000 plus prejudgment interest. (Report and Recommendation of the Magistrate, March 31, 1993)

What the court gave in the name of contract, it took away under tort. SGS, said the court, was liable for negligent misrepresentation, since it had made a representation that someone had relied on. It should have recognized that if it were to issue a certificate, the plaintiff would take no further precautions. At the same time, the plaintiff was also negligent because it had not brought home to SGS how important it was that the inspection be performed with great care. Had it been so informed, SGS might have performed a more careful inspection. Therefore, each was partly at fault. Holding them equally responsible, the court held SGS liable for 50% of the damage.

On appeal, the only thing that survived was the outcome. Judge Winter, agreeing with SGS that its only duty to Interore arose from contract, threw out the tort claim. Despite the fact that Interore had not appealed the treatment of its contract claim and that neither party had briefed the issue, Judge Winter held that *Vitol* was merely *dictum* and that Interore could recover its consequential damages. (The trial court had reduced the damages by 50% because of the plaintiff's contributory negligence. Judge Winter would have given Interore all the consequential damages, but held that its failure to appeal the contract claim precluded his increasing the award.) The *Vitol* reasoning, he said, "cannot be reconciled with the controlling New York case *Glanzer v. Shepard*." (p. 1284) This is a peculiar reading of *Glanzer*, because *Glanzer* was, after all, a tort case, because of the difference in the nature of damage in the two cases, and because in *H. R. Moch*, Cardozo himself had drawn an inference regarding the defendant's assumption of liability from the magnitude of the fees. Moreover, Cardozo's decision in *Glanzer* concerned only the existence of liability, not the financial consequences of a defendant's failure.

Judge Winter distinguished, unconvincingly, the court's *Sundance* decision.

> Our recent decision in *Sundance* . . . is not to the contrary. *Sundance* was an action for damages on a contract for the classification for insurance purposes of an ocean-going passenger vessel. The court held that the disparity between the fee charged on the contract and damages sought disclosed that the parties did not foresee the risk of such liability. However, the purpose of the contractual obligation of the ship classification society in *Sundance* contrasts markedly with that of the inspector in *Vitol* and in the present case. . . . In *Sundance*, the court therefore concluded that "the purpose of the classification certificate is not to guarantee safety, but merely to permit [the ship owner] to take advantage of the insurance rates available to a

classed vessel." The purpose of the inspection in this case, however, was precisely to guarantee the condition of the hold so as to insure the preservation of the cargo. There is no other reason to perform such an inspection and no other reason to pay for one, whatever the amount. (p. 1285)

That is a non sequitur. Regardless of the reason for undertaking the contractual obligation, the question remains: What is the promisor's liability if it fails to perform? Should it be liable for all the consequential damages, and can we infer anything from the disparity between the fee and the damage? The *Sundance* court concluded that the disparity between the asserted damage and the fee suggested that the parties did not intend to assign this risk to the provider of the service. The court might well have been wrong—the argument has a certain circularity—but it is, nonetheless, the argument on which the trial court in *Interore* relied.

Judge Winter put some emphasis on the fact that the classification society's task was ancillary to the purchase of insurance. But if Interore had wanted assurance, it did not have to purchase it from the inspector. It could have purchased insurance from third parties, and the availability of that insurance would have been contingent upon Interore's obtaining various inspection certificates. In its defense, SGS noted the commercial availability of insurance against the adverse consequences of its failure to find the barley:

Plaintiff's suggestion that [SGS] should have exercised a level of care commensurate with Interore's potential losses . . . is flawed on two grounds. First, [SGS] was not in this instance an insurer. It is possible to purchase— for a premium—insurance that will guarantee either or both of the quantity and quality of goods on arrival. It is also possible—again for a premium—to obtain so-called "full rejection coverage," insuring against rejection of a cargo for any reason. (Defendant's Post-Trial Brief, p. 21)

Had Interore purchased either form of insurance, the insurer would have almost certainly required inspection to cope with the inevitable moral hazard and adverse selection problems. Had it purchased the insurance, would Judge Winter have let SGS off the hook? Should liability depend on whether Interore purchased insurance or self-insured? Holding the surveyor liable for the losses arising from its negligence (or less than workmanlike performance) converts it into an insurer. If disclaimers will not be honored, then the surveyors are providing compulsory insurance with neither deductibles nor copayments nor any of the other devices that insurers use to limit their exposure.

There is nothing wrong, in principle, with a party having multiple sources of recovery against the same risk. Subrogation is, after all, common, and insurance rates will reflect the insurance company's expected net recovery from others. Their Lordships danced around that issue in *The Nicholas H.* Still, other things being equal, if compulsory insurance for surveyors would result in a system of costly transfers between insurers, that ought to make surveyor liability a less attractive policy. So, holding surveyors liable for consequential damages comes down to a matter of the effects of insurance that is both mandatory and duplicative.

5. The Evidence from Practice

If measurement errors are random, traders should expect that in the long run, the errors will balance out. Holding surveyors liable means that they in effect provide a form of insurance that is triggered by a finding of fault. If surveyors as a class are potentially liable for errors, their revenues must be sufficient to cover the costs of providing this insurance—their potential liability and the legal fees. With liability, then, the traders will pay a small amount in each transaction to cover the expected damages and legal fees and, on occasion, will receive compensation for a loss arising from the mismeasurement. The question is whether the gains to traders as a group from the incremental deterrence effect of legal liability exceed the net costs (essentially the litigation costs).

A trader might be involved in hundreds of transactions in a given year, purchasing surveying services from a small number of companies. The surveyor has a substantial incentive to take care even if there is no legal liability, since it must worry about its reputation and good will with the particular trader and with the trade itself. So, even absent liability, the surveyor has a powerful incentive to perform in a competent manner. Moreover, any incentive arising from the liability exposure is blunted by the surveyor's "errors and omissions" (E&O) policies, which will cover at least some of its exposure. Of course, if the E&O policy were experience-rated, then the liability exposure would have more impact on the surveyor's behavior. To further complicate the picture, the trader's direct insurance might well cover this contingency as well, in which case its direct insurer would, via subrogation, attempt to recover its payments from the surveyor's insurer.

Shifting the losses around in this way looks like a reasonably expensive proposition with little to show for it in the way of deterrence. My instinct is that the costs to traders as a class of holding surveyors liable exceed the benefits. If the surveyors are small firms with shallow pockets, and if the amounts in dispute are likely to be small, it would not be surprising to observe the parties accepting any default rule, including the *Glanzer* rule. In those instances in which surveyors are reasonably large entities with deep pockets and potential liability is large, I would expect that the common interest of the parties would best be served by limiting the liability of the surveyors to a modest multiple of their fee. While the first point seems to be confirmed in practice, the evidence on the latter is mixed.

Beans

If *Glanzer* were relitigated today, the contract would not present a hurdle to the buyer's recovery. Public weighers have not inserted liability limitations in their contracts. This suggests a nice, easy conclusion: Cardozo had it right. Weighers would pay compensation if they had erred, and buyers and sellers would find it in their mutual interest to have the weighers provide this limited insurance. In fact, the picture is more complicated than this. True, the weighers have not revised their contracts. But this observation is vitiated by two facts. First, their contracts are oral, not written. The absence of disclaimers and similar clauses in an oral contract is hardly noteworthy. Indeed, it could hardly be otherwise. Of course, if the issue mattered that much, the parties could have found it in their mutual interest to reduce at least one aspect of their relationship to writing. So, it is possible that they would have preferred a regime in which weighers were not legally responsible for errors, but the costs of putting it (and the rest of the agreement) in writing exceeded the benefits. Second, no one seems to care. I spoke with some industry veterans (one of whom had been a public weigher for forty years), and no one could recall a public weigher being sued for negligent weighing. The *Glanzer* rule, right or wrong, did not seem to matter.

Coffee Beans

Many international coffee transactions are made under standardized contracts published by the Green Coffee Association. Buyers and sellers agree that if a dispute arises, their only recourse will be to arbitration under the Association's rules. The arbitration clause encompasses all controversies "involving the principals, agents, brokers, or others who actually subscribe hereto," the final term including public weighers. The arbitration and the remedies are governed by New York law, except that consequential damages cannot be awarded. That is somewhat ambiguous, since *Glanzer* is still New York law and the damages could be deemed consequential. If the issue were to arise, I suspect that the arbitrators would find that the limitation on consequential damages applies only to the buyer and seller, so that the *Glanzer* rule would apply. The beans are weighed both at the load port and the discharge port. Since these weights might differ, the contracts must specify a mechanism for determining the transaction weight. The standardized contract provides for two options—delivered weights and shipping weights. The former is straightforward. The latter is qualified: "Coffee covered by this contract is sold on shipping weights. Any loss in weight exceeding _____ percent at port of discharge is for the account of Seller at contract price." (C&F Contract of the Green Coffee Assoc. on New York City, Inc., effective February 1, 1989) The blank term can be negotiated and is typically 1% or less. So, if the weight on arrival is within 1% of the invoice weight, the seller pays on the basis of the shipping weight. If the invoice weight exceeds the destination weight by more than 1%, the payment to seller will be adjusted downward. Weighing errors at the port of origin are likely to be skewed in favor of sellers, because of the possibility of corruption, so if the beans weigh more at the destination than at origin (probably because of a weighing error at the origin), the buyer gets a break. Regardless of which option is chosen, the contracts require that the coffee be weighed within fifteen days of delivery. The expenses of weighing are assigned to one party, usually, but not always, the buyer. The weigher's lack of privity with one of the parties, a feature of the *Glanzer* contract, continues to this day.

My industry informants suggest that the contract language is not taken seriously in arbitrations, quite the opposite of what Lisa Bernstein (1999) finds for other commodity arbitrations. Regardless of who hired the weigher, the weigher is viewed as an agent of both the seller and the buyer. Further, errors discovered outside the fifteen-day window will often be corrected despite the clear language. A five-month gap, as in *Glanzer*, however, would almost certainly be too long. The weigher would, under *Glanzer*, be liable to a disappointed buyer. However, the buyer's first recourse would, in practice, be against the seller. Only if the seller were to become judgment-proof in the brief interval between the initial weighing and the correct weighing, or if the seller were no longer subject to reputational sanctions, would it be necessary to pursue a remedy against the weigher. Industry veterans could not recall an instance of a weigher being asked to make up the quantity difference. If, however, the buyer believes that it has been short-weighted, even after the fifteen days have passed, it would expect the weigher to pay for the reweighing, despite a lack of contract language to that effect.

For coffee traded on the Coffee, Sugar and Cocoa Exchange, the rules are quite different. Weighers and other intermediaries (master samplers and graders) are licensed by the Exchange. If the weigher fails to comply with the appropriate procedures, it is subject to fines and penalties. Nothing in the Exchange rules suggests that the fines or penalties will be related to the market value of the shortfall or that the buyer will have any recourse against the weigher. The Exchange disclaims any liability to coffee traders for errors:

> The Exchange, its officers, committee members, or employees, whether or not negligent, shall not be liable: (i) in any way by reason of the fact that coffee delivered under Coffee "C" contracts was not sampled, graded, weighed, or certified in accordance with the Rules; or (ii) for the authenticity, validity, or accuracy of documents or any other information or data prepared by third parties (including samplers, weighers, and warehouses) not in the employ of the Exchange, notwithstanding the fact that the Exchange might select or license such third parties to take certain actions in accordance with the Rules, unless it is established that the Exchange, its officers, committee members, or employees acted in bad faith in failing to take action or in taking such action as was taken, and that such failure or action caused any loss. (Coffee, Sugar & Cocoa Exchange, Inc. Coffee "C" Rule (1990), Rule 8.10(e))

So, the Exchange, the one deep-pocket intermediary in the coffee business, contracted around the *Glanzer* rule. It is not liable to the contracting parties, barring some egregious behavior on its part. The weighers themselves are subject to discipline for failure to follow proper procedures, not for erroneous weighing; the discipline does not include making the buyer whole. That outcome conforms to my expectations.

Petroleum Products

I would have expected that contracts for the international shipments of petroleum products would limit the surveyor's liability. The surveyor is hired by buyer and seller, so there is no privity issue. The traders typically engage in a large number of transactions, and the number of surveyors serving this market is small. The surveyors tend to be large firms with reasonably deep pockets, and the potential damage is substantial. All of these factors suggest that the liability issue is important enough to warrant the attention of the parties. The fact that most, if not all, surveyors include liability limitations in their terms and conditions—recall the discussion of Saybolt's contract—seems to confirm this. However, the truth appears to be a bit more complex.

While it is true that the surveyors include the disclaimers on their price lists, the oil traders are not entirely happy about it. Their ex post discontent would not be noteworthy. We would expect that a firm that has suffered a $500,000 loss as a result of a surveyor's error would be upset. There appears to be ex ante resistance as well. Industry sources indicated that one response the traders make when they receive the price lists is to send back acknowledgment letters that state that the liability limitations are not accepted. In the remainder of this section, I will propose a number of explanations for the traders' apparent opposition to liability limitations, even if such limitations might be in their collective interest. Of course, even if the oil traders willingly accepted the terms ex ante, the courts' hostility to the disclaimers could trump, even if the traders unambiguously gave their consent.

One possible explanation might be a variant on the free rider problem. Suppose one oil trader accepts the disclaimer, while others do not. If the surveyor cannot charge a higher price for its services for the clients who refuse the disclaimer, then this trader will bear the costs of liability to others, but not reap the benefits. This explanation has an obvious problem. What prevents the surveyor from setting a higher price for the subset of customers who insist upon maintaining their right to sue? A standard response to this question is the invocation of adverse selection. Those sellers of surveying services who would insist upon a disclaimer might be systematically inferior to those who would not; or those oil traders who would insist upon maintaining their right to a legal remedy might deal in cargoes that have a greater likelihood for disputes, or they might be vulnerable to greater damage claims in the event of a surveying error. By haggling over the disclaimer, the party reveals unfavorable information about itself. This seems highly unlikely for the oil traders, since their repeated dealings would dampen any problems that could arise from such information asymmetries. Could negotiation over a disclaimer reveal much new information about either the surveyor or the oil trader, given a history of hundreds of similar transactions? I am skeptical.

The free rider explanation might be salvaged in another way. Lawyers have learned how to game the battle of the forms. Rather than negotiating the terms either one-on-one or collectively, they state their terms unilaterally and hope that their terms will be the ones honored by the courts if the dispute ends up in litigation. If the surveyors do not object to an acknowledgment letter rejecting the liability limitation, perhaps because no one in authority read the letter, then the trader gets the ex ante benefit of being treated like everyone else and the ex post benefit of preserving the right to sue. The oil traders are likely emboldened by the judicial hostility to liability limitations.

A second response is what Hanson and Logue (1990) label the first-party insurance externality. If the surveyors have broad protection under an errors and omissions policy, they might not reap much of a benefit from cutting their exposure. The gains accrue to their insurer, which might not fine-tune rates enough to make the no-liability policy sufficiently attractive. However, the insurance typically is experience-rated so that it amounts to temporally spreading the surveyor's liability costs; this externality, therefore, tends to disappear.

A third explanation relies on the peculiar nature of the marine insurance market, particularly the prominence of Lloyds in that market. If something goes wrong with a shipment, in many cases the costs will be borne by an insurer, and that insurer will have a right of subrogation against whoever caused the shipment to go awry. Within Lloyds, the risks are borne by individual syndicates that are at least as concerned with their own liability as they are with the total costs to Lloyds. It is possible that the distributional issue—where the losses ultimately fall—dominates the efficiency issue. Lloyds, unlike the Coffee Exchange, cannot or will not prevent the additional round of litigation. If this raises the costs of insuring through Lloyds, it need not hurt Lloyds insurers competitively if their way of doing business defines how competitors must do business as well. In effect, this argument relies on path dependency: traders are willing to pay additional costs for assigning legal fault in their dealings with surveyors because their insurers are willing to pay the additional costs for assigning fault and the historical development of the insurance market was such that the behavior remains shielded from potentially lower cost competition.

Of course, the simplest explanation is that my instincts are just wrong. The benefits to oil traders of holding surveyors liable for their negligence could, indeed, outweigh the costs. I would feel more comfortable with that conclusion if the courts were to routinely honor liability limitations in business to business (B2B) transactions and the gamesmanship in the battle of the forms were properly constrained.

6. Concluding Remarks

Glanzer and *Ultramares* taken together suggest a somewhat unusual rule. Cardozo did not pay much attention to how the rule that comes out of these two tort decisions interacts with contract law. In effect, the rule is: If it is easy to contract out, hold them liable; if it is difficult to contract out, do not. In the case of the negligent accountant, the ease of contracting is not symmetrical. It is hard for the accountant to contract specifically with the many people who might come across his report. If a disclaimer against the world is not enforceable, then he cannot protect himself from suits by plaintiffs who used his faulty work without paying for the privilege. If the default rule were no liability, then any potential user who wanted the accountant to provide some form of insurance could purchase it directly from the accountant.

For Glanzer and other traders, contracting out was relatively easy; indeed, oil traders usually were in privity. In some instances, reaching the potential claimants before performance would not be so easy; for example, a hold inspector in Florida might find it inconvenient to contract with a buyer in New Zealand. Even then it would not be terribly difficult to insist upon indemnification from the seller if the seller were to fail to extract acceptance of a disclaimer from the buyer. The greater hurdles to a contractual solution were judicial hostility to liability limitations and the traders' ability to game the battle of the forms.

Because the barriers to contracting are generally low for surveyors, it would seem the most sensible default rule would be no contract, no liability. If contracting were easy, there would be no need for tort. If, however, tort law were to define the default rule, then the barriers to contracting out should be lowered, particularly the hostility to disclaimers.

PART V

Option to Terminate

In Part IV, I suggested that in many instances it is useful to treat breach as the exercise of an option to terminate, with the appropriate damage remedy being the price of the option. In this part, I consider two cases in which the contract set an explicit formula for pricing that option. In both the court failed to appreciate the nature of the option. In the first, the contract for a movie star included a pay-or-play clause which, in effect, granted the studio an option on her time (at a considerable price). The court, in *Parker v. Twentieth Century-Fox*, managed to get to the right result, but in an unsatisfactory way. In the second, *Wasserman v. Township of Middletown*, a lease included a formula for calculating a termination charge in the event that the lessor chose to terminate the lease early. The formula would have resulted in an absurdly high termination charge in the final years of the lease. Nonetheless, when viewed from the option perspective, the formula makes sense. The court, however, chose to frame the issue in terms of the liquidated damages/penalty clause distinction.

Like many contracts scholars, I find the hostility to penalty clauses to be largely unfounded. Once we realize the inaptness of the pure expectation remedy, the doctrinal limits on penalties in contracts between serious commercial parties make no sense. Scott and Triantis (2004) provide a convincing argument to that effect. The option to terminate an agreement is a valuable one. The parties could price it by remaining silent and resorting to the default rules of contract damages; or they could establish a specific price (as in *Parker*) or a formula price (as in *Wasserman*). Because there are so many reasons for the option price to diverge from but-for expectation damages, the law should be deferential to the efforts of sophisticated parties to price the termination option.

In both cases I provide a framework for analysis which explains why the parties would choose to price the termination option as they did. I do not propose that courts engage in such an effort. Rather, my intent is to short-circuit the court's inquiry. As in the discussion of the misuse of the good faith standard in Chapter 5, the moral is for the courts to do less, not more.

CHAPTER 15

Bloomer Girl Revisited,
or How to Frame an
Unmade Picture

Nearly all contracts casebooks feature the saga of Shirley MacLaine's suit against Twentieth Century-Fox arising from the cancellation of the proposed film *Bloomer Girl*. None really get the story right. To be fair, none try. The case is a vehicle for exploring the obligation that the victim of the breach of an employment contract has to take alternative employment. If she refused an offer of alternative employment that was not "different and inferior," her failure to mitigate would mean that the earnings she would have received would be offset against the damages; so, asked the court, was the alternative proposed by Fox "different and inferior?" And for that purpose the case can be great fun. Is a western-style movie to be filmed in Australia different from and inferior to a musical about Amelia Bloomer to be filmed in Hollywood? If so, what would not be? A musical filmed in England? A western musical? What about a western set in Mexico in which MacLaine played a nun with an unsavory past? Could she have possibly settled for that?

Well, actually, she did. Universal released *Two Mules for Sister Sara* about one year before the California Supreme Court released *Parker v. Twentieth Century-Fox*, with Shirley MacLaine co-starring in both. Would the court have also found that project different and inferior as a matter of law? More importantly, should it matter? Suppose that the alternative film proposed by Fox was also a musical to be filmed in Hollywood, with the same director associated with the *Bloomer Girl* project, and with all contract terms identical. If she had rejected that alternative, would she still have been allowed to recover under the original contract? Or suppose that this alternative project had been proposed by a second studio. If she rejected their offer, would she still be able to recover from Fox? The hypothesized offer would not be "different and inferior"; regardless of its source, her rejection should take Fox off the hook. At least that appears to be the moral.

In fact, even if the second offer had been equivalent, she probably would have prevailed, perhaps even on a summary judgment motion. Moreover, she should prevail. By posing the problem in terms of the "different or inferior" question, the California Supreme Court deflected attention from the essence of the contract. The contract had a "pay-or-play" provision, common in the motion picture industry. The studio had, in effect, purchased an option on her time; they would pay her to be ready to make a particular film, but they made no promise to actually use her in making the film. When Fox canceled the project, they did not breach; they merely chose not to exercise their option. There was no breach and, therefore, there was no need to mitigate. And the Supreme Court knew it. Nonetheless, they chose to ignore it (or nearly so).

By framing the case as it did, the *Parker* court managed to convert an easy case into a harder one. That it gave the right answer is a fortuitous result. The contract language was clear and the function of the contract terms transparent. Had the court framed the issue properly, focusing on the nature of the pay-or-play obligation, the case would have been doctrinally less interesting, but of much greater interest to those concerned with the design of transactions. Why use a pay-or-play clause? If the studio does cancel a project that has been made pay-or-play, what determines whether the studio should encourage the artist to work with another studio during the pay-or-play period? Would the earnings from the project with a second studio be offset against the first studio's obligation? Could the first studio prevent the artist from working for the second studio during the pay-or-play period?

The chapter proceeds as follows. The background of the dispute is presented in Section 1. Section 2 tracks the case through the courts showing how the mitigation component of the case waxed while the pay-or-play component waned. Section 3 discusses the whys and wherefores of pay-or-play clauses, paying particular attention to an issue not explicitly raised by *Parker*, the relationship between the artist and other potential employers.

1. The Rise and Fall of the *Bloomer Girl* Project

Bloomer Girl was an adaptation of a stage musical, written by Harold Arlen and Yip Harburg, that ran for 654 performances on Broadway in the mid-1940s. Harburg's son summarized the play's plot and political themes:

> *Bloomer Girl* concerns the political activities of Amelia (renamed Dolly) Bloomer and the effect they have on the pre–Civil War family of her brother-in-law, hoopskirt king Horace Applegate, and his feminist daughter, Evalina. Evalina is the youngest and only remaining unmarried Applegate daughter; her older sisters are all married to company salesmen, and as *Bloomer Girl* begins, Horace is trying to unify business and family by encouraging his chief Southern salesman, Jefferson Calhoun, to court Evalina. On the eve of the Civil War, *Bloomer Girl* centers around Evalina's tutelage of Jeff in matters of gender and racial equality. Evalina, Dolly, and the other feminists of Cicero Falls not only campaign against Applegate's hoopskirts and sexism but also stage their own version of *Uncle Tom's Cabin* and conceal a runaway slave—Jeff's own manservant, Pompey. It was, said Yip, a show about the "the indivisibility of human freedom."
>
>   *Bloomer Girl* interweaves the issues of black and female equality and war and peace with the vicissitudes of courtship and pre–Civil War politics. . . . [I]t was at no point an escapist entertainment. "There were so many new issues coming up with Roosevelt in those years," Yip once said, "and we were trying to deal with the inherent fear of change—to show that whenever a new idea or a new change in society arises, there'll always be a majority that will fight you, that will call you a dirty radical or a red." (Meyerson and Harburg 1993, pp. 186–187)

Macaulay et al. (1995, pp. 63–65) speculate on whether the left-of-center politics of the play might have influenced Shirley MacLaine's decision to choose this project. Frug (1985, pp. 1114–1122) proposed a political interpretation of the *Parker* decision, emphasizing the feminist politics of Amelia Bloomer. As we shall see below, the politics of both Miss MacLaine and *Bloomer Girl* had nothing to do with the proper disposition of the case.

When she entered into her contract to make *Bloomer Girl* in August 1965, Shirley MacLaine was one of the biggest female stars in Hollywood, having received three Academy Award nominations for Best Actress in a five-year span. (The nominations were for *Irma La Douce* (United Artists, 1963) in 1964, *The Apartment* (United Artists, 1960) in 1961, and *Some Came Running*

(Metro-Goldwyn-Mayer, 1959) in 1960.) The contract negotiation had taken about seven months. Shooting was to begin the following May and was expected to take fourteen weeks. MacLaine would receive 10% of the gross profits of the film to be offset against her guaranteed compensation ($750,000) and expenses of $50,000. She had the right to approve the screenplay and the director. In fact, the director, George Cukor, had already been approved. His previous film, *My Fair Lady*, had been both an artistic and a commercial success, both the film and Cukor winning Academy Awards in 1964. If the movie had been produced, and if it had been as successful at the box office as *My Fair Lady*, MacLaine would have earned over $3 million from the domestic box office alone.

Her contract included a standard pay-or-play provision: "We shall not be obligated to utilize your services in or in connection with the Photoplay hereunder, our sole obligation, subject to the terms and conditions of this Agreement, being to pay you the guaranteed compensation herein provided for." (*Parker II*, p. 691, n.2) That is, she would receive the $750,000 guaranteed compensation so long as she was ready, willing, and able to perform. If Fox decided to replace her or to abandon the project, they remained obligated to pay her the $750,000.

While waiting for shooting to begin on *Bloomer Girl*, MacLaine turned down a role in *Casino Royale*, for which she would have received guaranteed compensation of $1 million plus an unspecified percentage. (Respondent's Brief, *Parker I*, p. 18) It is not clear whether she was to receive a percentage of the gross receipts, as in *Bloomer Girl*, or of some other amount. The large number of stars associated with *Casino Royale* (and her counsel's silence) suggests that the contingent compensation was less favorable for *Casino Royale*. She did, nonetheless, manage to fit one film in; according to her agent, she "consented to perform in the motion picture called 'Gambit' for Universal Pictures only because she knew at the time that the motion picture 'Bloomer Girl' would follow."

In March 1966, Fox decided to terminate the *Bloomer Girl* project for reasons unspecified. Fox's letter to MacLaine said, in part:

> Because of circumstances which have arisen since the date of the Agreement, we have determined not to proceed with the production of the photoplay as originally contemplated. Therefore, we cannot and will not utilize your services as contemplated by the Agreement nor otherwise comply with our obligations to you under that Agreement.

In order to avoid any damage to you, the Corporation hereby offers to employ you to portray the leading feminine role in a photoplay tentatively entitled "Big Country, Big Man," which role you previously expressed interest in performing. (Respondent's Brief, *Parker I*, p. 7)

Big Country, Big Man (BCBM) was a western-style drama, set, and to be filmed in, Australia. She had read the screenplay in June 1965 and had expressed interest in doing the film if there were a different director. (Respondent's Answer, *Parker II*, p. 18) The record is silent on the identity of the director and whether that director was still associated with the project when it was proposed in 1966. In the March discussions, her agent informed Fox that she was no longer interested in the alternative project. A few weeks later, Fox sent a letter (characterized by her counsel as artfully drafted) (Respondent's Brief, *Parker I*, p. 48) to MacLaine informing her that her services would not be utilized in *Bloomer Girl* and offering her the female lead in *BCBM* as a substitute, giving her one week to accept the offer. (Respondent's Brief, *Parker II*, p. 18) The terms of the second contract would be the same, with a few exceptions. In fact, of the thirty-four clauses in the *Bloomer Girl* contract, thirty-one were identical. The second contract eliminated the clause giving her approval rights regarding the dance director (since there would be none) and modified her approval rights of the director and the screenplay.

There are hints in the record that the *BCBM* offer was not entirely sincere. Her agent stated in his declaration that Fox had informed him in December 1965 that *BCBM* was off schedule and if it were to be done at all, it would probably be in 1967. (Respondent's Brief, *Parker I*, p. 48) In the March discussion of the termination of the *Bloomer Girl* project, Richard Zanuck (Fox's executive vice president in charge of production) purportedly told her agent that the script was much better now and could be produced in July or August 1966. (Respondent's Brief, *Parker I*, p. 77) Both her lawyer and the judge pointed to Fox's failure to name the proposed director and leading man as evidence that the offer was somewhat questionable. (Respondent's Brief, *Parker I*, p. 78; *Parker I*, p. 225, n.5) Fox's counsel characterized the lower court's response in strong terms: "The lower court apparently believed that defendant's offer, and its affirmative defense, were outrageous and in bad faith and expressed those sentiments in its strangely argumentative language at the conclusion of its Opinion." (Appellant's Opening Brief, *Parker I*, p. 40) In his declaration, Zanuck claimed the offer was "a bona fide good faith offer and the defendant would have complied with the terms of that offer, had plaintiff accepted them." (Appellant's Opening Brief, *Parker I*, p. 52) Fox's sincerity would have been a fact question and probably would have survived the summary judgment motion.

MacLaine refused the substitute offer and, according to her agent, was unable to find alternative employment in the *Bloomer Girl* shooting period. (Appellant's Opening Brief, *Parker I*, p. 4) She brought suit against Fox to recover the $750,000 guarantee, stating two causes of action: money due under a written contract, and damages for breach of a written contract. (*Parker II*, p. 691) She rejected a settlement offer of $400,000. Fox conceded that it had breached the original agreement and offered as its only defense her failure to mitigate damages by her refusal to accept the *BCBM* offer. Her failure to mitigate, claimed Fox, meant that MacLaine should receive only nominal damages. On a very thin record consisting of the *Bloomer Girl* contract, Fox's letter proposing the *BCBM* contract, short declarations by her agent and lawyer, Fox's in-house counsel, and Richard Zanuck, an affidavit by MacLaine that she did not work or receive compensation during the fourteen-week shooting period, and a few stipulations, MacLaine asked for and received summary judgment. That result was upheld on appeal.

2. The Opinions

Superior Court

The case was first heard by Judge Zack in Superior Court. His opinion is reprinted as an Appendix to Respondent's Brief in *Parker I*. He rejected Fox's mitigation defense because the pay-or-play clause meant that no mitigation was necessary and because, even if it were, the proposed alternative was "different and inferior." Judge Zack provided a straightforward characterization of the pay-or-play clause:

> The contract . . . is one in which the Defendant said, in substance, "We contemplate making a motion picture called 'Bloomer Girl.' We desire your services as 'Evalina,' the star thereof, to be filmed during a certain period, in Los Angeles, California. If the picture is made and if you appear recognizably in the photoplay, as released, and the contract has not otherwise been validly terminated, we will pay you the guaranteed compensation, the expenses, and the percentage of the gross. Also, if the picture is made,

you shall have absolute (subject to contingencies) approval of the director (Paragraph 29), reasonable approval of the dance director (Paragraph 31), and absolute approval of the screenplay for the photoplay (Paragraph 32)."

However, Defendant also says: "We do not promise we will ever make the picture or if we do, you will ever appear in it as released. The sole binding promise we make here and now (Paragraph 2) is that we will pay, in exchange for your commitment to perform at our election as provided in the agreement, the guaranteed compensation."

Thus defendant is not liable to Plaintiff, under Paragraph 2, for failure to make the picture or for failure to have Plaintiff appear in it. Since Defendant elected not to proceed prior to the time Plaintiff's performance was to commence, Defendant's only enforceable promise now is to pay the guaranteed compensation. (Appendix to Respondent's Brief in *Parker I*, pp. 6–7)

The clause, said the court, amounted to a waiver of any right to have damages mitigated. (Appendix to Respondent's Brief in *Parker I*, p. 18) Fox relied on the conclusory Declaration of its resident counsel, Frank Ferguson: "Nothing in Article 2 is intended to nor does it relate to any advance waiver by the producer of the doctrine of mitigation of damage." (Appellant's Opening Brief, *Parker I*, p. 13) Fox's admitted breach was not its failure to make the movie—it had never promised that. The breach was only the failure to pay the guaranteed compensation at the promised time. Judge Zack had a rather stinging characterization of Fox's position:

To destroy all rights under a contract, to assist a wrongdoer, is unconscionable. To paraphrase: Defendant is saying: "Yes, we admit we signed a contract giving you approval of director and subject matter in a picture if we made it. We also admit that provided you are not in default, the contract requires us, in any event, to pay the guaranteed compensation. But there is another *unwritten* clause in the deal, resulting from the rule of mitigation of damages which allows us to compel you to perform on our terms if you are to recover anything in the "Bloomer Girl" Contract. Under this unwritten clause we either get your performance on our terms, or we get off scot-free. It works like this: We totally breach the contract and make an offer to employ at the same salary, *but this time on terms we dictate*. If you accept the offer and sue us on the original contract, we can demur you out because Paragraph 2 eliminates all covenants other than the one to pay money. You have received the money; we are not liable for failure of the other conditions to occur because we did not promise they would. On the other hand, if you do not accept the later offer to perform on terms which only we decide, and then sue us for breach of the original agreement, we have a complete defense of failure to mitigate damages. Take your choice." (Appendix to Respondent's Brief, *Parker I*, pp. 27–28)

If MacLaine did have to mitigate, under the stipulated facts the only mitigation possible would have been acceptance of Fox's offer to star in *BCBM*. Neither this opinion nor the two subsequent opinions had to confront issues arising from an employment offer from a third party (although it comes up indirectly in the discussion of "offset"). Judge Zack ruled that, as a matter of law, the alternative employment was different and inferior and, therefore, she did not have to accept it. While he noted the differences in the films—a musical to be filmed in Hollywood versus a western to be filmed in Australia—he put no weight on those factors in determining that the substitute was different and inferior. Rather, he emphasized artistic control, her approval of the director and the screenplay: "Failure of Defendant to show . . . any facts at all, as to the comparability of the employments, leaves the Court in a position where there is only one conclusion that can be reasonably drawn from the absence of screenplay and director control in the second employment and that is that these powers were *important*." (Appendix to Respondent's Brief, *Parker I*, p. 23)

MacLaine did not have to work, but what if she had done so? Could she keep the income from the other employment, or would Fox's liability be reduced? The court emphatically stated that she would be required to offset her earnings: "Plaintiff . . . would have to deduct . . . all earnings, even those as a seamstress, during the contracted period of 'Bloomer Girl' employment." (Appendix to Respondent's Brief, *Parker I*, p. 19)

The Court of Appeal

Writing for a unanimous court, Judge Kingsley upheld the grant of summary judgment but on quite different grounds. The difference stems from his interpretation of MacLaine's position:

Plaintiff's cause of action, therefore, is not actually for a breach of her employment contract by an unlawful discharge; rather it is for a recovery under the contract according to its terms. The parties also are in agreement that defendant's alternative obligation to pay plaintiff $750,000 if it did not utilize her services in "Bloomer Girl" was subject to an implied condition that she mitigate defendant's obligation by accepting other suitable employment. (*Parker I*, p. 222)

He expands on this in a cryptic footnote:

We have decided the case at bench on the theory stated in the text. Since it was tried below, and was briefed and argued here, on that theory, we assume that the parties have correctly interpreted their mutual intention as to the particular contract herein involved. Our acceptance of the theory of mitigation for the purpose of this opinion, however, is not a determination that, in some other lawsuit, involving other parties to another similar contract, the validity of that theory might not be raised. (*Parker I*, p. 222)

Judge Kingsley's meaning is not entirely clear. I interpret this to mean that the pay-or-play provision would normally mean that MacLaine need not mitigate, but in this particular case and for purposes of summary judgment only, she conceded that she would have to accept an offer of comparable employment in mitigation. How he came to this interpretation, I do not know. He does not hold that the trial court erred. Perhaps her lawyer took the position in oral argument, but the written record does not support Kingsley's characterization. Fox's counsel, in its opening brief to the Court of Appeal, criticized the lower court's treatment of the pay-or-play clause "as being vitally significant—so much so, that the Court ruled that its very existence waived the only defense defendant proffered to the Complaint, the alleged failure of plaintiff to mitigate damages." (Appellant's Opening Brief, *Parker I*, p. 12) "Plaintiff," argued Fox, "took the position that as a matter of law, employees could sit out their term of employment without mitigating and that if she were wrong about this, defendant's affirmative defense 'would indeed present a triable issue of fact.' " (Appellant's Opening Brief, *Parker I*, p. 49) That hardly sounds like agreement on an implied condition that she mitigate. Indeed, in its petition for rehearing, Fox claimed that the two quoted passages from Judge Kingsley's opinion were inaccurate "because plaintiff never so agreed." (Appellant's Petition for Rehearing in the Court of Appeal at 9, *Parker I*)

Plaintiff, in fact, did not back off from her claim that she was entitled to the compensation regardless of whether she had attempted to mitigate:

It is that right of Respondent's—to receive the $750,000 anyway, *even if not used in "Bloomer Girl"*—which Appellant is seeking to take away from Respondent through the "mitigation" device. In other words, an express contractual provision which in effect eliminated mitigation by providing that Respondent was to be paid even if *not* used in "Bloomer Girl" is being threatened by Appellant's "mitigation" theory. If that theory were given effect, it would render meaningless Respondent's express contractual right to be paid under the "Bloomer Girl" contract, *even if her services were not used.*

And, of course, Respondent paid dearly for that contractual right, among other things because she turned down an offer of $1,000,000 plus royalties from Columbia Pictures because of the necessity to hold herself in readiness for "Bloomer Girl" during the period indicated.

Her sole present right of action, because of the election reserved to Appellant in the last unnumbered paragraph of Paragraph 2 of the "Bloomer Girl" contract, is to have the guaranteed compensation. (Respondent's Brief, *Parker I,* pp. 37–38)

Having determined that there was an implied condition that she mitigate, Judge Kingsley then had to give it content. There being no law regarding the failure to mitigate the nonbreach of a contract, the court turned to the only analogy available, mitigation of damages in unlawful discharge cases. Like Zack, Kingsley concluded that as a matter of law, the tendered employment was different and inferior; unlike Zack, he did not rely solely on the artistic control issues:

It is obvious that the two plays differed widely: One was a musical with opportunities for plaintiff to display her talents as a singer and dancer; the substitute offered no such opportunity. One was to be filmed in Los Angeles; the other in a foreign country. As to one, plaintiff had the right of detailed script approval; as to the other, she was required to accept a script already fixed. In one, she was to work under the direction either of a director named in the contract and, thus, approved by her in its execution, or by some other director satisfactory to her; in the substitute, she would work under a different director in whose selection she had had, and would have, no voice at all. Those differences are of a kind that, as a matter of common knowledge, are all significant to a star performer. The question is not whether or not plaintiff would have been wise to have accepted the offered substitute role. Her duty to defendant was not to exercise the wisest professional judgment. It was merely to accept employment that did not differ substantially from that which the original contract contemplated. Plaintiff had been employed in Los Angeles, to appear in a musical, based on a stage play of established reputation, under the direction of a director in whom she had confidence, using a script she had approved. She was offered employment in a foreign country, to appear in a non-musical, under a director whom she did not know or trust, and using a script which (so far as defendant's affidavits show) she had read only once and as to which she had indicated, at the most, only a general approval and not a detailed one. Those differences were substantial within the meaning of the cases in the field. The trial court properly ruled that, as a matter of law, plaintiff had no duty to defendant to accept its substitute role. (*Parker I*, pp. 224–225)

The California Supreme Court

In the California Supreme Court's decision, the one prominently featured in all the casebooks, the existence of the pay-or-play clause was acknowledged in a footnote, but it warranted no discussion from either the majority or the lone dissenter. The majority opinion concluded by noting that its finding on the "different and inferior" issue made consideration of the pay-or-play provision unnecessary:

In view of the determination that defendant failed to present any facts showing the existence of a factual issue with respect to its sole defense— plaintiff's rejection of its substitute employment offer in mitigation of damages—we need not consider plaintiff's further contention that for various reasons, including the provisions of the original contract . . . plaintiff was excused from attempting to mitigate damages. (*Parker II*, p. 694)

The court's entire discussion centered on whether the second offer was different and inferior as a matter of law. "The sole issue," said the court, "is whether plaintiff's refusal of defendant's substitute offer . . . may be used in mitigation." (*Parker II*, pp. 692–693) The majority said that it could not. The nature of the project made it different, and the loss of the screenplay and director approvals made it inferior. The majority asserted:

The mere circumstance that "Bloomer Girl" was to be a musical review calling upon plaintiff's talents as a dancer as well as an actress, and was to be produced in the City of Los Angeles, whereas "Big Country" was a straight dramatic role in a "Western Type" story taking place in an opal mine in Australia, demonstrates the difference in kind between the two employments; the female lead as a dramatic actress in a western style motion picture can by no stretch of imagination be considered the equivalent of or substantially similar to the lead in a song-and-dance production.

Additionally, the substitute "Big Country" offer proposed to eliminate or impair the director and screenplay approvals accorded to plaintiff under the original "Bloomer Girl" contract, and thus constituted an offer of inferior employment. (*Parker II*, pp. 693–694)

The dissent observed that the majority's conclusion amounts to proof by repetition and went on to claim that the relative merits of the second film were not so obvious that they could be determined without more facts. (*Parker II*, pp. 696–697)

The court's emphasis on the "different and inferior" question and the scant attention given the pay-or-play provision was only partially dictated by the parties' briefs. The bulk of their arguments was addressed to aspects of the mitigation defense. For example, plaintiff framed the dispute in terms of the mitigation defense:

> [T]he various admissions by Appellant in its pleadings and declarations and the various undenied facts and stipulated facts in this case all narrowed the issues to the mitigation defense. Even as to that one defense it was further limited to the question of whether one particular alternate offer of employment by Appellant to Respondent constituted a mandatory mitigation opportunity for her. (Respondent's Answer, *Parker II*, p. 4)

When she did raise the pay-or-play issue, the presentation was less than crystal clear. Nonetheless, the arguments were available to the court, which chose simply to ignore them.

Fox presented seven arguments; the first six concerned the mitigation defense. The seventh was most strange. The Court of Appeal, said Fox, erred when it stated that the suit was not for unlawful discharge, but for recovery under the contract according to its terms. It further erred when it said that plaintiff had agreed that it would have to mitigate damages. Fox claimed that it had anticipatorily repudiated and breached its contract and that MacLaine had been discharged; both parties had, Fox noted, stipulated to those facts.

Moreover, not only did plaintiff never agree that defendant's obligation to pay $750,000 was subject to an implied condition that she mitigate damages, plaintiff vigorously contended quite the opposite. Thus, when the Court of Appeal declared (1) this was not a case involving an unlawful discharge and (2) plaintiff had agreed that her right to receive $750,000 was subject to an implied condition to mitigate damages, it was inaccurate in the extreme. (Appellant's Petition for Hearing in Supreme Court, *Parker II*, p. 26)

If the court had been correct in labeling this a contract still in force, Fox contended, the mitigation defense would fail. It cited *Payne v. Pathe Studios, Inc.* (discussed below), which concerned a studio's liability under a pay-or-play clause for failure to make a film: "Here again we must bear in mind that this is not an action for damages for breach of the contract of employment, but an action on the contract itself for agreed compensation. The doctrine of mitigation of damages has no place in such an action." (*Payne*, p. 600)

Fox concluded by noting that the "inconsistency" with *Payne* "cannot help but lend confusion and inconsistency in what has been heretofore well settled law." (Appellant's Petition for Hearing in Supreme Court, *Parker II*, p. 26) This all seems like a pretty powerful argument, but *for the plaintiff*. The law is well settled that in a pay-or-play contract there is no place for mitigation—the plaintiff simply receives the guarantee. Fox's twist is the one described derisively by Judge Zack. By announcing a breach, Fox breaches the promise to employ (which is subject to the mitigation defense), not the promise to pay (which is not). That argument seems extraordinarily silly. Neither the Court of Appeal nor the Supreme Court overtly recognized it; but it is the implicit core of their analysis.

The Precedents

To be fair, the courts' failure to recognize the nature of the pay-or-play clause was not entirely their fault. While plaintiff did argue that the clause did not require her to mitigate, she did not even attempt to relate the case to the few other reported cases involving such a clause. In her lengthy briefs, she mentioned only one and did not bother to note that the case involved a pay-or-play clause. That case, *de la Falaise v. Gaumont-British Picture Corp., Ltd.*, was the only case concerning a pay-or-play clause cited by any of the courts. And, like the plaintiff, their invocation of the case ignored the pay-or-play nature of the contract. Fox, however, called three other cases to the court's attention.

The four cases taken together provide a good picture of the role of pay-or-play clauses. They also illustrate how, by forcing their analyses into Procrustean categories, the courts manage to make simple questions difficult. I will consider the four cases in chronological order.

1. Zazu Pitts *(Payne v. Pathe Studios, Inc.)*. She entered into a contract in May 1930 with Pathe Studios to star in *Beyond Victory*, to be completed before the end of December of that year. She was to receive a guarantee of $5,000, to be paid whether or not the picture was made. Her salary was to be $1,250 per week for a minimum of four weeks. The film was not made, and she (or rather her assignee) sued for the guaranteed amount. The opinion is silent on whether the filming was expected to take longer, but I think it a reasonable inference that it was not. Despite cancellation of the one film, Pitts still managed to appear in thirteen films that year. (See Zasu Pitts, IMDB.) She prevailed, with the court finding that this was "not an action for damages for breach of the contract of employment, but an action on the contract itself for the agreed compensation." *(Payne, p. 600)* Because of this, said the court, there was no occasion to mitigate. Any earnings between May and the end of December would not be offset against the $5,000 obligation. The court noted that "she was employed and received compensation during a large portion of the period in question" *(Payne, p. 600)*, but that did not preclude her fully performing the contract.

The court observed: "The question whether this contract was an option in favor of defendant on the services of [Pitts] . . . to be exercised at will, or was an agreement to engage her services for at least four weeks with a guarantee of $5,000 as a minimum compensation, became a question of fact for the trial court to determine." *(Payne, p. 600)* If the latter, the court would have had to deal with the question of whether the $5,000 was liquidated damages or a penalty. It is a distinction without a difference. The court managed to convince itself of the former, so it did not have to deal with the doctrinal niceties of liquidated damages. Of more interest than the doctrinal smokescreen is the court's characterization of the clause as an option. Pathe paid Pitts $5,000 to be ready to make a particular film in a seven-month period, but Pathe retained the right to cancel the film or to make the film with someone else.

2. Constance Bennett *(de la Falaise v. Gaumont-British Picture Corp., Ltd.)*[1]

Constance Bennett agreed to make two films in London in 1936, each to be made in eight weeks or less. The first was completed, but the second was never made. Her compensation for each picture was 10% of the American gross receipts to be offset against a guarantee of $30,000. In addition, she would receive a guaranteed $5,000 which was not to be recouped from her share of the gross receipts. So, if the American gross receipts were less than $300,000, she would receive $35,000. For every dollar of gross receipts above $300,000, she would receive an additional 10%. The start date for the second picture was to be between September 1 and November 14, and the studio promised to give notice of the starting date by August 1. The studio sought to cancel the contract in the spring of 1936, but she refused; the studio failed to give notice of a start date on August 1, whereupon she sued the studio for the $35,000 minimum guarantee.

In its defense, the studio noted that she had begun working on a picture for Twentieth Century-Fox in July *(Ladies in Love)* and that this would relieve them of their duty to notify on August 1. However, the court found, she would have been able to complete that film in time to appear in England by September 1, so her behavior did not excuse the studio. The only issue was whether any employment she had taken between September 1 and January 1 should be offset against the $35,000 guarantee. She received no movie offers during the period, but did perform in two radio programs, receiving $4,000 for the two.

The court distinguished this case from *Payne*, "which instead of being an action for breach of contract, was based upon the failure of respondent to pay the minimum compensation specified in an agreement very similar to the one here involved." (*de la Falaise*, p. 452) Because *Payne* was not an action for breach of contract, the doctrine of mitigation did not apply. Since this was an action for breach of contract, the doctrine would apply. This is a most peculiar syllogism, given that the action is for precisely the same thing—payment of the guarantee after the studio chose not to go forward.

The court cited the "well settled" rule that the damages for wrongful discharge were the salary less the amount the employee might have earned with reasonable effort from other employment; the employee need not enter into service that was different or inferior to mitigate damages. The rule, the same one at issue in *Parker*, was even less relevant here. She had not *turned down* any alternative employment; she had *accepted* employment on radio. The court conflated two distinct questions: (1) Should the defendant's damages be reduced by the revenues the plaintiff should have earned (but did not) in mitigation? (2) Should the plaintiff's actual earnings be offset against the damages? Having so boxed itself in, the court extricated itself with a nonsensical argument. The radio engagement, said the court, "might be denominated different in character from that required of a moving picture actress, [but] it cannot be said to be inferior thereto." (*de la Falaise*, p. 452) The radio earnings would, therefore, be offset against the damages so that Bennett recovered only $31,000.

3. Pare Lorentz *(Lorentz v. R.K.O. Pictures, Inc.)*. Lorentz agreed to write, direct, and produce a movie for $50,000 plus 10% of the net profits. The picture was over budget and behind schedule, and the studio finally stopped production. Lorentz had already received the $50,000; he sued for a number of items, including the percentage compensation he would have earned and the lost screen credits. The relevant contract clause was written in the form of a waiver.

> The Producer expressly waives and releases the corporation from all claims or causes of action based on the failure of the Corporation actually to utilize the services of the Producer or the results thereof, or on the failure of the Corporation to produce or to release or to continue the distribution of the Pictures; provided, however, that nothing contained in this Article of this agreement shall be deemed to relieve the Corporation of its obligation to pay the Producer the fixed compensation payable to him pursuant to Article 1 of Section 11 of this Agreement. (*Lorentz*, p. 86)

In granting the studio summary judgment on these claims, the court explained why it made sense for the studio to maintain the option of replacing the director or terminating the project.

> [T]he contract makes employment certain and as well the payment of the fixed compensation. Such obligation is fixed, but the work to be done and the results of the work must remain in the sound discretion of the moving picture corporation. The expensive business enterprise may by the turn of events at any time indicate the wisdom of discontinuing the production or the showing of a photoplay. Should events of such portent occur, the corporation is absolved from liability from prospective benefits to appellant. Appellee has reserved decision on such question to its own discretion. (*Lorentz*, p. 86)

4. Ann Sheridan (*RKO Pictures, Inc. v. Sheridan*). In April 1949, Sheridan accepted the leading female role in a motion picture entitled *Carriage En-*

trance. Her fee was $50,000 plus an additional $100,000 which was to be paid out of the gross receipts of the picture. The contract gave her approval of the script, the director, and the leading man. At the time she signed the contract she also signed a letter stating that she approved the script, director, and Robert Young as the leading male actor. Young subsequently rejected the role, and the parties could not agree on an adequate replacement. In August, RKO sent her a letter saying that it would not use her in the picture and would not pay her any compensation.

The dispute involved two mechanical issues with respect to the pay-or-play clause. What event would trigger the clause and, if it were triggered, what compensation should be paid? Neither the purpose of a pay-or-play clause nor the mitigation defense was at stake. The clause, which included an awkwardly worded proviso, read as follows: "Producer shall not be required to use Artist's services hereunder or to complete the production of 'Carriage Entrance,' and shall be deemed to have fully performed all its obligations to Artist by paying Artist the minimum compensation payable to Artist hereunder. (*Sheridan,* p. 169)

> However, if, because Artist does not approve any one or more of the items specified in paragraph 1 [the director, script, and leading man], Artist does not become obligated to, and does not, render any services pursuant hereto, Producer shall not be required to pay any compensation whatever to Artist hereunder. (*Sheridan,* p. 168)

RKO argued that the last sentence meant that the pay-or-play obligation would not be triggered if she failed to act in good faith by not approving the alternative leading men they had proposed *or* if she did not render any services under the contract. The court held that the contract said "and" and meant "and." Even if she had unreasonably withheld approval of alternative leading men, as long as she had rendered some services the clause would be in effect. Since the jury had found that her consultations regarding costumes and her fittings of gowns were services rendered pursuant to the contract, the clause was triggered.

Sheridan argued that the trial judge erred by ruling as a matter of law that the phrase "minimum compensation" meant $50,000. The phrase, she argued (and the court agreed), was definitely ambiguous, and parol evidence should have been admitted; the case was remanded on this point.

I find the first conclusion more compelling than the second. At worst, the second issue involves a one-shot drafting snafu which could easily be rectified by making clear that the minimum compensation and the guaranteed payment are one and the same. The first issue was highlighted by awkward drafting, but the problem can be deeper. The studio's pay-or-play obligation has to be triggered by a specific event; only in some circumstances will that event be the signing of the contract. In the other four contracts considered in this section *(Parker, Payne, de la Falaise, and Lorentz)*, the pay-or-play obligation began the instant the contract had been entered into. But, as *Sheridan* illustrates, that need not be the case.

5. *In sum:* This tour of the precedents suggests that while the raw materials for a sensible analysis of *Parker* were there, they would be easy to miss. The outcomes were not so bad, and there was some awareness of the function of the pay-or-play clause. But the attempt to pigeonhole the facts into traditional legal categories did more to obscure than to enlighten. The opacity of the precedents is starkly illustrated by the failure of the *Parker* litigants (and courts) to appreciate their implications. Three were raised by Fox's counsel, not MacLaine's, despite the fact that they should support her claim. Fox failed to recognize that by calling these cases to the court's attention, it was really undermining its own case. And the plaintiff returned the favor. Only one of the cases, *de la Falaise*, was cited by the plaintiff and the courts, and that only for the proposition that mitigation does not require the plaintiff to take employment that was different and inferior.

3. Pay-or-Play

The essential features of a pay-or-play clause were spelled out in a decision contemporaneous with *Parker* by none other than Judge Kingsley. The issue arose in the context of a divorce. *(Garfein v. Garfein)* Carroll Baker had a seven-picture deal with Paramount in which she had agreed to perform in at least one picture a year. Paramount agreed to pay her a fixed fee each year whether or not she worked, the fee being $200,000 per year in the early years and $300,000 in the later years. After she starred in *Harlow,* a 1965 release, Paramount did not call on her to make any more pictures. Paramount attempted to renege, prompting her to sue, and the court, in an unpublished opinion, found in her favor. In the divorce proceedings, the issue facing the Court of Appeal was whether the final $1.2 million of payments under the pay-or-play clause should be treated as property, as the husband contended, or future earnings. (The amount was for payments falling due after the date of separation. *(Garfein,* pp. 716–717)) The court found the latter. Judge Kingsley spelled out clearly the meaning of the pay-or-play clause:

> [The contract] required the wife to hold herself available for service in one picture each 12-month period; without the consent of Paramount she could not accept other potentially conflicting engagements, business or social. (Footnote: Under the contract, plaintiff could perform for another producer, provided she gave Paramount notice of her intent; in that event, Paramount was required either to consent or to schedule her for its own picture at the time or times involved.)

> The husband argues that the several payments were not "earnings" because the wife was entitled to them even though she did not "work"—i.e., appear in any motion pictures. But appearance in a picture was only one alternative of her obligations to her employer under the contract. Under a "play or pay" contract, the employer secures: (1) an option on the performer's services; and (2) the assurance that a performer will not, without its consent, create competition for other pictures of the employer by performing for some other producer. "They also serve who only sit and wait." We hold that the wife "earns" her agreed compensation by refraining from performing for anyone except the employer during the period of the contract, unless with the employer's consent. (Footnote: The effect of the contract, obviously, was to limit plaintiff in bargaining with other producers and subjected her to losing the opportunity to appear in pictures for other producers, which she might regard as important to her career or her bank account. . . .) Since the payments made after June 1967, were "earned" after that date, they were separate property. (Footnote: The duty to pay, where no picture was made, did not accrue until the final day of each 12-month period, since the wife was required to hold herself available for the full period. The compensation, thus, was not "earned" until that last day.) (*Garfein,* pp. 716–717)

Judge Kingsley turns *Parker* on its head. A pay-or-play clause does not *require* the talent to seek reasonable employment alternatives to mitigate damages. Rather, he suggests, it gives the studio the power to *prevent* the talent from working with a rival studio for a period of time. It is not clear whether this drastically revised vision reflects rapid learning on the part of Judge Kingsley; perhaps he already knew it and this knowledge was the basis for his cryptic footnote in *Parker.* What is clear is that for the last quarter century this alternative understanding of the pay-or-play clause has been on the books and was put there by the intermediate court judge who helped create *Parker.*

Carroll Baker's Paramount contract differed from the five discussed in the previous section. Those were all for specific films to be made in a reasonably well-defined time slot. The Baker contract was for seven unidentified (and unidentifiable at the time of contract) films to be made over a seven-year period. This, along with the *Sheridan* contract's variation on the triggering mechanism, underscores the point that not all pay-or-play clauses are created equal.

The two basic features, however, remain those identified by Judge Kingsley: the studio has paid for the option of using the talent for some time period, and the talent has agreed not to work for someone else during that period unless it receives the studio's permission or pays for the privilege. Indeed, these features are memorialized in the Director's Guild union contract. If the director is employed by a third party, the employer "shall be entitled to an offset of the compensation arising from such new employment for such remaining portion of the guaranteed period against the compensation remaining unpaid . . . [However,] the Director shall have no obligation to mitigate damages arising from his or her removal." (1990 DGA Basic Agreement §6–105; cited in Selz et al. 1997, §27.10, p. 34)

The Studio's Option

Moviemaking is a sequential process. A studio might begin with a concept, hire a screenwriter to draft a screenplay, hire the director and actors and other talent, and, if all goes smoothly, a finished feature film will be the result. But things do not always run smoothly. Most projects do not make it to the screen. Indeed, most die early before the studio has invested a significant amount. Even if a project does not die, its course can change constantly as information or circumstances change. The screenplay can be revised, another studio might be coming to market with a movie about a similar subject, a particular star might become available, the co-stars might lack chemistry, and so forth. For descriptions of the evolution of various film projects, see Bach 1985 *(Heaven's Gate);* Lee 1992 *(Malcolm X);* Pink 1989 (independent films, most filmed in Europe); Salamon 1991 *(Bonfire of the Vanities);* Schatz 1988 (major studio films from 1930 to 1950); and Hayes and Bing 2004 *(Legally Blonde 2: Red, White, & Blonde).* By maintaining the flexibility to react, the studio can adapt the project to changed circumstances. As the primary claimant on the film's earnings, the studio has the incentive to make adaptive decisions which enhance the expected value of the project.

However, other participants must make decisions which depend on the likelihood that the project will go forward, and they do not want their interests to be totally ignored. Prior to 1950, when much of the talent was under long-term contract to the studios and studios produced a large number of films, the studios internalized these concerns. If Ms. X were dropped from a particular film, the studio still had to pay her salary. The studio held a portfolio of talent. If someone were dropped from one film, or a project canceled, the studio had a large number of other projects in the works so that the studio's cost of carrying an inventory of contract players was not great. As the number of films produced declined, the long-term contracts disappeared. Talent was hired largely on a film-by-film basis, and the studio had to pay for the talent's readiness on that basis as well. (The per picture contracts of Constance Bennett and Zazu Pitts were exceptions in their era.) In the studio contracts of the 1930s and 1940s, the studio determined which roles the actor would play. If the actor refused, the studio could suspend the actor. The standard contract was described in *De Haviland v. Warner Bros. Pictures, Inc.* (p. 984):

> The contract gave the Producer, defendant, the right to suspend plaintiff for any period or periods when she should fail, refuse or neglect to perform her services to the full limit of her ability and as instructed by the Producer and for any additional period or periods required to complete the portrayal of a role refused by plaintiff and assigned to another artist. Plaintiff was to receive no compensation while so suspended or thereafter until she offered to resume her work. It was provided that the Producer had the right to extend the term of the contract at its option, for a time equal to the periods of suspension.

Olivia de Havilland (the court is quite free with the spelling of her name) had been suspended for twenty-five weeks over the course of her seven-year contract. The court continued:

> The several periods of suspension totaled some twenty-five weeks. The facts as to the suspensions are not in dispute; defendant's right to impose them is not questioned. Plaintiff's reason for refusing the several roles was

that they were unsuited to her matured ability and that she could not faithfully and conscientiously portray them. Her good faith and motives are not in issue, but according to the contract the Producer was the sole judge in such matters and she had to do as she was told. (pp. 984–985)

The actor would not be compensated while on suspension, and the clock would stop running. That is, the suspension time would be tacked on to the end of the contract. In modern multipicture agreements, the actor has some discretion as to acceptance of a particular role.

The opportunity cost of accepting a contract for a particular film project is the offers that might come along in the intervening months. In Shirley MacLaine's case, at least one offer, *Casino Royale,* was foreclosed by her acceptance of the *Bloomer Girl* contract. If the studio were free to adjust without taking this opportunity cost (or reliance) into account, the talent would be reluctant to commit to the project in the first place. The pay-or-play clause provides some protection of the artist's reliance. It is analogous to the "take-or-pay" or "demand charge" often used in long-term supply contracts. The seller (the artist) is promised some compensation even if the buyer (the studio) chooses to take nothing at all. Shirley MacLaine is to receive the $750,000 even if the movie is not made. By reducing the incremental costs of continuation, these devices provide some protection to the seller's (artist's) reliance, balancing that reliance interest against the buyer's (studio's) need for flexibility. The parties leave the decision to proceed entirely in the hands of the studio, with pay-or-play merely altering the price it faces.

The studio should be free to make that decision without second-guessing by the courts. However, in a recent case, *Locke v. Warner Bros., Inc.,* the court held that the studio's discretion was limited by an implied covenant of good faith and fair dealing. The facts are somewhat unusual, as the disputed contract was apparently part of a settlement following the dissolution of the personal and romantic relationship of Clint Eastwood and Sondra Locke. Immediately following the settlement, Warner (Eastwood's studio) signed a development deal with Locke which included a $750,000 pay-or-play arrangement to direct some future unspecified project. Warner did not approve any of her projects, paid her the $750,000 (plus another $750,000 for an exclusive first look), and argued that it had satisfied its contractual duty. Locke argued that the studio, to please Eastwood, had no intention of making any movie with her and that the deal was a sham. She sued for breach of contract and for fraud; the California Court of Appeals, reversing the trial court, denied Warner summary judgment. In contrast to *Parker's* implication that only the $750,000 guarantee was at stake, the court noted that

> [m]erely because Warner paid Locke the guaranteed compensation under the agreement does not establish Warner fulfilled its contractual obligation. As pointed out by Locke, the value in the subject development deal was not merely the guaranteed payments under the agreement, but also the opportunity to direct and produce films and earn additional sums, and most importantly, the opportunity to promote and enhance a career. (p. 926)

Studios do not give their assurance lightly. Recall that Shirley MacLaine's contract negotiations took seven months and were not concluded until the parties had agreed on the director. The record is silent on whether that director, George Cukor, had also signed his contract at the same time, but that is a common practice. The studio will try to delay triggering its pay-or-play obligations until the project is far along. Until the contract is formed, the studio has no obligation to pay anything. MacLaine might turn down roles that would conflict with this project because she anticipates that the project will go forward, but until the pay-or-play clause is triggered, she bears all the consequences. The parties bargain, in effect, over when, and how, the actor's reliance (forbearance) will be protected.[2]

The subtlety of the triggering mechanism is well illustrated by the contract of a supporting actor who would only be made pay-or-play upon receipt of a bona fide conflicting offer. In effect, the producer's option would be a variation on a right of first refusal. Upon signing the agreement, the artist commits to being available. The producer can terminate the artist without cost until the start of shooting or until it "matches" an outside offer that includes a pay-or-play provision.

> In the event that Artist receives a conflicting *bona fide* "pay-or-play" offer on another motion picture which Artist would otherwise accept, Artist shall accord Producer the right to pre-empt such other offer by furnishing Artist with a "pay-or-play" guarantee for his guaranteed compensation hereunder within five (5) business days of receipt by Producer of a written request therefore describing the conflicting "pay-or-play" offer. If producer so exercises said right of preemption, Artist shall render his services hereunder on the Start Date, as defined herein. If Producer does not so furnish

Artist with such guarantee, Artist may elect to be released from his obligations hereunder. (Redacted contract excerpt)

The star of the same movie had a more attractive pay-or-play clause, though, unlike Shirley MacLaine's contract, it was not triggered upon signing.

Offset

Judge Kingsley's characterization of the pay-or-play clause as "assurance that a performer will not, without its consent, create competition for other pictures of the employer" is slightly off on two counts. The primary motivating force is almost certainly not shielding the studio from the actor *creating competition,* although industry people might characterize it this way. It is not plausible that preventing the production of a film with a particular star in a particular narrow window of time (fourteen weeks for Shirley MacLaine) would have much of an impact on the individual studio. Because the studio with the largest box office share has averaged around 20% since 1975 (Murphy 1997, p. 194), the adverse effects of another studio's having a big hit would be diffused over the remaining producers; the rewards to thwarting a project would, therefore, be spread over the remaining studios, with the initial studio receiving only a small share of the returns.

Nor, as Judge Kingsley recognized, would the actor require the studio's consent. The contract gives the studio something akin to a first refusal right. It grants the studio a limited right to prevent the actor from working with another studio (and perhaps other potential employers) for a specified period. That right is protected not by a "property rule" but only by a "liability rule." (Calabresi and Melamed 1972) That is, the studio cannot prevent the actor from working with someone else during the production period; it can only collect damages by setting off payments from the third party against its fixed compensation liability.

It was not always so. When most artists were under long-term contracts in the 1930s and 1940s, the studio did have the right to prevent them from working elsewhere. This did not mean that the artist would not work elsewhere; it simply meant that the third-party employer had to bargain with the studio to "rent" the employee. If the artist's market value were greater than the contract price, the studio could pocket the difference. Renting talent from other studios was a common occurrence—an industry study found over 2,000 loan-outs of actors, directors, and cinematographers among the seven major studios in 1933–1939. (Schatz 1988, p. 223)

So, although the studio in the 1930s had the power to prevent an actor from "creating competition," it usually chose not to wield that power. Rather, it more typically attempted to allocate its "assets" (artists under contract) to their highest and best use, since the studio would benefit from both the direct payments on this film and, possibly, the enhanced reputation of the artist. That might entail having the artist "sit and wait," but the motive for refusing to loan out the artist would be management of the inventory of talent (a better use for that artist might come along), not preventing the creation of competition.

One-Picture Deals

In the modern era, the studio's right has been protected only by a liability rule, in both one-shot deals (Shirley MacLaine) and in multipicture deals (Carroll Baker). I will discuss some aspects of the multipicture deal below, but for now will focus on the one-shot deal. If the studio invokes the pay-or-play clause, the artist is free to contract with someone else in the time slot. However, any earnings must be offset against the original contract. Rather than requiring the artist or third-party employer to negotiate with the original studio, the rule fixes a price in advance. The rule appears to establish a 100% tax on the subsequent transaction, which would seem to dampen incentives. Why shouldn't Shirley MacLaine just go to the beach?

Even if the entire fixed compensation had to be set off, there are good reasons why an artist might choose to perform rather than remain idle. First, the fixed compensation is only one element in the compensation package. Shirley MacLaine stood to make millions on her gross participation. The expected value of the contract would be substantially greater than her *Bloomer Girl* fixed compensation. If opportunities for roles of equivalent economic value are few and far between, she might find the potential gains from the contingent compensation attractive despite the fact that the fixed compensation from the second movie would go to Fox, not her. Second, if the period between signing the original contract and the production period is long (over nine months in Shirley MacLaine's case), the artist's market value can change dramatically. If an actor had one box office hit in the interim, fixed compensation might well jump from $100,000 on the canceled picture to $1 million on the new one. Third, even if the expected compensation for the second picture just equaled the pay-or-play obligation (so that the expected net compensation was zero), the actor might still be willing to make the second picture because doing so might enhance future earnings. Recall that in *Locke* (p. 926) the court explicitly recognized that production of the film could enhance career prospects. Fourth, since salaries are paid weekly, the offset applies only to the overlapping period. So, for example, had MacLaine started a movie with a different studio in the last week of the pay-or-play period, only one week of her compensation ($53,571.43) would be offset.

The preceding paragraph presupposes that the initial studio would be willing and able to enforce the entire offset. That is unlikely. The first studio is, in effect, bargaining with the second, and its bargaining position is not terribly strong. Its only chip in the negotiations is a few weeks of the career of a particular artist. The second studio has two dimensions in which it can substitute. It could choose someone else to perform, someone not burdened by the offset "tax." Or it could shift the timing of the project to avoid the pay-or-play period. That flexibility should, in most instances, enable the second studio to bargain away a considerable portion of the offset. If the artist has the right to refuse any offer, no matter how reasonable, the duty to offset is not likely to be onerous.

Still, even though the tax is likely to be much less than 100%, that doesn't explain why there should be any tax at all. Why not simply let the artist take any new offer that comes along unencumbered by the previous arrangement with the studio? The most plausible reason is that the tax (whatever its effective rate) provides some incentive for the studio to terminate in a timely manner. The earlier the exercise of the pay-or-play option, the more likely it is that the artist will find alternative employment and provide some offset to the first studio's contractual obligation. This argument is, essentially, the same as the rationale for encouraging anticipatory repudiation by a party who has determined that it will not perform.

These arguments suggest that Judge Zack erred in stating that all earnings during the pay-or-play period, even those as a seamstress, must be offset against the studio's obligation. If the artist knew that such earnings—a small fraction of the studio's obligation—would be offset, then there is no reason for the actor to work (the tax is 100%) and no reason for the parties to bargain over it. The only reasons the artist might engage in such non-theatrical work would be ignorance (she didn't know the rule) or an expectation that the studio would not bother to enforce its legal right. That expectation is likely to be correct, since in most instances it would not be worth the studio's effort to litigate the matter, although if a case were litigated on other grounds, the studio would likely raise this point in its attempt to limit damages (as was the case in Constance Bennett's radio contracts). So, while application of the offset rule for nonentertainment alternative employment would be silly, it is unlikely to cause much harm, since the parties would not, in most instances, take it seriously. Constance Bennett's radio performances might be a closer case. These were, in part, an investment in developing a presence in an alternative medium; indeed, in the 1940s she devoted more attention to radio than to film. (See Constance Bennett, IMDB.)

Multipicture Deals

The modern multipicture deal differs markedly from the long-term contracts of yesteryear. In the pre-1950 long-term contracts, the artist's ability to reject a proposed role was drastically curtailed. The studio assigned the artist to a film and, if the artist refused, the studio could suspend the artist. If the artist wanted to make a picture with another studio, she needed permission from the first studio. Now, the studio has the obligation to offer projects, but the artist need not accept. Nor would the studio have the exclusive right to the artist's services. If the artist wanted to make a film with another studio, the first studio would have, in essence, a first refusal right. Technically, a first refusal right allows the holder to buy an asset (here the artist's time) at a price fixed by the third party. In this case, the relevant constraint is not the third party's offer price, but merely the existence of an offer that the artist finds acceptable. As Judge Kingsley noted in a footnote in his discussion of the Carroll Baker contract, "under the contract, plaintiff could perform for another producer, provided she gave Paramount notice of her intent; in that event, Paramount was required either to consent or to schedule her for its own picture at the time or times involved." (*Garfein*, p. 717, n.4) If the studio fails to offer a role for the time slot, the artist is free to make a film elsewhere. If the artist were the originator of the project, she might have to offer the contract studio a "first look." If the studio failed to pick up the project within a contractually determined time period, the artist would be free to shop it elsewhere.

Carroll Baker's contract made her pay-or-play for at least one film each year. An alternative, and I think more common, arrangement would give the studio an option to use the artist in one film each year for one fee (a guarantee). If the studio desired to use the artist in a particular film, it would offer the artist pay-or-play status for a second fee (at a predetermined rate). If the artist accepted, then the pay-or-play clause would be triggered; if the artist rejected, then there would still be consequences as described in the following paragraph. Regardless of the precise structure, the same two problems remain. First, if the studio cannot require the artist to work on a particular film, what consequences might the artist bear by refusing a project? Second, if, say, Fox offers a part to Carroll Baker and Paramount fails to match, should Paramount's "guarantee payment" (the $200,000) be offset by the earnings from the second studio's project? Or, turning that around, should Fox have to repay some or all of Paramount's guarantee payment as a cost of hiring Carroll Baker?

The artist's discretion is a crucial variable in a multipicture deal, and the outcome will reflect the bargaining power (marketability) of the artist. The more powerful artists will demand considerable freedom in their choice of roles, while relative unknowns would have much less discretion. The pay-or-play clause can be used to make the artist take the studio's reliance interest seriously, a reversal of the single-picture story. If the studio offers the artist a role and evidences its seriousness by offering to make the artist pay-or-play, and the artist refuses, the artist can be made to bear the costs in two dimensions. The contract could require that the fixed compensation which would have been triggered by the pay-or-play clause be offset against the guarantee. That would mean that the studio has met its obligation of employing the artist for one of the contracted pictures, but at a relatively modest cost. Additionally, the pay-or-play offer could define a time period during which the artist could not perform for another studio without the studio's consent (or at least a right of offset). By varying (1) the ease with which the studio can trigger the pay-or-play clause and (2) the artist's ability to accept offers from other studios (the length of time, the reasonableness of consent, the magnitude of the offset), the parties can customize to some degree the cost to the artist of rejecting the studio's proposed role.

With the multipicture deal, the breadth of the studio's option is much greater than with the one-shot deal. In the one-shot deal, the artist had committed to a tightly defined time period. The narrowness of that window constrained the first studio's bargaining power; the second studio could wait a few weeks (at a cost) and eliminate the problem. That is not so for the multipicture deal as a whole (although it is true for each individual project offered to the artist). I would suspect that an artist with considerable bargaining power when entering into a long-term contract (i.e., one that was very marketable) would eliminate the offset. That would allow pursuit of outside offers without penalty and would also enhance the employer's incentive to find attractive roles. The less successful (at the time of contract formation) are more likely to be stuck with a duty to offset.

In a related context, the offset issue was at the core of a dispute between John Calipari and the New Jersey Nets. Calipari entered into a five-year contract to coach the Nets. He had been coaching for a few months before the deal had been memorialized in a writing (heaven knows why). At that stage Calipari insisted that there be no offset if he were fired and subsequently hired as a basketball coach during the duration of the contract. Calipari ultimately prevailed. Contemporaneous press accounts suggested that the majority of National Basketball Association coaches (seventeen) were required to offset their earnings from the second coaching job against the unpaid balance of the first contract. More powerful coaches (Pat Riley and Larry Brown were named) did not have offset clauses. See McDonough (1996, p. D5) and Roberts (1996, p. B15).

The offset issue arises in guaranteed player contracts as well. Arbitrations in both the National Basketball Association and the National Football League held that where the contract was silent, guaranteed player contracts did not require the player to offset when signing with another team. See *NFL Players' Ass'n v. NFL Management Council* (Arbitration of Dante Pastorini & Oakland Raiders); *Arbitration of Rudy Hackett & Denver Nuggets* (1977). The NBA collective bargaining agreement was subsequently revised to provide for offset against guaranteed compensation. These arbitrations and the NBA collective bargaining agreement are discussed in Weiler and Roberts (1993, p. 299).

4. Concluding Remarks

Whether the parties would require offset in a particular contract, one-shot or multipicture, is a hard question. It should not, however, be confused with the much easier question raised by *Parker:* Must the artist take a reasonable offer to "mitigate" damages? No. Shirley MacLaine granted the studio an option on her services for a specific use and a specific purpose. For good and sensible reasons, the studio was prepared to pay a considerable sum for that option. It then chose not to exercise the option. The studio's breach was not the failure to make the film, but only the failure to pay the contracted for option price. Had the courts framed the question properly, they would have reached the right result for the right reasons.

Instead, the court took a "different and inferior" path (in both senses). The court asked whether the alternate employment was different and inferior as a matter of law and somehow concluded that it was. It is hard to imagine how a rational court could find the second contract "different and inferior" as a matter of law while at the same time citing with approval *de la Falaise*. After all, that court found radio plays (regardless of content) different but not inferior. If a radio play is not inferior to a movie, how could a court find one unmade movie necessarily inferior to another? *De la Falaise* could be justified if the court had recognized a distinction between cases in which the plaintiff had been employed (offset) and those in which (like *Parker*) it had not. The court could plausibly argue that a radio play, unlike a seamstress job, is close enough (not inferior) to warrant an offset of the earnings, if earnings there be, while still holding that the law did not require that the plaintiff accept a radio script in mitigation.

The fact that there were significant differences between *Bloomer Girl* and *Big Country, Big Man,* I suspect, encouraged the courts to go down the wrong track. Suppose that the second offer was virtually identical—a Hollywood musical with the same director, same approvals, same compensation, same timing, and same politics. Had MacLaine refused to make the second picture as "mitigation," then she could not have raised the "different and inferior" objection. Without the "different and inferior" crutch, the parties would have posed the problem properly, and the court, like Judge Kingsley in *Garfein*, would have disposed of it neatly.

Maybe. A less sanguine view would be that the *Parker* analysis is symptomatic of deeper problems. Why did the California Supreme Court ignore the purpose of the relevant contract language in determining whether Shirley MacLaine had to mitigate? Does the disjunction between contract law's analytic boxes and transactional lawyers' practical concerns lead to systematic error in contract litigation? In particular, is there a hostility against option arrangements, which could be viewed as a form of "penalty clause?" (The studio agrees, in effect, to pay a penalty if it fails to perform.) Indeed, when I presented an earlier draft of this chapter at workshops, the immediate response was to ask if contracting parties could use the option characterization to evade the penalty clause bar. Part of the problem, I suspect, is the notion held by many contracts professors that $750,000 (in

1965 dollars) is too much to pay Shirley MacLaine for "doing nothing." One wonders how they will cope with Sondra Locke's claim that $1.5 million for "doing nothing" is too little. Of course, as Judge Kingsley pointed out in *Garfein,* they are not doing nothing—"[t]hey also serve who only sit and wait." (*Garfein,* p. 717) There is no reason for wooden application of the rule barring penalty clauses. Shirley MacLaine is no Shylock. The studios are not being put upon by her or other artists; they include pay-or-play clauses in their contracts (and these are, after all, the studios' contracts) for good reason. The pay-or-play clause is a nuanced balancing of the studio's need for flexibility against the artist's reliance.

Perhaps the most disconcerting aspect of *Parker* is that the court's framing of the issue has seemed so appropriate and noncontroversial to legal scholars and courts for over a quarter of a century. The court might have drawn the "different and inferior" boundary in the wrong place, but there has been no questioning the notion that ascertaining this boundary is the relevant inquiry. Even the one attempt to reframe *Parker,* Mary Jo Frug's feminist discussion, stays within the "different and inferior" framework. Contracts casebooks, in general, and Dawson, Harvey, and Henderson (1982), in particular, she claimed,

> inexplicably . . . omit material that would confirm readers' intuitions that the social context and political significance of the films might explain the application of the "different and inferior" qualification in *Parker.* Dawson, Harvey, and Henderson thus subtly deter readers who are familiar with nineteenth century feminist activists and their work from utilizing their personal connections with the case to understand *Parker. . . .* Although readers' intuitions about the *Parker* case may in fact explain the otherwise baffling result of this decision, the casebook does not encourage them to draw on these intuitions. (Frug 1985, p. 1119 (footnote omitted))

The sociopolitical context receives at least lip service in a few casebooks. See Farnsworth and Young (1995, p. 513); Kastely et al. (1996, p. 1024); Knapp and Crystal (1993, pp. 949–951); and Macaulay et al. (1995, pp. 63–65). It makes no sense to interpret a standardized clause on the basis of the hypothesized idiosyncratic politics of a particular artist. The court, unfortunately, invited argument along these (and other irrelevant) lines and academics, alas, have accepted.

CHAPTER 16

Bloomer Girl:
A Postscript

Parker is in the casebooks to illustrate a proposition regarding mitigation, and, as the preceding makes clear, the issue should not have arisen. What, then, of the responsibility of a terminated employee to find substitute employment? In their casebook, Macaulay, Kidwell, and Whitford (2003, pp. 63–64) note a few cases in which the courts have held that lower level workers failed to mitigate by taking jobs, and hint at a class-based rationale:

> Can we say that the law benefits upper-middle and middle class employees more than working class employees? Why do the courts seem to assume that one school bus driving job is like another but "Big Country, Big Man" is not like "Bloomer Girl" or any managerial, professional, technical job is not comparable to a managerial type position in the tire industry? Isn't the result that Shirley MacLaine could have devoted her time to peace and environmental activism during the time "Bloomer Girl" was to have been made, but that the police officer could not attend college? Is this an unfair reading of these cases?

Of course, they are only asking, but my impression is that the answer they are searching for is that this is a fair reading of the case law and that many contracts professors would agree with them. I don't believe, however, that class bias is any more helpful in analyzing the problem than Shirley MacLaine's political preferences were in analyzing *Parker.* Nor is it useful to treat the question as a moral matter—should we discourage the discharged employee from remaining idle—as asserted by Theodore Dwight in *Howard v. Daly* over a century ago.

The "different and inferior" rule is only a default rule. It is a gap filler for those instances in which the employment contract did not provide for severance pay or a parachute (golden for some, lead for others). When Michael Ovitz was fired by Disney, his severance package was worth around $140 million. For some details on this, see *In Re Walt Disney Company Derivative Litigation* and Stewart (2005). The employment contract of Mark Hurd as CEO of Hewlett-Packard dealt explicitly with both the mitigation and offset issues: "Executive will not be required to mitigate the amount of any payment contemplated by this Agreement, nor will any earnings that Executive may receive from any other source reduce any such payment." (Onecle 2006) Severance packages are common. In some instances, the severance pay will be substantial, with few conditions. In others, the pay will be modest and conditional on the employee's good faith search for employment and his failure to obtain it. In still other instances, the employer would prefer that the employee not take a similar position and might make the compensation contingent upon honoring a covenant not to compete. The point is that any employment contract that is not at-will must have some package of compensation and impose some responsibilities or limitations concerning the employee's subsequent search for work. Severance pay and the conditions thereon are decision variables. If there are conditions, they might require interpretation, and that could raise issues of the "different and inferior" variety. But that is quite different from imposing an obligation to seek employment that is not "different and inferior."

It would not be terribly surprising to find that those closer to the bottom of the economic ladder would get less cash and have a greater responsibility to accept alternative employment. But that is not because the law is class conscious; it is simply a reflection of the underlying economics. In general, those nearer the top of the income distribution will place more value on attractive severance ex ante, both because their need for current income is less critical and because their taking this job meant foregoing an attractive alternative. That is, they are likely to have a substantial reliance interest in the particular job taken. They want the employer to feel at least some of their pain when contemplating termination. If the firm-specific and industry-specific human capital is low (that is, the worker's skills are redeployable in a wide range of alternative occupations) and job security is income elastic (a fancy way of saying that someone would pay more for it—that is, give up some current income—as income rises), then employment contracts for those nearer the bottom of the income distribution will have less attractive severance packages.

Perhaps I am wrong on these predictions. Determining the appropriate trade-off between current income and severance payments and conditions is a difficult problem for parties to solve. But it is even more difficult for courts to solve with a one size fits all rule. The best the courts can do is provide a default rule for those cases in which the parties did not find it important enough to spell out the parameters of the severance package. This is yet another example of a theme that recurs throughout this book. Given that the default rules will often be inadequate, the law should facilitate contracting away from them. So, returning to *Parker*, a court should recognize that, whatever the default rule, the pay-or-play clause trumped it.

CHAPTER 17

Wasserman v. Township of Middletown: The Penalty Clause That Wasn't

Wasserman v. Township of Middletown makes it into the casebooks because Judge Stuart Pollock provided an eloquent statement of the doctrinal attempt to draw a line between enforceable liquidated damages and unenforceable penalty clauses. Properly understood, that issue should not have arisen. The clause in question was neither; it was an option granted to the lessor in a thirty-year real property lease. Far from being a penalty, it was more generous to the lessor than the default rule would have been.

If the lessor opted to terminate the lease prematurely, it would have to compensate the lessee by a formula based on the lessee's gross revenues in the previous years. After the lessor terminated the lease with over ten years to go, it refused to pay, arguing that the clause was unenforceable. The lessor claimed that if the lease were terminated in the last year, it would have resulted in an absurdly high assessment, and therefore that the clause would result in a penalty. Its claim was correct, but the conclusion does not follow.

The option perspective is particularly useful in this case. For, if the suspect clause is viewed as liquidated damages, it does not make sense. However, when viewed as an option, the fact that the option is priced too high in the waning years does not present a problem. It is simply an out-of-the-money option at a time when the lessor's need for an option is minimal.

Decisions are often misleading regarding the facts, and before attempting to rationalize the reported facts, we should first determine that the court got them right. That is particularly true in this case since the trial judge had a very different version of the facts. He denied, in very strong language, that the termination clause would overcompensate in the final years of the lease. So, if he were correct, there would be nothing to explain. It turns

313

out that he was flat wrong, yet no one—the parties, the Appellate Court, or the New Jersey Supreme Court—challenged his interpretation directly. They just ignored it.

1. What Happened?

The Township of Middletown owned a piece of property and Wasserman had been its tenant for about twenty years. In 1970 the Township decided to put the lease out to bid; Wasserman was the only bidder. The parties then proceeded to negotiate over the terms of the lease and signed it in May 1971. At the time, the property was valued at $47,500. The lease was for a term of thirty years with a monthly rental fixed for the entire period at $458.33. Wasserman was required to make significant physical improvements, increasing the area from 3,200 to 5,600 square feet. If Wasserman failed to do so within two years, the Township would have an option to void the lease and Wasserman would forfeit a surety bond for two years rent. (Information for Bidders, pp. TO-3, IB-4)

Wasserman did make the improvements, spending about $140,000. Subsequently, he sublet the premises to Jo-Ro with the Township's approval. (There was an additional layer of subletting which has no impact on the case and can be ignored.) The rent in the sublease was $1,850 per month. It appears that the rent was fixed and not at all contingent on the net or gross sales, although that cannot be ascertained from the record. The lease also included a termination clause which allowed the Township to terminate if it paid for the unamortized portion of the improvement costs and paid 25% of the gross annual revenues, calculated by taking the average of the three previous years. In December 1987, the Township notified Wasserman of its desire to exercise its option, giving one year's notice. The premises were vacated in December 1988, and six months later the property was sold at auction for $610,000.

The termination clause, the crux of the litigation, read as follows:

[P]ayment to be made shall be (1.) total value of all improvements made by lessee at time of construction × (multiplied by) years remaining in Lease term / (divided by) total number of years in Lease term; and (2.) twenty-five percent of the lessee[']s average gross receipts for one year (to be computed by + (adding) the lessee[']s total gross receipts for the lessee[']s three full fiscal years immediately preceding the time of cancellation of the lease and / (dividing by) 12 (twelve). (*Wasserman*, p. 248)

The first part (recoupment) had been included in the original bid document; the second part (the share of gross revenues) was added in the course of the negotiations. Wasserman's counsel claimed that such a clause was the norm. "However, it must be kept in mind that Mr. Wasserman will have an active operating business on the premises and the trade custom for the purchase of such a business envisions the price as set forth in your formula, together with twenty-five percent of the gross receipts for the year proceeding. This simple addition to your formula would basically take care of any problems left remaining." (Letter from Howard Roberts, March 22, 1971)

When the contract was terminated, there were 11.75 years remaining. Under the first half of the termination clause, the lessee was entitled to 11.75/30 times the initial construction costs, about $55,000. That is uncontroversial. The battle was over the second half of the clause. Jo-Ro's sales in the three preceding years totaled roughly $3.5 million, which would have resulted in additional compensation of about $290,000. At trial (and on appeal), Wasserman argued that there had been no breach, just a termination as per the lease:

> In the present case, neither party breached the contract. The Township voluntarily elected to invoke their rights under the contract to terminate the lease. This was done with the consent of the tenant who voluntarily surrendered the property to the Township. This is not a situation where one party has breached the contract and the non-breaching party is seeking "damages." (Plaintiff Brief to Superior Court of New Jersey, Appellate Division, p. 27)

The Township argued that the clause was a penalty clause and that the penalty was unreasonable. Counsel's argument that the clause would produce absurd results was interrupted by the judge:

Mr. Dowd: Judge, I believe that what we've heard this morning is a discussion in semantics and with all due respect to Roy [Curnow, Wasserman's counsel], this is a 30 year lease. And there are facts before this court, the most striking of which is this, your Honor, what Mr. Curnow is telling the Court is that at the conclusion of the 30th year the lease was over and his clients would have received not a penny, whether we call it damages or whatever we call it. But if in the middle of the 29th year the Township found it necessary to exercise what he calls its option, Mr. Curnow would be entitled to roughly the same amount of money that he's seeking today, namely a lump sum in the hundreds of thousands of dollars pursuant to that formula.

The Court: How do you figure that out?

Mr. Dowd: Huh?

The Court: How do you figure that out?

Mr. Dowd: Well,—

The Court: It's based upon the numbers and years remaining over the total numbers of the years of the lease—

Mr. Dowd: Well, there's a—

The Court: —which would make it almost de minimus.

Mr. Dowd: Well, as I understand the formula it's keyed to the prior three years. I don't have the formula in front of me, Your Honor, but it's still a substantial sum.

The Court: That serves as the average and then you apply, if there were six months left, it would be one half . . . over thirty or one over sixty. One sixtieth of that amount as opposed to the numbers we're dealing with now. (Trial Court Opinion on Damages, pp. 5–6)

Later, the judge elaborated:

> The argument presented, that the Township would have to pay a fee to the plaintiff if he's terminated in the 29th year, is absolutely ridiculous. I just made an initial calculation that if there were six months to go on this lease, the pay-out figure wouldn't be more than $20,000 or $25,000. We had eleven and a half years to go on this lease and the formula is so designed to provide that the number of years remaining over the total number of years of the lease, eleven and a half over thirty . . . that that would be the formula against which the average gross receipts for the three years previous and the capital improvement would result in the pay-out figure. (Trial Court Opinion on Damages, pp. 13–14)

To say the judge was annoyed with the defense would be an understatement. "I think the Township's position . . . is both bogus, insincere, incredible, and not in keeping with the image that the Court would like to see public officials and their agents and servants present to the public in cases such as this." He held the clause enforceable and awarded the lessee the full amount plus interest dating from December 31, 1988, at 10%. (The decision does not say whether that would be simple or compound interest, but since New Jersey presently awards simple interest, I presume it was the former. For our purposes it doesn't matter.)

The trial judge was, of course, completely wrong. The language was clear; only the lessee's construction costs were to be prorated over the remaining years of the lease. Indeed, the damage calculation approved by the court did not apply the multiplier to the gross revenue part of the formula. That the Township's attorney could not correct the judge on the spot is perhaps understandable, although it is hard to justify showing up at the courtroom without a copy of the lease. What is harder to explain is the defendant's failure to challenge explicitly the judge's error as the case proceeded through the appeals process. The closest the Township came to challenging the interpretation was this ambiguous argument in its brief to the Supreme Court: "The lease was cancelled in the 19th of its thirty years, yet cancellation in the second or 29th year would have resulted in application of the same damages clause." (Defendant Brief to the Supreme Court, p. 13) Neither the Court of Appeals, in its unpublished opinion, nor the New Jersey Supreme Court acknowledged the trial judge's interpretation of the disputed clause.

The trial judge's misreading did not affect his conclusion on liability, although it should have affected his conclusion on damages. He agreed with Wasserman that there had been no breach: "[T]his contract is an integrated contract. It calls for the right of termination. If one exercises that right of termination it is not considered a breach of the agreement." (Trial Court Opinion on Damages, p. 13) The Appellate Court affirmed for the reasons set forth by the trial judge. For some unknown reason, Judge Pollock chose not to address the not-a-breach argument at all, confining his opinion entirely to the penalty versus liquidated damages issue.

2. The Damages

The line between liquidated damages and a penalty is pretty fuzzy. The Second Restatement (Contracts) and the UCC both refer to the reasonableness of the damages in light of the anticipated or actual loss caused by the breach. Neither says which loss is to count. Is it only losses that would be recognized in a breach of contract suit? Judge Pollock quotes a Wisconsin decision suggesting a broader view: "[stipulated damages] enable the parties to correct what the parties perceive to be inadequate judicial remedies by agreeing upon a formula which may include damage elements too uncertain or remote to be recovered under rules of damages applied by the courts." (249–250. Quoting *Wassenaar v. Panos*, 362) I do not want to get into the details of the doctrine, largely because the doctrine is (or should have been) irrelevant in this particular case, and because, regardless of which interpretation is accepted, the penalty clause doctrine itself makes no sense. What I do want to do here is sketch out what the damages might have been, given the information available in the very thin record.

First, I want to clear up a possible misconception. At trial the Township intimated that the negotiated lease was a sweetheart deal, although it could never prove this. The New Jersey Supreme Court gave credibility to this notion, noting that the value of the property increased by a factor of thirteen. That sounds like a pretty terrific deal. However, recall that right after the lease was signed, Wasserman was required to make an additional investment of about $140,000. If we include that in the initial valuation, then the annual appreciation over nearly twenty years is only about 6%. That is not much, and it is even less impressive when we recall that the time period included "stagflation" and years in which the prime rate exceeded 10%. They—the Township and Wasserman—would have been much better off buying Treasury bills.

The New Jersey Supreme Court remanded for a determination of whether the actual damages bore a reasonable relation to the stipulated damages. Leave aside for now that it is inappropriate to label the consequences of the exercise of the option as "damages." The court's framing requires a determination of actual damages. The damages, the court suggests, would have been the difference between the plaintiff's position had the lease run the full thirty years and the plaintiff's position because of the termination. The latter would take into account "the lessee's duty to mitigate damages; and the fair market rent and availability of replacement space" (p. 258) as well as relocation costs. Note that this is irrelevant for Wasserman—he's just a sublessor whose only interest is the money. Jo-Ro presumably did have an interest in continuing in business.

It will be instructive to consider two different paths for reckoning those damages. The second will be particularly useful as an introduction to the proper analysis of the case. The analysis illustrates both that the formula yielded a result that was in the ballpark and that it was a big ballpark—there is a wide range of defensible answers. By remanding the case to determine whether the stipulated remedy was reasonable, the New Jersey Supreme Court required that the parties perform a rather complicated exercise. The following illustrates why wise parties would design their arrangement to avoid that exercise. Warning: the following discussion will involve some tedious arithmetic involving the present value of cash flows; just take my word for it.

Wasserman would have received the spread between what he paid the Township and what he received from Jo-Ro ($1,850 − $458.33) for the remaining 11.75 years. The present value of that, assuming an interest rate of 8%, would be about $130,000. In addition, Jo-Ro lost something of value. The court seemed to think that Jo-Ro's earnings as reflected in its income tax returns were relevant. For the three years combined, these totaled less than $4,000. The court suggested that these numbers did not bode well for the plaintiff: "We recognize the difference between tax losses and actual losses. Yet, to the extent that tax returns reflect actual profit or loss, they demonstrate the unreasonableness of damages exceeding $290,000, which were calculated on the basis of gross receipts." (p. 257) Jo-Ro's profits, even if calculated accurately, were only one component of the loss. It lost an ongoing business at a particular location. The court noted that Jo-Ro's present owners had paid $95,000 for "the business" in 1977. If that payment were entirely for Jo-Ro's inventory, then this would have no impact on measured damages. That was not the case. Jo-Ro's tax returns for 1985–1987 suggest that inventory valuation would have been around $20,000. If we assume that the remaining $75,000 was a payment for the right to continue running this type of retail establishment at this particular location, then that would suggest a value to the subtenant of around $600 per month. If that were still the valuation when the lease was actually terminated, the value of that stream for the remaining 11.75 years was about $55,000. Added to Wasserman's loss, this would yield a combined loss of roughly $185,000. Note that it would be improper to add the unamortized portion of the original investment since that would amount to double-counting.

An alternative approach is simpler and yields a larger number. If Jo-Ro were to move, it would have to incur relocation costs and would have to rent new space. To simplify, we can ignore the relocation costs. Suppose that Jo-Ro could find equivalent space—a perfect substitute. The damages would be the value of the future stream of payments it would have to make for the new location less the payments saved by the termination, the rent paid by Wasserman. Since the original property was sold for $610,000, the market price for the perfect substitute should be the same. The question then would be: What is the present value of the first 11.75 years for a property worth $610,000? That depends on both the interest rate chosen and the expected pattern of payments. If the payments are constant and the interest rate is 8%, then the present value of that stream is about $370,000.[1] So, over half the purchase price was for the use of the property prior to the expiration of the thirty-year lease. The rent that would have been paid to the Township was $458.33 per month; the present value of that for the remaining years was about $40,000. On the assumption that Jo-Ro would roughly break even for that period, the damages so measured would be the difference between the two figures, roughly $330,000.

Should we have much confidence in these numbers? Probably not. By fiddling with the assumptions one could generate a wide array of measured damages. For example, changing the interest rate or the rate of increase in rental value by 1% changes the measured damages by about $15,000. Lower interest rates (or higher growth rates) mean that relatively less weight is put on the near term, so the present value of the stream would be lower. So, while there is substantial room for dispute as to what the "true damages" would have been, the formula yielded a result that was at least plausible. Upon remand, should a court find that the range of damage measurements was close enough to warrant ignoring them and substituting the amount produced by the formula? Should we have much faith in a court's ability to do so, especially when the only hint the New Jersey Supreme Court gave on calculating damages was the misleading reference to Jo-Ro's income as reported for tax purposes?

Recall that the Township attempted to argue that the formula would yield ludicrous results as the lease drew close to completion. I will examine that claim below. I should note, however, that the New Jersey Supreme Court's opinion did not hinge at all on that. It was concerned with whether a measure based on gross sales would relate to actual or projected damages at the time of the actual termination.

3. The Option

A lot can happen in thirty years. The business might prosper or it might fail. The tenant might want to move, perhaps to a sunnier clime. It might want to reconfigure the premises or change its line of business. It might want to sublet to someone who would continue with a similar business or change to something completely different. The land might become more valuable for a nonretail use. A government might want to take the land for a public purpose. The terms of the lease affect both the ease of adjustment to changing conditions and the manner in which the gains (or losses) are distributed. The Township's option to terminate can best be understood as one of the mechanisms for adapting to change.

The second measure of damages was simply the difference between the present value of the stream of rental payments given current market values and the payments specified in the lease for the duration of the leasehold. That has a name—the "bonus value." The leasehold interest had increased in value, and the question is: To whom did that increased value belong? The black letter law says that it belongs to the lessee. Indeed, the lessee has a property interest in the leasehold; if the lessor wanted to terminate the lease, it would have to get the lessee's permission. That is only the default rule; parties can contract around it, and they usually do. However, it is important to recognize that absent the suspect clause, the Township could not have terminated the lease without Wasserman's permission. To use the Calabresi-Melamed (1972) terminology, Wasserman would have been protected by a property rule rather than a mere liability rule. It was only by adding the termination option to the lease that the protection was reduced to a liability rule.

It is useful to compare the disputed clause with what would happen if the government were to take the property for a public purpose. Since the leasehold is a property interest, if the government were to take the property, the Constitution requires that it compensate the lessor and lessee for their respective interests. Commercial leases typically undo this constitutional mandate by including a condemnation clause in the lease. The simple space lease typically provides that the lease terminates upon condemnation and therefore all the award goes to the lessor. (Goldberg, Merrill, and Unumb 1987) If the tenant was supposed to make significant permanent improvements (as was the case in *Wasserman*), the condemnation clause gets more complicated, but the norm would be that the lessee would be compensated for the unamortized cost of the improvements, with the remainder going to the lessor. The *Wasserman* decision did not mention whether the lease included a condemnation clause. It did. And, as we would expect, it followed the usual pattern.

In a taking there is no reason to believe that the bonus value would be positive, after netting out any lessee expenditures on permanent improvements. Market prices can go up or down, and there should be no correlation between market conditions and the government's decision to take the property. However, if a lessor chooses to exercise its option to terminate a lease, on average the bonus value should be positive. The greater the reward from exercising the option, the greater the probability that the lessor would do so. The lessee runs the risk that if things go badly, it is stuck with an above-market lease, and if things go well, it gets booted out. We should expect, therefore, that the lessee would demand greater compensation for a lessor-initiated termination than for a taking, as was the case in the Wasserman lease.

Still, the Wasserman clause provides far too much protection in the last few years of the lease. Is this just a quirk, or is there some logic behind it? As liquidated damages it makes no sense. Why have damages of $300,000 for a lease that will expire in a week? However, it is more understandable when viewed in an option context.

In a plain vanilla lease, the lessee would be free to do with the property as it saw fit for the full thirty years, after which control would revert to the lessor. The lessor would, of course, be concerned with the condition of the property upon reversion, and the lease would include some mechanisms or conditions that would constrain the lessee's freedom. It could also include some restrictions that preclude the property's being used in a more valuable way without the lessor's consent. Restrictions on assignment, subletting, use, and additional construction could serve this purpose. If a better use came along, the lessor could use the consent requirement to capture some of the bonus value. Both lessor and lessee would be able to thwart the change. Each would have a holdout right, and the approval of both would be necessary to attain it.[2] The termination clause eliminated the holdout problem.

In the very early years of the lease, the option to terminate has little value since it is unlikely that the bonus value has changed much. The price of the option (25% of one year's sales) will likely exceed the bonus value, so, unless this had really been a sweetheart deal, the lessor would virtually never find exercising the option worthwhile in the early years. For some period, say between ten and twenty years, the option could be valuable—the lessor could repossess the property to either lease it out at a higher rental or sell it outright. If the option price were set too low, the lessee's incentives to make long-term location-specific investments would be dampened. To some extent, the compensation for physical improvements deals with that. (At first glance it appears that the formula at least covers the costs of adding the physical improvements. However, that does not take into account the time value of money. Sticking with the 8% interest rate, the expected value of that damage component after twenty years is less than 10% of the initial investment—not the third implied by a casual reading of the formula.) But, absent a higher option price, the lessee risks getting all the negative bonus value but none of the upside. The formula imperfectly links the option price to the bonus value, it is true. But it is doubtful that any other formula could do much better. In some instances termination would prove a profitable strategy. That might be because the formula inadequately reflected the value of the lease to the lessee. The Township might, for example, have a higher discount rate than the lessee. More importantly, if the property became valuable for a use other than the lessee's, the lessor could force a change to what it believed was a higher and better use, and it would be rewarded with a larger piece of the bonus value. The option eliminated the lessee's power to block change or to fight over the disposition of the bonus value.

The value of that option might be substantial in years 10 through 20. What about the later years, particularly year 29? As the defense noted, it would be ridiculous to charge the Township $300,000 if it terminated in the last year of the lease. Of course, it would be even more ridiculous for the Township to exercise its option in that year. It could wait. The fact that its option to terminate is way out of the money doesn't really matter. Waiting ten years to get rid of the tenant is expensive; waiting one year is not. In effect, in the last years of the lease, the lease reverts to the default rule—the bonus value belongs solely to the lessee, who is protected by a property rule. However, the costs of this rule in that circumstance—bargaining costs and a possible failure to adapt to changed circumstances—will most likely be low. The lessee has the right to say no, but its leverage is limited since the lessor can just sit back and let the lease expire.

4. Concluding Remarks

The parties did not accept Judge Pollock's invitation to explore the relation between the termination fee and true damages. They settled. The settlement, eight years after the termination, was for $360,000, which, after taking into account the time value of money, comes to about sixty cents on the dollar. As it turns out, it doesn't much matter whether we use the 10% simple interest rate that the trial court used or use compound interest (which assumes that the initial judgment could have been invested in the intervening eight years) with rates varying from 6% to 9%. By allowing the Township to muddy the waters with the penalty ploy, the court managed to effect a significant transfer of wealth from the lessee.

There are two morals to this story. The first concerns the liquidated damage/penalty clause distinction, and the second relates to the specifics of this case—the fact that the dispute involved a termination clause in a lease. A liquidated damages clause has two very attractive features. First, it allows the parties to bypass some messy measurement problems. If, as in *Wasserman*, a court will require the parties to show the reasonableness of the damages, this benefit is sacrificed. Second, the formula can be designed to serve an economic function. It might, as in *Parker*, convey the promisee's reliance to the party with discretion to terminate, and that reliance need bear no relation to traditional measures of expectation damages.

The second moral is that a termination option limits the lessee's holdup power. The plain vanilla long-term lease established by the default rules is unrealistic for commercial property. Parties can, and do, contract away from the baseline. By constraining the lessee with restrictions on use, subletting, and so forth, the lessor's bargaining position is enhanced; the lessee must pay for the lessor's consent. However, the lessee still would maintain the right to refuse; the lessor would have to pay for the lessee's consent. Giving the lessor the option to terminate changes the balance. It does not have to buy the lessee's consent. The exercise price must be set high enough to give the lessee a realistic chance to obtain some of the upside since it bears all of the downside. If, as would be the case under many scenarios, the option is out of the money, that only means that the lessor must bargain for the lessee's consent. My conjecture is that the termination option would be structured so as to give the lessee the holdup power when that power is least likely to be of value (near the beginning and end of the lease period). Allowing courts to interfere with the devices the parties have incorporated into the lease by raising extraneous matters like the penalty issue simply makes the task of contracting away from the baseline lease more difficult.

PART VI

Impossibility, Related Doctrines, and Price Adjustment

Because conditions are likely to change after parties enter into an agreement that is expected to last for a period of time, their contract should incorporate some mechanisms to adapt to the changed circumstances, and contract doctrine will, by necessity, establish a set of default rules. In Part III, I considered how the discretion to adapt the quantity was allocated between the parties and how the decision maker's flexibility was constrained by concerns about the opposite party's reliance. In Parts IV and V, the option to terminate, whether explicitly spelled out or as a remedy for breach, described another set of mechanisms for adapting to change.

In Part VI, I consider two more mechanisms for coping with change—excusing performance and adjusting the price. In the absence of explicit language, the doctrinal bases for excusing performance come under a variety of headings—impossibility, impracticability, frustration, and mistake. The flexibility of contract law allows the parties to do more. They could introduce additional grounds for excusing performance (for example, force majeure clauses and conditions). In this part, I provide an economic rationale for the doctrines. But I will begin with a brief chapter on price adjustment. Contrary to most economists and lawyers, I argue that price adjustment problems have little to do with attitudes toward risk. I argue that the variance of future prices is a significant factor in determining the desirability of an adjustment mechanism, but that the reasons are independent of risk attitudes. My concern in Chapter 18 is not with the judicial response, but with the reasons why parties would include price adjustment mechanisms in their agreements and the variety of tools (for example, indexing and meeting competition clauses) they have for doing so.

Posner and Rosenfield (1977) were the first to attempt to provide an economic explanation of the impossibility doctrine. They emphasized the importance of putting liability on the party that is the superior risk bearer. In part, this meant the party that was in the best position to avoid costs. But they also placed great emphasis on the risk aversion of the parties and the relative costs of insuring against risk. In Chapter 19, I propose two alternative explanations which do not require explicit assumptions as to the risk preferences of the parties. The first depends on the low correlation between the intervening event and market conditions. The second treats the intervening event as giving one party an option to terminate. The discussion concludes with an analysis of the interplay between reliance and restitution.

While it is not uncommon for German courts to revise the price term in a long-term contract (Dawson 1983), American courts rarely do so. In one of the cases generated by the first oil shock, *Alcoa v. Essex*, the court found that the failure of one component of the price adjustment mechanism to accurately track cost changes justified excusing Alcoa. However, rather than terminate Alcoa's obligation, the court reformed the agreement. Like most commentators, I conclude that the case was wrongly decided, but my take is quite different. I argue in Chapter 20 that the real problem in *Alcoa* was not the indexing failure. Rather, the contract itself was misconceived.

One line of argument in the excuse cases holds that if costs have changed by "too much," a party might be excused. The question of how much is too much often arises, and the case often cited for illustrating "too much" is *Mineral Park v. Howard*. In the final chapter in Part VI, I show that the high cost of completion was irrelevant in that case, since there was no reason to believe that it would be borne by the defendant.

CHAPTER 18

Price Adjustment in Long-Term Contracts

Economists commonly invoke risk aversion in analyzing contracts. It is an "easy" explanation, and it is tempting to end the search at that point. For example, in his analysis of the *Westinghouse* case, Paul Joskow (1977, p. 173) asked, "Why would somebody buy a long-term fixed price contract other than to insure against fluctuations in the price of uranium?" There are, I suggest, a lot of reasons, but risk aversion provides a convenient excuse for not bothering to look.

1. The Benefits of Price Adjustment

Business firms have ample incentives to include some form of price adjustment mechanism in their contracts, even if both parties are risk neutral. Firms do not generally enter into multiyear contracts because of their concern for the future course of prices. Rather, they enter into the agreements because there are benefits from coordination. Having entered into such an agreement, the parties have to make some decision regarding the course of prices during the life of the agreement. That is, price adjustment will probably be ancillary to the main purposes of the agreement.

Price adjustment can be difficult and costly. Why then bother? Why not simply establish a price or a schedule of prices for the duration of the agreement? I will suggest four reasons that might lead business firms to consider using some form of price adjustment. First, if the contract concerns a complex product that will be continuously redefined during the life of the contract, a price adjustment mechanism can price the "amendments" to the original agreement. Examples include cost-plus pricing of sophisticated defense hardware and complex construction projects. Second, to properly coordinate their behavior, the parties want correct price signals. If the price of an input were below the market price, the buyer would have an incentive to use "too much" of the input. Since this should be anticipated at the formation stage, the costs of poor coordination are borne by both parties. This is a pure moral hazard problem akin to an insured person consuming too much health care because the post-insurance price is too low.

The third and fourth reasons are, analytically at least, more interesting: reduction of pre-contract search and post-agreement jockeying. In both these explanations, the success of price adjustment depends upon its ability to reduce the variance of outcomes. The reduced variance is not, however, valued directly. Rather, it enables the parties to curtail mutually harmful behavior, thereby increasing the value of the agreement to both parties.

Assume initially that the parties are contemplating entering into a multiyear, fixed-price contract. The contract establishes how the gains are to be divided between the parties. Each party could attempt to increase its share of the gains before signing the contract by improving its information on the future course of costs and prices. The more each spends on this search, the smaller the pie. Other things being equal, the larger the variance of the outcomes, the more resources would be devoted to this effort. The parties, therefore, have an incentive to incorporate into the initial agreement a device that would discourage this wasteful searching. Price adjustment mechanisms can do precisely that by reducing the value of the special information. This argument is just a slight variation on the argument in Chapter 10 regarding price search for standardized commodities sold in thick markets. There, the timing of the contract execution influenced the private search for private information; here, the price adjustment mechanism is expected to reduce the value of information on future market price movements.

If after the firms enter into a long-term agreement the contract price fails to track changing market conditions, the loser will be reluctant to continue performance unless it can renegotiate the terms. It could breach and suffer the legal and reputational consequences, but other, less severe, alternatives to willing compliance exist. A buyer could, for example, insist upon strict compliance with quality standards. The aggrieved party could read the contract literally, "working to the rules" as in labor disputes or in centrally planned economies. The incorrect price induces the aggrieved party to expend resources in attempting to renegotiate the terms of the agreement. The costs can arise directly from the effort to renegotiate or indirectly through strategic bargaining. That is, the loser might threaten to engage in acts which impose costs upon the other party but do not constitute a legal breach. If the parties had easy access to market alternatives, they would not be vulnerable to such strategic behavior. Other things being equal, the more isolated from alternatives the contracting parties are, the more significant would be the potential losses. Again, to the extent that the parties can anticipate these problems at the formation stage, they both bear the costs from this wasteful behavior. If the probability of wasteful behavior increases as the divergence between contract price and the opportunity cost of the aggrieved party widens, price adjustment rules which narrow the gap become increasingly attractive.

2. The Mechanics of Price Adjustment

The easiest way to adjust the price is to index. But what should the parties be indexing? The overall price level? Input costs? Market price? Ideally the parties would index the market price. The payoff from indexing, after all, is from the reduction in the divergence between the contract price and the market price. However, practical exigencies usually lead parties to index other prices as proxies. Indeed, in a long-term contract there often is no unique external market price. Indexing has the advantage of being mechanical and generally nonmanipulable. Some contracts index to a price posted by the seller which, obviously, would be under the seller's control. In those instances, however, the seller would have a large number of customers so that strategic behavior vis-à-vis a particular customer would not be feasible. The disadvantage of indexing is that it might track market conditions poorly.

Cost changes would be a reasonably good proxy for changes in the market price if demand did not fluctuate too much or if industry supply were very elastic. However, even in that case, changes in *input prices* are not necessarily the same as changes in *input costs*. If the relative prices of inputs change, the firm has an incentive to alter factor proportions to take advantage of the new price relationships. Also, if factor productivity changes, the connection between input prices and costs deteriorates. Nevertheless, indexing to input prices is common. For example, in my co-authored study of long-term petroleum coke contracts (Goldberg and Erickson 1987), over half the contracts were indexed by the price of an input (crude oil). One alternative to indexing is cost-plus pricing. It tracks cost changes more closely, but is more subject to manipulation; it also gives the seller poorer incentives to control costs, and requires that the parties devote more resources to monitoring performance.

While indexing would be the easiest price adjustment mechanism to implement, it has the obvious disadvantage of tracking changing conditions imperfectly. Even if indexing tracked costs perfectly, it might prove inadequate because of changes on the demand side. The poorer the correlation between the index and what it is supposed to be tracking, the less attractive it will be.

One way to allow the contract price to track market conditions is to permit the buyer to solicit outside offers, with the seller having the right of first refusal (or to meet competition). The buyer could solicit bids from outside sources and if it were to receive a bona fide bid below the contract price, the supplier would be given the option to match. If the supplier chose not to do so, then the contract could be terminated or suspended. Such clauses would not be of much value if there were a thin market and the buyer could not rely upon the existence of external suppliers. Nor would they generally be used when there were extensive relation-specific investments. Where such investments have been made, giving the buyer an option to suspend or terminate performance would undermine the seller's reliance. The relative attractiveness of a meeting competition clause as a means of adjusting prices decreases the more extensive are the relation-specific investments.

Consider a market in which transportation costs were a large percentage of the delivered price and local demand conditions varied. Market price information would be available only for a few central shipping points, not at the buyer's actual locations. Movements of prices at a central shipping point could differ substantially from the movements of prices at particular locations. Thus, it seems reasonable to conclude that the likelihood that parties to a long-term contract would use some variation on a meeting competition clause for price adjustment would increase (a) the greater the availability of alternative suppliers, (b) the less significant the relation-specific investments by the parties, and (c) the lower the correlation between market-based price indexes with local supply and demand conditions.

Negotiation is, of course, always an option. Even if the contract explicitly utilizes one of the methods mentioned in the previous paragraphs or unambiguously states that the contract is a fixed-price agreement, one party could propose that the price be renegotiated. The contract price, the clarity of the legal rule, and the costs of invoking the legal rule provide the background against which the renegotiation might take place. Renegotiation allows use of accurate, current information in revising the contract; but reopening the contract could result in cost-generating strategic behavior, especially if one of the parties is vulnerable to the threat of nonrenewal. Renegotiation is not a zero-sum affair with one side's gains offset by the other's loss. In exchange for an increased price, for example, a seller could offer a contract extension and the prospect of not working to the letter of the contract. (A threat, after all, is just a promise with the sign reversed.)

The contract could explicitly establish the conditions under which renegotiation is to take place. It could require renegotiation at fixed intervals or have it triggered by specific events (for example, a rise in a price index of more than 20%). Gross inequity clauses call for renegotiation if the contract price is too far out of line, but typically do not spell out the criteria for determining when a gross inequity exists. The parties could agree to renegotiate in good faith and determine what would happen if the negotiations break down. The failure to negotiate a new price could result in continued performance at the current price, termination, mediation or arbitration, and so forth.

There are, in sum, a lot of mechanisms available for adjusting price within a long-term contract. All are imperfect. Their relative costs and benefits will determine which, if any, the parties should choose. I should note that one of the options is to do nothing. A fixed-price contract might be the best the parties can do. Consider again the petroleum coke contracts discussed in Chapter 5. (Goldberg and Erickson 1987) When it was clear that indexing was not working well in the mid-1960s, the majority of Great Lakes Carbon's agreements in 1966–1973 switched to "good faith renegotiation" to revise prices, with the agreements terminating after six to eighteen months if agreement was not reached. The aluminum producers were more likely to switch to fixed-price agreements. Their greater reliance made them more vulnerable to strategic renegotiation, and their less frequent participation in the market made the repeat-dealing sanction less effective.

3. Indexing and Inflation Risk

It is important to distinguish between the change in price or costs for the subject matter of a particular contract and a change in the overall price level—inflation or deflation. There are a number of reasons why perfect indexing against inflation is not feasible. Even if it were technically possible, there is a political reason that perfect (or even pretty good) indexing is often unavailable: because the government has chosen to make it so. For example, prior to the German hyperinflation, many German long-term contracts had gold clauses to protect against the government's inflating the currency. When the government made those clauses unenforceable, the lender (or seller or lessor) lost its protection. Today, parties in countries experiencing rapid inflation could avoid most of the pure inflation risk by contracting in dollars or euros rather than the local currency, but that might not be legally feasible.

Inflation is the equivalent of a tax, and its success in this role depends upon the government's ability to prevent indexing. The government can alter the incidence of that tax by allowing some transactions (e.g., pensions) to be indexed and preventing the indexing of others. The incidence is not likely to be the result of a deliberate policy choice; rather, it will most likely be an ad hoc set of responses to political interests. By accident or design, the government alters the rate of inflation and determines which constituencies would bear the brunt of the policy.

There is an interplay between the courts and the legislature in distributing the benefits and burdens of inflation. Given the legislature's decisions, the courts have some limited ability to alter the incidence. In the German hyperinflation, for example, the courts led the legislature in "revalorization." (See Dawson 1984.) It appears, however, that with rare exceptions the courts have deferred. Contracting parties attempting to protect against rapid inflation are in the same position as parties attempting to contract against future government actions (e.g., regulations and taxes) that both affect the outcomes and restrict the parties' ability to shield themselves from the consequences.

CHAPTER 19

Impossibility and Related Excuses

If conditions change after parties enter into a contract, one of them might want to be excused from performance, or at least have its obligations revised. Anglo-American law provides the disadvantaged party with a number of defenses that would extinguish that party's obligations— impossibility, frustration, impracticability, and mutual mistake. Although there are some technical distinctions between these, for analytical convenience I will lump them all together under the impossibility rubric. My purpose in this chapter is to explore some problems that have arisen in determining the appropriate scope of the impossibility defense.

The importance of the impossibility defense is circumscribed by the ability of the parties to contract around the law. If the law were too liberal in excusing performance, the parties could narrow the range of acceptable excuses by explicit contractual language. Conversely, if the law defined the grounds on which a party could be excused too narrowly, the parties could enumerate additional circumstances that would justify discharge of the contractual obligations. If the law were badly out of line in either direction, the problems could be vitiated by proper drafting of force majeure clauses. Such clauses, which are very common, will suspend or discharge a promisor's obligations for "acts of God." While most of the acts of God enumerated in such clauses are beyond the control of the contracting parties, there is one significant exception to this generalization. The clauses typically include strikes by the employees of either party. The purpose of this strike exception is, clearly, to protect the contracting parties from the threat of holdup in their dealings with labor. In the absence of such a clause, the possibility that a firm would be liable for damages for breach of contract would weaken its bargaining position vis-à-vis its employees.

It should not really matter whether we frame the problem of excuse in

333

terms of implementing the parties' decision or of identifying the conditions that would justify excusing performance. Even if a contract had no force majeure clause, a court might infer that the parties would have included one had they thought of it. That is, instead of recognizing an impossibility defense, the courts could achieve the same result by interpretation of a force majeure clause, express or implied.

Regardless of how the doctrine is labeled, courts, when considering a plea to excuse performance, should be constrained by the fundamental question: What would reasonable parties in this position have chosen? I will argue that, as a general rule, parties would not agree to excuse performance because of changed market conditions (neither supply nor demand shocks). The fact that market prices have doubled or tripled would be irrelevant. Parties are more likely to excuse performance if the supervening events adversely affect the costs of performing this particular contract for reasons that are essentially unrelated to overall market conditions. This does not, of course, mean that parties would never adjust the contract price. Price concessions in the face of changed market conditions are commonplace. But the grantor of the concession often expects a quid pro quo, either express (e.g., an increase in the term of the contract) or implied (e.g., enhanced good will). The grantor, that is, maintains the right to make (or not make) price concessions.

1. Excuse for Events Uncorrelated with Market Conditions

Many contracts include a force majeure clause which would discharge a seller's obligation if, for example, his factory were to burn down. If he did not want to deliver for other reasons, perhaps because he could get a better price elsewhere, he would not be excused. Why would reasonable businessmen agree to excuse performance for the first reason but not the second? It is useful to note first that not all contracts would discharge the seller's obligation even in the first situation. If the subject matter of the contract were fungible, the contract would be less likely to provide for discharge. For example, suppose that Smith agrees to pay $1,000 for an item. His wallet, with $1,000 in it, is consumed in flames. It is unlikely that the parties would want to excuse his performance on this ground, since there is no reason to presume that this $1,000 was connected in any way with performance of this contract. The loss of his wallet makes Smith poorer, but does not otherwise impair his ability to perform the contract. He simply substitutes other dollars for those destroyed in the fire. If, instead of cash, Smith had lost a ton of a fungible commodity or if his warehouse storing that fungible commodity had burned down, the same story holds. He does not need to produce the commodity; he can meet his contractual obligation by buying it on the open market.

Let us consider, then, a contract for delivery of something other than a fungible commodity from the seller, Smith, to the buyer, Brown. If Smith does not perform and remains liable for damages, then the court must assess damages and ascertain the reasonableness of Brown's cover. These tasks present some of the same problems that arise with monitoring specific performance. Because the good is not fungible, Brown has some leeway in choosing the goods with which to cover. If Brown bears the costs, he will have an incentive to choose the most efficient substitute. If, however, Smith must bear the costs, Brown's incentive to economize is weaker. For example, suppose that Brown was purchasing a computer system. His choice of alternatives to the original system that Smith had promised includes one provider with somewhat better hardware and somewhat inferior software and aftersale services. A second alternative has the opposite features and is considerably more expensive. If Brown had to pay out of his own pocket, he would choose the superior hardware at the lower price. If, however, the costs were to be borne by Smith, Brown would choose the latter.

This is a routine moral hazard problem. The greater the moral hazard, the greater the *joint* costs of the parties. It might appear that nondischarge would be good for Brown—he receives more than he initially bargained for. While this would be correct if we begin the analysis at the time at which Smith is no longer able to perform, it is not correct if we begin at the contract formation stage. Since in the long run the sellers must cover their costs, the costs of moral hazard will be reflected in the price of the goods. In this indirect way the buyers share in the costs.

If not excusing the seller would result in these increased costs, why would contracting parties ever fail to excuse? The obvious reason is that there are benefits from holding sellers to agreements. While these benefits will generally outweigh the costs, they are likely to be much lower in the event of the occurrence of a condition covered by a force majeure clause. If the plant for building a particular machine burns down or a farmer's entire carrot crop is destroyed, the overall market conditions do not change, although the costs of the individual producer do. If the occurrence of the particular event is uncorrelated with market conditions, then at the formation stage, the expected value of the change in price between the date of contract formation and the date of the occurrence is zero. If the seller were excused, the buyer would gain when the market price fell and lose when it rose; leaving consequential damages aside, those two effects should roughly wash out. That is, the buyer's *expected* damages from this source at the contract formation stage would be low. The *actual* damages could turn out to be very high, however. One cost of excusing performance is that the existence of a force majeure condition would be a question of fact which could be costly to litigate. The greater the contract versus market differential, the greater the incentive to allege the existence of such a condition.

The crucial point is this: If the occurrence of a force majeure condition is not correlated with market conditions, the expected change in market price is zero, and therefore, the benefits anticipated at the contract formation stage from holding the promisor liable are likely to be low. However, if the seller refuses to perform because events subsequent to the formation of the contract have shown that the contract price is too low, the buyer does suffer. If the seller could perform, but would prefer not to, we can reasonably infer that the reason is that the contract price is too low; the seller could do better selling elsewhere. The changed conditions affect the market for the good or service involved. There is a widespread drought, the Suez Canal closes, and so forth. Discharging the contract in this instance carries a greater cost. If a seller could be excused simply because the contract price was below the market price, the substantial benefits from entering into a contract in a timely manner, as discussed in Chapter 10, are sacrificed. While this sacrifice might be acceptable in some cases, it is clear that the costs of excusing a seller's performance when the contract price is too low are greater than excusing its performance in the event of a fire or other act of God.

Thus, it is at least plausible that contracting parties would find it efficient to excuse a seller in the event of a fire or similar seller-specific occurrence, but not on other grounds. It should be emphasized that discharge does not allow the seller to get off scot-free. If a fire destroys the seller's factory and its contract is discharged, it still bears all the costs of the destruction. The buyer bears the risk of a subsequent price change. It should also be noted that the "impossibility" label is misleading. It might be impossible for the seller to perform what had been promised, but it is not impossible for him to pay the damages. All he would have to do is write a check. The justification for discharge is that the expected value of the check at the contract formation stage is likely to be low compared to the costs associated with holding the seller liable.

The Suez cases illustrate how the correlation between the event and market conditions would determine whether performance should be excused. In 1956 and again in 1967, military operations in the Middle East closed the Suez Canal to shipping traffic. Parties that had entered into contracts before the canal was closed found that completing performance would be considerably more expensive. Carriers and sellers who had promised to deliver goods at a fixed price attempted to avoid their contractual obligations. In most instances, the courts enforced the contracts. In *Transatlantic Financing Corp. v. United States*, for example, a shipowner argued that its contract with the United States to transport wheat from the United States to Iran was discharged by the closing of the Suez Canal. Posner and Rosenfield (1977, p. 104) argue that the court's refusal to discharge the contract was correct:

> [T]he decision on whether to discharge the contract turn[s] on an examination of the key economic parameters that we have identified. The shipowner is the superior risk bearer because he is better able to estimate the magnitude of the loss (a function of delay, and of the value and nature of the cargo, which are also known to the shipowner) and the probability of the unexpected event. Furthermore, shipowners who own several ships and are engaged in shipping along several different routes can spread the risks of delay on any particular route without purchasing market insurance or forcing their shareholders to diversify their common-stock portfolios. And the shipping company could, if it desired, purchase in a single transaction market insurance covering multiple voyages. Of course, the shipper in the particular case—the United States Government—was well diversified too, but decision should (and here did) turn on the characteristics of shippers as a class, if an unduly particularistic analysis is to be avoided.

Perusal of current shipping contracts indicates that the basic shipping form contracts were not altered after the *Suez* decisions. Closing of the canal is not an enumerated excuse in force majeure clauses, although, as Treitel (1994, pp. 182, 185) notes, in some instances the parties added clauses that would increase the carrier's compensation if the Suez route were unavailable. See, for example, *D. I. Henry Ltd. v. Clasen* and *Achille Laura v. Total spA*. Nonetheless, these appear to be exceptions, so it would seem that the courts got it right. The Posner-Rosenfield explanation, however, does not work.

To see this, consider a closely related problem. How would the parties to a shipping contract deal with the possibility that the port of destination would be closed by a blockade? The reasons given by Posner-Rosenfield would apply at least as well to this problem. Nevertheless, ocean shipping contracts routinely include language that would discharge the carrier in this instance.

Why would the parties agree to excuse the carrier in the event of a blockade of the port of destination, but not excuse in the event that the Suez Canal was blockaded? To make the analysis even crisper, suppose that in both instances these are executory contracts. That is, the parties entered into the agreement before the supervening event had occurred, but had not loaded the goods on the ship. Consider first the blockade of the single port. The costs of getting the goods to the original destination increase. If the carrier were to attempt to deliver by sea, it would incur the increased risk of loss due to destruction of the ship or cargo. If it attempted to get the goods to the port by other means (shipping over land or substituting other goods for the goods named in the original contract), it would also incur additional costs. It is not at all clear that the shipper would want these additional costs to be incurred if it had to pay the costs out of its own pocket. Discharging the contract puts that question to the promisee directly. The supervening event raises the costs of performing this particular contract, but there is no reason to believe that there would be any effect on the market price of ocean shipping generally. This is a classic instance of the occurrence of a supervening event uncorrelated with market conditions. Ocean shipping services are sold in an international market. Since at the contract formation stage the expected change in the market price of shipping services due to the blockade of a destination port is approximately zero, the benefits of holding the promisor liable should be low.

This is not true for the closing of the Suez Canal. The closing of the canal had a substantial impact on the market price for ocean shipping services. Transatlantic argued that because performance would require going around the Cape of Good Hope, which added about 3,000 miles and $40,000 in costs to a trip that would otherwise have been 10,000 miles and for which the contract price was about $300,000, it should be excused. Actually, since it did perform, it asked that it be reimbursed for the additional costs. (I don't understand how one can invoke impossibility when it has in fact performed the "impossible," but I will leave that aside.) The big difference was not the additional cost of actual performance. There was a large increase in the short-term demand for ocean shipping services which, when coupled with the short-term inelasticity of supply of vessels, resulted in prices more than doubling. The fact that the journey was longer and more costly than originally anticipated should have been irrelevant. The key factor was that the opportunity cost of the ship had increased. Excusing the carrier in this case where the supervening event is correlated with market conditions makes it happier ex post, but both parties would be worse off ex ante.

It is worth noting in passing that the nondischarge of the contracts does not mean that all the contracts would be performed. The changed circumstances would not affect all shippers equally. There would be a reallocation of shipping services, with the ships tending to go to the highest bidders. Nondischarge means that the beneficiaries of the windfall would be those shippers who happened to sign contracts before the canal closing was anticipated. Discharge would give the windfall to the owners of the vessels.

2. Frustration and Options

In anticipation of the procession to be held in connection with the coronation of Edward VII, rooms were rented along the parade route at high prices. Edward's appendicitis forced the postponement of the procession, and considerable litigation ensued. In the litigated cases, rooms were being rented at £75 to £100. Since per capita gross domestic product (GDP) at the time was only £45, this was quite a substantial sum. The postponement did not, of course, affect the availability of the rooms, but it did affect the rooms' value to the hirers—they were worth approximately zero.

In *Krell v. Henry*, it was held that the cancellation of the procession frustrated the purpose of the contract and that the hirer was discharged from the contract. He did not have to make payments that were due after the procession had been canceled. Since he had withdrawn his cross-claim for restitution of funds already paid before the cancellation, the court did not have to deal with that issue. In *Chandler v. Webster*, the hirer did ask for a refund, but the court ruled that there could be no recovery for money that had been paid before the cancellation; furthermore, the hirer would be liable for any money due before the cancellation but not yet paid. This result has been subjected to considerable criticism. Professors Dawson, Harvey, and Henderson (2003, p. 679), for example, state that "the absurdity of this solution is at once apparent."

I think that the solution is not absurd. Before I begin the analysis, I should point out that *Krell* and *Chandler* are one-shot deals between amateurs. These are the sorts of cases that law professors love. One can play a lot of games attempting to divine how the parties might have dealt with the problem had they thought about it. There are few constraints upon the imagination. As such, these are terrible cases on which to build a commercial jurisprudence. Treitel (1994, pp. 286–296) provides some background on the Coronation cases and notes that not all the cases involved amateurs. In fact, Krell did not let his rooms directly; rather, he left that task to his solicitor, who, for whatever reason, did not see fit to plan for this contingency. However, a number of contracts did deal explicitly with the risk of postponement or cancellation. For example, in *Victoria Seats Agency v. Paget,* there were two contested contracts. One provided for the use of the room on June 27 "or such other day as the said processions should pass the premises. Should the processions not pass the premises, I agree to refund the money." The other provided that if there were no procession, the hirer should get back his money less 10%. In addition, at least some of the firms that constructed stands for viewing the processions had insured against the risk of cancellation or postponement. The judge put considerable weight on the notion that the supervening event could not have been supposed to have been in the contemplation of the parties. He did not have to explain why that same event was in the contemplation of other parties who did manage to explicitly assign the risks.

There are many commercial situations in which similar problems arise and in which it would be possible to observe how parties routinely deal with the problem. If, for example, the Chicago Cubs lose in the playoffs, hotel reservations in Chicago for the World Series will be worth considerably less; how would the contract treat the guest's obligation? If I make reservations at a ski lodge and when the time comes there is no snow, can I have the contract discharged, and will I get a refund for any money already paid? I will discuss *Krell* and *Chandler* on the assumption that the contracting parties were acting as reasonable businesspeople. This will be a useful prelude to consideration of the World Series or ski lodge type of problem.

It is useful to view the owner of the flat, Krell, as selling an option. By agreeing to make a series of payments at specified dates, Henry was in a position to exercise or not exercise the option. If after he had made one payment he decided that he did not really want to see the procession or that he would rather see it from a different location, he could refuse to make the subsequent payment, thereby allowing the option to expire. In this interpretation, all money that was due prior to the supervening event should be paid to Krell for performance of the contract. The cancellation of the procession does not require that the contract be discharged; rather, the option contracts are performed, with Henry simply allowing all the subsequent options to expire. That, in effect, is what the court held in *Chandler v. Webster.*

Now, the contract did not say that Henry had an option; nor did it explicitly state that in the event that the coronation had taken place as scheduled, Henry could refuse to make the payment due prior to the event and escape without liability. Nonetheless, I think it reasonable to infer that this is how parties would treat the problem had they dealt with it explicitly. Would the option price have been that high? Probably not, as the money-back-less-10% arrangement in *Victoria Seats* suggests. But it would have been a fruitless exercise for the court to search for the "true" option price.

The nature of the option is easier to see when we look at less exotic problems. There would typically be no need for invocation of the excuse doctrine, since the payment schedule would simply permit the buyer to terminate the agreement by letting the option expire. Suppose, for example, that a skier is contemplating a vacation at a popular ski lodge. She might make reservations six months in advance. If she changed her mind the following day and the contract was silent on the matter, she would be legally liable for the full amount. But the contract would probably not be silent on this point. The lodge would probably ask for a modest initial deposit and require some additional nonrefundable deposits at later dates. In the event that the skier changed her mind, her liability would only be for the nonrefundable deposits. It might well be that she could walk away from her reservations two weeks before the planned vacation date at a cost of only 10% of the contract price.

Posner and Rosenfield (1977, p. 110) argue that the contract should not be discharged because of the lack of snow. Their argument hinges on the relative ability of the contracting parties to diversify risks. The ski lodge, they claim, is less able to diversify the risks than are the customers, who could ski elsewhere. I doubt that the argument is correct, since it would probably be difficult for the skiers to book alternate accommodations on short notice. But we need not worry about whether their assertion is correct; the ability to diversify is a red herring. The contract would most likely include a schedule of payments. When it becomes clear to the skier that snow conditions will be inadequate, she stops paying. There would be neither a breach nor a discharge. The magnitude of the payments made by the skier will depend upon the timing of the decision, the popularity of the lodge, and so forth. If the contract did not require that the skier make any payments prior to showing up, then she would bear no liability. The contract might make the termination fee contingent upon the cause. For example, some or all of the deposit might be refunded if the lodge were to burn down or if the ski slopes were closed.

I have not collected any systematic information on how ski lodges, hotels, and others handle these problems. Anecdotal evidence suggests that the options are routinely sold. Hotels frequently require that someone booking a room pay for the first night in advance to assure reservations. In college towns during graduation week, hotels typically have high option prices. Restaurants rarely charge a price for reservations, although some high-priced restaurants have established a policy of billing no-shows, especially for very popular dates (like Valentine's Day). I am reasonably confident that a more systematic canvassing would show that the use of options is very common and that the judicial disposition of *Krell* and *Chandler* is consistent with what is routinely done in the hotel business.

3. Reliance and Restitution

If a contract involved a machine to be constructed by the seller and installed in the buyer's factory, and that factory were destroyed by fire prior to delivery, the contract would be discharged under both the Anglo-American case law and the Uniform Commercial Code. Force majeure clauses would also generally excuse the performance. There is less agreement on what should be done after the seller has been excused. Should the seller be compensated for costs incurred prior to the fire? Should the seller be required to return payments made by the buyer prior to the fire?

Let us begin with the simplest case. The fire occurred before the seller had started to perform, and the buyer had made no payment. If the buyer were not excused, for what damages would he be liable? He would be liable for the change in the market value of the machine between the date at which the contract was formed and the instant at which he breached. Since the fire at the buyer's factory is likely to be unrelated to overall market conditions for the machinery, the expected value of the price change is likely to be zero. By the previous argument, it is unlikely that the benefits of holding the promisor to the contract would outweigh the costs. Posner and Rosenfield (1977, pp. 92–93, 105–106) and Bruce (1982, pp. 330–331) reach a similar conclusion by a different route. They note that the seller is generally in the better position to salvage, and that courts have correctly discharged the contracts in such circumstances. There is a bit of confusion in the Posner-Rosenfield analysis in that they assumed "the machine has no salvage value" (p. 92) and then argued that the "loss depended not only on the salvage value of the machine if the fire occurred after its completion but also on its salvage value after various anterior stages." (p. 93) If the seller had not begun to perform or if the salvage value were zero, then the relative ability to affect salvage would, of course, be irrelevant.

Curiously, Bruce (1982, pp. 323–324) argued that *Taylor v. Caldwell*, the fountainhead of modern impossibility law, was wrongly decided. That case concerned a contract between a promoter and a music hall for four grand concerts, with the promoter paying £100 for each performance. One week before the first concert, the music hall was destroyed by fire. There is no practical distinction between that case and one in which the fire disrupted a contract for delivery of a machine. Bruce emphasized the incentives for the music hall owner to control the likelihood of the occurrence of the fire. However, the music hall owner bore the direct costs of that fire; it was his music hall that burned down. Moreover, if the defendant had been deemed responsible for the fire, it would not have been excused. The damage issues in *Taylor v. Caldwell* could have included the post-contractual change in the price of music hall services and the promoter's reliance costs, consequential damages, and incidental damages. In fact, the promoter sued only for reliance expenses for advertising and preparations for the concert, asking for £58. (Treitel 1994, p. 37) By excusing the music hall, the decision put the entertainer in exactly the same position as the manufacturer of machinery in the hypothetical.

In my hypothetical, unlike in *Taylor v. Caldwell*, the costs of reliance and the consequential and incidental damages were assumed to be zero. The assumptions will now be relaxed. If the fire occurred after the seller had begun to perform, and if only some of the costs of performance were salvageable, then responsibility for these additional costs must be assigned. In the absence of specific contractual language, this raises two new damages issues: (a) Should there be restitution of any payments made? and (b) Should the other party be compensated for expenditures made in reliance on the contract? Reliance might include the costs of acquiring inputs necessary for performance of this contract, costs incurred in performing the contract up to the point at which the fire occurred, costs incurred in anticipation that the contract would be performed (e.g., travel expenses, establishing a network of retailers, or initiating an advertising campaign), the time of salaried personnel that had been devoted to the particular event, and opportunities foregone.

How much protection should the seller's reliance get? We have seen this problem before. Pay-or-play contracts for movie actors (Chapter 15) and the many variations on take-or-pay contracts (Chapter 5) provide some protection for one party's reliance. The answer in those contexts and here is that there is no general answer. The question is too situation-specific. But that means that, to the extent possible, we should leave the balancing decision in the hands of the contracting parties. There are numerous contractual devices by which a seller could achieve some protection of its reliance. In particular, it could require interim payments from the buyer. The arrangement could be formalized with progress payments, as they are usually called, being required as the seller successfully completes particular phases of the project and with liquidated damages. If the contract were terminated prematurely (either deliberately or by an act of God), there would be no need to order restitution or to reckon the compensable reliance damages. By appropriately phasing their performance, the parties manage to balance their respective interests and to avoid wasteful litigation.

The questions of restitution and reliance are, therefore, interrelated. Prepayment should not be viewed as a mere happenstance. In serious commercial transactions, prepayment is a device for providing some protection of the reliance interest. A clear default rule that leaves the losses where they lie is a simple forcing default. Protecting reliance is, of course, not the only purpose of phased payment. As noted in the discussion of the Coronation cases, it can also be an effective way of creating options. Posner and Rosenfield (1977, p. 116) argue that because there are so many reasons for prepayment, we should not presume that prepayment is related to the possible occurrence of an event which would result in discharge of the contract. They, therefore, favor a rule which provides restitution of prepaid money. I think the leave-the-losses-where-they lie rule is a simpler default rule. If courts made it easy to contract out of the full restitution rule, then it probably would not matter too much. I would presume that if customized goods were involved, phased payment should be expected; the more nearly unique the goods, the greater the protection. By ordering restitution or attempting an independent assessment of reliance losses, courts would undo the balancing of interests achieved by the parties.

Returning to *Taylor v. Caldwell*, Treitel put much of his discussion in terms of the virtues of loss-splitting. He noted, only in passing, that the defendants were insured (p. 42), although I suspect that the insurance covered only the structure and would not have covered loss of use. He suggested that it would be unlikely that the hirers of the hall would have purchased insurance. (p. 515) While we don't know much about whether parties insured against such risks in mid-nineteenth-century England, or how they dealt with such risks in their contracts, information on the contemporary American response is available. For any live entertainment event, there are two obvious classes of risks: the artist(s) cannot perform, and the venue will not be available. It would, I believe, border on malpractice today for a lawyer to ignore these possibilities. Insurance for both the venue (for the structure and for business interruption) and artists is available. The *Taylor* impossibility rule is the default rule, but the contracts would likely be customized to take into account the reliance and opportunity costs of the parties. Other things being equal, the more valuable the talent (the higher its opportunity cost), the greater the payment it would receive if the venue were to become unavailable. And, likewise, the more significant the venue, the more it would collect if the artist were to become unavailable.

Anglo-American law appears to be moving in the wrong direction. *Chandler v. Webster*, after being subjected to a considerable amount of criticism, was overturned in England in *Fibrosa Spolka Akcyjna v. Fairbairn Lawson Combe Barbour, Ltd.* In that case, the Polish plaintiff ordered machines that were to be manufactured in England and delivered to Poland. The plaintiff had made a down payment and the manufacturer had partially completed performance when Germany invaded Poland, a condition that resulted in discharge of the contract. The House of Lords held that the plaintiff was entitled to a refund of the down payment, but that the defendant was not entitled to compensation for the costs it had incurred; that issue, it asserted, was a matter for the legislature to deal with. Shortly thereafter Parliament passed the Law Reform (Frustrated Contracts) Act, which allowed for some recovery of reliance expenditures. I wonder how a court should decide how much of the seller's reliance should be protected absent any theory other than vague notions of fairness to guide it. The net result of the decision and subsequent legislation seems to be that if courts do their job well, they will manage, at considerable expense, to replicate the balancing the parties had achieved in their agreement. But if they did so it would only be by accident.

4. Concluding Remarks

The first tentative conclusion I want to draw from this exercise is a methodological one. Because uncertainty over the future is a central element of the impossibility problem, there is a great temptation to invoke attitudes toward risk (relative risk aversion) and the ability to diversify risks in analyzing the problem. I hope that I have demonstrated the fruitlessness of that approach. This is one more piece of evidence in the case I have been trying to make against relying upon risk aversion to explain most contracting behavior or economic institutions generally.

The second conclusion is that the distinction between supervening circumstances which affect market conditions and those which affect the costs of performing this particular contract is the key to understanding much of the case law and the decisions of the parties as to when performance should be excused. Market fluctuations, even beyond the range that reasonable people might have foreseen, ought not be a ground for discharging a contract. That does not mean that the parties will set the price term and accept any subsequent price changes as part of their bargain. They have a number of devices at their disposal for adjusting the contract price to changed market conditions (Chapter 18), and they always have the option of making price concessions voluntarily.

The third conclusion is that private parties are pretty clever. Actually, individuals might be rather foolish, and most people in an industry could probably not tell us what the excuse clause looked like and why it took the form that it did. The cleverness is in part that of a few lawyers and in part the result of market forces rewarding the good contracts and penalizing the bad. Businesses do not use force majeure clauses indiscriminately. The grounds on which a contract would be excused can be nicely tailored to industry conditions. Moreover, force majeure clauses are only one aspect of the private response. Firms can set up their affairs to take into account the possibility that the contract might be terminated for any reason. Phasing performance with devices like progress payments can effectively protect the reliance interest of the performing party.

Finally, these points suggest that courts should be cautious when confronted with demands for discharge or demands for restitution in the event that a contract has been discharged. This does not mean that courts should never succumb to the demands. There is room for interpretation of ambiguities in force majeure clauses and of the intentions of reasonable parties in the absence of such a clause. This is especially true as we move away from commercial contracts between repeat players toward contracts between amateurs. Courts should not, however, take the existence of ambiguities, real or contrived, as license to remake deals in pursuit of ex post fairness. The preceding analysis suggests the principles that should be used to fill the gaps in these contracts.

CHAPTER 20

Alcoa v. Essex:
Anatomy of a Bungled Deal

When Essex, a manufacturer of copper wire and cable, entered the aluminum wire fabrication business, it considered a number of options for securing a supply of aluminum. It eventually agreed on a multiyear, partially indexed, fixed quantity contract with Alcoa. Following the oil shock of 1973, the indexed price failed to track either Alcoa's costs or the market price of aluminum, much to Alcoa's dismay. Alcoa brought suit asking for either rescission or reformation of the contract. The case was heard without a jury, and the judge ruled in favor of Alcoa, reforming the contract on the basis of mutual mistake, impracticability, and frustration. The mistake, according to the court, was in both parties believing that the index they chose for nonlabor production costs would accurately reflect those costs. Alcoa's purpose that was frustrated, said the court, was to make a profit.

The initial reactions to *Alcoa v. Essex* viewed it as a radical break with the past in two respects, hailed by some (for example, Speidel 1981 and Hillman 1987) and excoriated by others (for example, Dawson 1984). It appeared both to liberalize the excuse doctrines and to give courts the discretion to revise basic contract terms, including the price term. The latter was especially controversial. As White and Peters (2002, p. 1973) note, "the revolutionary part of the Alcoa decision was Judge Teitelbaum's rewriting the contract price formula to give Alcoa a small profit per pound. That was the act that made Jack [Dawson] apoplectic, that attracted the academic writers and that put Alcoa into most of the contracts casebooks." This, I believe, gets things backwards. If Alcoa were excused and had no further obligation to Essex, Alcoa could then take advantage of Essex's reliance and charge a higher price; once the court had decided to excuse Alcoa, protecting Essex from this opportunistic behavior required that the court devise some alternative pricing mechanism. Regardless, after the initial flurry of commentary, when the dust had settled, little had changed. *Alcoa* has not been followed in either respect, so the decision has become a casebook curiosity with little or no precedential value.

Still, I think *Alcoa* is worth examination for three reasons. First, it illustrates the court's difficulty in coping with a claim that an unexpected price change justifies excusing performance. Second, it illustrates the difficulty parties have dealing with changed circumstances. The contract was not quite a cost-plus contract, but the parties' intention was to make it cost-based. I want to argue here that this was a bad idea. The contract was poorly structured, something that neither the litigators nor the court ever acknowledged; it was pretty much doomed from the start. Third, *Alcoa* raises an interesting interpretation question. If we can infer from the structure of the contract that the parties really wanted to do X, but the language does not make this explicit, should we read X into the contract? Does it make a difference if we can also infer that X would have been unwise? Put concretely, if the Alcoa-Essex contract was supposed to mimic a cost-plus contract, should the failure of an index to achieve that justify rescinding or reforming the contract? And, if so, is that true even if we conclude that approximating a cost-plus contract was a really bad idea?

Given what the parties apparently wanted to do, the judge was probably right in finding, the explicit contract language notwithstanding, that the particular index Alcoa had chosen did not work. The court, in effect, took the parties' intention to mimic a cost-plus contract into account when interpreting the role of the price index. Should it have? I think not. Even if we could infer intent with confidence, I do not believe that we should allow the inference to trump a clearly worded, heavily negotiated substantive term. Reasonable people might disagree; in this chapter, I only intend to pose the question. My concern will be the shaky reasoning of the court and the dubious initial decision of the parties as to how to structure their agreement.

During oral argument on appeal, the panel expressed doubts about the remedy. The parties then settled before the court could deliver an opinion. They made a joint motion requesting voluntary dismissal of the appeal, vacation of the district court's judgment, and remand of the case with directions to dismiss. The Third Circuit granted this relief and the action was dismissed. (See Dawson 1984, p. 28; Macaulay 1985, p. 475; and Wladis 1988, p. 586.) I have synthesized the facts from the trial judge's lengthy opinion and the briefs prepared for the appeal. The contract itself was available in a second dispute involving Essex, *Amax v. Essex Group*. Because some data were redacted from the briefs, some of the numbers discussed below will be only approximations. That will not affect the overall analysis.

1. The Transaction

In the mid-1960s, Essex, a fabricator of copper wire and cable, decided to enter into the production of aluminum wire and cable as well. It explored a number of options both for locating its production facilities and for securing long-term access to aluminum. For its aluminum needs, Essex considered joint ventures to build a smelter with Amax and Conalco before entering into a long-term supply contract with Alcoa. Alcoa would add potlines to its smelter at Warrick, Indiana, and Essex would build a new fabricating plant in Boonville, Indiana. Molten aluminum would be trucked from the smelter to Essex so that Essex could skip the costly step of remelting the ingot. The agreement, which will be described in more detail below, was for sixteen years, with Essex having an option to renew for five years. It was for a fixed quantity, with Essex having the option to ask for the addition of discrete blocks of a fixed quantity. The contract allowed for four blocks, but by mutual agreement the last two were canceled, so the contract quantity was 75 million pounds. Alcoa's capital costs were about 40 cents per pound; Essex's investment in the new facility was $1.6 million.

Although Alcoa's capital costs were considerably greater than Essex's, the latter required greater protection for its reliance. Alcoa had an ingot plant at Warrick that required more aluminum than Alcoa could produce at its Warrick smelter. About two-thirds of the ingot plant's input came from inventory maintained at Warrick and produced at one of Alcoa's eight other smelters. Since the contract quantity was less than 1% of Alcoa's annual production, there is no doubt that, if for some reason Essex could no longer take its 75 million pounds, the increment could easily be absorbed. Essex, on the other hand, was vulnerable to the possible termination of the agreement. The favorable economics of its plant relied on the cost savings from the low transportation costs and the avoidance of the remelting stage. There was no direct evidence on the magnitude of these cost savings; nor was there any evidence regarding Essex's ability to melt ingot in the event that the supply from Warrick were cut off. I emphasize the relative reliance concerns because, I will argue, one of the mistakes in designing the contract was overprotecting Alcoa's reliance.

The contract was a "tolling" contract. Aluminum is made from alumina; according to the contract, 1.8894 pounds of alumina are required to produce 1 pound of aluminum. Essex would supply alumina to Alcoa, which would then smelt it and deliver the molten aluminum to Essex. The contract, therefore, was not for a good (aluminum), but for a service (tolling). Essex's alumina was not segregated, so Essex's obligation was only to deliver to Alcoa a specific amount of alumina meeting the contractual specifications. "Alcoa may commingle Alumina delivered to it by Essex with Alcoa's own alumina and reserves the right to deliver Aluminum to Essex hereunder made from alumina other than the Alumina delivered to it by Essex, but the quantity of aluminum delivered shall nevertheless be the same as that to which Essex is entitled to receive from Alumina under paragraph 19 hereof." (Clause 21) Essex could also meet its obligation by delivering alumina to other Alcoa smelters. "Essex shall deliver alumina to Alcoa at such plants of Alcoa in the United States and in such quantities as Alcoa shall from time to time designate for purposes of this Agreement." (Clause 11) Essex entered into a separate long-term contract with an Alcoa subsidiary to purchase its alumina and contracted with yet another Alcoa subsidiary for shipping the alumina. The trial judge found, and neither party disputed, that the contracts were independent and that Alcoa's left hand did not know what the right hand was doing.

The parties considered a cost-plus contract but concluded that it would be unworkable both because of Alcoa's concerns about confidentiality of its cost information and because of the poor incentives inherent in a cost-plus contract. Alcoa's chief executive testified: "Essex wanted a long term supply of aluminum . . . at a cost which would put them in, roughly, the same position as if they had gone into the primary aluminum business themselves . . . a situation where they could be paying our costs and a return on our investment, a reasonable return which they would have had to have calculated into their own economics if they had put their money into it." (Alcoa Brief, p. 6) While Essex denied that the contract was intended to be related to Alcoa's costs, the structure of the agreement clearly suggested that it was. I will argue below that both the attempt to track costs and the manner in which they did so were mistakes. Before getting to that, however, I will summarize the essential features of the contract.

The Contract

The contract was executed the day after Christmas, 1967. It ran for sixteen years, with Essex having an option to renew for an additional five. Essex's obligation to take aluminum was for four discrete blocks. Block A was for the nominal amount of 50 million pounds, and blocks B, C, and D were each for 25 million. There was some flexibility, with Essex having the right to order the nominal amount plus or minus 15%. However, as noted below, Alcoa also had the 15% leeway, thus limiting Essex's discretion. Essex had the option of activating any of the last three blocks through 1978. It elected all four blocks in 1971, but in 1973 both parties agreed to modify so that the options for C and D were terminated. Along with its obligation to take 75 million pounds per year, Essex had the concomitant obligation to deliver sufficient alumina for tolling purposes. The agreement was essentially a fixed quantity contract, not a requirements contract. There were no restrictions on what Essex could do with its aluminum, so that it could resell if it chose.

The initial contract price was 15 cents per pound to be adjusted as follows. Five cents was a "demand charge" that would roughly correspond to the capital costs required for the capacity at the Warrick smelter. For each block, the 5 cents would be multiplied by a demand charge index. That index would be the arithmetic average for the six months preceding a block being activated of a particular index, the *Engineering News Record* Construction Cost-20 Cities Average Index, as published in the *Engineering News Record*. The demand charge index would only be applied once so that once Essex designated a block, the demand charge for that block would remain constant for the life of the contract. In addition, Essex would pay a 10 cent production charge. Four cents would not be subject to adjustment. Three cents roughly corresponded to the labor cost and 3 cents the nonlabor production cost. However, in the course of the litigation, Alcoa's actual costs were revealed, and they turned out to be a bit different—2.174 cents for labor costs and 3.956 cents for nonlabor costs. In its brief, Alcoa notes how these add up to 6.1 cents, roughly the variable cost in the price adjustment formula. But it did not explain why the breakdown in the formula differed from the actual. (I suspect that the contractual breakdown reflects Alcoa's historical costs averaged over all its smelters, but there is no documentation of this.) Labor costs were indexed by the average hourly labor cost at Alcoa's Warrick Works, as determined by Alcoa. Nonlabor production costs were indexed by the Wholesale Price Index, Industrial Commodities (WPI-IC). The failure of the WPI-IC to track nonlabor production costs was the mistake that justified excusing Alcoa, according to the trial judge.

The price was capped at 65% of the price of a standard grade of aluminum ingot as published in *American Metal Market*. Since the price of aluminum when the contract was formed was 25 cents, the cap would have been 16.25 cents, only 1.25 cents above the base price. Essex was paying Alcoa only for the tolling service, so the price did not include the cost of the alumina that Essex purchased separately. The alumina cost was about 6.5 cents per pound of aluminum, so the base price discount was about 15%.

Alcoa provided the following rationale for this breakdown. The 5 cent demand charge included 4 cents for financial costs (depreciation, interest, etc.) and 1 cent "guaranteed profit." The first 4 cents of the production charge included 3 cents profit and 1 cent to cover general administrative and selling expenses. Three cents was for labor costs and 3 cents for material costs, about 75% of which was carbon based (power and calcined coke). In effect, the contract was designed to replicate a situation in which Essex invested in a smelter with a capital cost of 40 cents per pound with a 10% (4 cent) return. The demand charge would be paid by Essex regardless of whether it took any aluminum, so in that sense it was taking the risk of ownership.

The demand charge made the contract a form of take-or-pay contract with a modest makeup provision. At five-year intervals, if Essex had not taken five times the nominal quantity (75 million pounds after blocks C and D were canceled), it would have to pay Alcoa the demand charge times the shortfall. If Essex asked for less than the nominal quantity in any given year, it could make up the difference, but it could not ask for more than an additional 15%. It could only ask; Alcoa had the option of refusing. Essex argued that it alone had the option and attempted to exercise it by ordering 86.25 million pounds in 1979 (75 million × 1.15). In fact, Alcoa did deliver over 80 million pounds in three of the years between 1974 and 1978. It balked in 1979, citing its option. Essex argued that giving Alcoa the option made no sense, especially since that meant that Alcoa could prevent it from making up an early shortfall. The court found otherwise, and, given the clear contract language, that was the correct decision. "Essex shall give Alcoa notice . . . setting forth the quantity of Aluminum it desires Alcoa to produce. [Notice shall be for the nominal amount plus or minus fifteen percent.] Alcoa shall deliver and Essex shall take delivery of the quantity of Aluminum . . . as specified in each notice . . . plus or minus 15% during the year . . . but in no event more than the maximum or less than the minimum quantity." (Clause 7a)

The contract also included a limited "most favored customer" clause giving Essex some additional protection. As noted below, this clause could, in certain circumstances, have caused Alcoa the same problems that the court felt justified excusing Alcoa.

> If, at any time during the term of this Agreement, Alcoa enters into an agreement with any other party, who competes with Essex in the United States in the sale of aluminum electrical conductor, other than any subsidiary or affiliate of Alcoa, whereby Alcoa agrees to toll convert into Aluminum smelting grade alumina of substantially the same specifications as Alumina to be toll converted hereunder on substantially the same terms and conditions as provided in this Agreement, but for toll conversion charges and/or payment terms more favorable than those afforded Essex in this Agreement, such more favorable charges and/or payment terms shall become a part of this Agreement effective as of the next succeeding calendar month after such agreement was entered into by Alcoa with such other party but shall be a part of this Agreement only so long as such more favorable charges and/or payment terms remain in effect in such other agreement. (Clause 29)

Although Alcoa did not protect itself against the possibility that the WPI-IC would fail to track costs accurately, the contract did take account of the possibility that the indexes would no longer be available.

> In the event that any index referred to in paragraph 8 and 9 hereof is discontinued, no longer published in the sources indicated or become unavailable, the parties shall agree on a comparable substitute index and if they are unable to agree [on] the selection of a substitute index, the selection of a comparable substitute index shall be submitted to arbitration in accordance with the rules of the American Arbitration Association. In the event that the price of unalloyed primary aluminum ingot referred to in paragraph 9 hereof is no longer published in the American Metal Market, Alcoa's published price for such product shall be used for purposes of subparagraph (c)(5) of paragraph 9 hereof. (Clause 28)

The Problem

The contract performed satisfactorily until 1973. Three things happened which caused the contract price to be out of line with both Alcoa's costs and the price of aluminum. First, the oil shock sent carbon-based prices soaring far ahead of the WPI-IC, so the nonlabor variable production cost component failed to track the actual costs. Alcoa's nonlabor production costs at Warrick rose from 5.8 cents in 1973 to 22.7 cents in 1978, while the WPI-IC less than doubled. Second, the high inflation rates of the 1970s meant that even had the real aluminum price remained constant, the adjusted price would have fallen behind the market price. (For those unfamiliar with economic jargon, "real" means inflation-adjusted, as opposed to "nominal.") And, third, the demand for aluminum increased so that the real price of aluminum actually rose.

By 1979, the market price of aluminum ingot was around 73 cents, while Alcoa's costs were around 35 cents and the contract price was around 25 cents. Essex's costs for the alumina and transportation were about 11 cents, yielding it a nice profit of 37 cents if it resold the ingot rather than using it for itself. In fact, Alcoa claimed that Essex resold 22.8% of the aluminum (although it did not specify the time period for this calculation). The contract price of alumina appears to have lagged the spot market price, so that Essex was coming out ahead in its contract with Alcoa's alumina subsidiary as well.

If the indexed nonlabor costs had increased to 22.7 cents, Alcoa would have earned about 5 cents per pound. But even if the index had tracked the costs precisely, Alcoa would not have done so well because, recall, the base was 3 cents, rather than the actual 3.956 cents. Applying the perfect index to the 3 cent base would yield only about 17 cents, which would have meant that the profit would have been close to zero. (Because some data were redacted, the numbers in this and the preceding paragraph might not be precisely correct.) Since the only mistake the trial judge found was the poor performance of the nonlabor index, and since he emphasized that the index was designed to assure Alcoa at least a 1 cent profit, even had the index been perfect, it would have failed to yield that penny profit. Essex noted that the index would not accurately trace costs because it used the wrong base, but it did not emphasize that the result would have been zero profits at the time of the trial.

Alcoa wanted to renegotiate the contract, but Essex refused. Alcoa then brought suit asking for equitable reformation of the contract or, even better, termination. Termination would have meant that Alcoa, not Essex, would benefit from the increased demand for aluminum. Alcoa did not, however, base its argument for termination on the various excuse doctrines that it used to attack the failure of the WPI-IC. Instead, it argued that it could terminate pursuant to a side letter agreement. In the side letter, the parties agreed that if the contract were held to be a sale of goods, rather than services, either party could cancel the contract at will. The rationale for this odd agreement was that if the contract were deemed a sale of goods, it would be possible, albeit unlikely, that the contract would have violated the Robinson-Patman Act; the side letter was designed to limit the parties' exposure. The trial judge held that Alcoa's recital in the side letter of its good faith belief that the contract was for services estopped it from now arguing that it was for goods. In any event, the dispute over whether any of the excuse doctrines would excuse Alcoa centered on the poor performance of the WPI-IC in tracing Alcoa's costs, not on the bigger prize, the failure of the price adjustment mechanism to track the changing market conditions. "The Court recognizes that Alcoa has suffered even larger losses of potential profits which it might have earned but for the contract, in the strong aluminum market of recent years. Essex, rather than Alcoa[,] has enjoyed those profits. But their existence is immaterial to the questions raised in this case." (p. 65)

The crucial issue for the court was the rapid increase in the cost of power at the Warrick smelter and the failure of the index to capture that increase. Warrick was the only Alcoa smelter that relied on coal for its electric power. The remainder used hydroelectric power, power provided by the Tennessee Valley Authority (TVA), or natural gas. The costs at all of Alcoa's other smelters did not rise with the price of oil. So, while Warrick was Alcoa's low-cost plant when it was built, the changing fuel prices made it far and away the highest-cost plant, post-1973. As a result, Alcoa's overall profits were high in the years 1973–1979 despite the poor performance of the Essex contract. Indeed, Alcoa's return on equity in 1978 exceeded 14% for the first time in twenty-two years. This is not, clearly, a case in which a bad contract jeopardized the survival of a firm, as in *In Re Westinghouse*. Rather, this was one losing contract in the firm's much larger portfolio of contracts, a portfolio which was performing very well overall. As noted in Chapter 11, the existence of the other contracts should be irrelevant in adjudicating this one, but the court's refusal to take into account Alcoa's good fortune in the remainder of its business is somewhat surprising, especially in light of its distinction between actual losses and the failure to attain gains (discussed below).

Alcoa's coal was supplied under a contract with Peabody Coal Company from a mine owned by Alcoa. The coal was used as fuel in a power plant owned by Alcoa and operated by the local utility. So, ironically, had Alcoa used the same imperfect index in these two contracts in which it was a buyer, the "mistake" in the Essex contract would have been irrelevant.

2. The Decision

The decision hinged on one factual finding—the failure of the price index to track costs. The court had a number of grounds for modifying the contract. Because both parties presumed the index would work, its failure constituted a mutual mistake. The deviation was unforeseeable. Even if it were foreseeable, performance was impracticable. Alcoa's principal purpose for entering into this contract—to make between 1 and 7 cents per pound for the life of the contract—was frustrated. While the court could have used these doctrines to excuse Alcoa, it held that to do so would unfairly penalize Essex. (p. 79) Accordingly, it modified the contract, rewriting the price term. The price, recalculated quarterly, would be the lesser of the cap and a second price. That second price would be the greater of the price as defined in the contract and Alcoa's cost plus 1 cent. That would have meant that in 1979 Alcoa would have received about 11 cents per pound more than it would have absent the modification.

Anticipating wrongly that the precedent might be followed, the court suggested four factors to be considered in deciding whether to modify contracts: "(1) the parties' prevision of the problems which eventually upset the balance of the agreements and their allocation of the associated risks; (2) the parties' attempts at risk limitation; (3) the existence of severe out of pocket losses and (4) the customs and expectations of the particular business community." (p. 92) In the present case, the court concluded that the risk of index failure was something the parties did not anticipate and should not have anticipated (1 and 2) and that Alcoa suffered a severe out-of-pocket loss (3). The loss was greater than $60 million (pp. 66, 73) or $75 million (pp. 59, 88), depending on which part of the opinion you are reading.

Why Excuse?

The court offered three arguments for excusing Alcoa: mutual mistake (to which it devoted most of its attention), impracticability, and frustration. The mutual mistake, the court held, was the erroneous belief that the index would accurately track nonlabor production costs for the next twenty-one years. If contracts are entered into on the basis of predictions that years later turn out to be wrong, are these mutual mistakes at the time of contracting? Or are they just guesses that turned out to be wrong? A lot can happen in two decades; it is hard to imagine that there wouldn't be significant unanticipated events in that time period. I will show below that the notion that the WPI-IC had a long history of accurately tracking the nonlabor costs was false. But even if it had been extremely accurate, I do not see any virtue in treating a breakdown in that relationship years later as grounds for excusing performance. To treat the future failure of the index as a present fact is a linguistic stretch serving no useful purpose.

If the mutual mistake argument is weak, the impracticability argument is even weaker. There was nothing impracticable about producing aluminum at the Warrick plant. It was a perfectly sensible thing to do post-1973. Had the contract been rescinded, Alcoa would have been more than happy to continue producing aluminum at Warrick. Yes, its costs had increased, but the price had increased more. Impracticability, if it should be recognized at all, should be reserved for situations in which performing the contract would be a waste of resources for society. In this instance, bringing alumina to Warrick and converting it into aluminum was efficient. The rewards from doing so were skewed by the contract, to be sure, but that has nothing to do with whether or not the aluminum should be produced.

On first impression the frustration argument seems weaker still. Alcoa's principal purpose, said the court, was to earn money, and that purpose was frustrated. It is hard to imagine a serious commercial enterprise which does not have earning money as a "purpose." Surely, Alcoa's relevant principal purpose in this instance was to toll convert alumina into aluminum with economic consequences that it hoped would be favorable. The court's language cannot be taken seriously. However, the statement can be interpreted in a way that renders it less nonsensical. The parties intended the contract to be cost-based, with Alcoa receiving a return on its investment in capacity at Warrick. That return, according to Alcoa, was broken into two pieces—1 cent from the demand charge and 3 cents from the fixed component of the production charge. The contract was written with the expectation that Alcoa would make at least that 1 penny profit from the demand charge. If the nonlabor cost factor could be patched up, the purpose of tracking costs (including Alcoa's profit) could be achieved. Instead of invoking a "principal purpose" that wasn't, the court could have invoked the parties' intent, for which there was at least plausible evidence. That interpretation would at least narrow the scope of the frustration argument: in a contract that was supposed to mimic a cost-plus contract, the seller's failure to receive the "plus" could frustrate the intent of the parties. Given that it would have been easy enough for the parties to state this intent explicitly, I wouldn't want to read this interpretation into the contract. But at least it would make the court's frustration argument coherent.

Magnitude of the Loss

The two different loss numbers ($60 million and $75 million) correspond, more or less, to projections over the life of the contract and projections over the future life of the contract. The evidentiary base for either was extremely slim. In its brief (p. 49) Essex describes the basis for the projection: testimony by an Alcoa assistant controller that Alcoa's loss in the first half of 1979 was 9.503 cents per pound, and an assumption that these losses would continue through December 1988. There are three problems with this. First, the losses are undiscounted; a dollar in 1979 is treated the same as a dollar in 1988. Second, the sum of these losses would only be $71 million, so it is not clear how the court managed to conclude that future losses would exceed $75 million. Third, projecting losses for 9.5 years on the basis of the most recent six-month period is pretty tenuous. Essex made this last argument, but the court managed to give it a reverse twist:

> The Court rejects Essex's objection to the absence of expert testimony concerning future costs and prices. The objection is essentially based on the traditional refusal of courts to award speculative damages. But Essex presses the argument too far. The law often requires courts to make awards to redress anticipated losses. The reports are filled with tort and contract cases where such awards are made without the benefit of expert testimony concerning future economic trends. Awards are commonly denied because they are too speculative where there is a claim for lost future profits and there is insufficient evidence of present profits to form a basis for projecting

future profits. Similarly the courts often decline to speculate concerning future economic trends in calculating awards for lost future earnings. . . . This demonstrates the law's healthy skepticism concerning the reliability of expert predictions of economic trends. Where future predictions are necessary, the law commonly accepts and applies a prediction that the future economy will be much like the present (except that inflation will cease). Since some prediction of the future is inescapable in this case, that commonly accepted one will necessarily apply. On that prediction, ALCOA has proved that over the entire life of the contract it will lose, out of pocket, in excess of $60 million, and the whole of this loss will be matched by an equal windfall profit to Essex. (p. 66)

Both the court and Essex seem to have accepted the notion that projections of losses should be governed by the same rules as the measurement of damages. There is no particular reason for this to be so. Since the existence and magnitude of the projected losses are, ultimately, a red herring, this really shouldn't matter. In any event, it is a pretty dicey projection.

The $60 million projection takes into account that through 1978 Alcoa had received a net profit (undiscounted again) of $9 million. The court's response to Alcoa's making a modest profit in the first decade is remarkable: "If the contract were to expire today that net profit of $9 million would raise doubts concerning the materiality of the parties' mistake. But even on that supposition, the court would find the mistake to be material because it would leave ALCOA dramatically short of the minimum return of one cent per pound which the parties had contemplated." (pp. 65–66) However, as Essex noted in its brief (p. 52), since total sales through 1978 were a bit less than 800 million pounds, the undiscounted sum of the profits through 1978 was actually greater than 1 cent per pound; because profits were high in the early years, the present value of the profit stream in 1967 would have been even greater, so the factual statement itself is wrong. One does not have to pore over the briefs to learn this; the facts are available in the opinion itself. The interpretative statement, as it stands, is extraordinary: even a modest disappointment would justify excusing Alcoa. It only approaches plausibility if we explicitly treat the contract as one intending to mimic a cost-plus contract: because the contract did not (or will not) give the seller the "plus," there was a mistake, and the contract should be reformed to eliminate it.

The Index Was Bad, ex Ante

My impression is that most of the *Alcoa* commentary takes as correct the judge's claim that the WPI-IC had closely tracked Alcoa's nonlabor production costs in the past. Even if it were correct, I don't think the subsequent failure would warrant excusing Alcoa. But it was not correct. The court emphasized how the index chosen had been closely correlated with Alcoa's past nonlabor production costs:

> When Alcoa proposed the price formula which appears in the contract, Essex's management examined the past behavior of the indices for stability to assure they would not cause their final aluminum cost to deviate unacceptably from the going market rate. Alcoa's management was equally attentive to risk limitation. They went so far as to retain the noted economist Dr. Alan Greenspan as a consultant to advise them on the drafting of an objective pricing formula. They selected the WPI-IC as a pricing element for this long term contract only after they assured themselves that it had closely tracked Alcoa's non-labor production costs for many years in the past and was highly likely to continue to do so in the future. (p. 69)

Greenspan's involvement can usually be counted on for a good laugh in classroom discussions. Did it happen? Essex, in its brief, said not. "Contrary to the trial court's finding, George [Alcoa's key negotiator] testified that Alan Greenspan . . . was not consulted by Alcoa in connection with the Contract." (p. 16)

The court gave a numerical illustration: "If over the previous twenty years, the Wholesale Price Index had tracked within a 5% variation, pertinent costs to ALCOA, a 500% variation of costs to Index must be deemed unforeseeable, within any meaningful sense of the word." (p. 65) It is not clear whether this was meant to be a rhetorical flourish or an accurate rendition of the facts. If the latter, it missed. The Warrick plant was only seven years old at the time of the contract. As it expanded and took advantage of economies of scale, nonlabor costs fell by 60% while the WPI-IC was rising by 5%. If Alcoa was drawing on its cost history, it was on the cost performance of its eight other plants, which used different sources of power for electricity. So, the implicit assumption would have been that Alcoa's experience with plants located elsewhere and using a different power source would be an adequate predictor of the future course of this component of Alcoa's costs. That is a bigger leap than suggested by the court's description.

Suppose, for the sake of argument, that the indexing of the nonlabor costs had been perfect. And suppose further that the demand for aluminum had not shifted outward, since the court's argument was independent of demand conditions. Alcoa could still have been undone by the most favored customer clause. Alcoa's other plants were unaffected by the oil shock. If it entered into a tolling contract at one of them, the relevant costs would have been well below Alcoa's Warrick costs. The clause explicitly exposed Alcoa to the possibility that the correlation between the costs of coal-based power and other sources, especially hydro, would not hold for two decades. It was only because demand for aluminum and the cost of toll conversion had increased in the 1974–1979 period that the effects of the most favored customer clause were obscured.

So, if the purpose of the index was to track the nonlabor costs of the Warrick plant, the parties were indeed mistaken, but the mistake was one of bad judgment. There was no track record at Warrick, the implication of the court notwithstanding. Nor was there a historical basis for presuming that the costs of hydro and coal power would be closely correlated over a twenty-year period.

The Out-of-Pocket Loss

The judge distinguished between the case in which the seller actually lost money (which it referred to as "out-of-pocket losses") and one in which the contract resulted in the seller receiving less profit than it might otherwise have earned. "The existence of severe out of pocket losses should be essential to the award of relief." (p. 91) He used as an example a landlord whose variable costs are trivial. "Under these circumstances the landlord may suffer little or no out of pocket loss due to inflation, but he may suffer serious disappointment if his rent receipts fall greatly behind the current rental value of his property. This sort of disappointment seems less serious and relief from it seems more destructive of contract expectations than the disappointment of serious out of pocket losses and the destruction of expectations incident to their relief." (p. 91)

There is something tempting about this argument. The behavioral psychology literature, stemming from the seminal work of Kahneman and Tversky (1979) emphasized how people view gains and losses differently.

However, it also emphasized that whether they frame an outcome as a gain or a loss depends on context. That is, the landlord (or Alcoa) could view the out-of-pocket costs as the base, as the court suggests, or it could use the market price as the base, in which case the shortfall would be perceived as a loss. A priori, there is no reason to believe that parties would frame it one way or the other. Again, if the court rephrased this argument as the contract being an attempt to mimic a cost-plus contract, the argument would be more plausible: These parties cared more about covering costs than tracking market conditions because of the cost-based structure of their agreement; so, for them, the disappointment stemming from out-of-pocket losses would be greater.

3. It Was the Wrong Contract

Tracking Costs Is Hard

The contract was designed to mimic what would have happened had Essex vertically integrated, while achieving the scale economies of Alcoa's smelter. Nowhere in the contract does it say specifically that the contract was intended to mimic a cost-plus contract. Nonetheless, the structure of the agreement makes it quite clear that the intent was to make the contract cost-based. Pure cost-plus contracts have well-known difficulties in terms of measurement and incentive structures, and protection of confidential information. In this case, the measurement problem would have been complicated by the need to allocate the costs of the smelter between the Essex contract and Alcoa's other customers.

There are significant problems in designing a cost-based contract, especially one intended to last two decades. In this contract, the parties chose to index the major cost components, and, as they learned, at least one of these indexes performed poorly. However, even if all the base year numbers were accurate and all the indexes worked perfectly, the contract might fail to track costs accurately. The first reason is that the contract implicitly assumes that over the course of two decades there will be no technological changes and that the factor proportions will remain constant. If, for example, the price of nonlabor costs rose faster than that of labor costs, Alcoa would have had an incentive to switch to a more labor intensive technology over the course of the contract. If this were a "fixed proportion" production function, such substitution would not take place. The more flexible the technology, other things being equal, the more sensitive the costs would be to changing relative factor prices.

The second, and more significant, reason is that over half the price was not indexed. The production costs, accounting for 40% of the original contract, were indexed throughout the life of the agreement. The capacity costs were only indexed when Essex exercised its option to add another block. Thereafter, that cost remained constant, and Essex agreed to pay this amount in the form of a demand charge regardless of whether or not it took any aluminum. The rationale for this appears to be that Essex was, in effect, leasing new capacity at the average cost of building a new smelter; it, not Alcoa, would bear the risk of the smelter remaining idle. Alcoa was to recover the cost of the new capacity plus a reasonable return of 10% (4 cents per pound). That component was not indexed at all either. The new capacity would be a sunk cost, the parties reasoned, so Alcoa's reasonable return on its investment would be independent of future changes in the price level.

Treating the construction costs and associated profits as sunk costs appears plausible. However, there is a problem with this line of reasoning, and that is why the contract was destined to fail. Suppose, to simplify, that Alcoa was building new capacity for its own use and had a target rate of return of 10%. That target rate assumes something about future rates of inflation. If the rate of inflation were to increase after the investment was made, the 10% return would be inadequate. However, if the inflation were a general phenomenon, the price at which Alcoa sold its aluminum would increase and the nominal rate of return would increase accordingly. So, for example, if the initial inflation rate were 3% and it was expected to remain at 3%, Alcoa's nominal expected rate of return was 10% (by assumption) and its real expected rate of return would have been 7%. If the inflation rate doubled, if Alcoa continued to earn a nominal rate of 10%, the real return would have fallen to 4%. But if the real price of aluminum remained constant (that is, the nominal price of aluminum rose with the inflation rate), the real rate of return would have remained at 7% and the nominal rate would have risen to 13%. The point of this tedious exercise is that the failure to index the capital costs and rate of return meant that there was an implicit assumption that the rate of inflation would remain roughly unchanged for the duration of the agreement. To put this differently, in normal circumstances the capital costs would have been indexed implicitly by the demand side; the contract's failure to index them meant that this component of costs would be inaccurately measured for the life of the contract.

Tracking Production Costs Was a Bad Idea

In rationalizing his decision, the trial judge asserted (p. 92): "An indexed price term in a contract may prevent or minimize the hardship of inflation, but if it fails to do so, as was true in this case, a court should look beyond the fact of the parties' prevision of the general problem of inflation and should ask if the deviation between the index and the pertinent costs of the parties was adequately foreseen and its risk allocated in the contract." There is a difference between general inflation and an increase in a particular price. That, after all, is why the WPI-IC did not track the Warrick costs or aluminum prices. The judge did not recognize that the unindexed component made the contract incapable of dealing with the general problem of inflation. Nor, I believe, did the parties when they designed their contract.

Sixty percent of the initial contract price (the demand charge plus the fixed profit) was unadjusted for the life of the contract. A very simple example gives an indication of the type of problem this could cause. Suppose that the price level rises about 7% per year (doubling roughly every ten years); assume that the factors of production remain equally productive and that they continue to be used in the same proportions. The indexed production costs would then rise from 6 cents per pound to 24 cents per pound in the twentieth year. However, since the remaining costs were unindexed, the final contract price would rise only to 33 cents (24 + 9). To keep the real price of aluminum constant, the contract price would have had to increase to 60 cents. While an inflation rate of 7% per year might have seemed very unlikely in 1967, it was hardly inconceivable. The Vietnam War was heating up; by 1969 the inflation rate already exceeded 5%. In fact, because of the two oil shocks, the average inflation rate in the 1970s was substantially greater than 7%. Even if the inflation rate had remained constant at its 1968 rate, by 1988 the contract price would have only risen to 24 cents (15 + 9), while the nominal price of aluminum would have risen to 38 cents. Even that 14 cent differential was greater than the 10 cent deviation that had moved the court to bail out Alcoa.

It should have been clear at the time of contracting, therefore, that the failure to index 60% of the price would inevitably yield a growing divergence between the contract and market price. Only if the real price of aluminum plummeted would this be avoided. If, as I argued in Chapter 18, price adjustment mechanisms are a way of reducing the gap between the market price and the contract price, the contract was poorly designed to accomplish that. Even had the WPI-IC faithfully tracked nonlabor production costs, and even if the real price of aluminum had not changed, Alcoa would still have had strong incentives to attempt to renegotiate the price and to engage in behavior that would reduce the joint value of the deal. The *Alcoa* court did not concern itself with the gap between the market price of aluminum and Alcoa's production costs. The court's ex post indifference does not justify Alcoa's ex ante indifference.

The poor fit of the cap and the partial indexing provides another indication that the parties did not understand what they were doing. The cap, 65% of a published aluminum price, was only 8% above the initial contract price. If there were inflation, and if the real price of aluminum remained constant, the gap would have widened. Using the 1968 inflation rate, the cap would have grown to about 75% of the contract price. The higher the rate of inflation, the quicker the "cap gap" grows and the more the real price of aluminum would have to fall for the cap to come into play. If the real price of aluminum fell, we would expect a similar fall in the real costs of production, so for the cap to bind, there would have to be a disconnect between production cost and the indexed contract costs. There is no plausible rationale for the chance of hitting the cap becoming increasingly remote or for providing protection against this peculiar confluence of risks. On the other hand, a ceiling set at a constant percentage above a fully indexed base price is a common feature in long-term contracts, a perfectly sensible way of dealing with the inevitable imperfections of indexing.

The court's treatment of a lack of a floor is a further indication that it misperceived the implications of partial indexing. I suspect that was true for the litigators and transactional lawyers, but the only evidence I have of that is their failure to address the question. Consider the court's explanation of why there was no floor. "Clear hindsight suggests the flaw might have been anticipated and cured by a 'floor' resembling the 65% 'cap' that Essex wrote into the price formula. To the extent this possibility might be thought material to the case, the Court specifically finds that when the contract was made, even people of exceptional prudence and foresight would not have anticipated a need for this additional limitation to achieve the purpose of the parties." (p. 64) The "floor flaw" involved neither prudence nor foresight. A floor that resembled the cap in that it was a percentage of a quoted aluminum price would have drastically changed the contract—the cost-based indexing would have disappeared. Following the reasoning of the previous paragraph, if the inflation rate were positive and the real price of aluminum remained constant or at least did not fall by too much, the price would be determined by the floor. Again, using the 1968 inflation rate, if the floor were, say, 50%, the floor would have passed the indexed price in eight years (assuming the real price of aluminum remained constant). Perhaps the absence of a floor reflected the transactional lawyer's recognition of this absurd result, although I think that interpretation would be too charitable. Note that the court's remedy imposed a floor that bore no familial resemblance to the cap—a soft floor of a penny a pound above Alcoa's costs.

By framing their problem as one of treating Essex as if it owned the capacity to produce 75 million pounds of aluminum per year, therefore, the parties bungled the assignment of price risk. It also led them to err in assigning the quantity risk. The contract in effect made Essex the owner of capacity to produce 75 million pounds of aluminum per year. If it failed to use that quantity, Essex was still responsible for paying for it. It could either resell the unused portion or simply pay as if it had taken the aluminum. There was no good reason, however, for putting the quantity risk on Essex. Alcoa had other buyers for aluminum produced at Warrick. Its ingot plant at this location required more aluminum than could be produced at Warrick, so it was, on net, an importer at this location. Sales to Essex under the contract amounted to less than 1% of Alcoa's annual sales. Alcoa, therefore, had no reason to require significant protection of its reliance. While there was little reason to provide protection for Alcoa's reliance, that was not the case with Essex. The economics of its plant depended on the availability of molten aluminum. A more sensible contract would have given Essex the discretion to adapt to changing market conditions, probably in the form of a requirements contract for as much aluminum as necessary for fabrication at its nearby plant. Possibly, Alcoa might have wanted to include a minimum in order to limit Essex's ability to use the contract as an option—producing wire at this plant if the price here was better than at Essex's other plants and ceasing production here if the price elsewhere became more favorable. But the crucial point is that only one party had a significant reliance interest to protect, and the contract managed to get it backwards.

If the parties had chosen a requirements contract, that would still leave them with the pricing problem. There was nothing wrong, ex ante, with the two cost indexes the parties used. Their big mistake was the failure to index the remaining 60%. Beyond that, they had to recognize that, over time, indexing to costs reflecting some base condition is likely to lose touch with reality. Probably the best way to deal with that problem is to impose both a ceiling and a floor based on an external aluminum price. If either is triggered, there are a number of possible responses. These include continuing to perform with the price remaining at the ceiling (or floor), termination, giving one party the option to terminate at a predetermined pricing formula, and having a third party set a new price.

4. Concluding Remarks

The Alcoa-Essex contract provides a nice example of how sophisticated parties can go wrong when they misstate their problem. Mimicking ownership might have seemed a plausible way to proceed, but it resulted in a badly designed deal, one that was likely to fail. The likelihood of failure was enhanced by the erroneous notion that the capital costs should not be indexed. Moreover, it led the parties to ignore the critical question: Who should have the discretion to adapt to changed circumstances?

The Alcoa-Essex contract could be viewed as one component of two of Alcoa's contract portfolios. It was one small piece of Alcoa's aluminum sales portfolio, perhaps the only piece which was performing poorly. It was also a larger component of the Warrick portfolio which included the cost side. In that portfolio Alcoa's suppliers of coal and electric power generated from it did manage to index successfully, to Alcoa's disadvantage. And to make matters even worse for Alcoa, its subsidiary selling alumina to Essex apparently had not adequately indexed prices, so that the alumina contract price remained below the spot market price. They managed to guess wrong at every turn. Had their guesses in coal and power at least been consistent with their Essex guess, there would have been no basis for Alcoa's concern about costs. Had the alumina contract more closely tracked market conditions, much of Essex's windfall from escalating aluminum prices would have disappeared.

If Alcoa and Essex knew what they were doing, they would not have written this contract. A partially indexed long-term contract will inevitably result in a divergence between contract and market prices, and ex ante this divergence should be expected to have detrimental consequences. The court had to deal with the contract the parties did write, not the one they should have written. I have argued that the court, lacking an analytical framework, managed to misrepresent some of the facts and to come up with a weak rationale for bailing out Alcoa. (Alcoa's principal purpose was to make money!?!) The most charitable interpretation of the opinion, I believe, is that the judge imposed a cost-plus gloss on the contract which was not explicit in the contract, but most likely comported with the parties' intentions. If the opinion were read with the cost-plus gloss, it would at least be coherent, although such a reading would have drastically narrowed the opinion's reach.

Suppose that the capital costs were properly indexed. It would at least be a reasonable inference that the contract was intended to be cost-based. The failure of one of the indexes to track costs might, under those circumstances, justify an interpretation of the contract which substituted actual costs for the poorly performing index. I would be reluctant to make this argument, but at least this would be a plausible interpretation. It would be even more plausible if there were a recital to the effect that the contract was meant to track costs. Had the court understood what was happening in *Alcoa*, it could have directed debate to questions of this sort.

CHAPTER **21**

Mineral Park v. Howard:
The Irrelevance of
Impracticability

If it is impractical for a party to perform a contract because the costs are much higher than anticipated, should it be excused? And if so, how ought one determine impracticability? The doctrine of discharge by impracticability in the United States originated with *Mineral Park Land Co. v. Howard et al.* There the court found that because the cost of performance would have been ten times greater than had been anticipated, the promisor was excused. Had the court properly framed the inquiry, it would have been clear that the magnitude of the cost increase was irrelevant. Holding the promisor to the terms of the agreement would have created no great hardship for the promisor and would have led to an efficient outcome. That need not be true of all cases in which the impracticability defense is raised, but under the somewhat unusual circumstances of this contract, impracticability was a non sequitur.

The Howards had promised to build a bridge and entered into a contract to allow them to take all the gravel necessary for that purpose from Mineral Park's land. The removal of the gravel would be done by the Howards, who would bear all the costs. The contract stated the estimated amount of gravel, 114,000 cubic yards. The price was 5 cents per cubic yard for the first 80,000 yards, the next 10,000 yards were to be given free of charge, and the balance was to be paid for at the rate of 5 cents per cubic yard. It is not clear why the price term took this particular form, and nothing is lost analytically by treating it as constant at 5 cents per cubic yard.

After the Howards had begun to perform, they learned that a considerable amount of the gravel on Mineral Park's property was under water. It could have been recovered, but at ten to twelve times the cost of the gravel on dry ground. The Howards took 50,131 cubic yards under the contract and then completed the job by purchasing the remainder (50,869 cubic yards) from another supplier. Mineral Park sued, claiming that the contract required that the Howards had to purchase all the gravel from them and that the gravel was in fact on their property, albeit located in an inconvenient place. In their defense, the Howards claimed that taking all the gravel from Mineral Park would have been impracticable, and the court upheld that argument, emphasizing the magnitude of the additional costs. The issue posed by the decision is whether a multiple of 10–12 is enough to warrant a finding of impracticability; what if the multiple were only 5? Or 2?

We can reframe the issue by focusing on the Howards' decision, assuming that the law would not excuse them. They have agreed to pay 5 cents per cubic yard to Mineral Park for all the gravel necessary to complete the bridge. Either they pay directly for gravel taken from the Mineral Park land or indirectly in the form of damages. That amount is fixed regardless of the source of the gravel, unless damages were to be reckoned in some other way. If Mineral Park were to derive some benefit from having the gravel removed, then perhaps the damages would be greater. The usual presumption is that the excavation is a detriment to the landowner, so I doubt that there would be any benefit worth recognizing.

So, when deciding whether to take any additional gravel from Mineral Park, the Howards must compare their incremental costs of removing that gravel to the price of the best alternative supplier. Let me give a simple example. Suppose that gravel was available from an outside firm at 10 cents per cubic yard. As long as the cost to the Howards of removing the marginal unit of gravel remained below 10 cents, it would make economic sense for them to take the gravel from Mineral Park's land. If the incremental cost exceeded 10 cents, then the least-cost path would be to buy gravel from the outside supplier. The 5 cent payment doesn't affect its decision, because that 5 cents must be paid regardless of whether or not it takes the gravel. As long as the marginal cost of removal exceeds the price of the alternative source, the Howards should switch. That is true if the cost multiple were 10; it is also true if the multiple were 5, 2, or 1.2. The Howards' incentive is to do the right (efficient) thing, taking the lowest cost gravel, as they, in fact, did. The magnitude of the cost differential affects neither their incentives to behave in an efficient manner, nor the damages they must pay if they breach. As long as the marginal cost of removal exceeds the price of the best alternative, it is "impracticable" to take the gravel from Mineral Park's land rather than from the cheaper source. But that is no reason to excuse performance. The Howards can, and should, buy the cheaper gravel elsewhere and send Mineral Park a check for 5 cents for every cubic yard they take, regardless of its source.

The opinion included no discussion of why the contract was a requirements contract, nor why the fee was a flat per unit rate. In this case, I don't believe the reasons matter given that the grounds for enforcing the contract are so clear. Mineral Park's proximity to the bridge site gave it a locational advantage vis-à-vis other potential suppliers. I suspect that the expected marginal cost curve of extraction from Mineral Park's land was upward sloping. That is, there was a presumption that some gravel was near the surface and relatively inexpensive to remove, while some would have been more costly. So, suppose the expected cost of the first units (plus the 5 cents per unit fee) was considerably lower than the cost of the best alternative. Even if half the gravel were under water, the total cost to the Howards of the gravel from both sources plus the 5 cent fee might well have been less than if it purchased all the gravel from outsiders. Mineral Park's knowledge of the extraction costs would be imperfect; rather than trying to ascertain those costs, it simply set a per unit price that would allow it to capture much of the unique value of its locational advantage. If the court were to allow the buyer to walk away when the marginal costs of extraction exceed the cost of the alternative supplier, it would deprive the seller of some of the value of its unique location. The buyer gets the "sweet" and the seller keeps the "bitter."

I will add a bit of complexity to this story shortly. But the key point bears emphasis. The court based its decision on the exorbitant cost of removal, a cost that rational parties would not incur. The only issue should have been who would receive the 5 cents per cubic yard on the 50,000 plus cubic yards that were procured elsewhere. The decision on where the gravel should come from was unaffected by the 5 cent flat fee. Note that this argument depends on the remedy being money damages. If the remedy were specific performance, then Mineral Park would be in position to extort substantial payments from the Howards, and one could make a strong case against allowing that to happen. We needn't follow that path, since no one links the impracticability defense to anything other than money damages.

If the Howards expected to be excused, then they would have faced the same incentives: compare the marginal cost of excavation to the price of the alternative and choose the cheaper path. The incentive is the same whether or not they bear the 5 cent per cubic yard fee. It might appear, therefore, that we should be indifferent as to whether an excuse should be granted. Aside from the general argument that contracts should be enforced, there are two additional grounds for favoring enforcement over excuse. If the parties knew there would be a bailout, then the original pricing formula would likely be more complicated (or the seller might not even find entering into the contract worthwhile). So, if the flat fee were a device that allowed the seller to price its locational advantage, excusing performance would undercut that feature. In addition, the impracticability excuse would invite a costly debate over both the true costs of the disputed activity (costs never incurred) and the appropriate place to draw the line. So, had the case been properly understood, there was no good reason for the court to allow the defendants to offer the defense of impracticability.

I will now add a few wrinkles. The first two don't really change anything. The third, although seemingly minor, does make a difference. In the actual case, the Howards had an alternative supplier at a reasonable price, and they used that supplier. What if there were no other sources? It is, I should emphasize, not a good idea to promise to build a bridge if there is only one potential supplier of a particular critical input and no assurance that it has an adequate supply available to complete the bridge. Hold that aside for a moment. There are two alternatives. First, faced with the exorbitant cost of the gravel, the Howards might choose to default on the bridge contract. The only issue with regard to its Mineral Park contract (which the court did not reproduce, so we must speculate) is whether the contract was for gravel actually used to build the bridge, or the gravel that would have been used had a bridge been built. That is, it is possible that the contract could have bound the Howards to pay for a certain amount of gravel even if the bridge had not been completed. But unlikely. I am reasonably confident that this was a requirements contract and that if the Howards chose not to take gravel for the bridge, there would be no obligation to pay.

Second, the Howards could have gone ahead and incurred the additional costs and then sued for the difference. It would be a bit facile to argue that performance was impractical; after all, they performed. Nonetheless, some courts have chosen to treat such problems as impracticability cases. That was the argument proffered without success by the aggrieved party in *Transatlantic* and with success by Alcoa in *Alcoa v. Essex*. The remedy would not be excuse, it would be reformation. It is hard to imagine a justification—fairness, efficiency, or otherwise—that would shift the Howards' additional production costs back upon the passive landowner, barring some fraud or misrepresentation on the part of Mineral Park. Mineral Park had granted the privilege of removal at a fixed per unit fee. It would be quite remarkable if reformation required Mineral Park to pony up funds to partially bail out the Howards for their bad deal. Note that reformation would create a potential moral hazard problem. After the bad news was revealed, the Howards would decide whether to continue the bridge project and how much to spend on removal, but some fraction of the cost would be shifted to Mineral Park, which would have no say on the matter.

The moral hazard problem goes away if reformation would mean that the Howards were excused from paying the fixed fee, but still must bear all the production costs. That would make impracticability even more of a non sequitur. Because the extraction costs are so high, we still expect you to bear them. However, you will be excused from paying the fixed fee, which is unrelated to the actual extraction costs, regardless of its magnitude.

The peculiar feature of the Mineral Park contract distinguishing it from most other impracticability cases is that the seller was passive and the buyer had to incur the costs of removal. Let us turn our attention to the more common case, in which the seller incurs the costs of removal. Suppose that Mineral Park had promised to deliver all the gravel the Howards required to build the bridge for a flat rate of 10 cents per cubic yard. It turns out, however, that the actual extraction costs for the last 50,000 cubic yards are about 60 cents per cubic yard. Or worse, suppose that there were only 50,000 cubic yards in place originally so that providing the gravel from Mineral Park's land would be literally impossible. A case could be made for excusing performance in certain circumstances.

The starting point is the question: If parties had anticipated this contingency, what might their contract look like? Suppose that there were no feasible substitutes and that, given the contract price, gravel costs were only a small fraction of the expected final cost of the bridge. I would imagine that the buyer would demand strong assurance of an adequate supply, lest it be liable for the substantial costs of breaching its bridge building contract. Excusing performance in such circumstances would most likely be a very foolish policy. Unless the parties explicitly recognized such an excuse in a force majeure or hardship clause, the seller should be held responsible.

There could, however, be a set of circumstances in which the parties would have rationally chosen to excuse performance. Suppose, for example, that alternative suppliers were available at higher prices and that it was not at all clear at the time of contracting that the buyer would need the gravel if the price were higher. This would be similar to the case in which a seller's factory burned down or the port of discharge for a shipping contract was closed. The cost of performance of this contract could turn out to be higher than expected, although the costs of its competitors are not; and if the buyer had to bear those additional costs, it is quite possible it would choose not to go through with the transaction. In this instance, keeping the contract alive raises the moral hazard problems, while excuse would put the decision to adapt to new information in the hands of the party who would bear the consequences.

So, if the seller was the one bearing the costs of extraction, it is possible to make a plausible argument that in at least some circumstances it should be excused. But that was not the actual case. Here, the buyer incurred the costs and its payments to the seller were limited to the 5 cents per cubic yard fee. In that case there is no ground for excusing performance. Neither the *Mineral Park* court nor subsequent commentary failed to appreciate that distinction.

Conclusion

When Aaron Director turned his skeptical economist's eye on antitrust law in the 1950s, he stimulated the production of a stream of scholarly papers that, within a generation, resulted in a significant reshaping of antitrust law and policy. My hope is that this project will at least nudge contract law and interpretation in a similar direction. Adjustment of contractual relationships as circumstances change and new information becomes available can increase value, and contract law can facilitate that. The means for adjusting are many. Contracting parties could establish a governance mechanism that sets up a process for choosing a decision-making body and rules governing the domain and behavior of that body. A condominium, for example, might have a detailed set of rules for determining who governs and how (and rules for altering those rules). My primary concern has been with a lower level governance decision: the allocation of constrained discretion to one of the parties. As Scott and Triantis (2004) put it in their recent, important paper, a contract can often be viewed as an option with the grantor of the option setting a price for the option and an exercise price. The grantee has the discretion to adapt; the option price reflects the cost to the grantor of making itself vulnerable to the grantee's discretion. Twentieth Century Fox paid $750,000 for the option to use Shirley MacLaine to make a particular movie in a particular time slot. Robert Mattei paid $0 to Amelia Hopper for the option to buy her land for a particular use at a fixed exercise price. The Crushed Toast Company agreed to take all the bread crumbs Levy produced, but gave Levy the option of determining the quantity. Krell paid £25 for the option to use Henry's apartment and let the option lapse when the coronation events were postponed. In general, by giving one party the discretion to terminate or revise a contractual relationship, the parties increase the joint value of the contract.

376

Scott and Triantis use the option framework to argue against the expectation damage rule. Once we recognize the weak basis for the expectation damages, make-the-victim-whole rule, it is easy to treat damage rules as just another contract term. I recognize that there is an awful lot of entrenched doctrine to overcome, but I hope that this book, along with their paper, will at least nudge the discussion in the proper direction. I argued in Part IV for enforcing what I have labeled the narrow expectation interest, the market-contract differential. Scott and Triantis get to the same position by a slightly different route. Regardless of how we got there, the key point we agree on is that there is no basis for privileging expectation damage measures like lost profits over termination charges that the parties would choose. Breach sounds ugly; exercising an option to terminate sounds benign. Analytically, they are the same.

Scott and Triantis draw two policy implications. First, the law should be more accepting of liquidated damage clauses; indeed, it should encourage parties to make their damage remedies (or option prices) explicit. Second, the default rule should be specific performance. The analysis of Parts IV and V strongly supports the first. On the second I remain agnostic. I am less interested in the specific recommendations. What I want to underscore is the need to reframe the inquiry.

The wooden approach to protecting reliance of the "good faith" cases carries over to other areas of contract law and scholarship. Yes, parties will often want to get some protection for their reliance, but how much? All contracts casebooks include at least one case regarding the right of a subcontractor to retract its proposal after the general contractor has won a bid. Learned Hand's position in *Baird Co. v. Gimbel Bros., Inc.* holding that the sub was free to retract is juxtaposed with Roger Traynor's holding in *Drennan v. Star Paving Co.* that the general's reliance constrained the sub's freedom to retract. Traynor's position seems to have prevailed in the courts and the academic debates and has been enshrined in the Second Restatement as §87(2). I had always thought that Hand had the better argument, but it really shouldn't matter. This is a situation in which it should be extremely easy to contract around the default rule. The general contractor could simply state that as a condition of a bid being considered, the subcontractor agrees that the bid will not be retracted for a specific period of time (Traynor). Or, if the general believes that would discourage too many bidders, it could allow for an unlimited right of retraction (Hand). Or it could opt for some intermediary standard. There are costs and benefits from constraining the sub's right to retract, and generals might find that their weights differ depending on the context. (See Katz 1996.) Hand's is, I believe, a cleaner default rule, but for construction cases, there is no great cost in opting for Traynor's fuzzier rule instead. To the extent that §87(2) applies outside the construction context in areas in which contracting away from the default is more problematic, the Traynor interpretation might be the source of some mischief. The simple solution is subject to two doctrinal hurdles. First, there might not be consideration for the sub's promise not to retract, since the general does not bind itself in any way. Second, if the sub faxed in its bid with a disclaimer stating that it was free to retract, it could argue that either there was no contract or that the contract was formed on its terms (the last shot). I would imagine that courts could prevent both these moves without much tweaking of the law. Even if the legal loopholes remained, I suspect that a sub that tried to make either argument would face severe extralegal sanctions.

Termination looks like an all-or-nothing option. In practice, it can be less so. The option to terminate or walk away can be used as the basis for renegotiating the terms to cope with changed circumstances. A long-term, variable price contract could, for example, say that if the parties cannot agree on a new price (or if the contract price as indexed falls outside a predetermined band), the agreement will terminate; for examples of such contracts for petroleum coke, see Goldberg and Erickson (1987, pp. 388–391). More generally, the options need not be all-or-nothing. The contract can grant one party the discretion to adapt; it can, but need not, confront that party with a price for exercising that discretion. A requirements contract grants the buyer the choice of how much to take at the contract price. It can limit the discretion in a number of dimensions: by specifying the purpose (requirements for a particular use or plant); setting a minimum (or a formula or mechanism for determining the minimum); or setting a price for the option (perhaps with some variant on a take-or-pay contract). Chapter 5 is full of such examples. The doctrinal implication is that the law should encourage customization of the flexibility/reliance trade-off, rather than using a blunt instrument like good faith to restrict parties' ability to adapt to change.

In interpreting contracts we should not search for what the parties "really meant," but instead try to ascertain what reasonable parties should have meant, given the economic context (a "reasonable economic firm" test). Looking for a "meeting of the minds" sounds good, but it presents serious problems. The first problem is that it is hard to ascertain what was in the head of a party, especially if that party's incentives ex post are to be less than completely honest. The second problem is that it is not clear which head we should be looking into. The contract might be between X and Y, but X and Y can be organizations with numerous participants who might have different perspectives, knowledge, and goals. Moreover, in complex transactions, the words that might raise the interpretation issues were probably chosen not by any of these players, but by their transactional lawyers. Or, in the case of standardized forms, the relevant mind is that of a transactional lawyer who might have drafted that piece of the contract years ago for a class of transactions that might have some common features with the present one.

Focusing on the reasonable economic firm allows us to narrow the range of plausible interpretations. Even if the principals at Ballantine and Falstaff didn't realize that their royalty arrangement was a form of earnout, the contract should be interpreted as such, and that helps define "best efforts." Similarly, whoever negotiated American Bakeries' requirements contract with Empire Gas might not have considered the possibility that American Bakeries would fail to take any conversion units; nonetheless, the underlying economics makes it clear that no rational firm would pay a substantial price for the mere option to buy off-the-shelf units.

The reasonable-economic-firm test does not mean that each disputed contract must be subjected to a full-scale economic analysis. Its function is twofold. First is its negative role: to constrain courts from engaging in freewheeling interpretation. The use of the implied duty of good faith, for example, should be tightly cabined. Doctrinal tricks, like the liberal invocation of custom and usage, should not be allowed to undo clear contractual language (for example, the minimum quantity term in *Columbia Nitrogen* and the pricing formula in *Nanakuli*). Second, in its positive role, the approach should be used to resolve ambiguities. Some ambiguity is inevitable. For example, complex contracts often use terms like "materiality," "reasonable," "best efforts," and "good faith," which must be defined contextually. I recognize that clever litigators and judges can make virtually anything appear ambiguous. I don't believe, however, that their ingenuity would require a full-blown reasonable-firm inquiry in most contract disputes. A little economics can go a long way toward clarifying the issues.

This book could have been a lot longer. There are a lot of decisions out there just begging for a simple economic framework. I will briefly discuss one *(Chodos v. West Publishing Co.)*, which illustrates how a court operating in an analytical vacuum can lose its way. Chodos, a lawyer, entered into a contract to write a book on fiduciary duty for a particular publisher. His compensation was to be in the form of a 15% royalty rate; he received no advance. The publisher was sold to a larger company, West, which decided not to publish the book. The trial court held that the decision to publish was within the publisher's discretion and granted its summary judgment motion. On appeal, this was reversed and the court held that West had breached. *(Chodos I)* The publisher, the court held, could have terminated if the manuscript's content were unacceptable, but not just because it concluded that the book was unlikely to be a commercial success. It is not clear why a publisher would choose this standard; it is in business to make money, and it would prefer to retain the option to terminate if it believed publication would be a negative net present value exercise. If the intent were to protect the author's reliance, this could probably have been done better by paying a nonrefundable advance upon presentation of an acceptable manuscript, giving the publisher the option to publish, and, if it chose not to publish, to permit the author to market the manuscript elsewhere. Nonetheless, I will accept the court's position on liability; it is at least defensible. My concern here is with the treatment of damages, which is not.

Because the contract was silent on the matter, let us assume that the proper measure would have been expectation damages—to make the author as well off as he would have been had the publisher performed. The Court of Appeals held that measuring damages would be too speculative. A traditional response to the "too speculative" finding is to grant no damages. Instead, the court bought the plaintiff's argument that the appropriate remedy would be for restitution, in quantum meruit. The court expressed no opinion on how restitution should be calculated. Chodos did. He claimed to have put in 3,600 hours over a three-year period, time he could have spent earning his legal fees as a practitioner (which would have been more than $1 million). His compensation should, he argued, be the time spent multiplied by his hourly fee. On remand, a jury gave him only $300,000 and he appealed. The Court of Appeals *(Chodos II)* upheld the verdict. The standard it approved was the fee that West would have had to pay on the "open market" for another author to provide a similar service. It also approved the district court's allowing the jury to consider Chodos's lost opportunity in coming up with its measure. So, the jury could have come up with Chodos's pay-me-for-my-time measure had it been so inclined.

This is quite a comedy of errors. First, the open market test fails because West would not have paid a flat fee—it would have offered a royalty and, perhaps, an advance against royalties. Second, if we really wanted to compensate with expectation damages, the speculative nature of the damages should hardly have been a problem. It would have required a projection of book sales, but such projections are fairly routine. In *Bloor*, for example, Ballantine's potential sales were projected for a number of years. Moreover, the apparent lack of interest by other publishers suggests a simple way to calculate the maximum damages. What was the breakeven point for the least efficient publisher? From this we could determine the maximum expected volume of sales. (This is complicated a bit by the fact that the sales level depends on selling effort as well as production costs.) Implicitly, the court assumes that sales would have been $2 million (yielding royalties of $300,000). Third, and most important, the court never bothered to ask a very simple question: What publisher in its right mind would set an option price of $300,000 on a manuscript that did not even warrant an advance? If I were advising publishers, I would make the option explicit and make the price of the option be the advance. Or, if not that, at least it should include some sort of liquidated damages measure to prevent a clueless court from imposing such an irrational remedy.

I have not attempted to construct a general theory of contracting or contract law. I hope that I have indicated the fruitfulness of the transactional economic framework both for analyzing specific cases and doctrines, and for providing building blocks for constructing that more general theory. Litigated cases provide us with an immense data set, and the useful data go well beyond the holdings of the cases. I have taken a very micro approach, examining a fairly small number of cases intensively. Analyses of particular cases are sometimes disparaged as mere case notes or dismissed as "contract stories," sources of anecdotes to amuse our students. I have tried to go beyond this, and to provide a framework for making this a more respectable and valuable form of scholarly endeavor. Studies like this do not require superhuman strength. All that is needed is a simple economic framework, some skepticism, and the wherewithal to track down the case records and, perhaps, some related materials. I should note that my research assistant and I spent a lot of man-hours nailing down some very simple facts. We must have devoted over 100 hours to determining whether Otis was really Fernando Wood's son. A fun fact, perhaps, but not a very useful one. But from time to time, serendipity works. That search uncovered Wood's contract with Rose O'Neill, which turned out to be of critical importance.

I do not view this book as the final word. Rather, my intention is that it will map out a research agenda for others to build on. I envision extending the discussion in five ways. First, as much as I would like to believe that my take on every case was right, I suspect that there are a few misses. I would very much like to see debate joined on the analyses of particular cases. Second, I have only illuminated a few corners of contract law; we need more case studies on which to build, both to deepen our understanding of some of the matters discussed in this book and to extend the analysis to other matters. Third, my focus has been almost entirely on American law. That leaves open a wide array of comparative law questions. What happens abroad? Does the law differ? Do contracting parties respond differently? Fourth, I have used the transactional approach to shed light on doctrine. There is no reason why the feedback can't be reversed. That is, analysis of litigated cases can yield insights into how contracts ought to be structured. My *Alcoa* discussion in Chapter 20 is illustrative. And, finally, there is a second feedback loop. The theory suggests how cases should be analyzed, but the detailed analyses can, and should, have an impact on the evolution of the theory.

NOTES

REFERENCES

TABLE OF CASES

INDEX

Notes

1. The Net Profits Puzzle

1. A film's gross receipts comprise the total amount of revenue generated by the film. The sources of revenue include (1) theatrical revenue or film rental; (2) nontheatrical (armed forces and Red Cross; airlines; ships; oil rigs; and college campuses); (3) pay television; (4) network television; (5) television syndication; (6) home video; and (7) ancillary rights (music publishing, sound track recordings; merchandising interactive/computer game rights; and novelizations). (Nochimson and Brachman 1996)

2. In some instances the talent might forego an advance and simply take a share of the adjusted gross receipts. According to press accounts, Robert Redford took no upfront fee for *Indecent Proposal,* taking between 10% and 15% of the gross. He is said to have earned $20–$25 million. See Welkos (1995b, p. F5). Tom Hanks and Robert Zemeckis purportedly had a very small front-end compensation on *Forrest Gump* and a large enough share of the back end to yield them over $60 million. See Roddick (1995).

3. In 1996, actors with a fixed fee per film of $20 million included John Travolta, Mel Gibson, Jim Carrey, Harrison Ford, Sylvester Stallone, Tom Cruise, and Arnold Schwarzenegger. See Gilbert (1996, p. N1).

4. Despite claims of author Winston Groom's lawyer, Pierce O'Donnell, that the film would remain forever in the red, the net profits participants (Groom, screenwriter Eric Roth, and producers Wendy Finerman and Steve Tisch) did receive some contingent compensation from the movie. At the time the $62 million "loss" was disclosed, Paramount announced that it had paid a $3 million "advance against profits" to the net profits participants. See Munk (1995, pp. 42–43) and Weinraub (1995, C15).

5. The Complaint in *Garrison v. Warner Bros.* suggested that the studios were attempting to change their terminology. "In recent months, studio legal departments have reacted to court decisions on Talent contracts by attempting to place a new face on the old, discredited system. Studio lawyers have been replacing the term 'net profit' with some euphemisms like 'net proceeds' or

other terms designed to hide the fact that the unconscionable practice continues." (First Amended Complaint, *Garrison v. Warner Bros.*, pp. 25–26).

6. For a summary of the Bernheim and Buchwald contracts, see Plaintiffs' Preliminary Statement of Contentions Concerning Accounting and Damages Issues (*Buchwald I*, pp. 73–77).

7. For some background on the *Batman* case, see Griffin and Masters (1996, pp. 164–174).

8. See Friedberg (1992, pp. 345–346) and Reardon (1992, pp. 314–317. While there is considerable variation in the terms regarding the floors, according to Friedberg (1992, p. 348), "virtually every deal is a 90/10 deal."

9. Pierson provides numerous examples of the role of independent producers in actively promoting their films after they have signed a distribution agreement. The promotional role of the independent producer/director is emphasized by Deutchman (1992, p. 325), president of Fine Line Features: "[K]eeping the filmmakers happy is essential to a successful campaign, since we have to depend on them to go out on tour, doing interviews with regional press. Because independent movies are more director-driven and review-driven than studio pictures, much weight is placed on the filmmakers' shoulders to help us position the picture in the marketplace."

2. Reading *Wood v. Lucy*

1. A Westlaw citation count found 520 cases and 308 secondary source citations (November 22, 2005). The totals are growing at a rate of about three per month. For some background on the case, see Pratt (1988).

2. There is lots of public material on Lucy; see, for example, Etherington-Smith and Pilcher (1986). I received a tremendous amount of help from Randy Bryan Bigham, who is writing a biography of Lucy. See Lucy Christiana, Lady Duff Gordon (née Sutherland), www.encyclopedia=titanica.org/biography/101. On Otis Wood's family, Pleasants (1948) and Mushkat (1990) provided some background. The web has a number of short biographical notes on his father, Fernando, and his uncle, Benjamin. On the interaction between the fathers of Wood and Cardozo, see Kaufman (1998, pp. 12–14). I also received some useful information from Jerome Mushkat, a biographer of Otis's father. Additional information came from the archives of the *New York Times*, *Women's Wear Daily*, and *Printer's Ink*. On Rose O'Neill, see Armitage (1994) and O'Neill (1997) and the following websites: Rose Cecil O'Neill; Female Inventors: Rose O'Neill.

3. The contract has a certain quaintness befitting its age: "Said retailer shall . . . provide a clerk who writes a good hand and understands accounts and bookkeeping for the purpose of constantly assisting him in the management of said business." (p. 95)

4. The ad for the opening featured a letter from Lucy:

My Dear Mr. Bedell:

   After my visit today, I admire your courage in opening your beautiful new store in Thirty-fourth Street. We are much alike in that neither of us knows fear. I would have no hesitancy in opening such an extensive establishment myself.

   You have displayed wonderful taste in the selection of your models. And what a variety! I do not see how it is possible to offer such extremely attractive things at the prices you are asking. It is a revelation to me. I am glad to know that in reality I am your first customer in your new shop. The black-and-white coat which I have selected is perfectly adorable, and the gray motor coat will be exactly what I want for my personal use. I must send coats like these to my girls in England.

   You may tell the public that the blue evening gown which I admired so much I have christened with my first name (Christiana) and that this is the first time I have ever given permission to use my name in connection with a model. I shall be glad to visit your opening Monday. I wish you every success in your new establishment and I know it is assured. Sincerely yours,

   Lucie Christiana Duff-Gordon

5. This vulnerability is often cited as the basis for finding an implied covenant. A Lexis search of Wood/Lucy/Duff/Gordon/mercy turned up thirty-two hits. A typical statement goes as follows:

   A typical example of an implied covenant to exploit is found in a leading case in New York on the subject, *Wood v. Lucy, Lady Duff-Gordon.* There the defendant, a fashion designer, gave the plaintiff the exclusive privilege of marketing defendant's design. Although the plaintiff did not expressly agree to exploit the design, the court implied such an obligation, since defendant's sole revenue was to be derived from plaintiff's sales of clothes designed by defendant and defendant was thus at the plaintiff's mercy. In this and in similar cases the circumstances revealed that such an obligation was essential to give effect to the contract between the parties and was in accord with their intent.

   . . . In the *Wood* case, for example, the most important factor in the decision was that the fashion designer would not receive any revenue unless the plaintiff sold the designer's clothes. (*Permanence Corp. v. Kennametal, Inc.,* 1989, quoting *Vacuum Concrete Corp v. American Machine & Foundry Co.,* 772–773.)

   This passage illustrates the transmutation of facts in the legal process. Wood's job, recall, was to place endorsements, not to sell clothes.

6. See for example, Michigan's statute (M.C.L.A.) §600.2961 providing for treble damages for wrongful withholding of commissions to salespersons. See also *Kingsley Associates, Inc. v. Moll Plasticrafters, Inc.*

7. While damage remedies are more liberal today, a court could still find zero damages; see the ensuing discussion of *New Paradigm Software Corp. v. New Era of Networks, Inc.*

8. Her *New York Times* obituary (April 22, 1935) noted that in the course of her bankruptcy proceeding she "exhibited poor business ability in the hearings before the Recorder in Bankruptcy. That official asked her: 'Can you give me some particulars of your shareholding?' 'It is all Greek to me' she replied. 'I don't know what a share is.' "

9. Apparently, "due diligence" was changed to "best efforts" in the 1953 draft of the UCC; see Van Vliet (2000, p. 702).

10. See also *HML Corp. v. General Foods Corp., Vacuum Concrete Corp. of America v. American Machine & Foundry Co., Beraha v. Baxter Health Care Corp.*, and Eckstrom 2002, §2:28 ("For the most part, a best efforts obligation is implied only where the licensor has, as a practical matter, put the productiveness of the licensed property solely at the mercy of the licensee. A best efforts obligation is implied in such a situation on the ground that if the parties addressed this matter, such obligation would have been specified. Therefore, a best efforts obligation is usually implied only for exclusive licenses which do not include safety factors for the licensee, such as minimum royalty provisions.") (footnotes omitted)

11. The finding of zero damages was not inevitable, but was dictated by the plaintiff's framing of the damages issue and the judge's (magistrate judge, actually) annoyance with the quality of lawyering. In that portion of the opinion in which he found that the $2 million cash payment did not preclude an implied "best efforts" clause, he testily complained: "The Court notes that New Paradigm's counsel did not cite *any* of these cases. The Court is tired of attorneys who do a mediocre research job and thereby impose a heavy research burden on the Court. Nevertheless, this is not moot court, and this Court must determine the law, not decide which party would win based solely on the cases cited in the parties' briefs." (p. 13, n.21)

3. Mutuality and the Jobber's Requirements

1. As Farnsworth (1998, §12.12) notes, while the phrase "duty to mitigate" is commonly used, it is technically incorrect. If the nonbreaching party could have avoided a loss, but failed to do so, it would be precluded from recovering that portion of its damages.

2. Cooper was not, apparently, allowed to present evidence on this point. "Defendant was prevented from showing the reason for the change, although defendant offered to prove that it was for the sole purpose of allowing Schlegel to quote a price without being bound to buy anything from the defendant." (DB, p. 37)

3. The dissent in the Appellate Division seemed to think that the estimates were binding. "The defendant all through its dealings has treated the plaintiff with

great fairness and consideration. It did not hold the plaintiff to its contract in the year in which the contract called for the sale of 100 barrels, although it could have recovered substantial damages." (*Schlegel I*, p. 857)

4. Because of uncertainty about the future in the last months of 1916, glue manufacturers refused to quote prices for the following year. Schlegel solicited over thirty manufacturers, none of which was willing to quote him a price. (DB, p. 9)

5. Quantity is reckoned in both barrels and pounds. There is not a perfect conversion, since there were three different sizes of barrels, although it appears that in most cases it would be appropriate just to assume that a barrel equals 500 pounds. So, this would come to roughly forty to fifty barrels.

6. Molasses prices appear to have fluctuated violently. American Molasses entered into a contract in 1919 shortly after the decision at 8 cents a gallon. By mid-1920, the market price had risen to 26 cents a gallon. See *Globe Elevator Co. v. American Molasses Co. of New York*.

4. Satisfaction Clauses

1. If the contract gives a false recital of the payment of nominal consideration ("in consideration of buyer's payment of $20"), the majority position in the United States is that there is no contract. See *Lewis v. Fletcher* for the majority position and *Smith v. Wheeler* for the minority position.

5. Discretion in Long-Term Quality Contracts

1. In some instances, state and local governments have built capital intensive waste treatment facilities, set high prices for waste removal, and imposed "flow controls" limiting the ability of clients to dispose of their waste outside the jurisdiction. These fencing-garbage-in ordinances have generated a considerable amount of litigation. The Supreme Court found one such ordinance a violation of the dormant commerce clause. *C & A Carbone, Inc. v. Town of Clarkstown, New York*. For a sampling of post-*Carbone* flow control cases, many of which turn back challenges to the ordinances, see *Houlton Citizens' Coalition v. Town of Houlton; Automated Salvage Transport, Inc. v. Wheelabrator Environmental Systems, Inc.; National Solid Waste Management Association v. Williams; Sal Tinnerello & Sons, Inc. v. Town of Stonington;* and *Ben Oehrleins & Sons & Daughter, Inc. v. Hennepin County*.

2. Judge Posner's lengthy discussion in *Lake River* on the questionable wisdom of enforcing the rule against penalties in a contract between sophisticated commercial entities indicates that he is not happy with the outcome. See *Lake River* at 1288–1293.

3. In the former, Tennessee settled by paying Hamman $8 million. In the latter, Tennessee entered into a confidential settlement in 1985 revising the terms and paying a flat fee of about $600,000. After further hassles, the parties en-

tered into a second settlement in 1987, again revising the terms, with Tennessee paying an additional $6 million. The litigation in both cases involved unsuccessful claims by the lessors against the producer for royalties on the side payment.

6. In Search of Best Efforts

1. See, e.g., Bruno (1992, p. 76): "Falstaff agreed to distribute Ballantine beer, in addition to its own label, in exchange for payments to Ballantine"; Hadfield (1992, pp. 608–609): "The plaintiff signed a contract in which Falstaff, the defendant, agreed to use its 'best efforts' to promote the sale of Ballantine beer (which continued to be produced by Ballantine breweries)"; Long (1986, p. 1733): "Falstaff would not have agreed to spend money up front marketing Ballantine if Ballantine could later have come back and demanded a higher royalty"; Scott and Kraus (2002, p. 357): "What changes do you think would be made in a new agreement between these two companies? Is that relationship likely to be renewed after litigation?"

2. They attempted, unsuccessfully, to convert the brewery into an industrial park. On October 21, 1974, IFC and its wholly owned subsidiary IFC Collateral Corporation both filed for reorganization under Chapter X of the Bankruptcy Act. On November 1, 1974, James Bloor was appointed Trustee, replacing the Dansker management. On December 23, 1980, while other suits were still ongoing, Judge Bonsal approved a reorganization plan in which Helmsley Enterprises would inject new money. *IFC I.* Other litigation stemming from the IFC bankruptcy dragged on for over a decade. The Trustee Bloor had taken the position that a massive fraud had been perpetrated on the company, and he sued the Danskers, the banks, the accountants, IFC's outside legal counsel, various others, and, of course, Falstaff. The Trustee's claims against the principal accountants were dismissed. *IFC II.* Claims of the Trustee against the outside directors, IFC's outside legal counsel, and various other individuals were also dismissed. *IFC III* and *Bloor III.* Other claims of the Trustee against IFC's outside legal counsel were finally dismissed in 1986. *IFC IV.* In addition, holders of the stock and debentures of IFC filed five class actions against the Danskers, the accountants, and the banks which were consolidated for trial. The securities holders settled with the banks and the accountants on March 17, 1981. *IFC V.* In an unrelated matter, some of IFC's officers faced criminal charges stemming from the development of the George Washington Plaza shopping center. They were charged with conspiracy to give a $100,000 bribe to Burt Ross, the mayor of Fort Lee, New Jersey. On March 28, 1975, former IFC officers Norman Dansker, Donald Orenstein, and Stephen Haymes were convicted of bribery. See *United States v. Dansker.* They eventually served six months in jail. See Waggoner 1978, p. 1.

3. For the number of deals, see "1998 M&A Profile" (1999, p. 42). For the number including earnouts, see "Deal Structuring" (1999, p. 35).

4. Falstaff's Reply Brief raised, somewhat half-heartedly, the possibility that the proviso might be a penalty clause: "[A] construction of the proviso that would give it effect in any circumstances other than the near total cessation of Ballantine production would make of it, not a liquidated damages provision, but an unenforceable penalty clause." (Falstaff's Reply Br. at 37)

9. *Campbell v. Wentz*

1. The defendants noted that inability to pay might be grounds for specific performance but denied that it was relevant in this case. "Of course, if there had been proof that the defendants were insolvent or not financially responsible—and there was not even a suggestion that such a situation existed—there might have been some force to the plaintiff's contention that it could not obtain adequate relief by way of money damages." (Lojeski Brief, p. 12)
2. See also *R. N. Kelly Cotton Merchant, Inc. v. York; T. H. Taunton v. Allenberg Cotton Company, Inc.; Mid South Cotton Growers Association v. Woods; West Point-Pepperell, Inc. v. O. W. Bradshaw; Mitchell-Huntley Cotton Co., Inc. v. Waldrep; Cone Mills Corporation v. A. G. Estes, Inc.; R. L. Kimsey Cotton Company, Inc. v. J. D. Ferguson; Reigel Fiber Corporation v. Anderson Gin Company.*

11. The Middleman's Damages

1. Although it rejected the *Allied* result, the *KGM Harvesting* (p. 387) court also raised the reputational loss red herring: "The court apparently never considered anything other than whether the Japanese buyers would sue *Allied* Canners. For example, it did not consider whether the breach adversely affected Allied Canner's goodwill with its Japanese customers. Should the court not have also considered Allied Canner's potential loss of future contracts?"

14. A Reexamination of *Glanzer v. Shepard*

1. *Int'l Ore & Fertilizer Corp. v. East Coast Fertilizer Co., Ltd.* In *Glanzer*, the lawsuit was filed by the buyer, who was not party to the weighing contract; here, in the American case, the plaintiff was in privity. In fact, the fertilizer contract was a cost and freight ("c&f") contract, so title should have passed when the ship was loaded. The buyer should have borne the risk of contamination, and SGS should have been defending against the buyer, making the case more directly parallel to *Glanzer.*

15. *Bloomer Girl* Revisited

1. Henri Falaise, Marquis de la Coudraye, was the third of her five husbands. According to her mini-biography, "she feuded with the press and enjoyed lawsuits." (Crawford, Constance Bennett IMDB)

2. The contract formula will typically serve as the baseline for renegotiation. When, for example, Alan Arkin's contract was terminated two weeks before principal photography was to begin on *Bonfire of the Vanities*, the studio's only legal obligation was to pay his fixed compensation—$120,000. However, the co-producer suggested that the studio would do more. "We expressed our apologies to Alan—and we'll have to negotiate something. This is not the first time this sort of thing has happened—nor will it be the last, but we are concerned about his feelings." (Salamon 1991, p. 110)

17. *Wasserman v. Township of Middletown*

1. Assuming constant payments in perpetuity (X), the present value (V) of the property is $V = X/r$. So $X = rV = (.08)(\$610,000) = \$48,800$ per year, or a little over $4,000 per month. The present value of this stream for the 11.75 years remaining on the lease is the cost of the perfect replacement lease.

2. For a casebook example of a situation in which the parties reached such an impasse, see *Dickey v. Philadelphia Minit-Man Corp.* The rent was based on a percentage of gross sales with a fixed minimum. The lease restricted the use of the property to washing and cleaning automobiles. At some point the lessee discontinued all activity except that which was incidental to simonizing and polishing cars but continued to pay the minimum rent. The lessor brought suit asking that the lessee be ejected, asserting that the lease included an implied term requiring the lessee to operate the leased premises to the fullest extent possible. The court held otherwise, although it put considerable weight on the existence of the minimum rental, a red herring. Most likely, the crux of the dispute was that the land value had increased for some other use and the parties were bargaining over who was to get the bonus value. The use restriction gave the lessor some leverage, but the lessee could keep in the game by keeping a minimal operation alive.

References

Abelson, Reed. 1996. "The Shell Game of Hollywood 'Net Profits': Dreamworks May Be Shaking Up Some Time-Honored Accounting Habits." *New York Times,* March 4, p. Dl.

Anderson, Roy Ryden. 2001. "Of Hidden Agendas, Naked Emperors, and a Few Good Soldiers: The Conference's Breach of Promise . . . Regarding Article 2 Damage Remedies." *Southern Methodist University Law Review* 54: 795–866.

Armitage, Shelley. 1994. *Kewpies and Beyond: The World of Rose O'Neill.* Jackson: University Press of Mississippi.

Asbury, Herbert. 1928. *Gangs of New York.* New York: A. A. Knopf.

Bach, Steven. 1985. *Final Cut: Dreams and Disaster in the Making of Heaven's Gate.* New York: William Morrow & Co.

Baird, Douglas G., and Robert Weisberg. 1982. "Rules, Standards, and the Battle of the Forms: A Reassessment of §2–207." *Virginia Law Review* 68: 1217–1262.

Barzel, Yoram. 1982. "Measurement Cost and the Organization of Markets." *Journal of Law & Economics* 25: 27–48.

Ben-Shahar, Omri, and Lisa Bernstein. 2000. "The Secrecy Interest in Contract Law." *Yale Law Journal* 109: 1885–1925.

Bernstein, Lisa. 1999. "The Questionable Empirical Basis of Article 2's Incorporation Strategy: A Preliminary Study." *University of Chicago Law Review* 66: 710–780.

Bigham, Randy. *Lucile—Her Life by Design: The Story of Lady Duff Gordon.* Lubbock, TX: Texas Tech University Press, forthcoming.

Bruce, Christopher J. 1982. "An Economic Analysis of the Impossibility Doctrine." *Journal of Legal Studies* 11: 311–332.

Bruno, J. C. 1992. " 'Best Efforts' Defined." *Michigan Bar Journal* 71: 74–77.

Burton, Steven J., and Eric G. Andersen. 1995. *Contractual Good Faith: Formation, Performance, Breach, Enforcement.* New York: Little, Brown.

Bygrave, William D., and Jeffry A. Timmons. 1992. *Venture Capital at the Crossroads.* Cambridge, MA: Harvard Business School Press.

Calabresi, Guido, and A. Douglas Melamed. 1972. "Property Rules, Liability Rules, and Inalienability: One View of the Cathedral." *Harvard Law Review* 85: 1089–1128.

Chirelstein, Marvin A. 2001. *Concepts and Case Analysis in the Law of Contracts*. New York: Foundation Press.

Clark, John D. 1997. "The Proposed Revisions to Contract-Market Damages of Article Two of the Uniform Commercial Code: A Disaster Not a Remedy." *Emory Law Journal* 46: 807–866.

"Construction of Contract for Sale of Commodity to the Extent of the Buyer's Requirements." 1920. *American Law Reports* 7: 498–516.

Corbin, Arthur L. 1925. "The Effect of Options on Consideration." *Yale Law Journal* 34: 571–590.

Cowdery, Jabez F. 1905. *Cowdery's New Book of Forms*. San Francisco: Bancroft-Whitney Co.

Crawford, Rod. Constance Bennett IMDB. Internet Movie Database, *www.imdb .com/name/nm0000909/bio* (accessed September 29, 1998).

Dawson, John P. 1983. "Judicial Revision of Frustrated Contracts: Germany." *Boston University Law Review* 63: 1039–1098.

———. 1984. "Judicial Revision of Frustrated Contracts: The United States." *Boston University Law Review* 64: 1–38.

Dawson, John P., William B. Harvey, and Stanley D. Henderson. 1982. *Cases on Contracts and Contract Remedies*. 4th ed. New York: Foundation Press.

———. 2003. *Cases on Contracts and Contract Remedies*. 8th ed. New York: Foundation Press.

"Deal Structuring: Earn-outs Get into More Deals." 1999. *Mergers & Acquisitions* 33: 35–36.

Deutchman, Ira. 1992. "Independent Distribution and Marketing." In Jason E. Squire, ed., *The Movie Business Book*, 2nd ed., 320–327. Chicago: Fireside.

"Domestic Theatrical Film Distributor Market Shares, 1970–1995." In *1996–1997 Encyclopedia of Exhibition*. National Association of Theatre Owners.

Duff-Gordon, Lady (Lucile). 1932. *Discretions and Indiscretions*. London: Jarrods.

Eckstrom, Lawrence J. 2002. *Eckstrom's Licensing in Foreign and Domestic Operations*. St. Paul, MN: West.

Emmet, B., and John E. Jeuck. 1950. *Catalogues and Counters: A History of Sears, Roebuck and Company*. Chicago: University of Chicago Press.

Encyclopedia Titanica, *www.encyclopedia-titanica.org/biography/101* (accessed January 5, 2003).

Etherington-Smith, Meredith, and Jeremy Pilcher. 1986. *The "It" Girls: Lucy, Lady Duff Gordon, the Couturiere "Lucile," and Elinor Glyn, Romantic Novelist*. Orlando, FL: Harcourt.

Farnsworth, E. Allan. 1984. "On Trying to Keep One's Promises: The Duty of Best Efforts in Contract Law." *University of Pittsburgh Law Review* 46: 1–20.

———. 1998. *Farnsworth on Contracts*. 2nd ed. New York: Aspen.

———. 2004. *Contracts*. 4th ed. New York: Aspen.

Farnsworth, E. Allan, and W. F. Young. 1995. *Contracts: Cases and Materials Manual for Teachers*. 5th ed. St. Paul, MN: West.

Female Inventors: Rose O'Neill. *www.inventions.org/culture/female/oneill.html*.

Folkart, Burt A. 1987. "Paul Kalmanovitz, Beer Industry Magnate, Dies." *Los Angeles Times*, January 23, p. 28.

Friedberg, A. Alan. 1992. "The Theatrical Exhibitor." In Jason E. Squire, ed., *The Movie Business Book*, 2nd ed., 341–351. Chicago: Fireside.

Friedman, Robert G. 1992. "Motion Picture Marketing." In Jason E. Squire, ed., *The Movie Business Book*, 2nd ed., 291–306. Chicago: Fireside.

Frier, Bruce W., and James J. White. 2005. *Modern Law of Contracts*. St. Paul, MN: West.

Frug, Mary Joe. 1985. "Re-reading Contracts: A Feminist Analysis of a Casebook." *American University Law Review* 34: 1065–1140.

Fuessle. 1916. "Putting a Grand Air into Copy." *Printer's Ink*, October 26, p. 54.

Garrison, Jim. 1988. *On the Trail of the Assassins: My Investigation and Prosecution of the Murder of President Kennedy*. New York: Sheridan Square Press.

Gilbert, Matthew. 1996. "Box Office Star Power: In Summer's Films, Big Names Don't Always Deliver." *Boston Globe*, August 25, p. N1.

Gilson, Ronald J. 1984. "Value Creation by Business Lawyers: Legal Skills and Asset Pricing." *Yale Law Journal* 94: 239–314.

Goetz, Charles J., and Robert E. Scott. 1979. "Measuring Sellers' Damages: The Lost-Profits Puzzle." *Stanford Law Review* 31: 323–374.

———. 1981. "Principles of Relational Contracts." *Virginia Law Review* 67: 1089–1150.

———. 1983. "The Mitigation Principle: Toward a General Theory of Contractual Obligation." *Virginia Law Review* 69: 967–1024.

Goldberg, Victor P. 1980. "Relational Exchange: Economics and Complex Contracts." *American Behavioral Scientist* 23: 337–352.

———. 1984a. "An Economic Analysis of the Lost-Volume Retail Seller." *Southern California Law Review* 57: 283–298.

———. 1984b. "The Free Rider Problem, Imperfect Pricing, and the Economics of Retailing Services." *Northwestern University Law Review* 79: 736–757.

———. 1985. "Price Adjustment in Long-Term Contracts." *Wisconsin Law Review* 1985: 527–543.

———. 1988. "Impossibility and Related Excuses." *Journal of Institutional and Theoretical Economics* 144: 100–121.

———, ed. 1989. *Readings in Economic Analysis and the Law of Contracts*. New York: Cambridge University Press.

———. 1990. "Aversion to Risk Aversion in the New Institutional Economics." *Journal of Institutional and Theoretical Economics* 146: 216–222.

———. 1997a. "The 'Battle of the Forms': Fairness, Efficiency, and the Best-Shot Rule." *Oregon Law Review* 76: 155–171.

———. 1997b. "The Net Profits Puzzle." *Columbia Law Review* 97: 524–550.

———. 1997c. "The Gold Ring Problem." *University of Toronto Law Journal* 47: 469–494.

———. 1998. "Bloomer Girl Revisited, or How to Frame an Unmade Picture." *Wisconsin Law Review* 1998: 1051–1084.

———. 2000a. "In Search of Best Efforts: Reinterpreting *Bloor v. Falstaff.*" *Saint Louis University Law Journal* 44: 1465–1485.

———. 2000b. "Economic Reasoning and the Framing of Contract Law: Sale of an Asset of Uncertain Value." *Revue d'Economie Industrielle* 92: 111–123.

———. 2002a. "Discretion in Long-Term Open Quantity Contracts: Reining in Good Faith." *University of California Davis Law Review* 35: 319–385.

———. 2002b. "A Reexamination of *'Glanzer v. Shepard'*: Surveyors on the Tort-Contract Boundary." *Theoretical Inquiries in Law* 2: 476–510.

———. 2005. "The Enforcement of Contracts and Private Ordering." In Claude Menard and Mary M. Shirley, eds., *Handbook for New Institutional Economics.* Norwell, MA: Kluwer Academic.

Goldberg, Victor P., and John Erickson. 1987. "Quantity and Price Adjustment in Long-Term Contracts: A Case Study of Petroleum Coke." *Journal of Law & Economics* 30: 369–398.

Goldberg, Victor P., Thomas W. Merrill, and Daniel Unumb. 1987. "Bargaining in the Shadow of Eminent Domain: Valuing and Apportioning Condemnation Awards between Landlord and Tenant." *UCLA Law Review* 34: 1083–1137.

Griffin, Nancy, and Kim Masters. 1996. *Hit & Run: How Jon Peters and Peter Guber Took Sony for a Ride in Hollywood.* New York: Simon & Schuster.

" 'Gump' a Smash but Still in the Red, Paramount Says." 1995. *Los Angeles Times,* May 24, p. Al.

Hadfield, Gillian K. 1992. "Bias in the Evolution of Legal Rules." *Georgetown Law Journal* 80: 583–616.

Hanson, Jon D., and Kyle D. Logue. 1990. "The First-Party Insurance Externality: An Economic Justification for Enterprise Liability." *Cornell Law Review* 76: 129–196.

Hayes, Dade, and Jonathan Bing. 2004. *Open Wide: How Hollywood Box Office Became a National Obsession.* New York: Hyperion.

Hillman, Robert A. 1987. "Court Adjustment of Long-Term Contracts: An Analysis under Modern Contract Law." *Duke Law Journal* 1987: 1–33.

Hubbard, Glenn, and Robert J. Weiner. 1991. "Efficient Contracting and Market Power: Evidence from the U.S. Natural Gas Industry." *Journal of Law & Economics* 34: 25–67.

Hueth, Brent, and Philippe Marcoul. 2003. "An Essay on Cooperative Bargaining in U.S. Agricultural Markets." *Journal of Agricultural & Food Industrial Organization* 1, no. 1: Article 10. Available at *www.bepress.com/jafio/vol1/iss1/art10* (accessed December 7, 2005).

International Rose O'Neill Club Foundation, *www.kewpieroseoneillclub.com* (accessed December 7, 2005).

Issacharoff, Samuel, and John F. Witt. 2004. "The Inevitability of Aggregate Settlement: An Institutional Account of American Tort Law." *Vanderbilt Law Review* 57: 1571–1636.

Jackson, Thomas S. 1978. " 'Anticipatory Repudiation' and the Temporal Element of Contract Law: An Economic Inquiry into Contract Damages in Cases of Prospective Nonperformance." *Stanford Law Review* 31: 69–120.

Johnston, Louis, and Samuel H. Williamson. "The Annual Real and Nominal GDP for the United States, 1789–Present." *Economic History Services*. Available at *www.eh.net/hmit/gdp/* (accessed April 2002).

Jones, Leonard A. 1909. *Legal Forms*. Indianapolis, IN: Bobbs-Merrill.

Joskow, Paul L. 1973. "Cartels, Competition and Regulation in the Property and Liability Insurance Industry." *Bell Journal of Economics and Management Science* 4: 375–427.

———. 1977. "Commercial Impossibility, the Uranium Markets, and the Westinghouse Case." *Journal of Legal Studies* 6: 119–176.

Kahneman, Daniel, and Amos Tversky. 1979. "Prospect Theory: An Analysis of Decision under Risk." *Econometrica* 47: 263–291.

Kastely, Amy Hilsman, et al. 1996. *Contracting Law*. Durham, NC: Carolina Academic Press.

Katz, Avery. 1996. "When Should an Offer Stick? The Economics of Promissory Estoppel in Preliminary Negotiations." *Yale Law Journal* 105: 1249–1310.

———. 2004. "The Economics of Form and Substance in Contract Interpretation." *Columbia Law Review* 104: 496–538.

Kaufman, Andrew. 1998. *Cardozo*. Cambridge, MA: Harvard University Press.

Kenney, Roy W., and Benjamin Klein. 1983. "The Economics of Block Booking." *Journal of Law & Economics* 26: 497–540.

Kessler, Friedrich. 1957. "Automobile Dealer Franchises: Vertical Integration by Contract." *Yale Law Journal* 66: 1135–1190.

Kitch, Edmund W. 1977. "The Nature and Function of the Patent System." *Journal of Law & Economics* 20: 265–290.

Klein, Benjamin. 1980. "Transaction Cost Determinants of 'Unfair' Contractual Arrangements." *American Economic Review* 70: 356–362.

Knapp, Charles L., and Nathan M. Crystal. 1993. *Problems in Contract Law*. New York: Little, Brown.

Kraus, Jody, and Steven Walt. 2000. "In Defense of the Incorporation Strategy." In Kraus and Walt, eds., *The Jurisprudential Foundations of Corporate and Commercial Law*, 193–237. New York: Cambridge University Press.

Lee, Spike. 1992. *By Any Means Necessary: The Trials and Tribulations of the Making of "Malcolm X."* New York: Hyperion.

Lind, H. C. 1963. "Validity, Construction, and Effect of Contract between Grower of Vegetable or Fruit Crops, and Purchasing Processor, Packer, or Canner." *American Law Reports 2d* 87: 732–782.

Llewellyn, Karl. 1962. "A Lecture on Appellate Advocacy." *University of Chicago Law Review* 29: 627–639.

Long, Lawrence S. 1986. "Best Efforts as Diligence Insurance: In Defense of 'Profit uber Alles.'" *Columbia Law Review* 86: 1728–1740.

Lubove, Seth. 1995. "The Legacy of Mr. Paul." *Forbes*, May 22, 46–47.

Lucy Christiana, Lady Duff Gordon (née Sutherland). *www.encyclopedia-titanica.org/biography/101* (accessed June 1, 2006).

Macaulay, Stewart. 1963. "Non-contractual Relations in Business: A Preliminary Study." *American Sociological Review* 28: 55–67.

———. 1966. *Law and the Balance of Power: The Automobile Manufacturers and Their Dealers*. New York: Russell Sage Foundation.

————. 1985. "An Empirical View of Contract." *Wisconsin Law Review* 1985: 465–482.

Macaulay, Stewart, John Kidwell, and William Whitford. 2003. *Contracts: Law in Action.* 2nd ed. Vol. 1. New York: Lexis.

Macaulay, Stewart, John Kidwell, William Whitford, and Marc Galanter. 1995. *Contracts: Law in Action.* Charlottesville, VA: Michie Co.

Matthews, Daniel W. 1997. "Capping Market Damages at Lost Profit: An Unwarranted Limitation on a Middleman's Expectancy Interest." *Detroit College Law Review* 1997: 993–1020.

McDonough, Will. 1996. "Calipari Agrees to Stay with Nets." *Boston Globe,* November 21, p. D5.

Meyerson, Harold, and Ernie Harburg. 1993. *Who Put the Rainbow in "The Wizard of Oz"?* Ann Arbor: University of Michigan Press.

Munk, Nina. 1995. "Now You See It, Now You Don't." *Forbes,* June 5, pp. 42–43.

Murphy, A. D. 1997. "Domestic Theatrical Film Distributor Market Shares, 1970–1995." In *The 1996–97 Encyclopedia of Exhibition.* New York: National Association of Theatre Owners.

Murray, John E., Jr. 1986. "The Chaos of the 'Battle of the Forms': Solutions." *Vanderbilt Law Review* 39: 1307–1385.

————. 1994. "The Revision of Article 2: Romancing the Prism." *William and Mary Law Review* 35: 1447–1507.

————. 2001. *Murray on Contracts.* 4th ed. New York: Matthew Bender.

Mushkat, Jerome. 1990. *Fernando Wood: A Political Biography.* Kent, Ohio: Kent State University Press.

"1998 M&A Profile." 1999. *Mergers & Acquisitions* 33: 42–67.

Nochimson, David, and Leon Brachman. 1996. "Contingent Compensation for Theatrical Motion Pictures." *Entertainment and Sports Lawyer* 5: 3–6.

O'Donnell, Pierce, and Dennis McDougal. 1992. *Fatal Subtraction.* New York: Doubleday.

O'Malley, Thomas F. 1916. *Forms in Common Use.* Boston: Eugene W. Hildreth.

Onecle, 2006. Hewlett-Packard Company, Mark Hurd Employment Agreement, *http://contracts.onecle.com/p/hurd.emp.2005.03.29.shtml.*

O'Neill, Rose. 1997. *The Story of Rose O'Neill.* Ed. Miriam Formanek-Brunell. Columbia: University of Missouri Press.

Pierson, John. 1995. *Spike, Mike, Slackers & Dykes: A Guided Tour across a Decade of American Independent Cinema.* New York: Hyperion.

Pink, Sidney. 1989. *So You Want to Make Movies: My Life as an Independent Film Producer.* Sarasota, FL: Pineapple Press.

Pleasants, Samuel A. 1948. *Fernando Wood of New York.* New York: Columbia University Press.

Posner, Richard A., and Andrew M. Rosenfield. 1977. "Impossibility and Related Doctrines in Contract Law: An Economic Analysis." *Journal of Legal Studies* 6: 83–118.

Pratt, Walter F., Jr. 1988. "American Contract Law at the Turn of the Century." *South Carolina Law Review* 39: 415–464.

Reardon, D. Barry. 1992. "The Studio Distributor." In Jason E. Squire, ed., *The Movie Business Book*, 2nd ed., 309–319. Chicago: Fireside.

Restatement of the Law of Restitution. St. Paul, MN: American Law Institute, 1937.

Restatement of the Law Second, *Contracts.* St. Paul, MN: American Law Institute, 1981.

Revised Judicature Act of 1961, M.C.L.A. §600.2961.

Reynolds, Christopher. 1995. *Hollywood Power Stats.* Valley Village, CA: Cineview.

Robbins, William. 1965. "New G.M. Building May Rise around Two Tenants; Coffee House and Flower Shop Owners May Stay till Leases Expire." *New York Times*, December 12, Sec. 8, p. 1.

Roberts, Selena. 1996. "Calipari Resisting a Contract Addition." *New York Times*, November. 20, p. B15.

Roddick, Nick. 1995. "The Bigger They Come . . ." *The Observer* (London), July 2, p. 2.

Rose Cecil O'Neill. Women's Children's Book Illustrators, *www.ortakales.com/ illustrators/Oneill.html* (accessed December 7, 2005).

Salamon, Julie. 1991. *The Devil's Candy: "The Bonfire of the Vanities" Goes to Hollywood.* New York: Houghton Mifflin.

Sandler, Adam. 1995. "New Recipes Cooking for Net Profit Pie." *Variety*, June 5, p. 7.

Schatz, Thomas. 1988. *The Genius of the System: Hollywood Filmmaking in the Studio Era.* New York: Pantheon.

Schwartz, Alan. 1979. "The Case for Specific Performance." *Yale Law Journal* 89: 271–306.

Scott, Robert E. 1990. "The Case for Market Damages: Revisiting the Lost Profits Puzzle." *University of Chicago Law Review* 57: 1155–1202.

———. 2000. "The Case for Formalism in Relational Contract." *Northwestern University Law Review* 94: 847–876.

———. 2003. A Theory of Self-Enforcing Indefinite Agreements." *Columbia Law Review* 103: 1641–1699.

Scott, Robert E., and Douglas Leslie. 1993. *Contract Law and Theory.* New York: LexisNexis.

Scott, Robert E., and George G. Triantis. 2004. "Embedded Options and the Case against Compensation in Contract Law." *Columbia Law Review* 104: 1428–1491.

Scott, Robert E., and Jody S. Kraus. 2002. *Contract Law and Theory.* 3rd ed. Newark, NJ: Matthew Bender, Lexis-Nexis.

"Sears-Roebuck's Latest Advertising Coup." 1916. *Printer's Ink,* September 21, p. 28.

Selz, Thomas D., et al. 1997. *Entertainment Law.* 2nd ed. Colorado Springs: Shepards/McGraw-Hill.

Silkworth, Stacy A. 1990. "Quantity Variation in Open Quantity Contracts." *University of Pittsburgh Law Review* 51: 235–279.

Speidel, Richard E. 1981. "Court-Imposed Price Adjustments under Long-Term Supply Contracts." *Northwestern University Law Review* 76: 369–422.

Stewart, James. 2005. *Disney War.* New York: Simon & Schuster.

Sullivan, Lawrence. 1977. *Antitrust.* St. Paul, MN: West.

Tan, E. R. 1993. "Conclusiveness of Determination of Third Party Whose Approval Is Provided for by Contract for Sale of Goods." *American Law Reports 3d* 7: 555.

Those Indifferent People Involved in Titanic Tragedy, *http://my.execpc.com/reva/html3c6.htm* (accessed December 7, 2005).

Treitel, G. H. 1994. *Frustration and Force Majeure.* London: Sweet & Maxwell.

Unification of Certain Rules of Law Relating to Bills of Lading ("Visby Amendments"). 1968. Brussels: N.p., February 23.

Van Vliet, James M., Jr. 2000. " 'Best Efforts' Promises under Illinois Law." *Illinois Bar Journal* 88: 698–702.

Vogel, Harold L. 1994. *Entertainment Industry Economics.* 3rd ed. New York: Cambridge University Press.

Waggoner, Walter H. 1978. "Terms Cut for 4 in Ft. Lee Bribery." *New York Times.* February 4, p. 1.

Weiler, Paul C., and Gary Roberts. 1993. *Cases, Materials and Problems on Sports and the Law.* St. Paul: West.

Weinraub, Bernard. 1995. " 'Gump,' a Huge Hit, Still Isn't Raking In Huge Profits? Hmm." *New York Times,* May 25, p. C15.

Weinstein, Mark. 1998. "Profit Sharing Contracts in Hollywood: Evolution and Analysis." *Journal of Legal Studies* 27: 67–112.

Welkos, Robert W. 1995a. "Another Flap over a Movie's Net Profits." *Los Angeles Times,* September 12, pp. D2, D11.

———. 1995b. "Buchwald, Paramount Settle Film Dispute." *Los Angeles Times,* September 13, pp. D2, D11.

White, James J., and David A. Peters. 2002. "Essay: A Footnote for Jack Dawson." *Michigan Law Review* 100: 1954–1979.

White, James J., and Robert S. Summers. 1995. *Uniform Commercial Code.* 4th ed. St. Paul, MN: West.

Wladis, John D. 1988. "Impracticability as Risk Allocation: The Effect of Changed Circumstances upon Contract Obligations for the Sale of Goods." *Georgia Law Review* 22: 503–666.

Yeldell, Eric B. 1987. *The Motion Picture and Television Business: Contracts and Practices.* Los Angeles: Entertainment Business Publications.

Zasu Pitts. IMDB—Internet Movie Database, *http://us.imdb.com/Name?Pitts, +ZaSu* (accessed September 19, 1998).

Table of Cases

Index